KU-794-495

Explorations in Social Theory

LEEDS BECKETT UNIVERSITY
LIBRARY

Leeds Metropolitan University

17 0356229 0

Explorations in Social Theory

From Metatheorizing to Rationalization

GEORGE RITZER

SAGE Publications
London • Thousand Oaks • New Delhi

© George Ritzer 2001

First published 2001

Apart from any fair dealing for the purposes of research or
private study, or criticism or review, as permitted under the
Copyright, Designs and Patents Act, 1988, this publication
may be reproduced, stored or transmitted in any form, or by
any means, only with the prior permission in writing of
the publishers, or in the case of reprographic reproduction,
in accordance with the terms of licences issued by the
Copyright Licensing Agency. Inquiries concerning
reproduction outside those terms should be sent to the
publishers.

SAGE Publications Ltd
6 Bonhill Street
London EC2A 4PU

SAGE Publications Inc
2455 Teller Road
Thousand Oaks, California 91320

SAGE Publications India Pvt Ltd
32, M-Block Market
Greater Kailash - I
New Delhi 110 048

British Library Cataloguing in Publication data

A catalogue record for this book is
available from the British Library

ISBN 0-7619-6772-9
      0-7619-6773-7 (pb)

Library of Congress Control Number available

LEEDS METROPOLITAN
UNIVERSITY
LEARNING CENTRE
1703562290
HL-BV
CC-32277
31·03·03·   9·8·02
301.01 RIT

Typeset by SIVA Math Setters, Chennai, India
Printed and bound in Great Britain by Athenaeum Press,
Gateshead

To Casey Maxwell Ritzer:

Love Yet Again

CONTENTS

PREFACE

This constitutes a preface to both *Explorations in Social Theory: From Metatheorizing to Rationalization* and *Explorations in the Sociology of Consumption: Fast Food, Credit Cards and Casinos*. While each of these books can be read independently of the other, the two volumes taken together offer an overview of my contributions to these two fields. Included are journal articles and excerpts from some well-known books as well as some essays that I hope will get wider visibility as a result of their inclusion in these volumes. Some chapters are taken from material published some time ago, others are derived from more recent publications, and there are several that are being published in these volumes for the first time. Some of the material is derived from books that have been out-of-print for a decade or two. Thus, inclusion of excerpts from these books will bring these works to the attention of a generation or two of sociologists and other social scientists who might otherwise not have access to them.

Virtually all of the material in these two volumes was written with a professional audience in mind. However, as I make clear in Chapter 1 ('Writing to be Read') of *Explorations in the Sociology of Consumption*, I give great importance to writing in such a way that even the most abstract ideas in both social theory and the sociology of consumption are accessible to a wide range of readers. Thus, it is my hope that these volumes will not only be of interest to scholars, but also to many other readers, including both graduate students and undergraduates.

Not only are these two books designed so that they can be read independently of one another, but it is also the case that each of the individual chapters can be read on its own. While I would clearly like readers to proceed from cover to cover, there are many who, given their particular interests, might want to read only a chapter or two from each volume. The desire to have each chapter stand on its own has one drawback for the two volumes. That is, there is a bit more repetition in these books than one might like. Thus, for example, the reader will run into several versions of the basic types of metatheorizing and of the basic dimensions of McDonaldization. I trust that those of you who read the books in their entirety and are irritated by the occasional repetition will bear in mind that such repetition helps make each chapter more meaningful to those who are only reading a selected chapter or two.

The idea for these two volumes came from my dear friend and colleague – Chris Rojek – who also happens to be the sociology editor at Sage Publications in London. I owe him an immense debt for not only coming up with the idea, but allowing me to put together two volumes that I hope will give the reader a good feel for my work in both theory and the sociology of consumption. Other people at Sage have also been of great help including Jackie Griffin and Ian Antcliff.

I also need to thank a number of past and present graduate students at the University of Maryland who co-authored all or part of a number of the essays in these two volumes – Richard Bell, Pamela Gindoff, Doug Goodman, Terri LeMoyne, Elizabeth Malone, James Murphy, Seth Ovadia, Todd Stillman, David Walczak and Wendy Weidenhoft. Also to be thanked are undergraduate research assistants Jan Geesin and Zinnia Cho.

ACKNOWLEDGEMENTS

1-This chapter is derived from the Introduction and Chapter 1 of *Metatheorizing in Sociology*. NY: Lexington Books, 1991: 1–14; 17–21 and the Appendix to *Sociological Theory*, 5th edition. NY: McGraw-Hill, 2000, pp. 623–39.

2-This chapter first appeared as Chapter 4 of *Metatheorizing in Sociology*. NY: Lexington Books, 1991, pp. 67–92.

3-The bulk of the material covered in this chapter has appeared in several places including *Sociology: A Multiple Paradigm Science*. Boston: Allyn and Bacon, 1975; 'Sociology: A Multiple Paradigm Science'. *American Sociologist*, 10: 156–67; and *Metatheorizing in Sociology*. Lexington, MA: Lexington Books, 1991: 117–137. The Postscript to this chapter comes from 'Paradigm Analysis in Sociology: Clarifying the Issues'. *American Sociological Review*, 46, 1981: 245–48.

4-The material in this chapter is drawn from *Toward an Integrated Sociological Paradigm: The Search for an Exemplar and an Image of the Subject Matter*. Boston: Allyn and Bacon, 1981: 1–29.

5-The material covered in this chapter is derived from *Toward an Integrated Paradigm: The Search for an Exemplar and an Image of the Subject Matter*. Boston: Allyn and Bacon, 1981: 31–69; 107–29 and 'Emile Durkheim: Exemplar for an Integrated Sociological Paradigm'. (With Richard Bell) *Social Forces*, 59: 966–95.

6-The source for this chapter is 'Methodological Relationism: Lessons for and from Social Psychology'. (with Pamela Gindoff) *Social Psychology Quarterly*, 55, 1992: 128–40.

7-Original chapter

8-This chapter, co-authored with Jim Murphy, is published here for the first time. It will be published as part of a more general essay on metatheorizing (co-authored with Murphy and Shanyang Zhao) in a forthcoming *Handbook of Sociological Theory* edited by Jonathan Turner.

9-This chapter is derived from 'Rationalization and the Deprofessionalization of Physicians'. (with David Walczak), *Social Forces*, vol. 67, September, 1988: 1–22 and *Metatheorizing in Sociology*. Lexington, MA: Lexington Books, 1991: 95–104.

10-This chapter is derived from Chapters 1 and 8 of *The McDonaldization of Society*, 2nd edition. Thousand Oaks, CA: Pine Forge Press, 1996: 1–16; 143–60.

11-The source of this chapter is *Metatheorizing in Sociology*. Lexington, MA: Lexington Books, 1991: 93–115; this chapter was co-authored by Terri LeMoyne.

12-This is Chapter 2 of *The McDonaldization Thesis*. London: Sage: 16–34

13-The source of this chapter is Chapter 3 in *The McDonaldization Thesis*. London: Sage, 1998: 35–51.

INTRODUCTION

This is the first of two simultaneously published volumes that offer an overview of my work over the last three decades, primarily in the areas of social theory (this work) and the sociology of consumption (the second volume). While the chapters in this publication are mainly theoretical (and metatheoretical) in nature, and those in the second volume focus on the substantive sociology of consumption, there really is no clear dividing line between these two bodies of work. Some of the pieces in this volume touch on consumption and virtually all of those in the second book are rooted in social theory. Overall, the two books range from my metatheoretical work on such grand abstractions as 'methodological relationism', 'paradigms', 'multiple paradigms' ('social facts', 'social definition', and 'social behavior' paradigms), 'paradigm integration', and 'hyperrationality' to very concrete discussions of everyday social phenomena like fast-food restaurants, credit cards, shopping malls, and e-tail, as well as the concepts associated with them such as 'McDonaldization' and 'deMcDonaldization', 'hyperconsumption', the 'new means of consumption', 'cathedrals of consumption', and the 'dangerous consumer'. While it is a long way from paradigms to fast-food restaurants, from Thomas Kuhn to Ray Kroc, what unifies my interest in these diverse issues, and everything in between, is social theory. My work in metatheory is animated by a need to better understand social theory, while my interest in consumption stems from a desire to apply social theory in an effort to better understand the most mundane aspects of the social world. In a sense, much of my work can be seen as applied social theory, with theory being applied either to theory itself or to the everyday world of consumption.

Of course, understanding is often merely an intermediate objective in both bodies of work. In metatheoretical work, the better understanding of theory can provide the base for the creation of new theories and/or new overarching theoretical perspectives (metatheories). In the substantive sociology of consumption, understanding is the prerequisite to critical analyses and to the delineation of actions that can ameliorate some of the problems associated with fast-food restaurants, credit cards, and the new means of consumption.

In the first two decades of my academic life my work was primarily metatheoretical in nature. However it was not until a series of essays in the 1980s, and especially *Metatheorizing in Sociology* (1991b) and an edited volume *Metatheorizing* (1992), that I began to clarify the meaning of metatheorizing (see Chapter 1). It had become clear that theorists were not the only ones doing metaanalyses: methodologists were doing metamethodology (the study of research methods, often with the objective of combining several methods in a single research project) and empiricists in many disciplines were doing *meta-data-analysis* (the statistical reanalysis of a body of a research on a single topic in order to come to an overall conclusion about the subject in question). It also became clear that metatheorizing (defined as the process of studying and theorizing about theory) was badly in need of conceptual clarification and amplification. What eventually emerged was a threefold distinction among types of metatheorizing. First, M_u is oriented to studying theory in order to gain a better understanding of it. My essays on a sociological architectonic (Chapter 2) and sociology's multiple paradigms (Chapter 3) are examples of M_u. Second, M_p involves the study of theory as a prelude to theory development. That is, the creation of new theory almost always requires the systematic study of extant theory. Marx's study of Hegel, the young Hegelians, the political economists, and so on in order to develop 'dialectical materialism' would be an example, as would Parsons's action theory emerging from his study of the work of Weber, Durkheim, Pareto, Marshall, and so on. Finally, M_o entails the study of theory in order to produce a new overarching theoretical perspective, or a metatheory. For example, my study of sociology's multiple paradigms led to the creation of some of the basic elements of an integrated sociological paradigm (Chapters 4 and 5), an example of a metatheory.

As pointed out above, one example of M_u involves an effort to uncover the 'architectonic' that lies at the base of a range of social theories. A number of such underlying structures exist in social theory, but they are often obscured by the substantive and conceptual details of the theories involved. Chapter 2 entails an effort to delineate one of the major architectonics in social theory, one that undergirds the work of theorists like Marx, Weber, Simmel, Berger and Luckmann, and the like. This sociological architectonic consists of six basic components. First, it has a *philosophical anthropology* – an essentialist conception of human beings and what distinguishes them from all other forms of life. There are a number of philosophical anthropologies in social theory (and some theories have no discernible philosophical anthropologies), but the one of concern here assumes that people are endowed with the ability to think, and that action and interaction are largely based on this capacity. Second, there is a process of *institutionalization* through which the thoughts, actions, and interactions of people are transformed into larger social structures and social institutions. Third, the assumption is that people lose control, at least occasionally, over the larger structures and institutions that emerge out of thought, action, and interaction. *Reification* is the term most often used for this creation of, and loss of control over, macro-level phenomena. Fourth, once these structures and institutions are reified, it is assumed that it is likely that they will exert control and *domination* over the people who both created them and continue to create them. Fifth, these reified structures are likely to have *adverse consequences* for those who exist within them. Finally, there is concern for the ability of people to *emancipate* themselves from these reified structures and their adverse effects. The objective in Chapter 2 is to see how well this architectonic fits a group of theorists as well as how well it serves to distinguish them from other groups of theorists using other architectonics.

Chapter 3 is based on *Sociology: A Multiple Paradigm Science* (1975/ 1980), a book in which I used Thomas Kuhn's theory of science and scientific development (especially his concept of a *paradigm*) to do an M_u analysis of (largely American) sociology as it existed *circa* 1970. I took some liberties with Kuhn's theory, indeed I have frequently taken liberties with social theories (Eckberg and Hill, 1979; Ritzer, 1981a). I believe that while one must be scrupulous when doing exegeses of the work of social theorists, one needs to be much more flexible and creative in applying those ideas to either theory or the social world. In applied social theory an extant theory is a take-off point, not a final resting place. The point of such work is not necessarily to be true to the work of a social theorist(s) from whom one happens to be borrowing, but to use those theoretical ideas as a 'living legacy' to render a greater understanding of either some aspect of social theory or some element of the social world. Thus, just as I was not slavish in my use of Kuhn's theory of scientific development to analyze sociology, I was similarly flexible in my use of Weber's theory of rationalization to think about the McDonaldization of society (see Chapters 9 and 10).

I do not want to appear to be arguing for looseness in theoretical work. There are many places in my work where I have tried to be as true as possible to the thinking of a social theorist, often relying on the exact words of the theorist rather than trying to interpret and paraphrase them. And there are certainly times when being slavish in one's interpretation of a theorist aids in better understanding the social world. However, there are times when being slavish is an impediment to thinking about the social world. Too much time and attention is devoted to getting the ideas right and too little to gaining a better understanding of theory and/or the social world. Overall, social theorists and sociologists are often far better at getting the ideas right than they are at casting new and revealing light on the theoretical and social world. This is especially true of American (and British) theorists; French theorists (e.g. Foucault, Baudrillard), for example, are much freer in their metatheoretical work and this may help account for the fact that in the last several decades they have produced much more powerful theories offering far greater insight into the social world. (Erving Goffman is one example of an American theorist who was similarly free in his metatheorizing and creative in his theorizing.) It seems clear that too many theorists have come to spend too much time on exegetical correctness and too little on using theory to create new ideas and insights. Max Weber is famous for having little patience for methodological and theoretical details, but that did not prevent him from creating, and may well have helped him to create, an unparalleled set of insights into the Occident and its differences from other parts of the world. The application of my sense of Kuhn's model and what he meant by a paradigm led to the view that sociology in the 1970s (as well as today) was a 'multiple paradigm science'. By the way, Kuhn was famously obscure in what he meant by a paradigm, defining it, according to Margaret Masterman (1970), in about 21 different ways. Such ambiguity in many if not most theoretical ideas lends support to the view that what is of greatest importance is using theoretical ideas to better understand the social and intellectual worlds and not necessarily divining what a thinker 'really meant' by a certain idea. Thus, Weber is similarly obscure on what he meant by 'rationalization', and my guess is that if one did a count like Masterman's one would come up with far more meanings of rationalization in Weber's work (Kalberg, 1980; Levine, 1981) than of the paradigm concept in Kuhn's.

One of the important implications of viewing sociology as a multiple paradigm 'science'[1] was that it helped to explain why sociology was, and is, not 'advancing' in the way the hard sciences are (for example, the soon-to-be-completed work on mapping the human genome). While an agreed-upon paradigm gives a science a base upon which to build and to do 'normal science', the existence of multiple paradigms makes this impossible for a discipline as a whole. Even within a given paradigm, incessant criticisms from the supporters of other paradigms and the need to respond to them make normal science virtually impossible, at least for any length of time and with a high degree of concentration. If one thinks sociology needs to be a science, then a multiparadigmatic state is a serious problem. However, if one does not (as is the case with postmodernists and others), then a multitude of approaches is to be preferred because such a condition is more likely to lead to numerous and diverse insights.

Application of the paradigm concept to sociology yielded three extant paradigms – the social facts, social definition, and social behavior paradigms – with others as possible, or even likely, paradigms in the future. Supporters of an extant paradigm tend to have different views of the *subject matter* of sociology, to operate with different *exemplars*, to adopt different *theories*, and to use different *methods* than adherents of the other paradigms. Further complicating matters is the fact that there are major within-paradigm differences on each of these elements, especially among theories adopted and methods employed. Thus, differences between paradigms, differences within paradigms, and the existence of other would-be paradigms combined to create in sociology (*circa* 1975) a rather chaotic situation that militated against doing normal science. As we will see in Chapter 7, written expressly for this volume, the situation today in sociology in general, and social theory in particular, is, if anything, even more diverse and chaotic.

Based on the existence of multiple paradigms in sociology, and some of the dysfunctional aspects of the struggles between adherents of these paradigms for hegemony within sociology, I set out (Ritzer, 1981b) to do M_o in an effort to develop a more integrated sociological paradigm designed to supplement extant paradigms. The heart both of my sense of sociology's multiple paradigms and of an integrated sociological paradigm lies in the notion of 'levels' of social analysis. I am, of course, *not* arguing that the social world is 'really' divided into levels, but rather that thinking in these terms is *one* of many useful ways of thinking about the social world. While each of the paradigms divined in the 1970s tended to focus on one or two levels of analysis, an integrated paradigm would focus on all levels synchronically, diachronically, and dialectically. To put it simply, it would be concerned with the dialectical relationship among individual thought, action, culture, and social structure, not only at one point in time, but also over time. This kind of theorizing is, of course, part of the classical tradition (see Chapter 5). However, by the 1970s in the United States theorists tended to be locked into perspectives that focused on one, or at best two, levels of social analysis and saw the other levels as either determined by their preferred levels or subordinated to them. While I certainly cannot claim credit for it, I think that in the last two decades of the twentieth century social theory did witness movement in the direction of such a paradigm as reflected in the development and importance of micro–macro theory (e.g. Alexander, Collins) in the United States and agency–structure theory (e.g. Giddens, Bourdieu, Archer) and actor–network theory (Latour, Law) in Europe.

Chapter 5 involves a metatheoretical analysis of the work of two classical theorists – Durkheim and Marx[2] – in an effort to determine whether the work of one of these thinkers could be an exemplar for an integrated paradigm that deals, dialectically, with the relationship between thought, action, culture, and social structure. In spite of his well-known sociologism which predisposes him to focus on social structure (material social facts) and culture (nonmaterial social facts), Durkheim turns out to be a surprisingly strong candidate for an exemplar for an integrated sociological paradigm. However, in the end his focus on social facts undermines the adequacy of his work on thought and action. In any case, an analysis of Durkheim's work from this perspective sheds some new and interesting light on it.

Given Marx's commitment to the diachronic analysis of the various levels of capitalism, his synchronic analysis of various economic forms, and his dialectical approach to all of this, his work clearly qualifies as the exemplar for an integrated sociological paradigm. His well-known focus on the structures of capitalism is undergirded by a concern for the role and fate of species being in capitalism. Furthermore, that focus on structure reflects the realities of capitalism and not an overarching commitment to focus on such structures at all times and in all places. Although not without its flaws from that point of view, Marx's work provides a strong model for those interested in adopting an integrated sociological paradigm.

In Chapter 6 I examine, in an M_o analysis of social psychology (although the same points apply to sociology in general), what many consider its two major metatheories in sociology: methodological individualism and methodological holism. It is obvious that these two metatheories lie at the base of the micro–macro, agency–structure divisions within sociology. It is also obvious, following the logic of the integrated sociological paradigm, that there is a need for another metatheory to supplement methodological individualism and methodological relationism. The chapter proposes the creation of methological relationism as a metatheoretical base for more integrated thinking in social psychology and sociology.

Chapter 7 looks at the paradigmatic status of sociology at the millennium. It is clear that sociology remains a multiple paradigm science, but what those paradigms are, or how many of them there are, is not so clear as it was in the 1970s. The paradigms that existed then remain more or less in place, although they seem weaker and less clearly defined. Given the rise of micro–macro, agency–structure, and actor–network theory, and the proliferation of multimethod research, a strong case could be made that an integrated sociological paradigm has attained full-fledged paradigmatic status. However, the most powerful developments all lead one to question anew whether sociology can be considered a 'science' in any sense of the term and whether there are any paradigms in sociology in any of Kuhn's 21 senses of the term. I am thinking primarily here of the combined impact of postmodern social theory, feminist theory, and multicultural theory. The postmodern argument against grand narratives and totalizations, and its questioning of science and scientific advancement, tend to lead to incredulity about assertions on sociology as a 'science' and its 'paradigms'. Much of feminist theory leads to similar kinds of doubts and this is especially true of its defining perspective – 'standpoint theory' – which leads either to a rejection of notions of science or paradigms, or to so many different sciences and paradigms as to leave those concepts as faint glimmers of what they were intended to mean. Multicultural theory leads to a very similar set of conclusions.

However, it is also the case that many sociologists continue to act as if sociology is a science and as if they operate in paradigms of the type defined by Kuhn. The best examples are rational choice theory, arguably part of the social behavior paradigm, and exchange theory, a charter member of that paradigm. Practitioners of both theories continue to theorize with such a scientific model in mind and research is conducted that is designed to flesh out an extant paradigm. The coexistence of such scientific approaches with postmodern, feminist, and multicultural orientations means that sociology in the new millennium is in a much more ambiguous scientific and paradigmatic state than it was in the 1970s. There is far more dissensus today than in the 1970s about whether or not sociology is, or should be, a science in the Kuhnian sense. In one way, this is a highly positive environment in which there is much more freedom to do many different sociologies. In another way, it is a difficult, even schizophrenic, environment in which it is almost impossible to get one's moorings since everything seems up for grabs. At the minimum, it is hard to practice normal science in a sociology in which the very bases of such a science are being called into question by feminists, postmodernists, and multiculturalists. Yet paradoxically scientific sociology, while more open to question than ever before, remains in control, dominating the major journals, and its practitioners garner a disproportionate share of the discipline's rewards, at least in the United States.

The final chapter (Chapter 8) in Part One takes a closer look at postmodern social theory, especially in terms of its epistemological implications for metatheorizing in sociology. In some ways, postmodern theory stands in opposition to metatheoretical work of the type being discussed throughout Part One of this book. For example, the opposition of postmodernists to grand narratives and totalizations would lead one to oppose M_o and its objective of finding new metatheories which are, by definition, totalizations. However, while much of postmodern social theory points in this direction, there are aspects of it that can be seen as metatheoretical in nature. For example, deconstructionism leads to the idea, among many others, that one must study social theories in order to take them apart. While most metatheorists would have little problem with this, they would be more troubled by the associated idea that deconstruction is undertaken without the expectation that the disassembled parts need ultimately to be reconstructed into a new general orientation. Metatheorists have much to gain from postmodern social theory, both in terms of studying the latter's questioning of basic aspects of metatheoretical work and in utilizing various postmodern ideas to enhance the practice of metatheorizing.

Part Two of this book deals with a transitional set of works that are, in part, metatheoretical and hence in line with the theme of Part One, but are also more applicable to the social world and hence related to the more applied theoretical works that make up the second volume. The material discussed in Part One is totally metatheoretical and hence has no direct applicability to the social world.[3] What unifies the chapters in Part Two is a concern for the theory of rationality, mainly as it is expressed in Max Weber's work, but also that of Karl Mannheim. The work of these theorists is explored metatheoretically (M_u), with an eye toward the creation of new theoretical ideas (M_p). Furthermore, rationalization theory is applied to a range of social phenomena including the medical profession, the fast-food restaurant and related phenomena, and even American sociology.

Chapter 9 begins with an M_u analysis of Max Weber's work on rationality. An overview of his ideas is offered and some of the most important of the secondary works on the issue of Weber's theory of rationalization are reanalyzed. Perhaps the most important point in the first part of the chapter is that Weber worked with at least four major types of rationality – *practical, theoretical, substantive,* and *formal* – but his primary concern was with the last, as well as its conflict with substantive rationality. Much of his work is devoted to the issue of why formal rationality developed in the Occident and the barriers to such a development elsewhere in the world. It is the growth of formal rationality that is associated with the notion of rationalization (or McDonaldization) in my work.

The bulk of Chapter 9 analyzes contemporary changes affecting the medical profession. Three major types of changes are discussed: changes in government policies, the changing nature of medical delivery systems, and changes within medical delivery systems. It is argued that these changes are impelling the medical profession away from substantive rationality and in the direction of formal rationality. Increasing formal rationality is likely to lead to greater external control over physicians and to a decline in the ability of the medical profession to distinguish itself from bureaucrats and capitalists. These changes, in turn, are likely to lead to some degree of deprofessionalization of physicians. This essay, first published in 1988, anticipated many changes in the medical profession in the 1990s, culminating in mid-1999 in the dramatic shift in the American Medical Association and its announcement that it was in favor of unionization. Nothing could be a better indicator of the deprofessionalization of physicians. Nor could any other event better presage the fact that medicine is likely to deprofessionalize further in the coming years. Few things are more antithetical to professionalization than unionization.

Chapter 10 discusses the relationship between Weber's ideas on formal rationality and my notion of McDonaldization. Weber argued that the paradigm of the process of formal rationalization is the bureaucracy, while in my view by the late twentieth century the fast-food restaurant had become a far better model for this process. Neo-Weberians have defined what Weber meant by formal rationality in various ways, but for me the essence of the concept, and of its more contemporary manifestation, McDonaldization, lies in its major subdimensions: *calculability, efficiency, predictability,* and *control* through the substitution of nonhuman for human technology. Of great importance is the fact that formally rational and McDonaldized systems inevitably spawn a series of irrationalities, leading to the pivotally important idea of the *irrationality of rationality*. In my view, the contemporary world is growing increasingly McDonaldized, and while this brings with it a series of unquestioned advancements (including increased calculability, efficiency, predictability, and control), it also means a number of irrationalities that are rarely given the attention devoted to the positive effects of McDonaldization.

In addition to laying out the basic dimensions of McDonaldization, Chapter 10 also discusses its relationship to a number of contemporary theoretical ideas: postindustrialism, post-Fordism, postmodernism, and globalization theory. The McDonaldization thesis is at odds with the first three because it indicates the continuation of industrialism, Fordism, and modernism. In other words, it tends to cast doubt on the idea that we have moved into a postindustrial, post-Fordist, and post-modern society. It is also at odds with globalization theory since it demonstrates the importance of Americanization rather than global processes that are independent of any specific nation.

While the focus in Chapter 10, as well as in my work on McDonaldization, is on formal rationality, in Chapter 11 I deal with all four of Weber's types of rationality – formal, substantive, theoretical, and practical. As pointed out above, Weber's work on the Occident is defined by its focus on the triumph of formal rationality over the other types. However, it is possible to see that the ultimate in rationality, *hyperrationality*, is the result not of the dominance of formal rationality, or of any single type of rationality, but of the combination of all four types in one system. A hyperrational system is able to utilize not only formal rationality, but the other three types as well, in order to achieve its objectives. A synergy develops among the four types of rationality as they are applied in unison to practical situations that allows for the development of a far more effective system than if one relied merely on formal rationality. It is argued that the Japanese automobile industry, as it developed in the 1970s and 1980s, is a good example of a hyperrational system and this helps to account for its ascendancy relative to its American counterpart which remained locked in a formally rational system. Of course, the 1990s brought with it problems for the Japanese system in general, and its automobile industry in particular (although it remains powerful). Part of the Japanese automobile industry's problems is traceable to the fact that the American automobile industry learned from its mistakes as well as the successes of the Japanese and developed hyperrational systems of its own.

While Max Weber offers the most important theory of rationality, it is not the only such theory available. Chapter 12 involves a meta-theoretical examination of Karl Mannheim's theory of rationality. While heavily influenced by Weber's theory, Mannheim moves beyond it in many ways and his theory offers a number of advantages over it. For example, while for Weber the problem in the triumph of formal over substantive rationality is the loss of 'human values' associated with the latter, for Mannheim the problem in this conflict (although he uses slightly different terms) is the loss of the ability to think. Weber's sense of human values creates problems because it is possible to think of all value systems as 'human'. Thus, the set of values associated with Nazism that led to the Holocaust can be thought of as human, at least from the perspective of the Nazis. No such problem is created by Mannheim's notion that the threat of the triumph of formal rationality is to people's ability to think. And, it is certainly the case that formally rational systems discourage individual thought and creativity. Beyond this, Mannheim offers a number of other conceptual expansions and extensions (self-rationalization, self-observation, types of irrationality) that greatly enhance our ability to theorize about and apply the concept of rationality. Even when Mannheim's concepts seem wrong-headed or dated, they increase our ability to think about today's McDonaldized society.

This volume closes with Chapter 13 which serves to bring its concerns full circle. This chapter integrates my interest in metaanalysis with my concern with McDonaldization by discussing the McDonaldization of American sociology in general and sociological theory in particular. Here I use the concept of McDonaldization to do a metaanalysis of sociology. I demonstrate that sociology, like the rest of society, has undergone a process of McDonaldization and this helps us to better understand some of the problems in the discipline as a whole and in sociological theory. This demonstrates, once again, the more general point that the great abstractions of metatheory need not be as divorced from more concrete and applied ideas as it first appears.

Notes

1   By the way, while I used this notion of sociology as a 'science' because I was applying Kuhnian theory, I am personally agnostic on whether sociology is or should be a science. Some do sociology as if it is a science, and many others do sociology in various other ways. I favor a sociology characterized by a wide range of approaches, one of which should be a scientific approach. If the issue of which kind of approach to use needs to be resolved, it should be done on a case-by-case basis through an examination of which approach or combination of approaches yields the greatest insight into the social and theoretical worlds.

2   These are just two of a number of theorists surveyed with this objective in mind in *Toward an Integrated Sociological Paradigm* (1981b).

3   However, it is indirectly applicable and I often use it in my thinking about the social world. For example, the levels of analysis that are the heart of the integrated socio-logical paradigm *always* inform my thinking about the social world.

PART ONE

METATHEORIZING

1

METATHEORIZING IN SOCIOLOGY

There is strong antipathy, at least on the surface, among many sociological theorists to abstract (Stinchcombe, 1986) and grand (Hirsch et al., 1987) theorizing. Opponents argue that the abstraction of sociological theory should be greatly circumscribed and that theories should be derived from, and remain close to, the social world. This hostility is surprising because sociological theory, by its very nature, must be abstract, at least to some degree. It is also surprising because it comes from theorists; one would expect empiricists and practitioners to be hostile to the abstraction of sociological theory, but not theorists. After all, there is a need for at least some portion of the sociological community to think abstractly: if not theorists, who will function at this level?

This hostility to abstraction is related to an even stronger animosity among theorists toward those who analyze other theories, either theoretically or empirically. Such work is seen as doubly abstract: the study of abstract theories yields even more abstract results. Most sociological theorists are quite willing to allow sociologists to turn their theoretical arsenal and empirical tools on social and ideational phenomena but not on sociological theory. Clearly, however, sociological theory is a social and intellectual phenomenon that is, in turn, affected by a wide range of other social and cognitive phenomena. Thus, sociological theory, like any other social and ideational entity, can and should be studied theoretically and empirically.

In spite of the criticisms, the vast majority of theorists do, in fact, spend a good deal of time studying sociological theory in various ways. Some do this quite self-consciously in systematic efforts to deepen their understanding of various aspects of sociological theory. Others reflect on extant theories as a way of laying the basis for their own theories. Still others reflect on theory in order to get at basic principles that transcend theory.

As an example, let us focus for the moment on those who study theory as a basis for developing their own theories. Most such theorists (and this is true of most empiricists as well) in sociology do not spend large portions of their time studying the social world directly. Relatively few theorists develop and refine their theories while they study assembly-line workers or other denizens of the 'real' world.[1] Some may develop their theories as they analyze empirical data they have collected themselves. Others theorize on the basis of data collected and reported by other sociologists. Some may develop their theories, at least in part, on the basis of a careful study of, and reaction to, the work of other theorists. Still others may develop their theories by utilizing theoretical ideas drawn from other fields: economics, philosophy, psychology, etc. I suppose there are even those who practice 'cerebral hygiene' (which we usually associate with Comte and Spencer[2]) and whose theories emerge out of a kind of immaculate conception. The fact is that it matters little *where* the theories come from; what counts is whether they make sense and whether they help us understand, explain, and make predictions about the social world. Close contact with the social world *may* yield such theory, but so may intense involvement with the ideas of our theoretical predecessors and contemporaries. Similarly, such involvement can yield a deeper understanding of sociological theory as well as useful perspectives that overarch sociological theory.

My goal in this chapter is to describe and make the case for *metatheorizing*,[3] the systematic study of sociological theory, as an independent and significant endeavor, albeit one that is intimately involved in sound theoretical and empirical work. Most theorists (and other kinds of sociologists as well) do a great deal of metatheorizing. Thus, this chapter is not proposing something new, but rather is giving explicit recognition to a process that has been a reality in sociology since its inception.[4] My secondary objective is to help metatheorists come 'out of the closet'.[5] Too often, those who metatheorize have been subjected to vitriolic attacks, especially by fellow theorists (who themselves are often unwitting practitioners of this traditional form of work in sociology). There is nothing reprehensible about metatheorizing; some of the most important classic thinkers (Marx, Weber, Durkheim, Parsons) were, and many key contemporary theorists (Habermas, Collins, Giddens, Alexander) are, avid metatheorists.

As I stated above, and explain in much greater detail in related works, metatheorizing lies at the base of much of sociological theory. If that is true, then what is the distinction between a metatheorist and a theorist? To put it (too) strongly, a metatheorist is one who studies sociological theories of the social world, while a theorist is one who studies the social world more directly in order to create (or apply) sociological theory. However, despite this seemingly neat distinction between metatheorist and theorist (and they are ideal types), the categories overlap to a great extent. For example, most of those we consider metatheorists also study the social world[6] and most of those classified as theorists[7] also study theoretical works. Furthermore, both theorists and metatheorists study documents. The theorist often examines documents derived from the social world while the metatheorist usually analyzes documents produced by theorists. Finally, and perhaps most importantly, substantial metatheorizing often precedes, and helps lead to, advances in social theory.

I must distinguish between those metatheorists who seek to lay down the prerequisites for doing theory before theory is developed, and those who take developed theories as their subject matter (Turner, 1991). In most other fields metatheorizing (and *all* forms of metaanalysis) is done *after* theories have been developed. Such metatheorizing may seek a better understanding of those theories, or it may seek to create new theory, or it may seek to create an overarching theoretical perspective. However, in Turner's view[8] most metatheorists in sociology do not study extant theory, but rather seek to create a metatheory (i.e. an overarching perspective) that in their view must be articulated *before* adequate theory can be developed. That is, 'advocates of meta-theory usually emphasize that we cannot develop theory until we have resolved these more fundamental epistemological and metaphysical questions' (1991: 9). Turner concludes, quite rightly in my opinion, that 'such meta-theorizing has put the cart before the horse' (1991: 9). Not only is such metatheorizing misplaced, but it leads us into an arena of substantial difficulty and irresolvable controversy. Because of these and other problems, metatheorizing, as the term is used here, is not a process that occurs *before* theory is developed in order to lay down its prerequisites. Rather, metatheorizing is a process that occurs *after* theory has been created and takes that theory itself as the object of study.

Paul Furfey (1953/1965: 8) in *The Scope and Method of Sociology: A Metasociological Treatise* claims to have introduced the term *metasociology*, of which metatheory is clearly a part. Furfey (1953/1965: 9) defines *metasociology* as a science distinct from sociology; that is, sociology takes as its subject matter the social world, 'whereas the subject matter of metasociology is sociology itself'.[9] This definition is in accord with the more specific approach to metatheory taken in this chapter. That is, theory focuses on the social world, while metatheory takes theory as its subject matter. However, it is useful to take a closer, critical look at the details of Furfey's ideas because they will help us to clarify the meaning of *metasociology* and *metatheory*.

While he made an important beginning, Furfey has an orientation that involves a questionable approach to metasociology (and metatheory, in particular), an approach that has been attacked explicitly by Turner. Furfey *is* guilty of undertaking the kind of metasociology criticized by Turner.[10] In spite of the way he defines the term, Furfey's metasociology does *not* involve the study of sociology, but instead is a set of principles that is prior to, and presupposed by, sociology. He begins with the debatable assumption that sociology *is* a science and proceeds to argue that metasociology has three tasks to perform for the field. First, it is to develop criteria for distinguishing scientific from nonscientific sociological knowledge. Second, and reminiscent of Durkheim (but more than a half century later), metasociology is to differentiate between phenomena that are and are not relevant to the field of sociology. Third, 'metasociology is to provide practical procedural rules for applying in actual sociological research the two sorts of criteria mentioned' (1953/1965: 14).

Furfey's (1953/1965: 17) work is dominated by his view that sociology is a science and metasociology is 'an auxiliary science which furnishes the methodological principles presupposed by sociology'. In Turner's terms, Furfey is here putting the cart before the horse. Metasociology should *not* provide a service to scientific sociology (or, for that matter, antiscientific sociology) but rather should take sociology as a subject of study.[11] Where I part company with Turner is over the type of metasociology, particularly metatheorizing, that takes sociology as its subject of study. Turner has more sympathy for this type of metasociology, but even here he concludes that metatheorizing bogs us down in unresolvable philosophical controversies. Turner's criticisms here rest on practical grounds: metatheorizing prevents us from getting on with theorizing. While this may be the case, I will argue that a careful study of extant sociological theories can be a great aid in gaining a greater understanding of theory, creating transcendent perspectives, and creating and developing theories.[12] For instance, a number of examples come to mind of metatheorizing that proved highly useful in theory creation, including Marx's study of Hegel, the young Hegelians, the French socialists, and the political economists; Parsons's detailed analysis of Weber, Durkheim, and Pareto; and Alexander's similar work on Marx, Weber, Durkheim, and Parsons.

I also differ with Furfey over the idea that metasociology and implicitly metatheorizing are fields distinct from sociology. To my mind, metasociology in general, and metatheorizing in particular, are parts of sociology, subareas within the larger field (for a view – with which I am quite comfortable – that sees metatheorizing as an integral part of sociology, see the discussion of Bourdieu's 'socioanalysis' later in the chapter).

In spite of Furfey's position, and Turner's critique of his orientation, the overwhelming majority of metasociological and metatheoretical efforts have *not* sought to predefine the field, but instead have studied what actually transpires in the field. Gouldner (1970) labels this kind of work the 'sociology of sociology', or, more specifically, 'reflexive sociology'.[13] Without getting into the 'radical' rhetoric[14] that characterizes (and badly dates) *The Coming Crisis of Western Sociology* (1970) and Gouldner's specific thoughts on reflexive sociology, I am quite satisfied with his position that 'first and foremost, a reflexive sociology is concerned with what sociologists want to do and with what, in fact, they actually do in the world' (1970: 489). More specific to the narrower aims of this chapter, Gouldner (1970: 46) is interested in getting at the 'sub-theoretical level, the "infrastructure" of theory'. He is quite clear about the relationship between metatheory and metasociology: 'My concern with a theory of social theories is only part of a larger commitment to a "sociology of sociology"' (1970: 488). Gouldner's sociology of sociology, and more particularly his 'theory of social theories', is much closer to the approach taken in this chapter than Furfey's metasociology. However, as we will see, metatheorizing does not merely involve theorizing about theory; it also includes empirical studies of theories and theorists.[15]

Indeed, Gouldner had earlier done such an empirical study in *Enter Plato: Classical Greece and the Origins of Social Theory* (1965). Gouldner traced the roots of Plato's theory to the social structure and culture of Athens. In addition, he offered 'a critical case study of Plato as a social theorist' (1965: 168). He was interested not only in gaining a deeper understanding of Plato's theory, but also in deriving lessons from such an analysis relevant to contemporary theory. In the context of his discussion of Plato, Gouldner offered a good description of his meta-theoretical approach: 'Some social scientists are interested in studying industrial workers; some study physicians; and still others, drug addicts and prostitutes. I happen to be curious about social theorists, as part of a sociology of social science' (1965: 170–1).

Sociologists in general, and sociological theorists in particular, are not the only ones to do metaanalysis, that is, to reflexively study various aspects of their own discipline. Others who do such work include philosophers (Radnitzky, 1973), psychologists (Gergen, 1973; 1986; Schmitt et al., 1984), political scientists (Connolly, 1973), other social scientists (see the various essays in Fiske and Shweder, 1986), and historians (White, 1973). Some of these efforts are quite similar to at least some types of metaanalysis in sociology, while others differ considerably from the types of work done in sociology. The key point is that the reflexive study of one's own discipline is not the exclusive province of sociology.

Beyond the fact that metaanalysis is found in other fields, it is also true that various kinds of sociologists, not just metatheorists, do such analyses. We can group the various types of metaanalysis in sociology under the broad heading of *metasociology*, which we can define as the systematic study of sociology in general and of its various components: substantive areas (e.g. Hall's 1983 overview of occupational sociology), concepts (Porpora's 1989 analysis of the concept of 'structure'), methods (*metamethods*: e.g. analyses by Coleman, 1986 and Bailey, 1987 of the micro–macro problem in social research; Brewer and Hunter's 1989 effort to synthesize methods; Noblit and Hare's 1988 work synthesizing qualitative methods), data (*meta-data-analysis*:[16] e.g. Hunter et al., 1982; Fendrich, 1984; Wolf, 1986; Polit and Falbo, 1987; Hunter and Schmidt, 1989), and theories. It is the last, *metatheorizing*, or the systematic study of sociological theory, that will concern us in this chapter.

Types of Metatheorizing

A wide variety of work can be included under the heading of sociological metatheorizing. What distinguishes work in this area is not so
much the process of metatheorizing (it may vary greatly in a variety of
ways),[17] but rather the nature of the end products. In my view, there are
three varieties of metatheorizing, with each largely defined by differences in its end product. The first type, *metatheorizing as a means of
attaining a deeper understanding of theory* (M_u), involves the study of
theory in order to produce a better, a more profound understanding of
extant theory (Ritzer, 1987; 1988a). M_u is concerned, more specifically,
with the study of theories, theorists, and communities of theorists, as
well as with the larger intellectual and social contexts of theories and
theorists. The second type, *metatheorizing as a prelude to theory development* (M_p), entails the study of extant theory in order to produce new
sociological theory (Ritzer, 1989a). The third type, *metatheorizing as a
source of overarching theoretical perspectives* (M_o), is oriented to the goal of
producing a perspective, one could say a metatheory, that overarches
some part or all of sociological theory. All three types involve the
systematic study of sociological theory; they differ mainly in terms of
their objectives in that study (Ritzer, 1990d).

The third type of metatheorizing (M_o) is not identical to the kind of
overarching metatheory (O_m) (e.g. Furfey's positivism) rejected earlier
in this chapter. In fact, O_m does not even fit my definition of metatheorizing because it does not occur after theory has been created and
that theory then taken as a subject of study. M_o, like the other two types
of metatheorizing, occurs *after* theory has been developed, while O_m
occurs *prior* to the development of theory. Thus, M_o is derived from
theory rather than imposing itself on theory. In this sense, M_o is the
preferable approach because it at least allows us to assess the process
by which the transcendent perspective is created. In the case of O_m we
have no way of ascertaining the validity of the process through which
the overarching perspective came into existence.

Nevertheless, in spite of differences in how they reach their objective, both M_o and O_m produce overarching theoretical perspectives. In
so doing, they share the likelihood that they will, as Turner suggests,
embroil us in a series of irresolvable controversies. Elsewhere (Ritzer,
1991b), I examine six examples of M_o and O_m, as well as mixed types
that produce positivistic, dialectical, and postpositivistic perspectives
that transcend sociological theory. Needless to say, supporters of one
of these types of overarching perspectives are likely to reject, or at least
be extremely uncomfortable with, the other types. Overarching perspectives, whether they precede or come after theory, are likely to be
highly controversial and often counterproductive. Thus, I argue that M_o,

while it is not without utility, may be the most controversial of the three major types of metatheorizing.

In spite of their inherent problems, there has been a tendency to equate the third type of metatheorizing (M_o), as well as O_m, with metatheorizing as a whole. This is because they, unlike the other two types of metatheorizing (M_u, M_p), produce *a* metatheory in the sense of a perspective that stands above sociological theory. While it is distinguished by this end product, M_o involves essentially the same kind of metatheoretical processes as the other two types (M_u, M_p). As we will see, some sociologists do engage in M_o, but many more do M_u and M_p. Since all three are legitimate forms of metatheorizing, it would be much too restrictive to equate M_o with the field of metatheorizing as a whole. Furthermore, as I mentioned above, M_o is the most problematic of the three types of metatheorizing. As to O_m, the approach that comes before theory has been created, it poses, as we have seen, even greater difficulties. Thus, the production of overarching perspectives, as well as those perspectives themselves, constitute only a very small and highly controversial portion of sociological metatheorizing.

The three varieties of metatheorizing are, of course, ideal types. Actual cases are usually marked by considerable overlap in the objectives of particular metatheoretical works. Nevertheless, those who do one type of metatheorizing tend to be less interested in achieving the objectives of the other two types. Thus, for example, those who seek the creation of transcendent perspectives tend to be less interested in achieving a deeper understanding of theory or in new theory creation than those who engage in these latter types of metatheorizing directly. Of course, there are sociologists who at one time or another have done all three types of metatheorizing. For example, Alexander (1982–3) created overarching perspectives in the first volume of *Theoretical Logic in Sociology* (1982) and used them in the next three volumes to achieve a better understanding of the works of the classic theorists, and in later works sought to help create neofunctionalism as a theoretical successor to structural functionalism (Alexander, 1985; Alexander and Colomy, 1990; more recently Alexander has abandoned the latter effort).

Related Subfields

Metatheorizing (and more generally metasociologizing) is intimately related to several extant subfields within sociology. For example, it has much in common with the sociology (and philosophy) of science. However, the sociology of science is clearly more general than the sociological study of sociological theory as a specific scientific endeavor. Furthermore, many would contest the applicability of the sociology of science to sociological theory because of their view that sociology is not a science. There is more to sociology than its scientific aspects. In taking extant theory as its subject, metatheorizing need not make the assumption that sociological theory is scientific or that it is part of a scientific discipline. Nevertheless, to the degree that it is applicable to sociology, metasociologists have much to learn from the sociology (and philosophy) of science. In fact, ideas drawn from the sociology (e.g. invisible colleges, scientific networks) and philosophy (e.g. paradigms, scientific research programs) of science have played a central role in metasociology and metatheorizing.

Metatheorizing also has much in common with the sociology of knowledge, although the latter too is much more general than metatheorizing: there are certainly many other forms of knowledge than sociological knowledge. Furthermore, sociological theory is more than knowledge (e.g. schools, networks) and in that sense is broader than the sociology of knowledge. Again, in spite of the differences, metatheorizing has gained much from the sociology of knowledge.

Still another subfield with which there is overlap is the history of sociological theory. In my view, most histories of sociological theory involve metatheorizing, especially M_u. The objective of such histories is a more profound understanding of theory. There are, however, histories, or at least parts of some of them, that are interested in historical issues *per se* and because of this the history of sociological theory cannot be subsumed under metatheorizing. On the other side, not all metatheorizing involves historical analysis. In fact, all three types of metatheorizing can focus on contemporary sociological theory. Thus, I think metatheorizing is far broader than the history of sociology, although historians of sociological theory obviously go into historical issues in much greater depth than most metatheorists.

Thus, while metatheorizing overlaps with the sociologies of science and of knowledge and the history of sociology,[18] in some senses it is narrower than them and in other senses it is broader. This means that metatheorizing cannot subsume, or be subsumed by, these other fields and must be considered an independent subfield.

Major Critiques

Earlier in this chapter I mentioned those who are critical of abstract sociological theory and grand theory. It should come as no surprise that metatheorizing, which is even more abstract than theory or even grand theory, has itself come under substantial attack. However, most of these attacks are general and unfocused. Most critics have an unclear and undifferentiated sense of metatheorizing. Their criticisms cannot be taken seriously because they fail to specify exactly what type of metatheorizing they are attacking. While they seem to think that they are indicting all metatheorizing, it is clear, given the three types outlined above (as well as the rejected form O_m), that their criticisms are far narrower in scope.

Jonathan Turner (1991: 9; see also 1985) is critical of metatheorizing largely on pragmatic grounds because, as mentioned earlier, it 'often gets bogged down in weighty philosophical matters and immobilizes theory building ... meta-theory often stymies as much as stimulates the theoretical activity because it embroils theorists in inherently unresolvable and always debatable controversies'. Later, Turner describes metatheory as 'interesting but counterproductive' and contends that those who propound it 'never get around to developing theory' (1991: 24).

Turner is really criticizing those who seek to lay down prerequisites to adequate sociological theorizing (O_m) rather than those who do any of the three types of metatheorizing. If Turner is critical of any of the latter, it is of M_o because overarching perspectives emerge from analyses of extant theory. It is likely that such overarching perspectives plunge us into a series of irresolvable controversies. However, these works do come after theory has been created and in this sense Turner would be satisfied with them. Turner is far less likely to be critical of the other two types of metatheorizing. Neither M_u nor M_p involve us in irresolvable controversies. Few sociologists would be critical of the objective of attaining a deeper understanding of extant theory or of developing new theory (indeed the latter is what Turner, 1989 often seeks to do). A particular understanding and a specific new theory might be controversial, but such controversies can be resolved by analyzing and discussing the steps involved in the attainment of a given understanding or the creation of a particular theory. Furthermore, both *are* productive, of greater understanding of theory in the former case and of new theory in the latter case. Thus, it is clear that Turner (1990a) is not critical of all types of metatheorizing and he may well not be critical of any of the three types discussed in this chapter.

In a now infamous review of a book (Alford and Friedland, 1985) in political sociology, Theda Skocpol (1986) makes it clear that in her view what is good and useful in that subfield is substantive theory and research. She describes the Alford and Friedland work, pejoratively, as 'five hundred pages of nothing but metatheory' (1986: 10). She attacks the authors for 'pigeonholing' the work of political sociologists; for arguing for the need for an integrated theory that draws from every pigeonhole but never specifies what it is about; for arguing that different types of approaches fit best at different levels of analysis; and for ignoring the fact that the best work in political sociology has dealt with the interrelations among such levels. She hopes that Alford and Friedland will return to substantive work in political sociology, but in the meantime 'may the good lord protect other political sociologists from wandering into the dead end of metatheory' (1986: 11–12). The use of the phrase 'dead end' here, as well as in the title of her review essay, implies clearly that Skocpol sees *no* productive role for meta-theorizing within sociology.

Skocpol's critique of metatheorizing, like that of Turner, lacks specificity. What she is being critical of, in my view, is M_u and *not* the other two types of metatheorizing. Alford and Friedland practice M_u since their objective is to review work in political sociology in order to achieve a more profound theoretical understanding of it (as well as of the polity). Skocpol believes that such a deeper understanding comes not from thinking about the theoretical work of others, but from substantive investigations in the political world. I believe that Skocpol would find the other two types of metatheorizing less likely to be 'dead ends' because they produce either new theory (M_p) or overarching theoretical perspectives (M_o). Furthermore, I am far from being convinced that M_u is a dead end. In fact, I think such work can be, and has been, highly important to the development of sociological theory. A better understanding of extant theory is invaluable in the development of new theory.

Perhaps the most interesting critique of metatheorizing comes from Randall Collins (1986a). At first, Collins associates metatheorizing with the overarching perspective of antipositivism. This, implicitly, involves an attack on M_o and/or O_m. However, Collins quickly moves to a much broader critique:

> It is not surprising to me that metatheory does not go anywhere; it is basically a reflexive specialty, capable about making comments on other fields but dependent on intellectual life elsewhere that it can formalize and ideologize … or critique. That is why so much of the intellectual work of today consists of commentaries on works of the past rather than constructions that are creative in their own right. (1986a: 1343)

Collins, unlike Turner and Skocpol, is, I think, indicting implicitly all three types of metatheorizing, although he lacks a differentiated sense of the field. Like Turner and myself, Collins is critical of those (in this case the antipositivists) who seek to lay down prerequisites for the field.[19] His critique is more general than that of Turner and Skocpol since he is attacking metatheorizing, or all work that takes extant theory as the object of study. However, the implication is that Collins is most critical of M_u because it is the least creative of the three types of metatheorizing. The other two types of metatheorizing are clearly creative of new theory or overarching perspectives, and hence Collins would find them far more acceptable. In spite of his seemingly general critique of metatheorizing, Collins proceeds in the same essay to do what he condemns most (M_u) and undertakes a metatheoretical analysis of a variety of works of the (recent) past.

Perhaps the most telling response to the critics discussed above is to point out that they themselves, like most sociological theorists, do a great deal of metatheorizing. Given their criticisms, one would assume that none of these notables had ever uttered a metatheoretical word. However, even a cursory review of their work indicates significant metatheorizing. This is not the place to go into a full-scale review of the works of Turner, Collins, and Skocpol; a few examples will have to suffice.

Turner has done all three types of metatheorizing at one time or another in his work. Some examples of M_u include attempts to analyze and critique structural functionalism (Turner and Maryanski, 1978), neofunctionalism (Turner and Maryanski, 1988a), and the history of American sociological theory (Turner, 1990b). Most of his work on positivism would be included under the heading of M_o. However, this is being charitable to Turner and accepting the idea that his positivism is derived from his study of sociological theory. If, however, Turner's positivism was developed prior to his study of theory, and is a prerequisite to theory, then he is guilty of creating the kind of approach (O_m) of which he (and I) is highly critical. In fact, Turner's vocal adherence to a strict positivistic perspective does plunge us into the kind of irre-solvable controversies (e.g. with antipositivists, postpositivists) that he is so concerned about. Turner has also done M_p, including an effort to piece together a microtheory of motivation out of the contributions of a number of microtheoretical traditions (exchange theory, interaction-ism, ethnomethodology, structuration theory, and the theory of inter-action ritual chains) (Turner, 1987); the fifth edition of his theory text which, like the others, attempts to derive hypotheses from a variety of contemporary theories (Turner, 1991); and a similarly oriented book aimed at the development of elementary principles derived from work, mainly theoretical,[20] in the area of social stratification (Turner, 1984). Turner makes his use of M_p clear in the conclusion of the chapter in his stratification book devoted to prior theories: 'In this chapter, I have reviewed some of the weaknesses in the literature on stratification ... Yet, there have been numerous important contributions to theorizing about stratification processes ... I will borrow from Marx, Weber and Spencer; I will recast dramatically the functional argument; and I will use many elements of Lenski's synthesis' (1984: 55). Turner also makes a more general case for M_p, or what he calls 'theory cumulation': 'We selectively take the ideas of others and extend them in some way, producing a theoretical argument that is more powerful than the one with which we began. Unfortunately, we do not do enough of this kind of activity' (1989: 9–10).

As for Collins, among his works are efforts to review and build theo-retically upon the work of theorists like Weber (Collins, 1985), Goffman (Collins, 1986c), and Mead (Collins, 1989b). Even his best-known theoretical works on conflict (Collins, 1975; 1990) and interaction ritual chains (Collins, 1981b; 1981c; 1987b) are based heavily on an analysis and critique of the work of theoretical predecessors (e.g. Marx, Weber, Durkheim, Goffman, Garfinkel, etc.) within those traditions. Thus, Collins is one of our most prominent practitioners of M_p. I have already noted how he did M_u in a paper purportedly critical of metatheorizing. He also does M_o as, for example, in his work (Collins, 1989a) outlining and defending his view that sociology must be a science, albeit a more broadly defined positivistic science that avoids some of the excesses of Turner's positivism.[21]

Skocpol is the least metatheoretical of this triumvirate, but a portion of her major work, *States and Social Revolutions* (1979), is a metatheoretical analysis (M_p) of various theories of revolution. Indeed, Skocpol's preface to that book makes her metatheoretical intentions abundantly clear:

> Developed through critical reflection on assumptions and types of explanation common to most received theories of revolution, the principles of analysis sketched in the first chapter of the book are meant to reorient our sense of what is characteristic of – and problematic about – revolutions as they actually have occurred historically. Then the remainder of the book attempts to make the program of Chapter 1, a calling for new kinds of explanatory arguments, come alive in application. (1979: xi)

This is a remarkable position for someone who, as we saw above, came to label metatheory a 'dead end' (Skocpol, 1986). Chapter One of *States and Social Revolutions* is an avowedly metatheoretical endeavor involving a critique of extant theories of revolution and an effort to develop an alternative theory on the basis of that critique. The remaining 'empirical' (comparative/historical) chapters are merely meant to make the derived theoretical program 'come alive'.[22]

Thus, it is clear that the major critics of metatheorizing do a great deal of this kind of work themselves. If this is true of such critics, it seems obvious that metatheorizing is ubiquitous among sociological theorists. Such well-known contemporary theorists as Habermas, Giddens, and Alexander do a considerable amount of metatheorizing; it may well be the case they do more metatheorizing than theorizing. In fact, it appears that while theorists have always been inclined toward metatheorizing, today's theorists do a great deal more of it than the classic theorists. While there is much merit in metatheorizing, it might become a problem if our dominant theorists do increasingly more metatheorizing and correspondingly less theorizing about the social world. In line with the criticisms voiced (and largely rebutted) earlier in this chapter, such perspectives are in danger of growing too abstract and too removed from the social world.

This chapter, then, is about a ubiquitous form of sociology, a form that has been widely, albeit largely implicitly, practiced. It is also a form of sociology that has been often, and wrongly, maligned. One objective of this chapter is to make the practice of metatheorizing more explicit. I hope that by making it explicit, future practitioners will be able to develop and refine metatheorizing more self-consciously. Another function of making metatheorizing more explicit is that it will allow critics of the practice to refine their criticisms, if they still wish to make them. The continuing development of metatheorizing in general, as well of its various subtypes, will make it much more difficult to simply dismiss the approach out of hand. Critics will need to come to grips with the approach in general as well as with its various subtypes. They will need to specify the forms of metatheorizing of which they are critical, and why they are critical of them. The propensity to criticize may come to be mitigated by the fact that the critics will realize that they themselves are frequently metatheoreticians.

Another hope I have is that metatheoretical work will come to be accepted in its own right. Frequently, metatheoretical work is dismissed because it is 'not theory', that is, because it is not about the social world, but rather about theory. But metatheory is not theory and it should be judged on its own grounds. The study of theory is an acceptable, even desirable, type of sociological work that can be distinguished, at least in part, from theory. Those who do sound metatheoretical work are contributing to sociological theory (and empirical research as well) in a variety of ways and thereby, indirectly, to a better understanding of the social world.

Metatheorizing as a Means of Attaining a Deeper Understanding of Sociological Theory

We have briefly mentioned M_u above, but it is necessary to go into it in more detail here because it lies at the base of all metatheorizing. That is, it is impossible to create new theory or new overarching theoretical perspectives without first gaining a solid understanding of the relevant theories. There are several well-defined varieties of M_u. All these subtypes involve the formal or informal study of sociological theory. A fourfold diagram utilizing the dimensions *internal–external* (Smelser, 1989) and *intellectual–social* yields a typology that deals exhaustively with the varieties of M_u.[23] *Internal* refers to things that exist within sociology, while *external* deals with phenomena that are found outside sociology but have an impact on it. By *intellectual* I mean anything that relates to the cognitive structure of sociology: theories, metatheoretical

Figure 1.1 Major types of M$_u$

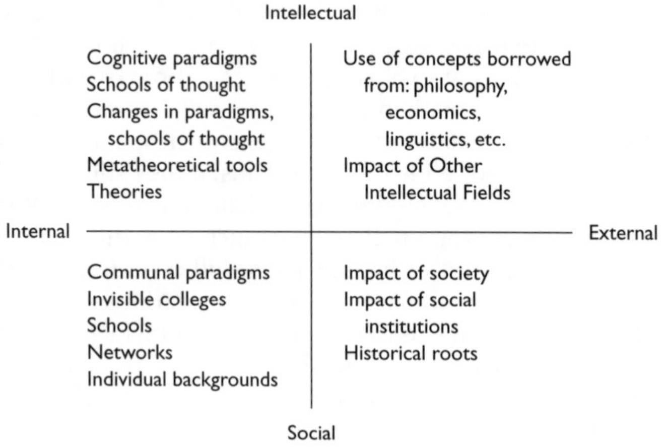

Intellectual

Cognitive paradigms	Use of concepts borrowed
Schools of thought	from: philosophy,
Changes in paradigms,	economics,
schools of thought	linguistics, etc.
Metatheoretical tools	Impact of Other
Theories	Intellectual Fields

Internal ————————————————————————— External

Communal paradigms	Impact of society
Invisible colleges	Impact of social
Schools	institutions
Networks	Historical roots
Individual backgrounds	

Social

tools, ideas borrowed from other disciplines, and so on. *Social* refers to the sociological structure of sociology: schools, the effect of individual background factors on sociologists, the impact of the larger society, and so forth. Figure 1.1 is the fourfold diagram that is created when we crosscut the internal–external and intellectual–social dimensions.

Four cautionary notes are in order before I proceed. First, the two dimensions (internal–external; intellectual–social) are continua with no hard-and-fast dividing lines between the poles of each. Second, the four types of M$_u$ developed by crosscutting these continua are not clearly distinct from one another. In other words, specific metatheoretical works may, as we will see, bridge two, three, or even all four types of M$_u$. Third, the enumeration of kinds of work to be discussed under each heading will likely require expansion in the future as other kinds of work under each evolve. Fourth, we should not reify the typology to be discussed below; its utility is in helping us to understand the diverse types of work going on in M$_u$. Thus, other typologies may be developed that could prove even more useful in analyzing M$_u$.

Internal-Intellectual

The first, and by far the largest, body of work in M$_u$ is derived from Thomas Kuhn's (1962; 1970b) philosophy of science (as well as that of others, e.g. Lakatos, 1978),[24] and attempts to identify the major paradigm(s) in sociology. Although Kuhn's paradigms encompass both intellectual and communal (social) components, most sociologists working within the Kuhnian tradition have emphasized the cognitive aspects.

At a cognitive level, paradigms are sometimes equated with theories (Friedrichs, 1970; Effrat, 1972; Leinhart, 1977; Colclough and Horan, 1983; Rosenberg, 1989), sometimes with groups of theories (Eisenstadt and Curelaru, 1976; Strasser, 1976), and sometimes with a variety of cognitive components including theories and/or methods (Ritzer's, 1975c, 1975d 'social facts', 'social definition', and 'social behavior' paradigms that encompass both theories and methods;[25] Albrow's 1974 distinction, focusing on methods, between the 'dialectical' and 'categorical' paradigms; Platt's 1986 more specific effort to study the linkage between structural-functional theory and the survey research method).

Many of the works discussed above and derived from Kuhn's approach have themselves spawned considerable thought and research. For example, Ritzer's multiple paradigm schema elicited a number of empirical tests (e.g. Snizek, 1976; Picou et al., 1978; Friedheim, 1979; Platt, 1986; Fuhrman and Snizek, 1987), theoretical extensions (Staats, 1976; Ritzer, 1981b), applications (Falk and Zhao, 1989; Rosenberg, 1989), heated critiques (Eckberg and Hill, 1979; Bealer, 1990), debates (Hill and Eckberg, 1981; Ritzer, 1981a; Falk and Zhao, 1990), and so on. These extensions are as much a part of M_u as the original works on the cognitive structure of sociology.

Efforts to map the cognitive structure of sociological theory are not restricted to those inspired by Kuhn. Examples of non-Kuhnian efforts to map the cognitive structure of sociological theory included H. Wagner's (1964) distinction between 'structural-functional' and 'interpretative-interactional' orientations and D. Wagner and J. Berger's (1985) differentiation among theoretical contexts: orienting strategies, unit theories, and theoretical research programs.

Also to be included as a non-Kuhnian cognitive strategy is the 'schools of thought approach' (Sorokin, 1928; Martindale, 1960). This is distinguished from the communal approach (to be discussed under the internal-social heading) by the fact that a school of thought is a larger, more far-flung group of theorists most of whom have little or no personal contact with one another.[26] They are tied together by their common identity with a particular theoretical orientation.

The metatheoretical approaches discussed above tend to be static orientations identifying what Harvey (1987) calls 'meta-scientific units': extant paradigms, idea systems, schools of thought.[27] These approaches have been criticized for their static character (Harvey, 1982) and they have led to an approach in which calls are made, and efforts undertaken, to develop a more dynamic approach to the underlying structure of sociological theory (Wiley, 1979; Wagner, 1984; Wagner and Berger, 1985). The focus here is on what causes paradigms, idea systems, schools of thought (Harvey, 1987) to change, grow, decline, etc. Included here would be various aspects of the history of sociology (e.g. works like that of Shils, 1970 on the general history of sociology, or more specific works like Lengermann's 1979 study of the founding of the *American Sociological Review*).

A very different internal-intellectual approach involves the development of general metatheoretical tools with which to analyze existing sociological theories and to develop new theories. Included here would be Gouldner's (1970) use of concepts like 'background assumptions' and 'domain assumptions' to analyze the underlying structure of sociological theory, Kalberg's (1983) effort to get at the underlying 'architectonic'[28] of at least a portion of Weber's work, efforts to deal with 'levels' of analysis[29] within sociological theory (Edel, 1959; Blau, 1979; Berger and Chaffee, 1988; Wiley, 1988; Ritzer, 1989c; Wiley, 1989), and more specific attempts to analyze 'micro–macro' linkages in sociology (Wagner, 1964; Wallace, 1969; Kemeny, 1976; Collins, 1981b; 1981c; 1987a; 1987b; 1988; Ritzer, 1981b; 1988a; 1990b; Alexander et al., 1987).

The last body of M_u work to be discussed in this section is also far and away the most common: the reexamination of sociological theories as well as the work of sociological theorists. The list here is almost literally endless, but some examples include Camic's (1987) reexamination of the methods of the early Parsons, Marske's (1987) look at Durkheim's 'cult of the individual', Hilbert's (1987) subjectivistic interpretation of Weber's views on bureaucracy, Elster's (1985) micro interpretation of Marx, and at least a portion of Collins's (1989b) analysis of Mead.[30] Such work is characterized by direct and careful examination of a theory in order to shed new light on it. This work is generally unfettered by the kind of metatheoretical paraphernalia (e.g. 'paradigms', 'level', 'micro–macro linkage') discussed above and instead looks quite directly at the theories themselves.

Internal-Social

The main internal-social approach is also indebted to Kuhn (as well as to others, such as Price, 1963 and Crane, 1969, and their notion of 'invisible colleges') and emphasizes the communal aspects of various sociological theories. The tendency in this approach is to focus on relatively small groups of theorists who have direct links to one another. Of utmost importance are the various approaches that have sought to identify the major 'schools' in the history of sociology (Tiryakian, 1979; 1986; Besnard, 1983a; 1983b; Bulmer, 1984; 1985; Wiley, 1989). The greatest amount of work and the strongest documentation exist on the Chicago and Durkheimian schools, but some sociologists doubt whether there have been any true 'schools' in the history of sociology.

Also worth noting here is a related, but more formal, approach to the study of the ties among groups of sociologists. For example,

Mullins (1973; 1983) used a network approach to identify the major 'theory groups' in sociology.

As with the paradigm concept, work on schools has now created an independent, developing body of scholarship. For example, Tiryakian's work on schools has led to a variety of efforts to critique, clarify, and extend his ideas (e.g. the various essays in Monk, 1986 and Harvey, 1987).

Another internal-social metatheoretical approach involves turning to the sociological theorists themselves and examining, among other things, their training, their institutional affiliations, their career patterns, their positions within the field of sociology, etc. (Gouldner, 1970). The view here is that these and many other experiences shape a sociologist's theoretical orientation. As Gouldner puts it, 'much of theory-work begins with an effort to make sense of one's experience' (1970: 484). Of importance here are the biographies (e.g. the various works on C. Wright Mills: Horowitz, 1983; Tilman, 1984) and autobiographies (Homans, 1984) of sociologists.

External-Intellectual

The third M_u orientation involves turning to other academic disciplines for ideas, tools, concepts, theories, and the like that have been, or can be, used in the analysis of sociological theory. Paradigm analyses in sociology obviously owe a great debt to philosophy and the ideas of Kuhn, Lakatos, and others. Another example of this orientation is found in the efforts to look at sociological theories as forms of discourse and to analyze them using an array of linguistic tools (Brown, 1987; 1990). Sociologists in general, and sociological theorists in particular, are seen as using rhetoric in order to persuade others of the adequacy of their approaches. Thus, sociological rhetoric, especially sociological theory, can be studied using the same linguistic tools used to study everyday forms of discourse. Sociological theory is seen, from this perspective, as not being a privileged form of discourse.

External-Social

Finally, the external-social approach (also suggested by Gouldner) involves shifting to the more macro level to look at the larger society and the nature of its impact on sociological theorizing. For example, Tiryakian (1979) suggests that we look at the national setting,[31] the sociohistorical setting, the relationship between sociology and various institutions, the relationship between sociology and its funding agencies, sociology as an institution, and the process of institutionalization (Shils, 1970), as well as sociology as a profession. In his essay on external influences on sociology, Smelser (1989) examines cultural influences, trends in the larger society, the influence of science, and the impact of the polity. Very suggestive in this realm is the work of Michel Foucault (1965; 1975; 1979) and his thoughts on the historical roots of the human sciences (including sociology) as well as the power–knowledge (especially sociological knowledge) linkage.[32]

Postscript on Pierre Bourdieu's 'Socioanalysis'

An important contemporary metatheorist (although he would resist that label, indeed any label) is Pierre Bourdieu. Bourdieu calls for a reflexive sociology: 'For me, sociology ought to be meta but *always vis-à-vis itself*. It must use its own instruments to find out what it is and what it is not doing, to try to know better where it stands' (Bourdieu and Wacquant, 1992: 191). Or, using an older and less well-defined label ('sociology of sociology') for metasociology, Bourdieu says, 'The sociology of sociology is a fundamental dimension of sociological epistemology' (1992: 68). Sociologists, who spend their careers 'objectivizing' the social world, ought to spend some time objectivizing their own practices. Thus, sociology 'continually turns back onto itself the scientific weapons it produces' (1992: 214). Bourdieu even rejects certain kinds of metatheorizing (for example, some forms of M_u) as 'a complacent and intimist return upon the private person of the sociologist or with a search for the intellectual *Zeitgeist* that animates his or her work' (1992: 72; for the discussion of Bourdieu's more positive view of even these kinds of metatheorizing, see Wacquant, 1992: 38). However, a rejection of certain kinds of metatheorizing does not represent a rejection of the undertaking in its entirety. Clearly, following the logic of *Homo Academicus* (1984a), Bourdieu would favor examining the habitus and practices of sociologists within the fields of sociology as a discipline and of the academic world, as well as the relationship between those fields and the fields of stratification and politics. *Distinction* (1984b) would lead Bourdieu to concern himself with the strategies of individual sociologists, as well as of the discipline itself, to achieve distinction. For example, individual sociologists might use jargon to achieve high status in the field, and sociology might wrap itself in a cloak of science so that it could achieve distinction *vis-à-vis* the world of practice. In fact, Bourdieu has claimed that the scientific claims of sociology and other social sciences 'are really euphemized assertions of power' (Robbins, 1991: 139). Of course, this position has uncomfortable implications for Bourdieu's own work:

> Bourdieu's main problem during the 1980s has been to sustain his symbolic power whilst simultaneously undermining the scientificity on which it was

originally founded. Some would say that he has tied the noose around his own neck and kicked away the stool from beneath his feet. (1991: 150)

Given his commitment to theoretically informed empirical research, Bourdieu would also have little patience with most, if not all, forms of M_o which he has described as 'universal metadiscourse on knowledge of the world' (Bourdieu and Wacquant, 1992: 159). More generally, Bourdieu would reject metatheorizing as an autonomous practice, setting metatheorizing apart from theorizing about and empirically studying the social world (see Wacquant, 1992: 31).

Bourdieu makes an interesting case for metatheorizing when he argues that sociologists need to '*avoid being the toy of social forces in* [*their*] *practice of sociology*' (Bourdieu and Wacquant, 1992: 183). The only way to avoid such a fate is to understand the nature of the forces acting upon the sociologist at a given point in history. Such forces can be understood only via metatheoretical analysis, or what Bourdieu calls 'socioanalysis' (1992: 210). Once sociologists understand the nature of the forces (especially, external-social and external-intellectual) operating on them, they will be in a better position to control the impact of those forces on their work. As Bourdieu puts it, in personal terms, 'I continually use sociology to try to cleanse my work of ... social determinants' (1992: 211). Thus, the goal of metatheorizing from Bourdieu's point of view is not to undermine sociology, but to free it from those forces which determine it. Of course, what Bourdieu says of his own efforts is equally true of metatheoretical endeavors in general. While he strives to limit the effect of external factors on his work, Bourdieu is aware of the limitations of such efforts: 'I do not for one minute believe or claim that I am fully liberated from them [social determinants]' (1992: 211).

Similarly, Bourdieu wishes to free sociologists from the symbolic violence committed against them by other, more powerful sociologists. This objective invites M_u analyses of sociology in order to uncover the sources and nature of that symbolic violence. Once the latter are understood, sociologists are in a better position to free themselves of them, or at least limit their effects. More generally, sociologists are well positioned to practice 'epistemological vigilance' in order to protect themselves from these distorting pressures (Bourdieu, 1984b: 15).

What is most distinctive about Bourdieu's metatheoretical approach is his refusal to separate metatheorizing from other facets of sociology.[33] That is, he believes that sociologists should be continually reflexive as they are doing their sociological analyses. They should reflect on what they are doing, and especially on how it might limit the amount of 'symbolic violence' against the subjects of study.

Although Bourdieu is doing a distinctive kind of metatheoretical work, it is clear that it is, at least in part, metatheoretical. Given his growing significance in social theory, the association of Bourdieu's work with metatheorizing is likely to contribute further to the growth of interest in metatheorizing in sociology.

Notes

This chapter is derived from the Introduction and Chapter 1 of *Metatheorizing in Sociology* (1991b: 1–14, 17–21) and the Appendix to *Sociological Theory* (2000c: 623–639).

1   Although, maybe they should. See the discussion of Bourdieu's perspective on this, below.

2   I could say that what we have here are bad practitioners of metatheory. Spencer (1904: 289), in his autobiography, describes how he had read only the first few pages of Kant's *Critique* and had read no books in psychology or philosophy. Spencer was apparently not much of a reader and was content to pick up what he could from casual conversations and popular publications. In other words, Spencer was not a serious student of other theoretical works. He was a metatheorist (he certainly did not bother to venture into the field to collect data); he was just not a very good one. Turner and Maryanski (1988b) would disagree with this characterization of Spencer, but it seems to me that the thrust of their work is that Spencer was a better empiricist (albeit one who relied on secondary data) than he was a metatheorist.

3   Thus, this chapter is not about metatheory which, as we will see, is one possible end product of metatheorizing, but about the *process* of metatheorizing which may have several end products. This constitutes one change from my early work on this issue (Ritzer, 1987; 1988b) where I discussed metatheory rather than metatheorizing.

4   The first 'true' sociological theorists were not able to study the work of other theorists, but they metatheorized about the work of philosophers and social thinkers in neighboring fields like political economy.

5   This idea, of course, was first applied to homosexuals. In fact, there are a number of similarities between homosexuality and the practice of metatheorizing. For example, both homosexuals and metatheorists have been judged in negative terms and practitioners have been stigmatized for their activities.

6   For example, while most of my work is metatheoretical, I have done work using Weberian theory to analyze society in general (Ritzer, 1983), the professions (Ritzer, 1975b), and the medical profession in particular (Ritzer and Walczak, 1988).

7   For example, that sophisticated theorist of capitalist society, Karl Marx, did a great deal of metatheorizing.

8   While I too see this kind of work as problematic, I do not agree that the majority of metatheorists do it.

9   Furfey (1953/1965: 8) also is cognizant of metatheory which he sees, unlike this author, as dealing with the 'logic of a theory'.

10   I also think that most of the authors in Fiske and Shweder's *Metatheory in Social Science: Pluralisms and Subjectivities* (1986) are guilty of this charge.

11   This is in line with Harvey's definition of metascience, following Radnitzky (1973), as 'research into science ... coming "after" science, or "about" science' (1987: 271).

12   In fact, Turner (1991) himself does this type of metatheorizing when, for example, he uses his study of sociological theories to generate a wide range of hypotheses.

13   For a comparison of Gouldner's 'reflexive sociology' and Bourdieu's 'auto-analysis', see Swartz (1990).

14   *The Coming Crisis in Western Sociology* is a product of the late 1960s. Gouldner sympathizes with the radical movements of that period both in and out of sociology, and thus tends to take positions that sound naive and antiquated today.

15 In fact, Parsons (1937/1949: 697) describes his own work of this genre as an 'empirical monograph'. Merton (1968: 4), another key figure in the history of meta-theoretical work, argues in a similar fashion that the works of classical theorists are 'crucial source materials'.

16 I have labeled this (somewhat awkwardly) as meta-data-analysis in order to differentiate it from the more generic metaanalysis. In meta-data-analysis the goal is not to study methods, but to seek ways of cumulating research results across research studies. In his introduction to Wolf's *Meta-Analysis*, Niemi defines metaanalysis as 'the application of statistical procedures to collections of empirical findings from individual studies for the purpose of integrating, synthesizing, and making sense of them' (Niemi, in Wolf, 1986: 5).

17 While I focus here on the end products of metatheorizing, similar work is needed on the process of metatheorizing, especially the methodologies employed by metatheorists.

18 See Ritzer (1991b: Chapter 13) for a discussion of some of the things that metatheorizing has to gain from these subfields.

19 As we will, Collins (1989a) does just what he is critical of here when he outlines a pro-science position for sociology.

20 Turner recognizes his comparative lack of involvement with the empirical literature: 'critics will decry ... the lack of an extensive literature review of empirical findings' (1984: 207).

21 In outlining such an M_o position Collins is likely to create (again) an unresolvable controversy involving his position and that of the more extreme positivists and hermeneuticists.

22 The bulk of *States and Social Revolutions*, however, is a comparative/historical analysis of various societies. As is the case in all such research, Skocpol's data base is secondary historical documents. One might well ask why the analysis of historical documents is acceptable, but the study of theoretical documents is such a heinous endeavor? To put it another way, much of metatheorizing *and* much of Skocpol's empirical work involve documentary analysis.

23 I would like to thank Shanyang Zhao for suggesting this kind of differentiation. Jonathan Cole and Stephen Cole (1973) employ a similar fourfold diagram of influences on scientific development utilizing identical internal–external and intellectual–social dimensions to develop their typology.

24 For one metatheoretical effort influenced by Lakatos and his notion of a 'scientific research program', see Tiryakian (1986).

25 For a discussion of my work on paradigms as well as on an integrated sociological paradigm, see Chapters 3 and 4.

26 This distinction is made by Tiryakian (1979).

27 This label can be affixed to the 'schools' approach to be discussed shortly.

28 See Ritzer (1981a; 1991b) for discussion of levels of analysis.

29 See Chapter 2 for a utilization of this tool.

30 Collins does M_p in this essay.

31 See Vidich and Lyman's *American Sociology* (1985).

32 For more on the applicability of Foucault's ideas to metatheory, see Ritzer (1991b).

33 This is at odds with my notion that metatheorizing should be an autonomous subdiscipline, but I am comfortable with Bourdieu's position. In arguing that metatheorizing should be autonomous, I was really trying to legitimate this kind of work in sociology. Given such legitimacy (which I'm not so sure metatheorizing has in everyone's eyes), I can see the advantages of metatheorizing as an inherent part of all sociology.

2

THE DELINEATION OF AN
UNDERLYING ARCHITECTONIC

This chapter is based on my conviction that the works of a number of seemingly diverse sociological theorists share a limited number of architectonics (defined for the moment as underlying structures). By employing the concept of architectonics as an M_u tool, we can gain better insight into the most fundamental similarities and differences among sociological theorists. Beyond this, and perhaps more importantly, architectonics can give us a firm understanding of the various bases used – in the past, present, or future – to systematically erect sociological theories of social phenomena.

Involved here is an effort to delineate *one* of the most important architectonics in sociological theory. It is clear to me that a number of other architectonics exist; I will hint at the natures of a few of them in the closing pages of this chapter. A major utility of this kind of work will lie ultimately in comparative studies of architectonics. At this point, I can only suggest what such comparative work might look like.

The importance of the architectonic that will be delineated in this chapter will be demonstrated by the fact that it will be shown to undergird a significant portion of the work of three of the most important theorists in the history of sociology: Karl Marx, Max Weber, and Georg Simmel.[1] In addition, in order to demonstrate the breadth of the applicability of the architectonic, it will also be applied to a more contemporary work by Peter Berger and Thomas Luckmann, *The Social Construction of Reality* (1967).[2] This is not an exhaustive list of those whose work can be analyzed using such an architectonic; others (e.g. Gerth and Mills, 1953) are easily identified.

While of crucial importance to an understanding of the works of the theorists mentioned above, this architectonic does not undergird the entirety of their work. Furthermore, there is considerable variation in the degree to which it informs the work of these thinkers. Thus, for example, while I believe it lies at the base of much of Marx's work, it is largely confined to those aspects of Weber's work devoted to the economy and bureaucracy. Despite such variation, the fact that it underlies a significant portion of the work of these thinkers shows a continuity among a range of theorists who are not often thought to be linked so strongly.

The term *architectonic*[3] has been used by the Weberian scholar Stephen Kalberg (1983) to mean 'the underlying themes', 'the comprehensive analytic', the 'universal-historical' analytic that penetrates Weber's 'entire opus'. I too associate 'architectonic' with underlying themes: a comprehensive, universal-historical analytic. While I borrow the term 'architectonic' from Kalberg, I must here note important differences between the way in which he uses the concept and the way in which I use it. For one thing, Kalberg's objectives are narrower than mine. While Kalberg's sole objective is to identify Weber's architectonic, my goal is to identify a more general sociological architectonic that undergirds the work of a number of sociological theorists. For another, even within Weber's work my objectives are broader than Kalberg's. His goal is to 'identify major theoretical possibilities for economically-oriented action at the level of civilizational analysis' (1983: 256). He admits that this is *'one small step* toward a reconstruction of Weber's entire historical sociology of comparative civilizations' (1983: 255, emphasis added). In contrast, rather than identify a small portion of a very detailed architectonic, I have attempted to identify in broad terms the parameters of Weber's architectonic.[4]

Although she does not use the term 'architectonic', an effort that bears a strong resemblance to the one undertaken here, at least as far as the analysis of Marx is concerned, was made earlier by the philosopher Carol C. Gould (1978). Gould's basic description of Marx's 'social ontology' or his 'metaphysical theory' of social reality is, as will be seen, very close to the image of the architectonic developed in this chapter:

> Such a metaphysical theory would give a systematic account of the *fundamental entities and structures of social existence* – for example, persons and institutions – and of the nature of social interaction and social change. Such an ontology is only implicit in Marx's work. Nevertheless, my thesis is that his concrete analysis of capitalism and of the stages of social development *presupposes such a systematic ontological* framework. Thus, for example, Marx's account of the transition from precapitalist societies to capitalism, his theory of surplus value, his analysis of technological development and his outline of the communal society of the future *cannot be adequately understood apart from ... his fundamental philosophical ideas about the nature of social reality and the systematic interrelations among those ideas.* (1978: xi–xii, emphasis added)

Although Gould's analysis of Marx is similar to the analysis of his ideas presented below, there are significant differences. As a philosopher, she is led in some very different directions than those taken by a sociologist. Thus, while some elements of Marx's social ontology identified by Gould are similar to the elements of his architectonic outlined here, others (e.g. freedom and justice) are significantly different or encompassed by broader concepts (e.g. praxis, emancipation). Furthermore, Gould seeks simply to identify Marx's social ontology, while I seek to uncover a more general sociological architectonic. Thus, while there are some efforts that presage my own, they are far narrower in scope than this attempt.

It could be argued that the approach taken here parallels Marx's own orientation to the study of capitalism.[5] Marx (1857–8/1973: 247, 509, 595, 639) sought to probe beneath the surface economic appearances of capitalism (e.g. money, wages, profits) to examine the underlying economic structure of capitalism (e.g. capital, value, surplus value) (Godelier, 1972: 3). I seek to probe beneath Marx's analysis of the underlying economic structure of capitalism (as well as the theories of Weber, Simmel, and Berger and Luckmann) to examine the sociological architectonic that undergirds and informs it. In other words, a sociological architectonic does inform Marx's analysis of the hidden economic structure of capitalist society. One could say that this sociological architectonic informs Marx's analysis of the underlying economic structure and that the two together guide his analysis of the surface economic structure.[6] More generally, it can be argued that the same architectonic is at the base of Weber's theory of the iron cage of rationality in the economy and the bureaucratic structures of Occidental society, Simmel's theory of the tragedy of culture involving the growing gap between individual and objective culture, and Berger and Luckmann's theory of the social construction of reality.

The sociological architectonic of concern to us here consists of six basic components. It begins with a set of fundamental assumptions about the nature of human beings and their thoughts and actions. This first element can be called a *philosophical anthropology*. Brubaker, in his work on Weber, defines a philosophical anthropology as the 'conception of the essence of human being, of what it is that distinguishes human life from other natural processes' (1984: 92). Not all sociological architectonics have a philosophical anthropology, and of those that do, some differ in their specifics from the philosophical anthropology of concern here. In this particular philosophical anthropology it is assumed that people are endowed with the ability to think, and that action and interaction are largely based on this capacity. Second, this architectonic assumes a process of *institutionalization*, a series of steps whereby the thoughts, actions, and interactions of people are transformed into larger social structures and social institutions. Third, it is assumed that in at least some cases people lose control over the larger structures and institutions that emerge out of thought, action, and interaction. This loss of control over macro-level phenomena is most often thought of as *reification*. Fourth, once larger structures and institutions take on a reified existence, the architectonic assumes that it is likely that these creations will come to exert control and *domination* over the people who created them both historically and on a continuing basis. Fifth, the existence of reified structures that dominate individuals is seen as creating the likelihood that they will have *adverse consequences* on the individuals who exist within those structures. Sixth, there is a concern in this architectonic for how people can achieve *emancipation* from these reified structures and their adverse effects. Given these six elements of one sociological architectonic, the goal in the rest of the chapter is to systematically examine the way in which it informs the work of Marx, Weber, Simmel, and Berger and Luckmann.

Philosophical Anthropology

The basic element of Marx's sociological architectonic is his concept of *praxis* (encompassing his – actually Feuerbach's – earlier idea of *species being*). It can be argued that *everything* that is sociologically (and economically) meaningful in Marx's work is derived from his conception of praxis (Henry, 1983: 14). The concept of praxis informs not only the manuscripts of 1844, but also the notebooks of 1857–58 and the late writings on capital. Praxis is *more basic* to Marx's work than his fundamental economic concepts.

In the end, economics in Marx's work is subordinated to his sociology.[7] The admittedly enormous body of work done by Marx on the economy represents a specific application of his sociology; his work on capital is a case study utilizing his sociology. Marx focused on the economy because it was, by far, the dominant institution in capitalist society. In fact, this dominance was a problem that had to be overcome. The point is that the nature of capitalism, *not* the nature of his architectonic, led Marx to focus on the economy.[8] That sociological architectonic could have been, and could be, as easily focused on the family, religion, or any other (predominant) institution.[9] This perspective is consistent with one taken by Engels (e.g. 1890/1972: 642) in various writings.[10]

As I indicated above, the focal concern in Marx's philosophical anthropology is with praxis, although it is important to discuss the earlier concept of species being.[11] Species being, 'at least in its most developed form, has *never* fully existed historically. It is a *potential*, the fulfillment of which has always (at least to the present time) been thwarted by the conditions of material life. Thus, in looking for a full expression of species being one cannot look to some "fictitious primordial condition"' (Marx, 1932/1964: 107). Capitalism, while denying species being, provides the material conditions necessary for the future full expression of species being. As Heller put it: 'capitalism creates needs that are rich and many-sided at the same time as it impoverishes men' (1976: 47). In the future communist society people will be able to 'bring their species powers out of themselves' (Marx, 1932/1964: 73; see also Barbalet, 1983: 47, 53).

In earliest times, people were too busy desperately trying to survive to be able to approach anything like a full expression of species being. They were able to develop and express only a limited number of needs (Marx, 1857–8/1973: 398). The ability of people to think, their consciousness, was limited and amounted to little more than animal, 'sheep-like', consciousness (Marx and Engels, 1845–6/1970: 51). In spite of limited needs and limited abilities to think, people needed to act.[12] Indeed, they had to act in order to acquire the food, clothing, and shelter they needed to survive (1845–6/1970: 48). The production[13] of material life cannot be accomplished by isolated individuals, but requires cooperation with other people; in other words, production requires social relationships (Marx, 1857–8/1973: 84). Out of human action and interaction consciousness is shaped. 'Consciousness is, therefore, from the very beginning a social product, and remains so as long as men exist at all' (Marx and Engels, 1845–6/1970: 51). Out of people's activities, social relationships, and production of material life comes an expansion of consciousness (Marx, 1857–8/1973: 494). There is, then, a dialectic between activities, social relationships, products, and consciousness. In his effort to separate himself from German idealism, Marx gave priority to material (activities, relationships, products) factors over ideal (conscious) factors.

While Marx gave the material world priority, he certainly did not ignore the ideal domain of consciousness. Among the characteristics associated with consciousness by Marx are the ability to choose, to plan, to concentrate, to be flexible and purposive, and to set the self off mentally from the action being taken (Ollman, 1971). McMurty (1978) argues that to Marx the special property of human nature is its creative intelligence: the ability to raise a structure in one's imagination and then to erect that structure in reality. McMurty (1978: 23) calls this distinctive human capacity 'projective consciousness'.[14] But projective consciousness is not enough; people are endowed with the need to express that consciousness in 'creative *praxis*' (1978: 32).

In sum, species being involves an interrelated set of ideas about people, their actions, thoughts and social relationships, and the world they create and that in turn creates them. It encompasses Marx's philosophical anthropology, his philosophical presuppositions about the nature of human beings.

Yet, as Marx's work progressed, he used the philosophical concept less and less, although he retained its essential ideas. Barbalet (1983), for example, sees a shift as early as *The German Ideology* (Marx and Engels, 1845–6/1970) away from an essentialist conception of man (species being) and toward an empirical view of man in *praxis*; rather than referring to species being (with its bothersome combination of historical and ahistorical components[15]), Marx focuses on 'real individuals' in action. Nevertheless, his discussion of praxis is informed by his earlier notion of species being. Whereas in the Feuerbachian notion of species being intuition is the essence of reality, for Marx that essence lies in practice.

We can conceive of praxis as productive activity (Meszaros, 1970: 78) carried out in conjunction with other people. Thus, involved in the idea of praxis is action, interaction (Lefebvre, 1968: 34), production, and consciousness (Avineri, 1968: 138). In other words, in its essential components, praxis is indistinguishable from species being. But while species being is a philosophical concept, praxis is ontological.[16]

Let us turn now to Weber. Weber bases his architectonic on a philosophical anthropology (what Brubaker, 1984: 49 calls his 'philosophical psychology') of *action* that is very similar to Marx's ideas on praxis (and species being). Kalberg sees Weber's four types of action (traditional, affectual, *wertrational*, and *zweckrational*) as 'universal capacities of *Homo sapiens*', 'anthropological traits of man' (1980: 1148). Involved in Weber's conception of action is the ability to think[17] (Weber, 1903–17/1949: 40), and to link that thought to action and interaction: 'We shall speak of "action" in so far as the acting individual attaches a subjective meaning to his behavior – be it overt or covert, omission or acquiescence. Action is "social" in so far as its subjective meaning takes account of the behavior of others and is thereby oriented in its course' (1921/1968: 4).[18] While all action involves subjective meaning, motive ('a complex of subjective meaning … ground for the conduct in question': 1921/1968: 11), and the ability to think, rational action is distinguished by the capacity to consciously regulate or control (Kalberg, 1980) and to deliberately plan (Brubaker, 1984: 92) action. Here is the way Weber describes rational mental processes and their linkage to action:

> the acting person weighs, *in so far as he acts rationally*, the 'conditions' of the future development which interests him, which conditions are 'external' to him and are objectively given as far as his knowledge of reality goes. He mentally rearranges into a causal complex the various 'possible modes' of his own conduct and the consequences which these could be *expected* to have in connection with the 'external' conditions. He does this in order to decide, in accordance with the (mentally) disclosed 'possible' results, in favor of one or another mode of action as the one appropriate to his 'goal'. (1903–17/1949: 165, first emphasis added)

In contrast, those who engage in nonrational action act blindly on the basis of affect or tradition; their actions are not controlled by conscious processes. In other words, much of Weber's philosophical anthropology is embedded in his work on rational action: *zweckrationality* and *wertrationality*. In sum, Weber's work, like Marx's, is premised on a philosophical anthropology that links thought, action, and interaction.

Despite this general similarity, crucial differences separate the philosophical anthropologies of Weber and Marx. For one thing, while Marx's philosophical anthropology is richly developed, Weber's is comparatively undeveloped with bits and pieces scattered throughout his work. As Brubaker put it in terms of Weber's ideas on rational action, they are 'terse, undeveloped, fragmentary' (1984: 49). Moreover, while Marx's actors create things, Weber's are largely endowed with thinking ability, self-consciousness, intentionality, meaning, and motives. The result is that Weber's actors, while endowed with the capacity to act and interact, do not seem to have the same capacity as Marx's actors to *create* things. I will return to this idea and its implications in the section on institutionalization.

Simmel's philosophical anthropology (Oakes, 1984: 15) is manifested throughout his work, but usually in an indirect way. In the range of essays devoted to forms of interaction and types of interactants Simmel clearly operated with the assumptions that human beings possess creative consciousness and this consciousness lies at the base of their ability to act, interact (especially through exchange, which 'is the purest and most developed level of interaction': Simmel, 1907/1978: 82), and create the larger society. While Simmel believed that consciousness allowed people to create their social worlds, he also believed that it gave them the ability to reify social reality, to create the objects that enslave consciousness. As Simmel said, 'Our mind has a remarkable ability to think of contents as being independent of the act of thinking' (1907/1978: 65). While Simmel bases his work on a sense of creative human consciousness, 'he does not try to discover or to explain what goes on in the mind itself' (Aron, 1965: 5–6). On the other hand, Simmel was quite interested in social action and interaction and devoted considerable attention to the forms that they might take.

Simmel's philosophical anthropology is expressed nowhere better than in his sense of *individual culture*. Individual culture encompasses, among other things, the ability to think, act, create, and objectify. In other words, individual culture is intimately linked to *objective culture*. Through individual culture people produce objective culture and objective culture, in turn, shapes and expands individual culture. However, the crucial problem for Simmel is that objective culture can become detached from, and come to control, individual culture.

Finally, we come to Berger and Luckmann's *The Social Construction of Reality* (1967). We should not be surprised to learn that the philosophical anthropology that underlies that work is consistent, at least in part, with the other philosophical anthropologies discussed in this section. The authors explicitly state that their 'anthropological presuppositions are strongly influenced by Marx' (1967: 17). They also acknowledge their debt to Weber and his interest in the subjective meaning of action. Although affected by the ideas of Marx and Weber (and Simmel, among many others), Berger and Luckmann are most heavily influenced by phenomenology. But the powerful influence of phenomenology still leaves Berger and Luckmann with a philosophical anthropology of thoughtful individuals who act, interact, and create social reality that is quite consistent with the one discussed in this section. However, as we will see later, the phenomenological influence pushes Berger and Luckmann in some crucially different directions on other elements of the architectonic.

Berger and Luckmann see people as unique in the animal kingdom. Their uniqueness stems from people's 'world-openness'. Their sense of human nature lies in this openness, or the plasticity of instincts, and not in any fixed structure that determines social life. Thus, people construct their own nature rather than being determined by it. Basic to that nature is human consciousness. Influenced by phenomenology, Berger and Luckmann see that consciousness as intentional rather than as a mental substratum; that is, consciousness is always consciousness *of something*. As a result of the influence of phenomenology, every aspect of Berger and Luckmann's work focuses on consciousness. They recognize various kinds of consciousness, but the most important is the consciousness of everyday life. Action and interaction are determined by consciousness. Of all of the realms of interaction, it is face-to-face interaction that is most important because the actors are in the presence of each other's subjectivity. That subjectivity is also expressed, as we will see in the next section, in the things that people produce.

Also inherent in Berger and Luckmann's sense of 'human nature' is human sociability: 'Man's specific humanity and his sociality are inextricably intertwined' (1967: 51). People cannot develop as human beings without social relationships. People cannot produce a human environment in isolation from other people. In other words, 'Men *together* produce a human environment, with the totality of its socio-cultural and psychological formations' (1967: 51).

Institutionalization

Built into Marx's notion of praxis (as well as his idea of species being[19]), but worth separating out for our purposes, is the concept of *objectification*. As Ollman says, 'Man's productive activity [praxis] ... is objectified in his products in all societies' (1971: 143). By 'objectification' Marx is referring to the fact that people must produce the objects (food, clothing, shelter, etc.) that they need in order to survive. While we often associate economic phenomena with the process of objectification, we can also think of the family structure, religious institutions ('spiritual goods': Heller, 1976: 28), organizations, and governments (among others) in the same way (Marx, 1932/1964: 136). This extended meaning of objectification is close to what we now think of as *institutionalization* in contemporary sociology.

People, through their thoughts and actions, and in concert with other people, produce the objects (economic and otherwise) that they need in order to survive. In other words, objectification is an inherent part of praxis (and species being). The objects that people produce, in turn, act back upon them, helping to expand human capacities. This ongoing process continually accelerates with more and more varied objects eliciting extended human capacities. People and the objects they produce are dialectically related (Marx, 1867/1967: 177).

In praxis, at least in its potential form, objectification is a natural process; it is not a problem; it does not create problems. In fact, objectification is a positive process in a variety of senses, including the fact that we produce 'objects which confirm and realize … individuality' (Marx, 1932/1964: 140). People express their essential powers, they express themselves, in the objects that they produce.

However, the process of objectification, like praxis in general, can be perverted.[20] For example, in capitalism objectification, at least within the economy, is reduced to production: 'Man objectifies himself in production' (Marx, 1857–8/1973: 89). Within the capitalist economy production becomes 'the predominant moment' (1857–8/1973: 94). On the one hand, this means that the process of objectification within other institutions becomes stunted and subordinated to economic production. On the other hand, the process of objectification within the economy is itself limited. That process comes to be defined by the nature of the relationship between capitalist and proletariat. In the production process it is the proletariat that objectifies and it is the capitalists that control the objects (commodities) produced. Thus, the proletariat loses control over its objects; indeed, it loses control over the entire process of objectification. These objects (products), as well as the market for them, come to have a separate and external existence, a life of their own. In effect, the process of objectification becomes separated from the other elements of praxis. People are no longer able to express themselves in the process of objectification. Instead, man 'loses his way among the products of his own efforts, which turn against him and weight him down, become a burden' (Lefebvre, 1968: 8).

While Weber had a clear sense of objects[21] and, more generally, of institutions, one of the crucial problems in his work is often thought to be that he lacked a clear sense of objectification or institutionalization. As I pointed out above, Weber's actors often do not seem to create anything, with the result that they appear to lack the capacity for institutionalization (or objectification). In Levine's view, Weber lacked 'a viable theory of institutionalization, such that he did not have at his disposal a ready and precise way of distinguishing the term "objective" in the sense of *valid* from "objective" in the Durkheimian sense of supra-individual or institutionalized' (1981: 11). Udehn (1981: 131) puts this issue in slightly different terms by arguing that there is a conflict between Weber's 'individualist and subjectivist methodology' (in my terms, his philosophical anthropology) and his work on the development of rational structures in the Occident.

Although it is true that Weber's architectonic is weak on institutionalization (at least in comparison to Marx's), it must not be assumed that the process is ignored entirely. There is at least one notable place in which Weber has a sense of objectification that is very close to that of the other thinkers discussed in this chapter:

> An inanimate machine is mind objectified. Only this provides it with the power to force men into its service and to dominate their everyday working life as completely as is actually the case in the factory. Objectified intelligence is also that animated machine, the bureaucratic organization, with its specialization of trained skills, its division of jurisdiction, its rules and hierarchical relations of authority. (1921/1968: 1402)

Furthermore, the processes of objectification and institutionalization appear in several strategic areas of Weber's work. One crucial area is in his discussion of the routinization of charisma. Clearly, the process by which the extraordinary abilities of the charismatic leader are turned into day-to-day authority involves institutionalization. Under this heading we can also include the transformation of the authority of the prophet into permanent congregation and of the sect (a group of charismatic individuals) into a church.

Also of note is Weber's concern with the institutionalization of formal (as well as substantive and theoretical) rationality. According to Kalberg, formal rationality does not 'remain simply amorphous sociocultural regularities of action ... [but is] institutionalized as normative regularities of action in "legitimate orders", organizations, traditional ... and rational-legal ... forms of domination, types of economic structures, ethical doctrines, classes and strata' (1980: 1161). In contrast, practical rationality does not lead to institutionalization, but is confined to that 'domain of routine, everyday, pragmatic difficulties' (1980: 1161).

Finally, I should note Weber's discussion of the transformation from nonstatutory norms to customary law that indicates a clear concern with both objectification and institutionalization:

> The psychological 'adjustment' arising from habituation to an action causes conduct that in the beginning constituted plain habit, later to be experienced as binding; then with the awareness of the diffusion of such conduct among a plurality of individuals, it comes to be incorporated as consensus into peoples semi- or wholly conscious 'expectations' as to the meaningfully corresponding conduct of others. Finally, these consensual understandings acquire the guarantee of coercive enforcement by which they are distinguished from mere 'conventions'. (1921/1968: 754)

In spite of these and other examples of a concern for objectification and institutionalization in Weber's work, it seems clear that these processes are less well developed there than they are in Marx's work. This difference in the treatment of institutionalization is of significance in understanding the differences in the specific architectonics (and substantive theories) of Marx and Weber.

Simmel's actors are closer to Marx's than to Weber's in that they are clearly endowed with the capacity to create their social worlds. In other words, Simmel does have a sense of objectification. At one level, objectification is clearly implied by the notion of objective culture. That is, it is through the process of objectification that people produce objective culture. For example, Simmel (1921/1968: 11, 42) talks of 'the spiritual dynamic' and 'the creative processes of the soul' that create objective culture. At another level, however, objectification lays the groundwork for the development of an objective culture that grows more and more remote from individual culture. Thus, objectification is a normal process, one that enables individual culture to grow and expand. However, objectification inevitably leads to a massive expansion of objective culture and a growing gap between it and individual culture.

Simmel (1907/1978: 174) sees 'the interaction between individuals [as] the starting point of all social formations'. But out of interaction emerge macro-level phenomena: 'Further development replaces the immediacy of interacting forces with the creation of higher supraindividual formations, which appear as independent representatives of these forces and absorb and mediate the relations between individuals. These formations exist in great variety; as tangible realities and as mere ideas and products of the imagination' (1907/1978: 174). In other words, interaction produces social objects that can take the form of what we today would call either social structures or social institutions.

As far as Berger and Luckmann (1967: 52) are concerned, 'externalization' is 'an anthropological necessity'. People must produce things, most importantly the social order in which they live. What people externalize may take subjective or objective forms; when they take objective forms we are talking about objectivation (1967: 60). Berger and Pullberg (1965: 199–200) clarify this process by differentiating between 'objectivation' and 'objectification'. *Objectivation* is the process by which human subjectivity is embodied in objective products. In other words, there is a sense in Berger and Pullberg of the production of objective reality. However, not only is the production of objects anthropologically necessary, but so too is *objectification* which (in their work) is the process by which people distance themselves from these objects so that they can take cognizance of them, so that the products can become objects of consciousness. Thus, externalization for Berger and his coauthors has both an objective and a subjective component, but, as we will see, it is the subjective aspect that interests them most.

Reification

The perversion of objectification within capitalism, *reification*, is the third element of Marx's sociological architectonic. Ollman (1971: 143) clearly links the perversion of objectification with reification when he argues that what distinguishes objectification in capitalism is that people's products have a separate existence and become a power on their own confronting man. The term 'reification' is usually associated not directly with Marx, but with the neo-Marxist Georg Lukács (1922/1968: 135). Reification can be conceived of as a process whereby people lose control over the 'objects' that they created, come to believe that those objects have a natural life of their own that is fixed and immutable, and come to be controlled by those objects. In objectification people control objects; in reification objects control people. People express themselves in the process of objectification; they deny themselves in the process of reification.

Although Marx does not use the term 'reification',[22] the phenomenon appears in his work in a variety of places. The most notable source of the idea of reification is in Marx's work on the *fetishism of commodities*.[23] This is the process by which laborers in capitalism lose sight of the fact that it is their labor that gives commodities their value. They come to believe that value arises from the natural properties of the things themselves, or that value is conferred on commodities through the impersonal operation of the market. In effect, it appears that things themselves, or the relationship among things in the marketplace, are the source of value. 'A definite social relation between men ... assumes, in their eyes, the fantastic form of a relation between things' (Marx, 1867/1967: 72).[24]

The process of the fetishism of commodities, as well as the resulting commodities and the marketplace for them, are an example of reification occurring within the economy. But there is more to reification within the economy than the fetishism of commodities. For example, Marx (Marx and Engels, 1845–6/1970: 54) describes a reified division of labor[25] within capitalist society and has an even broader sense of a reified economy (Marx, 1857–8/1973: 307, 831; see also Gould, 1978: 156–7). But Marx (cited in Bender, 1970: 176) goes even further than this, arguing that reification occurs in other institutions such as the state (as well as religion: Barbalet, 1983: 147). Finally, and most generally, Marx (Marx and Engels, 1845–6/1970: 53) seems to have a world-historical conception of reification. Thus, Marx is not restricted to the fetishism of commodities; underlying his work is a general conception of reification.

As I made clear earlier, Weber does not have a strong, explicit sense of objectification (or institutionalization), but it is certainly at least implicit in his architectonic because his actors, like Marx's, end up being confronted by the problem of reification.[26] Reified structures can only come about as a result of the perversion of the process of institutionalization. The idea that Weber deals with reification is well recognized by sociologists. Swingewood, for example, says that in 'Weber's discussion rationality and technology have become reified' (1975: 107). Mitzman (1969: 176) argues that in many places Weber does 'a sociology of reification'. Weber's image of the reified world is clearest in his ideas on the 'iron cage' of rationality in the economy and bureaucracy. Take the following statement by Weber on the rationalized economy of the Occident: 'Capitalism is today an immense cosmos into which the individual is born, and which presents itself to him, at least as an individual, as an unalterable order of things in which he must live' (1904–5/1958: 54).

The capacity of Simmel's actors to objectify leads, as we have seen, to the production of *objective culture*. Although objective culture need not be reified, the problem in the modern world is that it does take on a reified existence. Simmel describes the structure of the reified society in these words: 'They [the elements of culture] acquire fixed identity, a logic and lawfulness of their own; this new rigidity inevitably places them at a distance from the spiritual dynamic which created them and which makes them independent' (1921/1968: 11). Swingewood notes that for Simmel 'the social world was a world dominated by reification' (1975: 87).

Oakes (1984) describes reification in Simmel's work as both a process and a state of cultural development. He sees four stages as necessary for the development of reified structures. First, the actor must objectify, specifically by producing cultural artifacts. Second, this set of cultural artifacts 'becomes a relatively independent entity, self-contained, self-perpetuating, and developing according to its own immanent principles' (1984: 12). Third, this objective culture grows increasingly remote from the individual culture that created it. Fourth, and finally, 'the development of this form outstrips the ability to master or control it' (1984: 12). In a reified world, people are controlled by objective culture rather than exerting control over it.

Berger and Luckmann's (1967) actors also reify social reality. Reification is intimately related to the processes of objectivation and objectification. As we saw, objectivation involves the production of the objective world and 'as soon as an objective social world is established, the possibility of reification is never far away' (1967: 89). Once the world has become objectivated, and people have objectified it, reification can occur as the world 'loses its comprehensibility as a human enterprise and becomes fixated as a non-human, non-humanizable, inert facticity' (1967: 89).

Reification, like most of Berger and Luckmann's other concepts, is defined *subjectively* as 'the apprehension of human phenomena as if they were things, that is, in non-human or possibly supra-human terms ... such as facts of nature, results of cosmic laws, or manifestations of divine will' (1967: 89). Berger and Pullberg (1965: 200) directly link reification to alienation: '*reification is objectification in an alienation mode'*. As we will see, Berger and Pullberg define alienation, following Marx, as the breakdown of the interconnection between producing and the product. Thus, actors are taking cognizance of objects that are separate from them, that have acquired the character of 'things'. For Berger and Luckmann, reification is *not* the process by which objects acquire the character of 'thinghood', but rather the cognitive process by which actors *think* of these things as objective facts: 'It must be emphasized that reification is a modality of consciousness' (1967: 89). Once they have reified the world, people forget that they created the world and that they can re-create it, they lose control over it, and they see themselves as products of the world rather than producers of it.

Domination

In Marx's work, in one sense, it is the capitalists who come to control and benefit from the reified economic structures of capitalist society. The capitalists are able to dominate the proletariat because the workers must sell the capitalists their labor time in order to gain access to the means of production (reified structures) (Gould, 1978: 157). The domination of the proletariat by the capitalists is closely related to exploitation.[27] The capitalists *exploit* the workers because they appropriate at least part of the products of the proletariat without recompense. The capitalist only pays for part of a day's labor (enough to keep the laborer and his family alive), but gets a full day's work. The rate of surplus value (the amount of surplus labor divided by the amount of necessary labor) is 'an exact expression of the degree of exploitation of labour-power by Capital, or the labourer by the capitalist' (Marx, 1867/1967: 218; see also Marx, 1857–8/1973: 646). Marx also depicts the domination and exploitation of the proletariat by the capitalists in a more graphic manner: 'Capital is dead labour, that vampire-like, only lives by sucking living labour, and lives the more, the more labour it sucks' (1867/1967: 233). This domination and exploitation by those who control the reified structures of capitalism leads to alienation. 'Indeed, exploitation and alienation are the same process viewed from two sides: the first from the side of capital and the second from the side of labor' (Gould, 1978: 145).

But while it is possible to discuss domination in terms of the relationship between capitalist and proletariat, there is another and perhaps sociologically more important form of domination embedded in Marx's work. This form is the domination *of both* proletariat *and* capitalists by the reified structures of society. While he sometimes writes as if capitalists do things *to* workers, more often he makes clear that both classes are embedded in a coercive system that compels them to act in certain ways (1867/1967: 309–10, 592). Marx indicates that it is not just the proletariat that is affected by reified structures: '(and this applies to the capitalist) all is under the sway of *inhuman* power' (1932/1964: 156).

Weber makes it clear that his reified system exerts domination over people: 'It forces the individual, in so far as he is involved in the system of market relationships, to conform to capitalist rules of action' (1904–5/ 1958: 54). Later, in *The Protestant Ethic*, and even more strongly, Weber says: 'the tremendous cosmos of the modern economic order ... is now bound to the technical and economic conditions of machine production which to-day determine the lives of all the individuals who are born into this mechanism, not only those directly concerned with economic acquisition, with *irresistible force*' (1904–5/1958: 181, emphasis added). More specifically, he described bureaucracies as systems of domination that are 'escape proof', 'practically unshatterable', and from which the bureaucrats could not 'squirm out' once they were 'harnessed' in them. Weber wrote of bureaucracies in these terms:

> Objectified intelligence is also that animated machine, the bureaucratic organization, with its specialization of trained skills, its division of jurisdiction, its rules and hierarchical relations of authority. Together with the inanimate machine it is busy fabricating the shell of bondage which men will perhaps be forced to inhabit some day, as powerless as the fellahs of ancient Egypt. (1921/1968: 1402)

While Marx saw domination stemming from both individual capitalists and reified systems, Weber emphasized the domination of the latter. However, like Marx, Weber (1904–5/1958: 54–5) saw the reified system of capitalism as coercive over *both* workers and capitalists.

Simmel too had a sense not only of reification, but also of actors dominated by reified structures: 'Society transcends the individual and lives its own life which follows its own laws. It, too, confronts the individual with a historical, imperative firmness' (1908/1950: 258). Coser argues that these structures 'confront the individual as if they were alien powers' (1965: 5). Heberle argues that for Simmel society is 'an interplay of structural factors in which the human beings appear as passive objects rather than as live and willing actors' (1965: 117). Frisby writes of the 'reified objective culture' within which 'each individual's opportunity for creativity and development becomes increasingly restricted' (1984: 108). Thus Simmel, as well as numerous commentators on his work, have pointed to his concern for the domination of individuals, of individual culture, by an increasingly reified objective culture.

Berger and Luckmann's (1967) actors are dominated by objective structures and institutions. For example, social institutions 'control human conduct by setting up predefined patterns of conduct' (1967: 55). Not only is control exerted by the institutions themselves, but they also tend to develop mechanisms of social control that further dominate people. In their work on domination, Berger and Luckmann are borrowing from Durkheim and thinking of social facts (e.g. social institutions) as external to and coercive on people. Thus, there is a sense in Berger and Luckmann in which actors are dominated by objective structures, but of greater importance is the domination exerted by their own reified consciousness.

Adverse Consequences

To Marx, the major adverse consequence of the existence of reified structures is *alienation*. Following Ollman (1976), I define alienation as the breakdown of the natural interconnectedness that is praxis (and species being[28]). This separation is clear in a number of places in Marx's work (e.g. 1857–8/1973: 489). In capitalism, people are separated from their praxis: productive activity (and nature), their products, other people, and their species being. Alienation has disastrous consequences for people; it is a condition that is in many ways the antithesis of praxis (1867/1967: 350, 360, 508). The individual 'does not affirm himself but denies himself, does not feel content, but unhappy, does not develop freely his physical and mental energy but mortifies his body and ruins his mind' (1932/1964: 110). As a result of alienation, instead of engaging in distinctively human praxis, people are reduced to the status of lower animals (1932/1964: 111).

What causes alienation and the disastrous consequences outlined above? The domination of reified structures (and the exploitation practiced by those – capitalists – who control reified structures) that interpose themselves between people and productive activity, products, other people, and themselves. Among the reified structures within the economy discussed by Marx are capital, commodities, the market, private property,[29] the division of labor, social class, etc. Meszaros makes this same point using somewhat different terms: 'Man's productive activity cannot bring fulfillment because the institutionalized second order mediations [division of labor, private property, exchange] interpose themselves between man and his activity, between man and nature, and between man and man' (1970: 83).

As I discussed earlier, Marx's concern with the economy led him to focus on reified economic structures, domination, and the alienation produced by them. However, since people can and do reify non-economic structures, it is possible to talk of alienation in other social institutions (e.g. the state, religion). Furthermore, reified structures are not restricted to modern capitalist societies: they existed in precapitalist societies. Finally, reified structures can be thought of as existing in contemporary communist and socialist societies (if it is still possible to refer to the few remaining such societies in those terms) since modern man has disassociated reification from the capitalist economy in particular and the economic institution in general.

While alienation is certainly not the focal concern for Weber that it is for Marx, Weber was clearly interested in alienation (Swingewood, 1975: 87) and, more importantly, in the adverse consequences for individuals of the reified structures of rationalized society. At one level, Weber took pains to show that alienation existed in institutions (e.g. the military) other than the economy. At another level, Weber's interest in the individual within the rational society can be seen as a concern for the adverse effects of such a society on people. Weber clearly has a sense of the actor as capable of distinctively human thought, but that thinking process is limited, if not destroyed, by the structures of capitalist society. Thus, for example, Weber argues that rational calculation within bureaucracies 'reduces every worker to a cog in this bureaucratic machine and, seeing himself in this light, he will merely ask how to transform himself into a somewhat bigger cog' (1921/1968: liii). In other words, the wide range of thought open to humans is reduced to a concern with how to get ahead in the bureaucratic system. 'Specialists without spirit, sensualists without heart; this nullity imagines that it has attained a level of civilization never before achieved' (1904–5/1958: 182).

The domination of individuals by reified structures is linked in Simmel's work, as it is in Marx's and Weber's, to the problem of adverse consequences (Swingewood, 1975: 87). For example, Simmel says of 'the objective culture' that 'the diversity and liveliness of its content attain their highest point through a division of labour that often condemns the individual representative and participant in this culture to a monotonous specialization, narrowness and stunted growth' (1907/ 1978: 199). Such a view is strikingly similar to what Weber has to say about the negative impact on people in the rationalized society and what Marx says about the alienated individual in capitalism.

Simmel's most general point is that the growth of individual culture cannot keep pace with the expansion of objective culture. Rather than being produced and controlled by people, objective culture comes to have a life of its own that increasingly produces and controls people. This could be termed a process of 'cultural alienation' (Frisby, 1984: 107). Instead of being naturally connected to objective culture, people come to be increasingly separated from it and dominated by it. In other words, the natural interconnection between individual and objective culture is progressively severed in the modern world. As Simmel put it: 'Thus far at least, historical development has moved toward steadily increasing *separation* between objective cultural production and the cultural level of the individual' (1908/1971: 234, emphasis added).

Although Berger and Luckmann eschew dealing with the concept of alienation because of the confused way in which it had come to be dealt with in the contemporary literature, Berger and Pullberg do deal with alienation and, as we have already seen, in a manner very similar to the way in which the concept was dealt with by Marx. According to Berger and Pullberg: *'By alienation we mean the process by which the unity of the producing and the product is broken'* (1965: 200). We could hardly be closer to the Marxian definition of alienation, especially as it is defined by Ollman in terms of breakdown of natural interconnectedness.

Emancipation

The final component of this general sociological architectonic, and Marx's in particular, is *emancipation*.[30] As I have detailed from Marx's work, through a perversion of the natural process of objectification, people have produced reified structures (in capitalism, in particular) that have served to dominate (and exploit) and alienate them. The political goal for Marx is the overcoming of these reified structures: the emancipation of people from the domination of reified structures. The community that would be created 'does not rule over the individuals and is nothing in itself beyond the concrete individuals in their social relation to each other' (Gould, 1978: 166). This would serve to eliminate alienation ('the human condition in the pre-communist stage': Barbalet, 1983: 53) and reunite people with their products, productive activities, other people, and themselves. In other words, the goal of emancipation is praxis (species being). 'Human emancipation will only be complete when the real, individual man has become a species being' (Marx, cited in Bender, 1970: 66). Another way of saying this is that the goal of emancipation is communism,[31] which is 'The first real emergence, the actual realization for man of man's essence and of his essence as something real' (Marx, 1932/1964: 187). In Avineri's view, 'Marx's postulate about the ultimate possibility of human self-emancipation must be related to his philosophical premise about the initial creation of the world by man' (1968: 65). In other words, communism cannot be understood without understanding praxis and species being.

The clear implication is that people have yet to engage in praxis and become species beings; they can only achieve that state in the future. Praxis can only be attained by building on the achievements of capitalist society, overcoming the reified structures that are an inherent part of capitalism, and creating a society without exploitation, alienation, and reified structures (Marx and Engels, 1845–6/1970: 50, 86).

One of the specific reified structures to be destroyed is the arbitrary and oppressive division of labor, leaving people free to pursue their interests to the best of their ability (Marx and Engels, 1845–6/1970: 108, 109). However, not all structures can or should be abandoned. For example, people cannot abandon the technological advances produced by capitalist society because these advances themselves help make praxis possible for the first time. While these technologies are needed, they cannot be allowed to become reified in a future society. Technologies need to be controlled by people and subordinated to their species needs.

Like Marx, Weber is concerned not only with the problem of the adverse consequences of a reified society, but also with the emancipation of people from the source of this problem.[32] However, emancipation represents a far greater intellectual problem for Weber than for Marx. Nevertheless, Weber (cited in Mitzman, 1969: 978) urges that people fight against the bureaucratic machine 'in order to preserve a remnant of humanity from this parcelling-out of the soul, from this exclusive rule of bureaucratic life ideals'. More specifically, he urges that professional politicians 'be the countervailing force against bureaucratic domination' (Weber, 1921/1968: 1417). On the other, more general level, he urges people to live by an ethic of responsibility in which ends are chosen by *wertrationality* and means by *zweckrationality*. Only in this way can individuals live a 'truly human life within the modern rationalized world' (Brubaker, 1984: 110). But while Weber details these and other ways of struggling for emancipation, he does not seem to recognize the possibility of any meaningful success.

Thus, while Marx foresees the overthrow of the structures of capitalist society, Weber is not nearly as optimistic as Marx about the structures of the rationalized society. In fact, Weber is strongly pessimistic about the possibilities of emancipation. This is manifested in his view that 'the future belongs to bureaucratization' (1921/1968: 1401). More generally, he felt that the kind of socialist revolution envisioned by Marx would only serve to heighten the level of rationalization. This pessimism about the possibility of emancipation led Weber (cited in Gerth and Mills, 1958: 128) to conclude: 'Not summer's bloom lies ahead of us, but rather a polar night of icy darkness and hardness, no matter which group may triumph externally now.'

Simmel is closer to Weber than Marx on the issue of emancipation in that he saw the problems of reification and its adverse consequence as inherent to the nature of human life (Weingartner, 1959; Aron, 1965: 139). Furthermore, in the modern world he saw an increasing tendency of objective culture to expand at the expense of individual culture. There is little hope of emancipation because Simmel saw the modern world becoming an 'iron cage' of objective culture. Simmel also shared with Weber a pessimism about socialism, which he felt would only serve to heighten cultural alienation rather than help to alleviate the problem.

Finally, Berger and Luckmann's (1967) thoughts on emancipation are embedded in their ideas on 'alternation'. This is the possibility of the transformation of subjective worlds 'in which the individual "switches worlds"' (1967: 157). In other words, since the problems of reification and its adverse consequences (as well as their sources) are subjective, emancipation from them will come in the form of a subjective transformation. Berger and Pullberg talk more concretely about the sociohistorical situations that make 'dereification', or doubting the taken-for-granted, possible. First, natural or man-made catastrophes can lead to the disintegration of social structures and, as a result, of taken-for-granted worlds. Second, culture contact can lead to culture shock and a questioning of the way in which people perceive the world. Third, those individuals or groups who are socially marginal have a proclivity toward dereification. Whether emancipation comes from alternation or dereification, it is clear that it lies in subjective change.

Conclusions

This, then, is the sociological architectonic that undergirds a significant portion of the work of Marx, Weber, Simmel, and Berger and Luckmann. That architectonic, which is potentially applicable to *any* institution and to *any* social structure in *any* society, as well as to entire societies, involves the relationship among *philosophical anthropology, institutionalization, reification, domination, adverse consequences*, and *emancipation*.

Now, I do not want to press this architectonic similarity too far. There *are*, as we have seen, important differences between the specific architectonics of Marx, Weber, Simmel, and Berger and Luckmann. For example, Weber's actors often lack the ability to objectify that is possessed by Marx's actors. Simmel (and Weber) take a pessimistic view on the issue of emancipation, while Marx is optimistic about the possibility of emancipation. Berger and Luckmann's architectonic is purely subjective while that of Marx integrates subjective and objective dimensions. In spite of these important differences, there clearly *are* striking similarities in the architectonics discussed in this chapter.

On a more general metatheoretical (M_u) level, there is the issue of the utility of comparative architectonics. On the surface, the substantive sociologies of Marx, Weber, Simmel, and Berger and Luckmann seem very different. It is difficult to say what it is that serves to unify their sociologies of capitalism, rationalization, cultural domination, and knowledge. However, when one strips away these substantive concerns, one is able to see the underlying similarities in sociological approach. While increasing the ability to see underlying similarities is one use of sociological architectonics, this approach also allows us to get at basic sources of differences among sociological theorists. Among the theorists discussed here, major theoretical differences between Marx and Weber are traceable to differences in their philosophical anthropologies. Furthermore, because Marx's actors objectify, they are endowed with the capacity to destroy the structures they create. Because Weber's actors are largely lacking in the capacity to objectify, they are doomed to living life in the iron cage. Thus, an architectonic is useful *both* for uncovering underlying similarities in superficially different theories and for tracing the sources of the differences in these theories.

This chapter has been restricted to theorists who can be subsumed largely under a given architectonic. It seems clear, however, that theorists such as Durkheim, Mead, Garfinkel, Goffman, and Homans operate with very different architectonics. What is needed is M_u work oriented to uncovering the architectonics of thinkers such as these. The analysis of a wide range of architectonics, once we know them, should allow us to get a truer sense of the basic similarities and the truly fundamental differences within sociological theory. We may even be able to come up with a limited number of basic types of architectonics. If we do, my view, as I have tried to show throughout this chapter, is that the bulk of the work of Marx, Weber, Simmel, Berger and Luckmann, and many others is informed by the same architectonic.

How might other architectonics differ from the one delineated here? A genuine answer to this question is far beyond the scope of this chapter. In order to get at this question, I would need to identify and delineate the other sociological architectonics. Lacking such elaboration at this point, all I can do is suggest a few of the ways in which other sociological architectonics might differ from the one outlined above.

While the architectonic discussed here is based on a philosophical anthropology of people who think, act, interact, and create, other architectonics may not operate, explicitly or implicitly, with a philosophical anthropology. Still other architectonics may have a philosophical anthropology that does not endow people with the ability to think, may relegate that ability to insignificance, and/or may not link thinking ability to people's actions and interactions.

The architectonic of concern here emphasizes institutionalization, the process by which large-scale structures and institutions emerge out of microprocesses. Other architectonics may not accept the existence of macro-level phenomena; may reject the idea that larger structures and institutions emerge out of these microprocesses; or may begin at the structural and institutional levels without linking them to the micro levels.

The architectonic outlined in this chapter accepts not only the emergence and reality of macro-level phenomena, but also the fact that these structures and institutions can come to have lives of their own that control, rather than are controlled by, the people who created them. Other architectonics that do not accept the idea of emergence also reject the notion of reification. In addition, some architectonics may accept the idea of emergence, but reject the possibility of reification.

In the architectonic analyzed in these pages, the emphasis is on the way reified structures dominate people. In other architectonics, such reified structures may not exist and therefore cannot dominate people. In still other architectonics people are not dominated, or if they are, it is by other people rather than by reified structures.

The emphasis in the architectonic discussed here is on the adverse effect of reified structures on people. In other architectonics the focus may be on how larger, nonreified structures positively affect individuals.

Since the emphasis in the architectonic discussed above is on the negative effects of reified structures on people, there is a parallel interest in emancipating people from such structures. In other architectonics that emphasize the positive effects of structures on people, the concern may be with increasing the control of such nonreified structures over individuals, not emancipating them from that control; in still other architectonics, the problem may be the emancipation of people from the control of other people, not from the control of reified structures.

Finally, it must be said that other architectonics have been discussed in terms of the dimensions of the architectonic outlined here. It is highly likely that these other architectonics have a range of other dimensions that have not even been suggested by the architectonic of concern to us here. Returning to the more general theme of this book, this chapter can be seen as an effort to demonstrate the utility of one M_u tool, the architectonic, as well as a series of subsidiary tools like philosophical anthropology, for enhancing our understanding of the work of some of the leading sociological theorists.

Notes

This chapter is Chapter 4 of *Metatheorizing in Sociology* (1991b: 67–92).

1 This correspondence in the work of Marx, Weber, and Simmel finds support in the work of Habermas (1987: 1) who sees them as part of a '"German" line of social-theoretical thought' dealing with the 'rationalization/reification' problematic. As we will see, the latter problematic is an essential aspect of the architectonic to be outlined here.

2 This discussion will be supplemented with an analysis of a paper Berger coauthored with Stanley Pullberg (1965) that was designed as a precursor to the *Social Construction of Reality*. In fact, Pullberg was to have been one of the coauthors of that book.

3 The term *architectonic* (like other terms used here, e.g. philosophical anthropology) has been used in many different ways in philosophy. See the many definitions in the Compact Edition of *The Oxford English Dictionary*.

4 Also by way of contrast, it is worth noting that I use *architectonic* as a noun to denote underlying structure and not, like Cohen (1981: xliii), as an adjective meaning an approach that is static, not dynamic. Furthermore, there is no contradiction between an architectonic and dynamism; the architectonic I will present *is* processual.

5   However, while Marx is doing theoretical work on social reality, I am doing a metatheoretical analysis of sociological theory. While the realities of capitalism were Marx's data, my data are the various theories.

6   Mandel makes at least part of this explicit when he argues that 'Underlying Marxist economic theory is an anthropological paradigm: man is a social animal; the human species can only survive through social labor' (1983: 189). As we will see, Marx's (philosophical) anthropology, embodied in his ideas on praxis (and species being), is one component, the most basic aspect, of his sociological architectonic.

7   For a similar view, see Mazlish (1984: 117–18).

8   In other words, the position taken here is in accord with those who argue that Marx was *not* an economic determinist (e.g. Meszaros, 1970: 118; Ollman, 1971: 9).

9   This implies that the dominance of *any* institution constitutes a problem for society. While Marx could have focused on other institutions, it is notable that he did not. As Worsley says, 'It is significant that Marx's greatest intellectual achievement is *Capital*, a study in political economy, and that he never produced any parallel study of non-economic institutions, or a systematic *sociology* of society (or even of any particular society) as a whole' (1982: 53).

10   However, to be frank, it is *inconsistent* with many statements made by Engels (and Marx) that reflect economic determinism. See Worsley (1982: 47–51) for a discussion of some of the vacillations of Marx and Engels on this issue.

11   There is little dispute that the concept of species being lies at the base of Marx's early works, especially the manuscripts of 1844. More controversial is the assertion that it informs the later work. But in *The Grundrisse* (1857–8/1973) Marx not only uses the term 'species being' (p. 243), but uses other terms that reflect the basic concept (e.g. the workers' 'creative powers', p. 307). In discussing the individual in a classless society in *The Grundrisse* (p. 51), Marx writes of 'all-sided, full, rich development of needs and capacities'. In *Capital*, vol. 1, the term *species being* does not appear, but the concept is clearly there in, among other things, Marx's (1867/1967: 167, 508) discussion of labor and labor power. Thus, in my view, the idea of species being informs the entire range of Marx's economic works. However, as we will see, the concept of praxis comes to subsume the idea of species being. It is in the concept of praxis that we find Marx's philosophical anthropology.

12   As Ollman (1971) makes clear, the concepts of activity, work, and creativity are interrelated in Marx's work. While they may be separated in capitalism, 'in communism, as far as possible, all activity and work is creative' (1971: 105).

13   Marx adds production to Feuerbach's conception of consciousness, emphasizing 'production as conscious life activity' (Barbalet, 1983: 54).

14   McMurty (1978: 30–1, 35) clearly sees Marx's notion of species being, or more specifically 'projective consciousness', as part of Marx's architectonic since he sees it as underlying, or being the ground for, his entire work.

15   Walliman (1981: 11) differentiates between the biological and social historical aspects of species being. More specifically, Heller (1976: 28) differentiates between 'natural' needs and 'socially produced' needs. This duality leads to interpretive difficulties. Thus, on the one hand, Avineri (1968: 71) can talk of ever-changing human nature, while Ollman (1971: 76) is led to emphasize the fact that Marx has 'a conception of man outside of history'. These views can be reconciled (Geras, 1983) by arguing that there are universal human characteristics (e.g. thought, action, interaction, production), but their specific manifestations are shaped by the nature of the given historical epoch. However, although reconciliation was possible, Marx obviously felt it best to move away from the notion of species being and toward praxis.

16   Many observers echo the position taken here on the centrality of the concept of praxis in Marx's work (e.g. Meszaros, 1970: 79; Rockmore, in Henry, 1983: ix; Lefebvre, 1968: 8, 34).

17   In fact, Weber is not mainly interested in mental processes *per se*, but in how they are translated into patterns of social action (Kalberg, 1980).

18   In fact, to Weber 'the specific task of sociological analysis [was] the interpretation of action in terms of its subjective meaning' (1921/1968: 8).

19   For example, Heller linked the concept of need associated with species being and objectification: 'Marx considered the object of need and the need itself to be always interrelated ... Types of need are formed in accordance with the objects toward which they are directed' (1976: 28).

20   The 1844 manuscripts are ambiguous on this topic. At times, objectification itself is seen as leading to problems, but later it is clearer that the problems stem from the form taken by objectification in capitalism (Nicolaus, 1973: 50).

21   Although I am arguing that Weber had a clear sense of objective structures, there are many places in his work (e.g. Weber, 1903–17/1949: 99; 1921/1968: 13, 14) where Weber discusses objective structures as if they were nothing more than the sum of micro processes. Many Weberian scholars (e.g. Kalberg, 1980) interpret his work in this way. Other observers walk a tightrope on this issue. For example, Cohen admits that Weber does not 'focus on the desiccated short-term strands of social action undertaken by discrete individuals. Rather he devotes the largest part of his analyses to patterns of action within and between large-scale institutions, modes of domination, and cultural ways of life' (1981: xxix).

22   Although it sometimes appears in translations as an appropriate word for what Marx is describing.

23   In fact, Ollman (1971) equates the fetishism of commodities and reification.

24   Elsewhere, Marx makes similar points (see, for example, 1857–8/ 1973: 157, 161; 1867/1967: 72).

25   Walliman (1981) places great emphasis on this reified structure; see also Rattansi (1982).

26   As on the issue of objectification, there are many places where Weber (e.g. 1921/1968: 27) explicitly rejects the idea of reification and reified structures.

27   According to Worsley, Marx 'put at the heart of his sociology – as no other sociology does – the theme of exploitation' (1982: 115).

28   As Barbalet puts it, the 'concept of "alienation" ... is a derivative of the concept "species being" in so far as the meaning of alienation can be understood only in terms of man's divested species being' (1983: 53).

29   Ollman argues that '"private property" is Marx's most general term for the objects produced by alienated labor, and encompasses all the products that come out of the capitalist society' (1971: 159).

30   Barbalet links the idea of emancipation to alienation: 'All theories of alienation entail a concept of the transcendence of alienation' (1983: 102). Similarly, Swingewood says: 'Freedom from alienation thus becomes indissolubly bound to total revolution' (1975: 93).

31   According to Berki, communism is 'the *only thing* that is important about Marx's thought' (1983: 1).

32   Still another parallel between Marx and Weber is the linkage between their philosophical anthropologies and their political philosophies. While Marx wanted to create a society in which praxis (species being) is possible, Weber wanted a society that had room for a 'personality' endowed with dignity, integrity, and autonomy (Brubaker, 1984).

3

SOCIOLOGY: A MULTIPLE PARADIGM SCIENCE

A variety of tools have proven attractive to metatheorists interested in gaining a deeper understanding of theory (M_u) and more generally to metasociologists seeking to better understand the nature of sociology as a whole. While the architectonic employed in Chapter 2 is a somewhat unusual tool, the paradigm concept has been widely employed and is extremely useful; that concept provides the basis for the analysis undertaken in this chapter. While the focus here is on American sociology as a whole, special attention is devoted to attaining a more specific comprehension of American sociological theory.

The period of concern here is primarily the 1960s, although the multi-paradigmatic status of sociology certainly predated that decade and did not disappear with the arrival of the 1970s. But the coexistence of multiple paradigms best defines the 1960s.

The Ideas of Thomas Kuhn

The work of Thomas Kuhn (1962; 1970b) has provided an attractive metasystem to sociologists interested in analyzing the status of their field. One of the best known of these efforts is Robert Friedrichs's *A Sociology of Sociology* (1970), but there are others, including works by Effrat (1972), Lodahl and Gordon (1972), Phillips (1973), Eisenstadt and Curelaru (1976), Strasser (1976), Colclough and Horan (1983), Falk and Zhao (1989; 1990) and Rosenberg (1989), as well as my own (Ritzer, 1975c; 1975d; 1981b), on which this chapter is based. My goal here is to apply Kuhn's ideas, especially the paradigm concept, to sociology in general, and to sociological theory in particular, as they existed largely in the 1960s.

Kuhn sees a science at any given point in time as dominated by a specific paradigm (defined for the moment as a fundamental image of a science's subject matter). Normal science is a period of accumulation of knowledge in which scientists work on, and expand, the reigning paradigm. Inevitably, however, such work spawns *anomalies*, or things that cannot be explained within the existing paradigm. If these anomalies mount, a *crisis* stage is reached, which ultimately may end in a *revolution* during which the reigning paradigm is overthrown and a new one takes its place at the center of the science. Thus a *new reigning paradigm* is born and the stage is set for the cycle to repeat itself. It is during the period of revolution that great changes in scientific status take place. This view clearly places Kuhn at odds with the lay and text-book conceptions of scientific development, which suggest that scienti-fic 'progress' is cumulative.

The key term in Kuhn's model, and the one that is the backbone of this chapter, is his concept of a *paradigm*. Unfortunately, the concept of a paradigm is elusive; according to Masterman (1970), Kuhn uses the term in at least 21 different ways. In response to those who criticized his vagueness about the concept in his first edition, Kuhn offers a very narrow definition of a paradigm in the epilogue to the second edition. There he equates paradigms with exemplars, or 'the concrete puzzle solutions which when employed as models or examples, can replace explicit rules as a basis for the solution of the remaining puzzles of normal science' (1970b: 175).

There is another reason for this narrow definition of a paradigm. As Kuhn (1970b: 191) himself notes, his original work was criticized for its 'subjectivity and irrationality'. The thrust of the first edition pointed in the direction of a very broad definition of a paradigm (as a 'disciplinary matrix') encompassing 'the entire constellation of beliefs, values, techniques, and so on shared by the members of a given community' (1970b: 175). (By 1970, Kuhn views this as an 'inap-propriate' use of the term *paradigm*, primarily because it makes science appear to be irrational.) The paradigm defines what scientists should and should not study; the paradigm tells scientists where, and where not, to look for the entities of concern to them; the paradigm tells scientists what they can expect when they find, and examine, the enti-ties of concern to them. Thus the entire scientific craft is determined by the nature of the dominant paradigm. Furthermore, that craft will be radically altered when one paradigm is superseded by another paradigm. Kuhn sees the emergence of a new paradigm, at least in the first edition of his work, as a distinctly political phenomenon. One paradigm wins out over another because its supporters have more *power* than those who support competing paradigms and not neces-sarily because their paradigm is 'better' than its competitors. For example, the paradigm whose supporters control the most important journals in a field and thereby determine what will be published is more likely to gain preeminence than paradigms whose adherents lack access to prestigious outlets for their work. Similarly, positions of leadership in a field are likely to be given to supporters of the domi-nant paradigm, and these leadership positions give them a platform to enunciate their position with a significant amount of legitimacy. Supporters of paradigms that are seeking to gain hegemony within a field are obviously at a disadvantage since they lack the kinds of power outlined above. Nevertheless, they can, by waging a political battle of their own, overthrow a dominant paradigm and gain that position for their own orientation.

In general, supporters of one paradigm make little effort to understand the basic tenets of its competitors. Instead, they are likely to launch attacks aimed at discrediting the validity of competing paradigms. The goal is not to understand the other paradigms, but to annihilate supporters of competing paradigms with verbal assaults.

In these, and many other ways, the emergence of a new paradigm, or the failure of one to emerge, may be attributed to political factors rather than to the relative 'scientific' merits of the paradigms. This is not to deny that the relative 'scientific' merits of a paradigm are important to its success. The point is that a meritorious paradigm cannot gain hegemony without first engaging in, and ultimately winning, the political conflict. Moreover, a less meritorious paradigm can first gain and then maintain hegemony through political means despite its lack of 'scientific' assets.

In a later article, and in response to his critics, Kuhn argues that one paradigm wins out over another for 'good' reasons, including 'accuracy, scope, simplicity, fruitfulness and the like' (1970a: 261). Thus Kuhn seems to be retreating to a more 'scientific' conception of scientific revolutions. 'Good reasons' have replaced irrational and political factors. This equivocation, like others in his later work, has, in my opinion, worked to the detriment of Kuhn's perspective. Phillips argues that Kuhn's later work has left open the question that Kuhn began with: 'Are there good objective reasons for scientists proceeding as they do, or do we merely term them good because they are endorsed by the members of a certain scientific community?' (1973: 19). In Phillips's view, and mine too, the weight of the evidence points in the direction of the latter interpretation. That is, notions like 'accuracy, scope, simplicity, and fruitfulness would be regarded as paradigm dependent' (1973: 18). Put another way, paradigms rise and fall as a result of political factors.

As a result of my rejection of some of Kuhn's later ideas, I offer the following definition of a paradigm which I feel is truer to the thrust of Kuhn's earlier work and one which is highly relevant to attaining a deeper understanding of sociology (and other fields):

> *A paradigm is a fundamental image of the subject matter within a science. It serves to define what should be studied, what questions should be asked, how they should be asked, and what rules should be followed in interpreting the answer obtained. A paradigm is the broadest unit of consensus within a science and serves to differentiate one scientific community (or subcommunity) from another. It subsumes, defines, and interrelates the exemplars, theories, and methods and instruments that exist within it.*

It is important to underscore the point that in my view a paradigm has four basic components: (1) an exemplar,[1] or body of work that stands as a model for those who work within the paradigm; (2) an image of the subject matter; (3) theories; and (4) methods and instruments. Although a number of other components could conceivably be added (e.g. values), these additions would not increase significantly our ability to analyze the basic sociological paradigms.

The paradigm concept, as it is defined here in cognitive terms, can be used to analyze either scientific communities or subcommunities. At a given point in the history of some sciences, when consensus exists on a single paradigm, a paradigm can be seen as coterminous with the scientific community. These are what Masterman (1970) calls paradigmatic sciences: physics, during the era when the Newtonian perspective was preeminent, is a good example. However, most sciences, including contemporary sociology, lack a single overarching paradigm. They are, according to Masterman, multiple paradigm sciences. In such sciences paradigms are related to the major subcommunities. It is this characteristic that allows us to apply the concept with equal facility to Newtonian physics and contemporary sociology.

American sociology, especially in the 1960s, was (and is) a multiple paradigm science: each of its paradigms was competing for hegemony within the discipline as a whole as well as within virtually every sub-area within sociology. Before identifying and delineating what I view as the three competing paradigms in sociology in the 1960s, I must first examine critically some early efforts to apply the paradigm concept to sociology.

Working with Kuhn's inadequate definition of a paradigm, Friedrichs (1970) examines the subject matter of sociology and proceeds to label almost every theory a paradigm, or at least a would-be paradigm. Thus system theory and conflict theory emerge as dominant sociological paradigms, with such a diverse lot as Marxism, dialectics, action theory, exchange theory, and phenomenology described as pretenders to that lofty status. However, as the definition used in this chapter makes clear, theories are *not* paradigms. Rather, theories are components of far broader paradigms. Because he lacks an adequate definition of a paradigm, Friedrichs mistakes theories for paradigms and thereby arrives at an overly splintered conception of the state of sociology.

Later in his analysis, Friedrichs seems to become concerned with his excessively fragmented conception of sociology and decides to differentiate between first- and second-order paradigms. He recognizes that the theories he has been calling paradigms may not be the 'most controlling' fundamental images in sociology. So he relegates these theories to the status of second-order paradigms. The first-order or most controlling paradigms in sociology relate to the image the sociologist has of 'himself as a scientific agent', rather than to the scientist's basic image of the subject matter. There are only two such self-images in Friedrichs's view, the priestly and the prophetic, and they are the most controlling. This idea of first-order paradigms allows Friedrichs to make a much more parsimonious analysis of the paradigmatic status of sociology.

I have no quarrel with the differentiation between priestly and prophetic self-images, but I do not accept the necessity of resorting to this type of analysis. Friedrichs was forced to look for paradigms based on self-images because he was working with an inadequate definition of a paradigm as it relates to the subject matter of sociology. In my view, different images of the subject matter *are* the key paradigmatic splits in sociology.

Like Friedrichs, Effrat (1972) is faced with the problem of parsimony in his effort to analyze the paradigmatic status of sociology. Although he uses a reasonably good definition of a paradigm, Effrat also makes the error of mistaking theories for paradigms. This flaw leads him to create a cumbersome list of 'paradigms' including Marxism, exchange theory, Freudian theory, Durkheimian theory, Weberian theory, Parsonsian theory, phenomenology, ethnomethodology, and symbolic interactionism. In addition, he enumerates a number of other theoretical perspectives that he is willing to call paradigms, and he implies that there are even more that he has not had time to discuss. If there really were so many paradigms in sociology, then the concept would be a useless tool for analyzing the status of the discipline. In fact, the paradigm concept *is* a useful instrument for analyzing sociology; its utility can be demonstrated by identifying and analyzing what I consider to be the three basic paradigms that characterized sociology in the United States in the 1960s: the social facts, social definition, and social behavior paradigms.

The Social Facts Paradigm

Exemplar

The exemplar for the social factist is clearly the work of Emile Durkheim, in particular *The Rules of Sociological Method* (1895/1964) and *Suicide* (1897/1951). In these works Durkheim developed and applied his concept of a social fact. Durkheim argued that social facts were to be treated as things external to individuals and coercive on them. He did not argue that they were things. They were only to be treated as things for purposes of sociological analysis. Social factists have tended to ignore this crucial equivocation in Durkheim's work and have proceeded to argue that social facts are things, real material entities. In addition, social factists have neglected the reality that a major type of social fact for Durkheim was the 'social current', which is best seen as an intersubjective phenomenon rather than as a material entity. Paradox arises because, although Durkheim coined the term 'social fact', some of the basic tenets of the social facts paradigm would be unacceptable to him. He would, I think, be comfortable with some aspects of the social definition paradigm. At numerous points in his work Durkheim makes it clear that he is concerned with the kinds of issues of concern to the social definitionist.[2]

Just to give one example, Durkheim (cited in Lukes, 1973: 498) contends 'that sociology has not completely achieved its task so long as it has not penetrated into the mind of the individual in order to relate the institutions it seeks to explain to their psychological conditions'.[3]

A more proximate piece of work can be seen as a clearer exemplar for the social facts paradigm: Charles K. Warriner's 'Groups Are Real: A Reaffirmation' (1956). Although Warriner focuses on only one social fact, the group, the case that he makes could be made for any other social fact. Basically, Warriner upholds what he calls the realist position 'that (1) the group is just as real as the person, but that (2) both are abstract, analytical units, and that (3) the group is understandable and explicable solely in terms of distinctly social processes and factors, not by reference to individual psychology' (1956: 550–1). This position, which best expresses the social facts paradigm, is the one Warriner defends: 'The purpose here is calling attention to and defending the legitimacy and validity of the realist position, and to propose that this is the most valid and potentially fruitful sociological approach to the study of group and society' (1956: 551).

Following Warriner, social factists accept the reality of such social facts as groups, norms, institutions, or social systems. They focus on the study of these social facts and their coercive effect on the individual and they argue that a given social fact can only be explained by other social facts.

Image of the Subject Matter

The basic subject matter of sociology to those who adopt this paradigm is the social fact. A large number of phenomena could be labeled social facts, including roles, values, groups, society, the world system, etc. Peter Blau (1960) performed a useful service by differentiating between two basic types of social facts: social structures and institutions.[4] Social factists are those sociologists who contend that the subject matter of sociology is social institutions and social structures. They argue further that an institution or structure can be explained only by other social facts. They view individuals, their social behavior, and their social activities as largely determined by social structures and social institutions.

Theories

A number of theories could be included within the social facts paradigm, but the two most important are structural functionalism and conflict theory.

In perhaps the most important essay on structural functionalism, Robert Merton makes it clear that it is oriented to the study of social facts when he says that the objects that can be subjected to structural-functional analysis must 'represent a standardized (i.e. patterned and repetitive) item' (1968: 104). He offers the following examples of these items, all of which are clearly social facts: 'Social roles, institutional patterns, social processes, cultural patterns, culturally patterned emotions, social norms, group organization, social structure, devices for social control, etc.' (1968: 104).

Structural functionalism is oriented to the analysis of social structures and institutions. The structural functionalist is concerned with the (functional) relationship between structures, between institutions, and between structures and institutions. While not oblivious to the individual, the structural functionalist, following Durkheim, sees the individual as primarily controlled by social facts that are external and coercive.

Conflict theory, especially the variant represented by the work of Ralf Dahrendorf (1959), while remaining firmly within the social facts paradigm, tends to take a series of positions directly antithetical to the ideas of structural functionalism. While functionalists see society as static, or in a state of moving equilibrium, Dahrendorf and the conflict theorists see every society at every point subject to change. Where functionalists emphasize the fact that society is orderly, conflict theorists see dissension and conflict wherever they look. Functionalists (at least early functionalists) tend to argue that every element in society contributes to stability, while exponents of conflict theory see each societal element contributing to disintegration and change. Functionalists tend to see society as being held together informally by norms, values, and common morality, while conflict theorists see whatever order exists in society as stemming from the coercion of some members by others who rank higher in the system.

In spite of these differences, Dahrendorf, as well as conflict theorists in general, focus on social facts.[5] Central to Dahrendorf's thesis is the idea that differential authority is an attribute of various positions within society. The central concepts here are *authority* and *positions*, both of which are social facts. Authority resides not in individuals, but in positions. Thus societal positions and the differential distribution of power among them should be the concern of sociologists: 'The structural origin of such conflicts must be sought in the arrangement of social roles endowed with expectations of domination or subjection' (1959: 165). The first task of conflict analysis to Dahrendorf is identification of various authority roles within society.

I should point out that I do *not* include the work of Karl Marx and a number of his followers under the heading of conflict theory. Marx is, as I point out later in this chapter, a 'paradigm bridger'. Although Marx is certainly interested in analyzing social facts, in particular those in capitalist society, he is also interested in social action ('praxis') and mental processes, both cornerstones, as we will see, of the social definition paradigm. In fact, Marx's architectonic, as it was delineated in Chapter 2, precludes the possibility of considering him a social factist. Marx was interested in reified social facts, but he was also interested in the microprocesses by which those facts come into existence (and through which they can be changed). Dahrendorf and other conflict theorists, although they contend that they are working in the Marxian tradition, have focused on social facts and have either ignored actors or seen them as determined by external social facts. Although Marx saw social facts as coercive on the individual, much of his analysis was specific to capitalism. His hope was the creation of a society in which social facts would not determine social action. In any case, his theoretical system, unlike Dahrendorf's and other conflict theorists, does take significant account of social definitions. It is this that will lead me, in Chapter 5, to view Marx's work as the exemplar for another, integrated, paradigm.

Methods

Those who accept the social facts paradigm should *tend* to use historical/comparative methods when they do empirical research (Snizek, 1976). This methodology fits best with the social facts paradigm. It allows the social factist to focus on macro-level phenomena (social facts) in historical and cross-cultural contexts. While there are some fine examples of historical/comparative research (e.g. Mann, 1986; Wallerstein, 1974; 1980; 1989), this method is not utilized as often as might be expected because it is so demanding and time-consuming and because it appears to be inconsistent with the positivism that dominates most research in contemporary sociology.

Snizek finds that, in fact, social factists rely heavily on the interview/questionnaire[6] *and* that this was also the dominant methodology in the other two paradigms. This widespread acceptance of questionnaires and interviews is traceable to the ease with which data derived from them can be compiled and analyzed utilizing advanced statistical techniques. The use of the questionnaire and interview by the social factist points to a basic paradox in contemporary sociology. These methods elicit replies from individuals, but a basic tenet of the social factist is that the whole is more than the sum of its parts. Social factists accept the idea of emergence, that is, the idea that out of the interaction of individuals a social reality *emerges* that is more than the sum of the individuals. Thus, the sum of individual replies does not equal a social fact. In addition, individual replies yield *their* definition of a social fact, not what that social fact *really* is. No less a social theorist and student of the interview and questionnaire techniques than James Coleman recognizes that these methods do not tap social facts: 'Survey research methods have led to the neglect of social structure and of the relations among individuals ... The *individual* remained the unit of analysis ... As a result, the kinds of substantive problems on which research focused tended to be problems of "aggregate psychology"' (1970: 115). More recently, Marini (1988: 45) criticized the specific area of gender research for studying macro-level phenomena with micro-level data.

In spite of these liabilities, many of those who study social facts use questionnaire and interview methods. Social factists prefer these methods because they make data collection and analysis easier, and because the other major methods available to them do not lend themselves as well to the study of social facts. Social factists tend to reject the observation technique because they view it as unscientific and crude. They are equally likely to reject the experimental method because it is not easily applied to the study of the kind of macroscopic questions of interest to the social factist.

The Social Definition Paradigm

Exemplar

The exemplar for the social definitionist is a highly prominent, albeit very specific, aspect of Max Weber's work: his analysis of social action. Weber defines sociology as the study of social action: 'Sociology is a science which attempts the interpretative understanding of social action in order thereby to arrive at a causal explanation of its course and effects' (1947: 88). He defines social action as 'all human behavior when and in so far as the acting individual attaches a subjective meaning to it ... Action is social in so far as by virtue of the subjective meaning attached to it by the acting individual (or individuals), it takes account of the behavior of others and is thereby oriented in its course' (1947: 88). This definition constitutes the basis of the social definition paradigm.

The paradox here is that while Weber's work is viewed as the exemplar for the social definition paradigm, he spent most of his life analyzing social structures (and doing historical/comparative research).[7] Gerth and Mills echo this view:

> Were one to accept Weber's methodological reflections on his own work at their face value, one would not find a systematic justification for his analysis of such phenomena as stratification or capitalism. Taken literally, the 'method of understanding' would hardly allow for Weber's use of structural explanations: for this type of explanation attempts to account for the motivation of systems of action by their function as going concerns rather than by the subjective intentions of the individuals who act them out. According to Weber's method of understanding, we should expect him to adhere to a subjective theory of stratification, but he does not do so. (1958: 57)

In short, Weber, although the exemplar for the social definitionist, was at least in part a social factist. Similarly, as we saw above, Durkheim is considered the exemplar of the social factists, even though he is, at least partly, a social definitionist.

Image of the Subject Matter

Four theories will be discussed under the heading of social definitionism: action theory, symbolic interactionism, ethnomethodology, and phenomenology. There are clearly many differences among them, but they share several overarching commonalities in their image of the subject matter of sociology. Perhaps the major theme consistent for all four theories is that people are active creators of their own social reality. The converse is another consistent theme in the social definition paradigm: social structures and institutions are not a static set of coercive social facts. Social definitionists stand in stark contrast to social factists who view people as controlled by such things as norms, values, and social control agencies. They are also, as we will see, at variance with the social behaviorists, who see people as controlled by 'contingencies of reinforcement'. In fact, the high priest of behaviorism, B.F. Skinner (1971), takes the extreme position and denies completely the view of people as active and creative (what he calls 'autonomous man').

Social definitionists tend to be interested in the mental process[8] as well as the resulting action and interaction. Although they cannot examine it directly, those who accept the social definition paradigm are generally interested in what takes place in the minds of people. Something occurs in a person's mind between the time a stimulus is applied and the time a response is emitted – the creative activity that is at the base of the interests of the social definitionist. This interest in the mental process is manifested in Mead's 'I' and 'Me', Cooley's 'looking glass self', Parsons's voluntarism, Berger and Luckmann's 'social construction of reality', Garfinkel's criticism of social factists for treating actors as 'judgmental dopes', and most importantly, given the label applied to this paradigm, W.I. Thomas's 'definition of the situation'. In addition to a concern for such mental processes, social definitionists are interested in the resultant actor and interaction.

Theories

Action theory, symbolic interactionism,[9] phenomenology, and ethno-methodology are all concerned with people as active creators of social reality. Conversely, they deny that social structure is merely a static set of coercive social facts.

Action theory has often been linked with symbolic interactionism. In fact, Hinkle (1963) views action theory as an intellectual antecedent of symbolic interactionism and he argues that the two theories share a number of common assumptions. It is somewhat less usual to link phenomenology with action theory and symbolic interactionism. Although the three theories share a common basis, the relationship between phenomenology and the other two theories has been obscured by the fact that phenomenology is believed by many to be more philo-sophical than sociological. Alfred Schutz (1932/1967; 1962; 1964; 1966), one of the major figures in phenomenology, has made it abundantly clear that his orientation is intimately related to both action theory and symbolic interactionism. Schutz points out that he is in accord with Weber's action theory, and in particular with the study of action that is meaningful to the actors involved. Subjective meaning is crucial to interaction both for the actor intending the behavior and for the others who must interpret it and act accordingly. Schutz is also in accord with Weber's method of *verstehen* which suggests that social scientists must involve themselves with interactants using a form of sympathetic introspection in order to understand the meaning contexts that serve as the impetus to action. Schutz also makes clear his admiration for the work of several symbolic interactionists (e.g. Mead and Thomas) and approves of their interest in how actors are socialized to internalize and share socially differentiated contexts of meaning that are experienced subjectively and serve as the basis for social action. Thus, it appears that Schutz would accept the association of phenomenology with action theory and symbolic interactionism and the inclusion of all three in the social definition paradigm.

Heritage offers a definition of ethnomethodology (one that fits well with the other theoretical varieties of social definitionism) as the study of 'the body of commonsense knowledge and the range of procedures and considerations by means of which the ordinary members of society make sense of, find their way about in, and act on the circumstances in which they find themselves' (1984: 4). There is a micro-level focus on actors dealing with their social situations and acting on the basis of their decisions. The actors, following Garfinkel, are endowed with the ability to make judgments that decisively affect their actions. However, there is a stronger emphasis on the social situation than in the other forms of social definitionism. That is, the ethnomethodologists are concerned with 'the body of commonsense knowledge' and the social practices and procedures through which actors deal with their social worlds. This is particularly true of a branch of ethnomethodology, conversational analysis, in which the focus is on 'the procedures by which conversationalists produce their own behavior and understand and deal with the behavior of others' (Heritage and Atkinson, 1984: 1). While there is focal concern with extant 'procedures', there is also a concern, in line with other social definitionists, with people 'producing' their actions.

Although action theory has a clear link to symbolic interactionism, phenomenology, and ethnomethodology, it also has a number of basic differences. In fact, I believe that action theory, more than the others, combines an interest in social definitions with an interest in social facts. Social definitionists have often failed to see the interest in social facts in action theory, just as they have often failed to recognize Max Weber's interest in social facts. A major reason for both oversights lies in a misrepresentation of the concept of *verstehen*. The symbolic interactionists tend to see *verstehen* as a method for gaining insight into actors' mental processes, to understand the way they come to define a given situation. However, Weber, following the German intellectual tradition (e.g. Dilthey), saw *verstehen* not as a method for understanding the mental process, but rather as a method for gathering data on social institutions and social structures ('the meaning context'). Researchers put themselves in the place of the actor, not in order to understand the actor, but rather to understand the cultural and societal milieu in which the actor exists. Despite these and many other misinterpretations, action theory can still be seen as a theoretical component of social definitionism, even though in many ways it fits better into the social facts paradigm. After all, at its base, action theory sees the actor as possessing a dynamic, creative, voluntaristic mind. In contrast, social factists tend to see the actor as strongly determined by the broader social structure.

Although there are problems with assigning action theory to a single paradigm, I have no problem seeing symbolic interactionism, phenomenology, and ethnomethodology as theoretical components of the social definition paradigm. These theories share an interest in intrasubjectivity, intersubjectivity, action, and interaction, although each maintains a difference in emphasis. The symbolic interactionists tend to focus on action and interaction, the phenomenologists concentrate on intra- and intersubjectivity, and the ethnomethodologists target the way actors use the body of commonsense knowledge (action theorists combine these interests with a concern for the social context).

Methods

Those who accept the social definition paradigm, like those who employ the social facts paradigm, most often use questionnaire and interview techniques. However, despite their obvious allure for all sociologists these methods are generally ill fitted to social definitionism (as they are to social factism) because they tend to gather information on static variables rather than the processual information on action and interaction of interest to the social definitionist. (The laboratory experiment is also ill suited to this paradigm because of the comparative lack of ability of those relying on it to study spontaneous and natural action.)

The observation technique is best suited to the demands of social definitionist research because it allows the researcher to examine process over time in a natural setting. This accounts, among other things, for the attraction of symbolic interactionists to participant observation and the ethnomethodologists' focus on such things as conversations between people. Social definitionists *should* be more likely to use observational techniques than the supporters of the other major paradigms.[10]

However, I must also ask whether observation is really well suited to the study of the topics of concern to the social definitionist. In fact, we cannot actually observe intra- and intersubjectivity, action and interaction. The best we can do is deduce information about these processes from the bits and pieces that we can observe. There is a very real question whether observation fulfills all of the demands of the social definition paradigm. Whatever its liabilities, observation comes closer to fitting the needs of social definitionists than any other methodology.

The Social Behavior Paradigm

Exemplar

Behaviorism has a long and honorable history in the social sciences, in particular in psychology. However, its modern resurgence in all of the social sciences, and in particular in sociology, can be traced to B.F. Skinner, whose work is the exemplar for the sociologists who have endeavored to adapt behaviorism to their discipline.

Image of the Subject Matter

Social behaviorists are interested in the relationship between individuals and their environment. Bushell and Burgess define the nature of the subject matter of sociology to the behaviorist as 'the behavior of individuals that operates on the environment in such a way as to produce some consequences or change in it which, in turn, modifies subsequent performances of that behavior' (1969: 27). Thus the focus is on the functional relationship between behavior and changes in the environment of the actor.

Social behaviorists claim that they are focusing on an interaction process, but this process is conceptualized very differently from that of the social definitionists. Actors, to the social definitionist, are dynamic, creative forces in the interaction process. They are not simply responding to stimuli, but interpreting these inputs and acting on the basis of the way they define them. But the social behaviorist allows individuals far less freedom. Believing that people's responses are determined by the nature of the external stimuli, the behaviorist's image of people is much more mechanical than that of the social definitionist.

The social factist's image of people is almost as mechanistic as the social behaviorist's. The social factist sees the individual as determined by norms, values, structures, and the like. The difference between the social factist and the social behaviorist lies in the source of control over the individual. To the social factist, macroscopic structures and institutions exert control, while to the social behaviorist the contingencies of reinforcement are the source of control.

Theories

Behavioral sociology (Burgess and Bushell, 1969) constitutes a theoretical effort to apply the principles of behaviorism to sociological questions. Take, for example, their effort to define socialization as 'an interactional process whereby an individual's behavior is modified to conform to the rules and standards of the groups to which he belongs' (1969: 275). In the hands of the behavioral sociologist, socialization becomes a process of behavior modification. A similar tendency to reduce social processes to behavior is found in the way behaviorists treat a variety of other traditional sociological topics and concepts (e.g. self, social structure, and so on).

The major sociological theory encompassed by the social behavior paradigm is exchange theory. Although exchange theory can be traced to the work of Chavannes (Knox, 1963) and Mauss (1954), it enjoyed a boom in interest in the 1960s as a result of the work of George Homans (1961/1974). Deeply indebted to Skinner's work on pigeons, Homans developed five basic propositions concerning elementary social behavior. Those propositions form the basis of Homans's exchange theory. Others participated in the development of exchange theory in the 1960s, the most notable being Peter Blau (1964).[11] Exchange theory is differentiated from behavioral sociology by its more traditional sociological orientation.

Methods

As was true for the other two paradigms, the most often used method in social behaviorism is the interview/questionnaire. However, once again, there is a poor fit between social behaviorism and the most often used method. Coming from psychology, social behaviorists prefer much more controlled scientific research than is possible in interviews of questionnaires. (An even greater lack of control leads social behaviorism to a rejection of the 'soft' observation techniques.) Because of their linkage to psychology, their preference for studying behavior in a controlled setting, and their microscopic orientation, behaviorists are more likely to feel comfortable with the experimental method in their research. Behaviorists are also more likely to use laboratory experiments than those who accept the other paradigms (Snizek, 1976).

Conclusions and Implications

There is some support in the literature for the tripartite differentiation of sociology in the 1960s into social factist, definitionist, and behaviorist paradigms. Brown and Gilmartin (1969), in a study of articles published in the *American Journal of Sociology*, found that articles focused on three variables: individual, individual–group, and group. Those three variables tend to parallel the three paradigms discussed in this chapter. The weakest correspondence is between the individual variable and the social behavior paradigm. Many of those researchers who focused on the individual did not support the social behavior paradigm. Nevertheless, the Brown and Gilmartin study is generally supportive. So is Theodore Abel's (1970) analysis of the way sociologists theoretically analyzed social collectivities. Abel argued that there are three theoretical conceptions of collectivities, and his conceptions parallel precisely the three paradigms discussed here. Again, this support is far from definitive since Abel only examined theories and focused on only one issue, collectivities.

The support offered above for the position outlined in this chapter is far from conclusive. The only true test is whether it enables the reader to better understand the status of American sociology, in particular sociological theory, in the 1960s. There are, of course, other classification schemes to which the one offered here can be compared. However, most such schemes – such as the work of Friedrichs and

Effrat discussed above – list theories rather than true paradigms. Thus, the analyses of Friedrichs and Effrat are of a lower level of generality than the one offered here.

There are also a number of efforts at classifying the components of sociology (especially in the 1960s) that focus explicitly on theory. Some of these come to conclusions very different from the one offered here, for example Martindale (1960), Timasheff (1967), Wallace (1969), and Mullins (1973), while others, for example Abel (1970), are much closer. However, all of these classification systems are far more narrow than the one developed here. I have not tried to develop a classification system for sociological theory; rather I have attempted to classify the basic approaches in sociology. Since paradigms are far broader than theories, the paradigm approach allows us to do much more than simply understand our theoretical differences. It allows us to see our methodological differences and to see how methodological differences are intimately related to theoretical differences. It also enables us to see how theoretical and methodological differences are tied to our discipline's history in the work of the exemplars. Finally, it allows us to see how theories, methods, and exemplars are related to our fundamental images of the subject matter of sociology.

There are a number of important implications of this analysis of the paradigmatic status of sociology in the 1960s. First, spokespeople for each paradigm tend to claim to be able to explain all of the phenomena of concern to sociology.[12] Thus they are competing to gain hegemony within the discipline as a whole. In addition, they are competing within virtually every subarea within sociology. In my view, this competition and conflict have negative consequences for the discipline. Each of the paradigms, standing alone, is inadequate. Each needs insights from the other paradigms in order to fully explain any social phenomena. Therefore, we need less competition and conflict and more effort at paradigmatic integration (see Chapters 4 and 5). The discipline is rife with political conflict. Much of it is interparadigmatic, although some of it is also intraparadigmatic (e.g. structural functionalism versus conflict theory). This political conflict has more negative than positive consequences and often serves to divide the discipline unnecessarily.[13]

Second, in the 1960s, and to some extent to this day, sociologists were often deceived into believing that the basic split in sociology was between structural functionalism and conflict theory. I have sought to show that these two theories share the same paradigm and have far more commonalities than differences. The truly fundamental differences in sociology are among the three paradigms discussed in this chapter.

Third, theory and method are often practiced in virtual isolation from each other. A paradigmatic approach emphasizes the general link between the methods and theories.

Fourth, behaviorism is not often accorded the central place in sociology that it receives in my paradigmatic approach. Its elevation to paradigmatic status in sociology in this discussion is based more on its anticipated significance than on its position in the 1960s. In my view, social behaviorism is likely to become a powerful force in sociology.[14] This view is not idiosyncratic and is reflected in a variety of examinations of the status of sociology in the 1960s (Tarter, 1973; Friedrichs, 1974).

Fifth, there is a considerable amount of irrationality in sociology. Sociologists often use methods that are not well suited to the paradigm from which they operate. The works of Weber and Durkheim are viewed as the exemplars for paradigms with which these two men would be highly uncomfortable. Action theory has been erroneously viewed as being akin to symbolic interactionism. The erroneous view that the basic split in sociology is between structural functionalism and conflict theory has already been discussed, as has the ubiquity of destructive political conflict. Finally, and perhaps most importantly, sociologists in the 1960s (and to this day) never truly understood their most basic differences.

Sociologists need to overcome their political differences and begin to create an integrated sociological paradigm. Although I doubt that sociology is likely to become a single-paradigm science in the near future, and such a goal is not necessarily desirable, I do think that there are a number of points of reconciliation among the paradigms that have been obscured by the political allegiances and political efforts to destroy competitors by adherents of each of the paradigms. Sociologists need to spend less time destroying their political opponents and more time deriving useful insights from their perspectives. No single paradigm is adequate for explaining all social phenomena. There is a need for a halt to *destructive* interparadigmatic debates. Some of these debates are useful (e.g. the ideas of one paradigm can be sharpened as a result of attacks from adherents of other paradigms), but most have had far more negative consequences than positive effects. A more common base in sociology exists than paradigmatic differences have allowed sociologists to realize. Nevertheless, Kuhn's insights into the political character of paradigmatic differences in all sciences make it clear that we are unlikely to overcome completely our narrow political interests.

While I favor reducing, or eliminating, destructive interparadigmatic debates, the point needs to be underscored that constructive paradigmatic debates should, and will, continue. Destructive debates are preventing sociologists not only from seeing their common base, but also from doing the normal science within their paradigm through which anomalies can be uncovered and which, in turn, could lead to scientific revolutions. Sociologists are too busy defending their basic assumptions to themselves and others to concentrate on normal science. Kuhn (1970b: 160) supports this position when he argues that fields like sociology can make progress when they 'achieve consensus about their past and present accomplishments'. The multiple paradigms in sociology will continue to exist even after we find our common core, but the debates among them will be more likely to have positive consequences.

Although paradigmatic reconciliation will not come tomorrow, a number of efforts offer hope to those interested in bridging at least some of these differences. Historically, theorists like Weber, Durkheim, Marx, and Parsons have been able to bridge paradigms. Their work can serve as a starting point for those who seek an integrated sociological paradigm (see Chapters 4 and 5).

Durkheim bridged the social facts and social definition paradigms, in particular in his analysis of material social facts and nonmaterial, intersubjective social currents. Weber bridged the same paradigms, most notably in his studies of religion. Marx devoted most of his attention to the social structure of capitalism, but his dialectical approach led him to recognize the significance of the actor's social definitions (Bender, 1970). Parsons was the only one to deal with all three paradigms. His early action orientation, the influence Tolman's behaviorism had on him in the 1940s, and his later preoccupation with social structure and culture reflect Parsons's propensity to 'leap' from paradigm to paradigm.

In the 1960s and early 1970s several pieces of work appeared that sought to integrate paradigms, or aspects of paradigms. For example, Blau (1964) sought to integrate social behaviorism and social factism. Singelmann (1972) attempted to integrate social behaviorism and social definitionism, although his effort was met by a political attack from the behaviorists (Abbott et al., 1973). Warriner (1970) combined social definitionism and social factism. Although all of these works were hopeful signs, paradigmatic integration did *not* immediately follow. The political goals and allegiances of sociologists continued to stand in the way of paradigmatic reconciliation, at least until the 1980s and 1990s and the rise of the micro–macro and agency–structure theories.

Postscript

The paradigm analysis presented above elicited a great deal of reaction, both pro and con. (For a summary and analysis of the debate, see Abrams et al., 1980.) In this postscript I want to deal with the most important of those critiques.

Eckberg and Hill's (1979) essay is one of a spate of research studies (e.g. Snizek, 1976; Picou et al., 1978; Friedheim, 1979; Platt, 1986; Falk and Zhao, 1989; 1990) and conceptual essays (e.g. Martindale, 1979; Snizek, 1979; Wilke and Mohan, 1979; Rosenberg, 1989) dealing at least in part with my application of Kuhn's paradigm concept to sociology in the 1960s. My objective in this postscript is to point to some basic differences between myself and Eckberg and Hill and in the process to help clarify the paradigm concept and its applicability to sociology.

There are three basic differences between Eckberg and Hill's (1979) work and my own. First, their main focus is the sociology of science, specifically Kuhnian theory. My major interest, and the interest of many others in this field, is metasociology: specifically, the paradigmatic status of sociology. Although these two interests are related, there is a significant difference in emphasis. Second, Eckberg and Hill are greatly concerned with being true to Kuhnian theory. My prime interest is in gaining as deep an understanding as possible of sociology and its future prospects. While these objectives are not necessarily incompatible, Eckberg and Hill's Kuhnian purism is not the best way of enhancing our understanding of sociology. Unlike Eckberg and Hill, I am willing to deviate from a strict interpretation of Kuhnian theory if it will help achieve a greater understanding of the discipline. Third, Eckberg and Hill and I disagree on which of Kuhn's definitions of a paradigm is best suited to the analysis of sociology. They prefer his later definition of a paradigm as an exemplar. In spite of the fact that he later rejected it, I prefer Kuhn's earlier definition of a paradigm as a disciplinary matrix, or the shared intellectual commitments of an intellectual community.

Operating from their three basic assumptions, Eckberg and Hill are virtually unassailable in their contention that the paradigm concept has been misused by those who have attempted to apply it to sociology. They are correct in recognizing the ambiguities of Kuhn's initial formulation. They understand that it is possible on the basis of his early work to equate paradigms with disciplinary matrices. They also recognize Kuhn's later equation of paradigms with exemplars, concrete solutions to problems. Eckberg and Hill argue that most sociologists either are unaware of the differences in and subtleties of Kuhn's conceptualization, or ignore them. Although they recognize that I understand the complexities of Kuhn's work, they criticize my work for disregarding those complexities in the study of the paradigmatic status of sociology.

While Eckberg and Hill are correct in both their formulation of Kuhn's perspective *and* their accusation that I ignore some of his distinctions, their strict adherence to Kuhnian theory leads them to some questionable assertions about sociology. Because they are tied to a strict usage of Kuhnian theory, they define paradigms as exemplars and thus focus on specific areas of research that are 'guided by concrete examples of scholarship, which serve to generate and to solve puzzles' (1979: 935). They argue that potential exemplars (paradigms) in sociology can be found in such areas as 'political socialization, status attainment, ethnic relations' (1979: 933).

If we were to take both Kuhn and Eckberg and Hill literally, we would end up with hundreds, or maybe even thousands, of paradigms. Because paradigms (exemplars) are, in their view, found within substantive areas, and because numerous such areas exist in sociology, presumably it would be possible to have an enormous array of paradigms. For example, within one substantive area in sociology – occupational sociology – we could identify such paradigms (following the model of status attainment) as job satisfaction, alienation, commitment, role conflict, professionalization, and innumerable others. Even if we had and were able to identify numerous exemplars, they would be useless tools for making sense out of the broad structure of the field. In fact, if we had so many exemplars, we would probably need another concept to help us divide them into reasonable groupings so that we could discern the basic structure of sociology. That basic structure would best be delineated then, as it is now, by paradigms as disciplinary matrices rather than exemplars.

Because I continue to believe that the disciplinary matrix is the more useful definition of a paradigm in so far as sociology is concerned, my sense of not only the present but also the future of sociology is not the same as that of Eckberg and Hill. While they believe that sociology needs more exemplars, my view is that what sociology needs is a new disciplinary matrix, one that deals in a more integrated fashion with the social world than extant paradigms. The next two chapters are devoted to the issue of an integrated sociological paradigm.

Notes

The bulk of the material covered in this chapter has appeared in several places including *Sociology: A Multiple Paradigm Science* (1975c); 'Sociology: A Multiple Paradigm Science' (1975d); and *Metatheorizing in Sociology* (1991b: 117–37). The postscript to this chapter comes from 'Paradigm Analysis in Sociology: Clarifying the Issues' (1981a).

1   *Exemplar* is used here very differently from Kuhn's conception of it as a concrete solution to a scientific puzzle. In sociology, we have few such solutions and our exemplars tend to be more general bodies of work that stand as models for others.
2   See Chapter 5 for a further discussion of this aspect of Durkheim's work.
3   Durkheim's tendency to accept at least some elements of social definitionism has been underscored by Robert Nisbet (1974) who argues that there is not 'one iota of difference' between Durkheim's approach and that of such preeminent social definitionists as Mead and Cooley. Of course, not all analysts of any sociological theorist offer the same interpretation. In contrast to Nisbet (and earlier, Talcott Parsons), Pope (1973: 414) argues that 'Durkheim never embraced a theory of action.' Since action theory is a component of the social definition paradigm, Pope is taking a position in opposition to Nisbet's. Nevertheless, it is my view that a careful reading of Durkheim's work, in particular *Suicide*, reveals a deep interest in the mental process and social action (see Chapter 5).
4   Durkheim offers a similar distinction between material and nonmaterial social facts.

5   Collins (1990) clearly acknowledges this point by arguing that his own contribution to conflict theory (Collins, 1975) was designed to add a micro level to the traditional macro-level concerns of conflict theory.

6   Platt (1986), however, has failed to find support for this association.

7   This wider set of concerns is also clear in the discussion of Weber's architectonic in Chapter 2, which demonstrates considerable interest in reified social structures.

8   Ethnomethodologists are less interested in this than the other theorists associated with this paradigm. However, the former's focus on everyday practice assumes such mental abilities.

9   I am basically discussing here the Chicago brand of symbolic interactionism. Iowa symbolic interactionism (e.g. Manfred Kuhn) fits less well, but it still can be subsumed by the social definition paradigm.

10   Although Snizek (1976) found social factists more likely to use the observation method than social definitionists.

11   More recently, the work of Richard Emerson (1981) and his colleagues (especially Karen Cook, 1987b) has become centrally important to exchange theory.

12   I will discuss these issues in the present tense since while they were particularly true in the 1960s, they remain true to at least some extent to this day.

13   There are innumerable examples of political attacks including, among others, Talcott Parsons's (1964) attack on George Homans's behaviorism, and Homans's (1971) response, which was an attack on Parsons's sometime social factism; Kurt Back's (1970) social definitionist attack on behaviorism; James Coleman's (1968) acid critique of ethnomethodology; and Becker and Geer's (1957) praise of participant observation and assault on all other methods.

14   This assertion, made in 1975, has I think been borne out by the substantial interest today in exchange theory and the work of people like Emerson and Cook (although it is true that exchange theory has moved far from its behaviorist roots).

4

TOWARD AN INTEGRATED SOCIOLOGICAL PARADIGM: IMAGE OF THE SUBJECT MATTER

Thomas Kuhn's (1962; 1970a) work on the structure of scientific revolutions has sparked reflexive activity in a variety of disciplines (e.g. Stanfield, 1974 in economics), including my own work (Ritzer, 1975c; 1975d), in which I concluded that sociology is a multiple paradigm science. Most analysts of the state of sociology agree with this conclusion, although there is considerable disagreement on the nature of sociology's multiple paradigms. The heart of this chapter lies in the case made for the creation of still another sociological paradigm that deals in a more integrated fashion with social reality than any of the extant paradigms. Such a paradigm would not replace existing paradigms, but rather is designed to supplement them by dealing with issues that are beyond their scope. In my view, existing sociological paradigms seem best able to cope with specific 'levels' of social reality and what is needed is an integrated paradigm that deals with the relationship among various levels.

Toward Paradigmatic Integration

Because of the one-sidedness of extant sociological paradigms, I perceive a growing interest in, and awareness of, the need for an integrated approach among a wide range of sociologists. Among those identified with structural functionalism we find Robert Merton (1975: 30) arguing that structural analysis 'connects with other sociological paradigms, which, the polemics notwithstanding, are anything but contradictory in much of what they suppose or assert ... recent work in structural analysis leads me to spheres of agreement and of complementarity rather than to the alleged basic contradictions between various sociological paradigms'. More specifically, Merton (1975: 31) later says: 'Many ideas in structural analysis and symbolic interactionism, for example, are opposed to one another in about the same sense as ham is opposed to eggs: they are perceptively different but mutually enriching.' Among the social definitionists, Mehan and Wood (1975: 180) say that ethnomethodology 'begins by accepting the reality of an external and constraining world. To this assumption is added an acceptance of the facticity of ceaseless reality work. The problem of a general theory of social order is thus determining the properties that relate structural activities to structural "facts".' Among social behaviorists we find people like Staats (1976) returning to the original Meadian project of integrating the minding (i.e. creative mental) process with traditional behaviorism. Even sociobiologists are able to see the reconcilability of their approach with other sociological orientations. For example, Edward O. Wilson (in Barash, 1977: xiv) admits: 'Human behavior is dominated by culture in the sense that the greater part, perhaps all, of the variation between societies is based on differences in cultural experience. But this is not to say that human beings are infinitely plastic.'

Despite the lengthy list of thinkers who recognize the need for theoretical integration, we continue to see the tendency to emphasize, and often overemphasize, the importance of a particular set of variables. Thus for many social factists individuals are seen to be determined largely by macrostructures, whereas for a large proportion of social definitionists it is individuals who determine social structures. Similar claims are made by the supporters of the other paradigms or would-be paradigms. The weakness of these efforts underscores the need for an integrated paradigm, and I would like to turn now to a discussion of a preliminary effort in that direction.

Levels of Social Analysis and an Integrated Sociological Paradigm

The metatheoretical (M_u) tool of 'levels of social analysis' is implicit in Chapters 2 and 3. The architectonic described in Chapter 2 begins at the micro level of philosophical anthropology and moves progressively to the macro level of reified social structures. The paradigms outlined in Chapter 3 descend from the social facts paradigm focally concerned with macro-level phenomena to the social definition and social behavior paradigms whose concerns are with more micro-level phenomena.

In this chapter I employ levels of analysis much more explicitly to form the basis of an integrated sociological paradigm. As we progress in this chapter we will see that levels of analysis are often too general for our needs. Thus we will need to develop two additional M_u tools that come under the broad heading of levels of analysis. These are the microscopic–macroscopic and objective–subjective continua. Beyond their independent utility, we will find that their interrelationship and the resulting formation of four major levels of social analysis (micro-objective, macro-objective, micro-subjective, macro-subjective) will prove particularly useful in the delineation of an integrated sociological paradigm.

Although the idea of levels of analysis is implicit in much of sociology, it has received relatively little explicit attention (for a recent work utilizing this idea, see Collins, 1999). In fact, the idea of levels is so foreign to most sociologists, at least at a conscious level, that on the rare occasions when it is discussed it often encounters stiff opposition. The term 'levels' is frequently attacked for distorting the nature of social reality and also for offering a static image of the social world. Although the idea of levels can be defended against these charges (as we will soon see), my guess is that it will still prove controversial. The irony of this situation is that sociology has long been dominated by a conception of levels of social analysis even though it has rarely been made explicit. In concentrating on levels here, I believe that I am doing little more than making explicit a metatheoretical idea that has been implicit in sociology since its inception.

To underscore this point, I want to further clarify the fact that the three paradigms discussed in Chapter 3 differ most basically in the views of their adherents on what is the most important 'level' of analysis in the social world. The social facts paradigm focuses on large-scale social structures and social institutions; the social definition paradigm concentrates on the more microscopic aspects of action, interaction, and the social construction of reality; and the social behavior paradigm focuses on the similarly microscopic patterns of behavior. Levels of social analysis inform each paradigm's image of the subject matter of sociology. Furthermore, the adherents of each paradigm tend to believe that their paradigm focuses on the level(s) of social analysis that adequately explains all of the others. Such beliefs lie at the root of all political conflicts among the adherents of the three major paradigms. Yet, despite their focal concern with levels, the adherents of each of these paradigms rarely address the issue directly, or in these terms. However, some work on the issue of levels of social analysis has been published and can be used to help us orient our thinking on this matter.

Before getting to that work, I want to make it clear that we are dealing with levels of social *analysis, not* levels of social *reality*. That is, levels are either theoretical or metatheoretical (M_u) tools; they are *not* ontological realities. The idea of levels of analysis does not imply that the social world is divided into levels. This crucial distinction constitutes one response to critics who feel that a levels approach distorts the social world. Levels are simply one way of thinking about the social world (and sociological theory); their use as tools does not imply that there are levels in that world. All such tools are distorting, but analysts are free to use a wide array of tools in their study of the social world. In spite of the distortions they cause, we must use such tools either explicitly or implicitly, for we have no other way of approaching the social world. Most of the work to be discussed in this section uses the idea of levels of social analysis to analyze the social world; that is, it is used theoretically to analyze that world. My interest, however, is metatheoretical in that I wish to use this tool to analyze sociological theory. Thus, most of the work to be discussed below will need to be translated to fit my particular needs and interests.

Levels of Social Analysis: A Review of the Literature

One of the most sophisticated treatments of levels of social analysis available in the literature was written by the philosopher Abraham Edel (1959). Edel immediately and directly addresses one of the most crucial issues in using the idea of levels to analyze social reality: he confronts the question of whether it is inevitably a structural orientation that gives social reality a static and unchangeable character. While he admits that in the hands of some analysts the use of levels might yield a static conception of society, Edel (1959: 168) is unwilling to reduce it to such a conception, arguing that the levels concept is 'not merely a concern with the relations of qualitatively distinct bands of coexistent phenomena in a static field'. Instead, what Edel does is to embed the whole issue of levels within a very dynamic conception of social life, a conception that goes to the very heart of the field of sociology as a distinctive endeavor. That is, Edel views levels within the context of the emergence of the sociological aspects of the world. The essence of this perspective is that more macroscopic social phenomena emerge out of the interaction that takes place at the more microscopic levels. To put it another way, people create a macroscopic social reality that is more than the sum of the individuals who create and compose it.

By placing the idea of levels within the process of emergence, Edel gives it an inherently historical and dynamic quality rather than the static structure into which it could easily degenerate. Edel sensitizes us to the fact that people in the course of history have produced today's macrostructures. His idea of emergence also attunes us to the fact that larger structures are produced and reproduced on a daily basis by actors in the process of action and interaction. Both historicity and dynamism are built into Edel's conception of the levels of social analysis, and they are also inherent in the way levels of social analysis are dealt with in the integrated sociological paradigm.

Within the context of this developmental and dynamic perspective, Edel offers a conception of levels of social analysis that begins at the microscopic level and moves to more macroscopic levels:

1   states of consciousness, actors' attitudes, and so on
2   individuals
3   interpersonal relations

4   groups
5   culture.

Although this is a useful first approximation of some of the major levels of social analysis, it has a number of omissions and failings that will become clear as I move toward my own conception of these levels.

Not only does Edel identify the nature and the dynamics of the levels of the social world, but he also identifies the political problems associated with the traditional sociological perspectives that focus on one, or a few, levels. In identifying these problems, Edel differentiates between the reality claims and the ultimacy claims of those who support a specific perspective. *Reality claims* simply involve a preference for dealing with one level rather than another. *Ultimacy claims* involve the tendency to claim that one level is the ultimate subject matter of sociology. It is the ultimacy claims of the adherents of each of the paradigms discussed in Chapter 3 that lead to much of the political conflict in sociology.

Finally, I would like to underscore an aspect of Edel's work that will become progressively more important as I proceed in this chapter. Although he has an obvious interest in the range from microscopic to macroscopic levels of social analysis, he has a less obvious but equally important interest in the continuum ranging from objective to subjective levels of social analysis. On the one end, he is very much aware of the objective level: 'Ongoing human activity is seen as crystallizing into structured forms on various historical levels' (1959: 183). He complements this awareness with an equally vivid sense of the subjective level of the social world: 'mind or intellectual reflection is to be viewed as an event in nature' (1959: 184). Edel also manifests his interest in the objective–subjective continuum by embedding himself in Marx's distinction between base and superstructure and by talking of the 'underlying distinction between the material and the expression of spirit' (1959: 188). Despite the fact that he has a sense of an objective–subjective continuum, Edel does little with it and leaves it largely unrelated to the macroscopic–microscopic continuum.

Although Edel's work attracted relatively little attention in sociology (perhaps because he was a philosopher, not a sociologist), a similar, although somewhat less sophisticated, work on levels of social analysis by Helmut Wagner (1964) did attract some attention. Wagner is more specifically concerned with the macroscopic–microscopic continuum in terms of large-scale to small-scale sociological theories, or what he calls differences in 'scope' in sociological thinking. Wagner clearly sees sociological interest in the macroscopic–microscopic issue as lying along a continuum: 'Empirically, sociological interests range all the way from the study of interactional encounters between two persons to the analysis of whole societies ... most sociologists operate, at least in particular phases of their work, either within small-scale, or intermediate, or large-scale ranges' (1964: 572). In other words, the scope of socio-logical phenomena is one way sociologists divide up the work of studying social reality. Although Wagner is to be applauded for this insight, one of the problems with his work is that he fails to be either microscopic or macroscopic enough. The microscopic end of the con-tinuum should be extended to include the concerns of ethnomethodo-logists and phenomenologists, and the macro level should be extended beyond the 'society' to such suprasocietal units as the 'world system' (Wallerstein, 1974; 1989).[1] Wagner chooses to focus on the poles of his micro–macro continuum in order to highlight some basic differences, and some inherent problems in traditional sociological theories. Here, then, Wagner is using levels of analysis metatheoretically rather than theoretically. In his view, sociology emerged in the nineteenth century with a macroscopic focus in order to be able to carve out a clear niche for itself in academia. Durkheim, with his focus on social facts, is accorded key significance in this development. Microsociology devel-oped slightly later, in the early twentieth century through the works of such people as Mead and Cooley, but can be traced as well to the ideas of Simmel and Weber. In Wagner's view, a basic dualism was intro-duced into sociology, a dualism that went largely unrecognized at the time.[2] Furthermore, this dualism has yet to be reconciled adequately.[3]

I have great sympathy for Wagner's characterization of the dualism within sociology, although there is a considerable difference between the way he classifies thinkers like Simmel, Weber, and Durkheim and the way I think about them. To put it succinctly, they are much more integrative thinkers than Wagner leads us to believe. The theoretical ideas of people as sophisticated as Weber, Durkheim, and Simmel are done a great disservice by simply being compressed into micro or macro camps. In fact, Wagner himself recognizes this flaw as he proceeds further in his analysis. For example, despite his classification of Simmel as a microsociologist, Wagner (1964: 573) later says: 'Simmel defies classification. It is often forgotten that he, with ease and elegance, trans-ferred his statements about the relations between two and three persons to the relations between religious sects, political parties, economic groupings, power constellations of nations, and others.' As was typical of theoretical works of that epoch, Marx is pointedly ignored by Wagner. As we will see in Chapter 5, Marx's work offers a highly integrated sense of social reality.

Wagner is also to be praised for his metatheoretical recognition of the relationship between theoretical orientation and level of social analysis. For example, he argues that structural functionalism, a theo-retical component of social factism, 'starts with the conception of social system and sees smaller units, down to the individual, as struc-tural subparts whose functions are essentially defined and confined by the whole system' (1964: 575). In the same way, Wagner (1964: 576) is also very good on recognizing the political character of paradigmatic claims: 'In fact, most of them claim that their theory is applicable to the whole range of the micro–macro sociological continuum.' In a clever turn of phrase, Wagner labels this the 'fallacy of displaced scope'.

Although he focuses almost exclusively on the micro–macro continuum, Wagner hints in his analysis about the objective–subjective continuum. In addition to a variety of indirect comments, Wagner addresses this issue directly in a footnote. He argues that structural functionalism tends to be an objective theory while interpretive sociology tends to be a subjective theory. While I do not agree with the specific associations – that is, I think that structural functionalism and interpretive sociology have *both* subjective *and* objective orientations – I find it promising that Wagner at least recognizes subjectivity and objectivity. However, Wagner does almost nothing with this recognition. Furthermore, Wagner, like Edel, fails to relate the objective–subjective continuum to the micro–macro continuum.

Blalock and Wilken (1979) explicitly adopt a micro–macro orientation in their analysis of intergroup relations. At the micro end of the continuum, Blalock and Wilken (1979: 6) focus on the subjective states of the actors, 'subjective probabilities', and utilities or subjective values attached to the importance of goals. At the other pole, they define the macro level as group phenomena. Although they have a very limited conception of the macro level, the authors do include a great deal under the group category including country clubs, colleges, and social categories (such as blacks and whites). Their goal is to operate between these two poles, at what they call the macro–micro level. They are basically interested in the impact of 'contextual effects' on actors.

Blalock and Wilken's sense of the micro–macro continuum is limited in two ways. First, since they do not make explicit theoretical provision for individual behavior and action, they are not microscopic enough. By ignoring units larger than the group (such as society and the world system) they are also not macroscopic enough. Second, they have no clear sense of the difference between the micro–macro and objective–subjective continua. In fact, the two are hopelessly confused in their theoretical scheme. Nevertheless, Blalock and Wilken are to be applauded for their interest in integrating levels and for their criticisms of traditional sociology for its failures in this domain: 'Ideally at least, the two perspectives (macro–micro) should be mutually reinforcing. Yet there has been surprisingly little systematic attention given to specifying the exact linkages between levels or to exploring the methodological difficulties one encounters when one attempts to move back and forth between them' (1979: 8). Their view, one that is in accord with the emerging thrust of this chapter, is that 'micro- and macro-level theories each need to be making some provision for variables located at the other level' (1979: 27).

There seems to be little controversy involved in the use of the microscopic–macroscopic continuum of levels of social analysis. Few would argue against the point that we can think in terms of large-scale and small-scale phenomena in social life, with most sociological entities falling somewhere in between. And most would have no difficulty thinking metatheoretically about sociological theories in these terms. What is far more difficult to explain, and to defend, is the objective–subjective continuum. However, my view is that this continuum is as important and as defensible as the micro–macro range. It is nothing more than another major theoretical and metatheoretical (M_u) tool that can be used to help us deal with the infinite complexity of the social world and of sociological theory. There are, of course, many other metatheoretical tools, including various other sociological continua that could be developed; but these two, as well as their interrelationship with one another, are the underpinnings of the concerns of this chapter.

Since it is less intuitively obvious, I need to devote some attention to explaining and defending the objective–subjective continuum.[4] I could go back to the philosophical roots of sociology and recast the continuum in terms of the split between idealism and materialism. But, given the vagaries of that philosophical debate, such an excursion might cause more harm than good. Instead of addressing this issue at a general philosophical level, I think it would be more relevant to the concerns of this book to discuss the objective–subjective continuum in terms of its influence on the work of Karl Marx.

It is well known that one of the early and important influences on Marx was German idealism, particularly the work of Hegel. The Hegelian dialectic is a subjective process taking place within the realm of ideas. Although affected by this view, Marx and before him the 'young Hegelians' were dissatisfied with the fact that the dialectic is not rooted in the real, material world. Building on the work of Feuerbach and others, Marx sought to take the dialectic and extend it to the material world. On the one hand, this means that he is concerned with real, sentient actors rather than with idea systems. On the other hand, he focuses on the material structures of capitalist society, primarily the economic structure. What came to interest Marx increasingly were the real material (reified) structures of capitalism and the contradictions that exist among and within them. This is not to say that Marx lost sight of subjective ideas; in fact, notions of false consciousness and class consciousness played a key role in his work. It is the materialism–idealism split, as manifested in the work of Marx and others, that is one key philosophical root of the objective–subjective continuum in modern sociology.

We can also find this continuum, although in a different guise, in the work of Emile Durkheim (1895/1964). In his classic work on methodology, Durkheim differentiates between material (objective) and nonmaterial (subjective) social facts. In *Suicide*, Durkheim (1897/1951: 313) says: 'The social fact is sometimes materialized as to become an element of the external world.' He discusses architecture and law as two examples of material (objective) social facts. However, most of Durkheim's work emphasizes nonmaterial (subjective) social facts:

> Of course it is true that not all social consciousness achieves such externalization and materialization. Not all aesthetic spirit of a nation is embodied in the works it inspires; not all of morality is formulated in clear precepts. The greater part is diffused. There is a large collective life which is at liberty; all sorts of currents come, go, circulate everywhere, cross and mingle in a thousand different ways, and just because they are constantly mobile are never crystallized in an objective form. Today a breath of sadness and discouragement descends on society; tomorrow, one of joyous confidence will uplift all hearts. (1897/1951: 315)

These social currents do not have material existence; they can only exist within and between consciousness. In *Suicide*, Durkheim concentrates on examples of this kind of social fact. He relates differences in suicide rates to differences in social currents. Thus, for example, where there are strong currents of anomie, we will find high rates of anomic suicide. Social currents, such as anomie, egoism, and altruism, clearly do not have a material existence, although they may have a material effect by causing differences in suicide rates. Rather, they are intersubjective phenomena that can only exist in the consciousness of people.

More contemporaneously, Peter Blau (1960) differentiates between institutions (subjective entities) and social structures (objective entities). He defines subjective institutions as 'the common values and norms embodied in a culture or subculture' (1960: 178). Objective social structures are defined as 'the networks of social relations in which processes of social interaction become organized and through which social positions of individuals and subgroups become differentiated' (1960: 178).

While Marx, Durkheim, and Blau all demonstrate a concern for the objective–subjective continuum, their work is dominated by an interest in macro-level objective (e.g. the economy) and subjective (e.g. social currents) phenomena. We must turn to the work of Georges Gurvitch to find a more balanced use of both the micro–macro and objective–subjective continua.

The Work of Georges Gurvitch

Although all of the works discussed thus far are at least in some part related to the conception of levels of social analysis being developed in this chapter, the most directly relevant work on this issue is that of the French sociologist Georges Gurvitch. He is focally concerned with the four major interests of this chapter: levels of analysis, the macroscopic–microscopic and objective–subjective continua, and the dialectical relationship of one to the other. These foci are quite explicit in Gurvitch's definition of sociology (which is characteristically complex and jargonistic): 'Sociology is the qualitative and discontinuous typology based on the dialectic of the total social phenomena in all their astructural, structurable and structured manifestations. It studies all their depth *levels*, scales and the sectors directly with the aim of following their movement of structuration, destructuration and restructuration and rupture' (1964: 11, emphasis added).

The key point is the fact that Gurvitch operates with a sense of levels of social analysis; in fact, he is the only thinker discussed to this point who has a strong sense of *both* the micro–macro and objective–subjective continua and their dialectical relationship to each other.

> The social reality to the practiced eye of the sociologist is arranged in levels, strata, planes, or in layers. These strata, or levels, interpenetrate and mutually impregnate each other. Moreover, they do not cease to enter into conflict: their rapport is tenuous, paradoxical, and dialectical. This has to do with the inextricable tensions inherent in all social reality, which one can qualify on a vertical scale. To these relative polarizations are added, at each depth level, the horizontal conflicts and tensions; the antagonism of classes is a good example. (Gurvitch, cited in Bosserman, 1968: 79)

Let us examine the two different levels of continua that interest Gurvitch.

Depths (or Vertical) Levels   Although I will discuss each of Gurvitch's ten depth levels (Bosserman, 1968) in this section, I should make clear from the outset that Gurvitch (like this author) is well aware that these levels are clearly differentiated from one another *only* for purposes of analysis; that is, levels (and a clear differentiation among them) do not exist in the social world. In addition, I also want to indicate that there is no magic associated with the number ten; the number of levels can be extended or contracted depending on the immediate needs and interests of the sociologist.

Gurvitch arranges his ten depth levels on the basis of the degree of difficulty of direct external observation. The first depth level is most easily observed, the last is least easily observed. Although Gurvitch does not use the same terms, this conception of depth levels is very close to the objective–subjective continuum that is being evolved in this chapter. That is, the initial depth levels are the most objective, the later ones more subjective. The following are the ten depth levels:

1 *Morphology and Ecology*   This surface level is the most superficial and the easiest to observe. Included here would be such phenomena as population density, mobility rates, kinds of churches, means of communication, and so on.

2 *Social organization*   Organizations in Gurvitch's view involve 'preestablished collective behaviors'. They are centralized, possess a hierarchy, and are managed by those at or near the top. They serve to fix the behavior of participants in a more or less rigid manner.

3 *Social patterns*   Here too Gurvitch is interested in social forces that guide and direct human beings. However, while social organizations primarily guide behavior, social patterns guide not only behavior but also individual and collective mental life. Included in the stratum of social patterns are customs, signs, signals, and rules, as well as the more temporary fads, modes, and fancies. They are influential not only within social organizations, but also in the collective behavior that takes place outside organizations.

4 *Unorganized collective behavior*   These are irregular, nonconformist, and insubordinate forms of behavior.

5 *Web of social roles*   Unlike most sociologists, Gurvitch does not look at individual social roles, but rather at the webs or 'skeins' of social roles. There is a tendency to look at these roles in process, and in tension with each other, rather than in harmony. In Gurvitch's system, roles represent the bridge between the more organized, more objective forms discussed before and the less organized, more subjective forms to be discussed next.

6 *Collective attitudes*   It is here that Gurvitch moves to the realm of what he thinks of as the more unorganized, spontaneous, immediate, and subjective aspects of social life.

7 *Social symbols*   These are more spontaneous than the social patterns discussed in level 3: 'Some examples of social symbols … are the statues of Joan of Arc calling forth certain collective values evoking national loyalty, the totem which symbolizes the god of the clan, the cross which reveals a whole gamut of values and ideas … and the national flag which brings forth the responses of patriotism' (Bosserman, 1968: 124).

8 *Creative collective behavior*   This is group behavior oriented toward innovation and invention.

9 *Collective ideas and values*   The broad values and fundamental ideas of a collectivity.

10 *The collective mind*   This concept is deeply related to Durkheim's notion of the collective conscience. It overarches and interpenetrates all of the other depth levels. Although heavily indebted to Durkheim here and elsewhere, Gurvitch is also aware of Durkheim's theoretical shortcomings. For example, he argues, unlike Durkheim,

that the collective mind is not totally transcendent. He also rejects
the idea that there is just one collective mind; to him there are several collective minds.

Gurvitch's depth levels are extremely useful from the perspective of
this chapter, especially to the degree that they parallel the objective–
subjective continuum. But there are a number of problems with his
system. For example, he postulates so many depth levels that using
them is cumbersome. We need a much more parsimonious system.
Second, it is sometimes hard to differentiate between some of the levels.
This is especially true of levels 6 through 10. In fact, in her analysis,
Korenbaum (1964) omits levels 8 and 9 (as well as 4). Finally, the overarching role played by the collective mind in Gurvitch's system, even
with his criticisms of Durkheim, is difficult to defend.

The Horizontal Continuum   In addition to the ten depth levels that he offers as
a vertical continuum, Gurvitch also has a sense of another hierarchy, one
he thinks of as a horizontal continuum. However, what he is really interested in here, and he is quite explicit on the point, is the micro–macro
continuum. In fact, the two key elements of Gurvitch's conceptualization
of the horizontal continuum are microsociology and macrosociology.

At one pole of Gurvitch's horizontal continuum is microsociology,
which, as he sees it, deals with the most basic and elementary forms
of social life. They are the forms of sociality, the patterns of action
and interaction. These represent the more spontaneous aspects of the
social world. Gurvitch's macrosociology deals with progressively more
organized forms of social life and progressively more large-scale
phenomena. Within his macrosociology, Gurvitch differentiates among
four levels:

1 *Groupings*   Following Durkheim, Gurvitch sees the group as a real
   collective entity that is more than the sum of its individual parts.
   Groups are created by people and those who belong to a group have
   a sense of identity with it. Groups are capable of acquiring a structure, although they are not necessarily structured.
2 *Social class*   Here Gurvitch supplements his Durkheimian influence
   with a Marxian influence. Social classes are seen as important enough
   to deserve a separate category.
3 *Social structure*   Gurvitch does not see these as hardened structures,
   but rather as composed of multitudes of hierarchies that are in
   constant tension. There is a precarious equilibrium that must be
   maintained by constant work. Structures are held together, but
   precariously, by 'cultural cement'. The various parts of the structure
   are in a constant dialectical process of structuration–destructuration–
   restructuration.

**Figure 4.1 Intersection of Gurvitch's horizontal
and vertical levels of social reality**

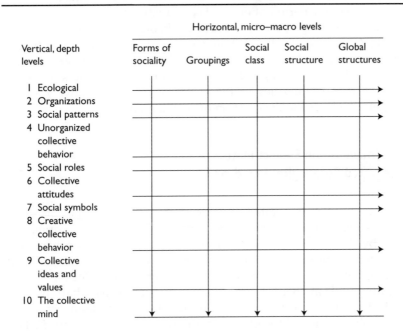

	Horizontal, micro–macro levels				
Vertical, depth levels	Forms of sociality	Groupings	Social class	Social structure	Global structures
1 Ecological					
2 Organizations					
3 Social patterns					
4 Unorganized collective behavior					
5 Social roles					
6 Collective attitudes					
7 Social symbols					
8 Creative collective behavior					
9 Collective ideas and values					
10 The collective mind					

4 *Global structures* Finally, at the most macroscopic level, Gurvitch deals with such global structures as city-states, nations, empires, and so on.

Gurvitch's thinking on the micro–macro (horizontal) continuum is not as sophisticated as his work on the depth levels, the objective–subjective (vertical) continuum. Perhaps this weakness reflects his roots in phenomenology and Durkheimian notions of collective conscience, both of which tend to be preoccupied with subjectivity.

Gurvitch's work is useful not only for developing these two continua, but also for dealing with their interrelationship. He argues that each of the components of the horizontal continuum can be analyzed using each of the depth levels: 'All those social microcosms and macrocosms represent totalities with depth levels of their own' (1964: 5). Bosserman has attempted to depict this interrelationship, but his image does not reflect the complexities of Gurvitch's thought. Figure 4.1 represents the way I depict the relationship between the two continua.

Despite a number of problems, Gurvitch comes closer than anyone discussed in this chapter to developing the conception of levels of social analysis that I am attempting to evolve here. He has a clear sense of both the micro–macro and objective–subjective continua; but the complexity of his model makes it cumbersome and ineffective. There are far too many permutations and combinations to make this a usable model for analyzing the social world (theoretically) and sociological theory (metatheoretically). While it is true that the world is infinitely complex, its complexity does not mean that we need similarly compli-cated models. In fact, a good case can be made that what is needed to analyze the complexities of the social world is a relatively simple model. I now turn to the creation of such a model.

The Image of the Subject Matter of an Integrated Sociological Paradigm

The model of an integrated sociological paradigm (actually, its image of the subject matter of sociology) to be presented here is informed not only by the preceding discussion of levels of analysis in general, and the microscopic–macroscopic and objective–subjective continua in par-ticular, but also by the discussion in Chapter 3 of sociology's multiple paradigms. That chapter included a discussion of paradigm bridgers and of the need to develop a more integrated paradigm. Since, as I noted above, each of the extant paradigms is linked to a specific level or levels of analysis, it should come as no surprise that an integrated paradigm must cut across levels of analysis. (The integrated paradigm seeks to integrate levels and *not* the extant social facts, social definition, and social behavior paradigms.) Furthermore, given my more specific focus on the microscopic–macroscopic and objective–subjective continua in this chapter, it should come as no surprise that an integrated paradigm must deal with the interrelationship of these continua.

Following the four dimensions of a paradigm laid out in Chapter 3, an integrated paradigm would include a unique set of those compo-nents: image of the subject matter of sociology, exemplar, theories, and methods. The delineation of all of the elements of an integrated para-digm is beyond the scope of this chapter. However, in this section I will give a brief, schematic representation of the image of the subject matter of sociology for such a paradigm. In Chapter 5 I will examine the ideas of two potential exemplars for an integrated paradigm. When, and if, such a paradigm develops – that is, attracts a group of adherents and supporters – I presume that distinctive theories[5] and methods[6] will evolve.

My intention is to try to cope with some of the problems in extant paradigms by trying to 'create' an exemplar for a new integrated para-digm.[7] That is, I want to outline a model that I hope will prove attrac-tive to a number of sociologists who are dissatisfied with available

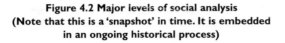

**Figure 4.2 Major levels of social analysis
(Note that this is a 'snapshot' in time. It is embedded
in an ongoing historical process)**

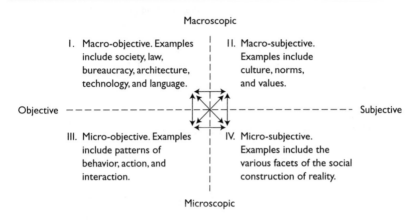

Macroscopic

I. Macro-objective. Examples include society, law, bureaucracy, architecture, technology, and language.

II. Macro-subjective. Examples include culture, norms, and values.

Objective — — — — — — — — — — — — — — — — — — Subjective

III. Micro-objective. Examples include patterns of behavior, action, and interaction.

IV. Micro-subjective. Examples include the various facets of the social construction of reality.

Microscopic

sociological paradigms. I hasten to add, and shall show in the next chapter, that this paradigm has existed in sociology since its inception as a distinctive discipline. I simply wish to call attention to an alternative that has always existed, albeit implicitly, in sociology.

The key here, of course, is the notion of 'levels' of social analysis. As I have made clear above, for my purposes the major levels of social analysis can be derived from two basic social continua – the microscopic–macroscopic and objective–subjective continua – and their interrelationship. The microscopic–macroscopic dimension relates to the magnitude of social phenomena ranging from whole societies (or even more macroscopic world systems) to the social acts of individuals, whereas the objective–subjective dimension refers to whether the phenomenon has a real material existence (e.g. bureaucracy, patterns of interaction) or exists only in the realm of ideas and knowledge (e.g. norms and values). Figure 4.2 is a schematic representation of the intersection of these two continua and the four major levels of social analysis that are derived from it.

It is my contention that an integrated sociological paradigm must deal in an integrated fashion with the four basic levels of social analysis identified in Figure 4.2. An integrated sociological paradigm must deal with the interrelationship of macroscopic-objective entities like bureaucracy, macroscopic-subjective structures like culture, microscopic-objective phenomena like patterns of interaction, and microscopic-subjective facts like the process of reality construction. Remember: in the real world all of these gradually blend into the others as part of the larger social continuum, but I have made some artificial and rather

Figure 4.3 Levels of social analysis and the major sociological paradigms

Levels of social analysis	Sociological paradigms	
Macro-subjective		
	Social facts paradigm	
Macro-objective		
Micro-subjective	Social definition paradigm	Integrated sociological paradigm
Micro-objective		
	Social behavior paradigm	

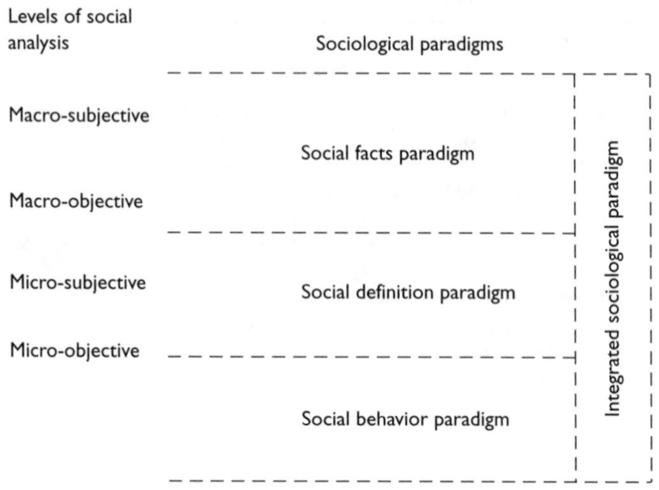

arbitrary differentiations in order to be able to deal with social reality. These four levels of social analysis are posited for heuristic purposes and are not meant to be depictions of the social world.

An integrated paradigm is concerned not only with these four major levels of social analysis, but also with the dialectical relationship among and between them. Thus, there is a dynamic sense of this interrelationship.

An obvious question is how the four levels depicted in Figure 4.2 relate to the three paradigms outlined in Chapter 3 as well as the image of the subject matter of the integrated paradigm being developed here. Figure 4.3 relates the four levels to the four paradigms.

The social facts paradigm focuses primarily on the macro-objective and macro-subjective levels; the social definition paradigm is largely concerned with the micro-subjective as well as that part of the micro-objective world that depends on mental processes (action); and the social behavior paradigm deals with that part of the micro-objective world that does not involve conscious processes (behavior). Whereas the three extant paradigms cut across the levels of social analysis horizontally, the integrated paradigm cuts across the levels vertically. This depiction makes it clear why the integrated paradigm does not supersede the others.

Although each of the three existing paradigms deals with a given level or levels in great detail, the integrated paradigm deals with all levels, but does not examine any given level in anything like the degree of intensity of the other paradigms. Thus the choice of a paradigm depends on the kind of question being asked. Not all sociological issues require an integrated approach, but it is certain that at least some do.

What is discussed above is a brief sketch of the image of the subject matter of sociology of the integrated paradigm, as well as those of the three other paradigms. Those images are all sketched in terms of the major concerns of this chapter: levels of social analysis, microscopic–macroscopic continua, and objective–subjective continua.

Conclusions

The preceding constitutes an effort to sketch out the image of the subject matter of a sociological paradigm that deals in an interrelated fashion with the basic levels of social reality. In Chapter 5 we will examine the work of Emile Durkheim and Karl Marx in search of an exemplar for such a paradigm, but before we do we need some conclusions based on the analysis to this point.

First, the paradigm being outlined here is not intended to replace any extant sociological paradigm. The already existing paradigms *are* useful for analyzing given levels of social reality. The social facts paradigm is most useful for the study of macro-objective and macro-subjective social phenomena. The social definition paradigm works best at the levels of micro-subjective and micro-objective social reality. The social behavior paradigm has the greatest application to the micro-objective world. As long as the adherents of each of these approaches refrain from claiming to explain all of social reality, their paradigms can be of great utility to sociology. Although attempting to explain all social phenomena is a laudable goal, it cannot be done with a paradigm which is inherently based on one, or at best two, levels of social reality.

Second, the essence of the new, integrated sociological paradigm lies in the interrelationship of the four basic levels of social reality: (1) the macro-objective, for example law, language, and bureaucracy; (2) the macro-subjective, for example norms, values, and culture; (3) the micro-objective, for example patterns of behavior and action; and (4) the micro-subjective, for example mind, self, and the social construction of reality. The key point is that these levels must, within the paradigm being proposed here, be dealt with integratively. That is, any specific subject of study must be examined from an integrated point of view. For example, the coming of the so-called postindustrial society (Bell, 1973) must be examined as an interrelated process involving changes in diverse social entities such as bureaucracies, norms, patterns of interaction, and consciousness. It may be that in such a case macroscopic variables are most important, but that should not permit us to ignore the other levels. Conversely, on other issues microscopic factors may be of greatest explanatory power, but that does not mean that macroscopic variables are of no significance. Many questions require an integrative approach, although the significance of any given level will vary from situation from situation.

Third, I think that even with an integrated paradigm, the greatest attention in contemporary sociology is likely to be focused on macroscopic levels of social reality. This will occur for the same reason that people like Marx and Weber were led to focus on this level: that is, the nature of large-scale modern society tends to overwhelm the microscopic level. Despite this, I believe we must never lose sight of the existence and significance of both the micro-objective and micro-subjective realms. People act, interact, and create social reality in even the most reified societies, and those actions do at some time and to at least some degree have an impact on the larger society. Real people act on behalf of, or are acted on by, macrostructures, and sociology *must never lose sight of this fact*. When we do, we tend to create arid intellectual systems that do little more than further support an already reified social structure. In addition, sociologists must not omit the more ephemeral modes of social action and interaction in their focus on macro-objective and subjective entities. Some of the noninstitutionalized realms of social reality may someday lead to the alteration of institutionalized realms or themselves become the accepted way of doing things.

Fourth, despite the fact that we have identified four basic levels of social reality, we should bear in mind that the social world is a world in flux and is not neatly divided into four levels. Thus the various microscopic phenomena are at some point rather arbitrarily transformed into the macroscopic level. The four-level schema does violence to the real world, and we must never forget that. However, all such schemata have this problem, but they must be created in order to be able to handle the complexities of the social world. We must be careful not to reify this, or any other conceptual schema. It is the real world, and not the schema, that is the subject matter of sociology.

Fifth, the paradigm being espoused here must inherently be comparative either over time or cross-societally. The interrelated character of this approach allows us to collect data by any or all methods (questionnaire, interview, experiment, observation, etc.), but if we are truly interested in understanding the dynamics of the interrelationships among various levels of social reality, we must be able to compare different societies in order to get a sense of the differences (and similarities) in the way in which the various levels work with, or against, each other. I believe that most of the truly great sociologists like Marx, Weber, and Durkheim utilized comparative methodology and they also operated with an implicit integrated paradigm.

Sixth, an integrated paradigm must be historical; it must eschew the idea that a single abstract theory can be developed that can explain all of social reality in all societies throughout history. Although all levels can be found in all societies, the weight of each and the relationship among them will vary from one society to another. This paradigm must also be oriented to the study of the changing nature of social reality over time. Although we might be interested in the study of contemporary reality, it must always be seen in the context of the changing nature of society.

Seventh, the integrated paradigm being proposed here has much to gain from dialectical logic, although the wholehearted adoption of the dialectic would seem to be prohibited by the political ideologies associated with it and sometimes infused in it. I am not the first to propose the resurrection of the mode of thought associated with Hegel and Marx. Friedrichs (1972) made a similar effort, although his major goal seemed to be bridging the differences between system and conflict theory and not the broader objective undertaken here. The dialectic is notoriously difficult to deal with, in part because it is hard to capture in static words and sentences. Furthermore, the dialectic carries with it certain radical political implications that have made it anathema to many sociologists. Nevertheless, there are a number of aspects of the dialectic that are useful to sociology, particularly to the kind of integrated analysis being proposed here.

The Marxian dialectic is rooted in the real world of individual thought and action. It sees people producing larger social structures and those structures coming, in turn, to constrain and coerce actors. It therefore has a very clear image of the interrelationship between the microscopic and macroscopic realms. Yet it does not give primacy to one or the other; they are seen as dialectically related.

The dialectic begins with the epistemological assumption that in the real world 'everything is interconnected and forever in flux' (Ollman, 1971: 54). There are therefore no hard-and-fast dividing lines between social phenomena. This sort of imagery is clearly in line with the one behind the integrated approach being offered here. Despite this image, dialecticians realize that in order to be able to deal with this world in flux, they must develop conceptual schemata. A schema clearly implied by the dialectic is one that carves the real world up into various levels. This, of course, is the schema employed here, although innumerable other schemata are possible, even desirable, in order to gain greater insight into the complexities of the modern world.

Whatever schema one adopts, the dialectic attunes us to look for the interrelationships among the various components. We should not be satisfied with merely dividing up social reality and then categorizing bits and pieces of social life. Rather, we must always be attuned to the manifold ways in which each of the entities is related to all of the others.

Not only does the dialectic lead us to look for levels, or other components, of social reality, but it also attunes us to the likelihood of contradictions within and between the various levels. The existence of such contradictions is a basic finding of virtually every major sociologist. Marx, of course, focused on the contradictions that exist within capitalist society, but insights into contradictions also exist in the work of Weber (rationalization versus individual freedom), Simmel (subjective versus objective culture), and many others. The study of such contradictions lies at the heart of a dialectical approach to social reality.

The dialectic also leads the sociologist to look beyond the appearance of social reality to its essence. To use Peter Berger's (1963) term, this means that sociology is engaged in the business of 'debunking'. We must never be content with individual rationalizations or group ideologies, but must look instead for the 'real' nature of social reality.

In sum, the dialectic focuses on the real world and the relationship between the microscopic and macroscopic levels of social reality; sees the world as forever in flux, thereby necessitating the creation of conceptual schemata to deal with it; looks to the relationship between the various levels of society (as long as we keep in mind that there are no hard-and-fast dividing lines in the real world); attunes us to the likelihood of contradictions between levels; and pushes the sociologist to look beyond appearances to the essence of social reality.

The dialectical mode of logic has much to offer to the integrated paradigm being espoused here. We may prefer less ideologically loaded terms like 'relational' or 'multicausal' to describe the approach taken here, but we should not lose sight of the fact that we shall be borrowing a good number of our insights from the dialectic.

I have only been able to present an outline of an image of the subject matter of an integrated sociological paradigm in this chapter. There is clearly much to be done with it, but as Kuhn points out, one of the things that makes a paradigm attractive is the fact that it does not answer all of the questions and leaves much to be done by others. It is hoped that the need to fill in the bare bones will make this integrated paradigm attractive to some sociologists who are dissatisfied with the existing ways of dealing with social reality and who see some utility in a more integrated approach.

Notes

The material in this chapter is drawn from *Toward an Integrated Sociological Paradigm: The Search for an Exemplar and an Image of the Subject Matter* (1981b: 1–29).

1   To be fair to Wagner, the perspectives (ethnomethodology, phenomenology, world systems theory) that point to these additional levels of analysis either did not exist, or were much less significant, when he wrote his essay.

2   Kemeny (1976) said the same thing in the 1970s. However, it certainly is recognized now.

3 Giddens (1984) is critical of the use of dualisms in social theory, while Archer defends their utility.

4 Actually, of course, objective–subjective is far less defensible as a continuum than the micro–macro relationship; it is more of a dichotomy. However, we can think in terms of objective and subjective poles with mixed types in the middle.

5 It may be that the integrative and synthetic theoretical efforts of the 1980s and 1990s (see Ritzer, 1991b) will form the bases of these theories.

6 These methods may also be developing in an array of works that seek to integrate methods (e.g. Noblit and Hare, 1988; Brewer and Hunter, 1989).

7 Thomas Kuhn, especially in his later work, would clearly be uncomfortable with the idea of 'creating' an exemplar. Moreover, Kuhn, at least in his later works, thinks of exemplars as concrete puzzle solutions. There are few, if any, of these in sociology. Our major exemplars are program statements like Durkheim's case for social facts as the subject matter of sociology. This is an attempt to create an exemplar in the Durkheimian tradition.

5

POTENTIAL EXEMPLARS FOR AN INTEGRATED SOCIOLOGICAL PARADIGM

Given the image of the subject of an integrated sociological paradigm outlined in the preceding chapter, the objective here is the search for an exemplar for such a paradigm.[1] In this chapter I will review the bodies of work of Emile Durkheim and Karl Marx to ascertain whether one or the other could be that exemplar.[2]

In the case of Durkheim, however, this review is merely academic; his work is not really a serious candidate for such exemplary status (see below). I undertake a review of Durkheim's work from the point of view of being an exemplar for an integrated paradigm because it points up some surprising things about it, especially Durkheim's level of interest in micro-level concerns. Thus, in the case of Durkheim, looking at his work as an exemplar merely serves to cast some new metatheoretical (M_u) light on it. But Marx's work, as we will see, proves to be a strong and obvious candidate for the exemplary role within an integrated paradigm.

Emile Durkheim

Emile Durkheim is an unlikely choice as a possible exemplar for an integrated sociological paradigm, in part because Durkheim is already an exemplar for the social facts paradigm (see Chapter 3), and that would seem to eliminate him as a possible exemplar for an integrated paradigm. It was Durkheim (1895/1964) who argued that sociology should focus on social facts, or what I have termed the macro-objective and macro-subjective levels of social reality. This implies, and Durkheim at times rather baldly took the position, that the micro-objective and micro-subjective levels are not part of sociological explanations. As Durkheim (1895/1964: 110) said, 'The determining cause of a social fact should be sought among the social facts preceding it.' It is this kind of orientation, as well as Durkheim's effort to carry it through by using social facts to study such individual acts as suicide,[3] that led Tiryakian (1962: 11) to see Durkheim as the prototype of sociologism, 'the viewpoint of those sociologists who, making sociology a science completely irreducible to psychology, consider it as necessary and sufficient for the total explanation of social reality'. If Durkheim in fact consistently took such an extreme position, then there would be little point in analyzing his work from the viewpoint of an integrated paradigm. But Durkheim does take a softer position on this issue, a position that is highlighted when we analyze his work from such a viewpoint.

Despite this enunciation of a general integrative interest, there remains the issue of whether Durkheim tells us enough about the microscopic levels to warrant further investigation. In fact, there is sufficient evidence of his interest in the microscopic level to at least begin such an exploration. Nisbet (1974), for example, argues that there is little difference between the approaches of Durkheim and George Herbert Mead. If this were only partially true, it would lend considerable weight to the idea that Durkheim has something to offer on the microscopic levels since these were Mead's primary foci. Alpert (1939) argues forcefully that Durkheim not only understood the micro levels of social reality, but gave them a significant role in his system. He says that Durkheim 'was keenly aware of the recalcitrant nature of human beings, of the give and take element in the process of acculturation, and of the fundamental tendency of individuals to be refractory to social discipline. It is erroneous to attribute to Durkheim, as Malinowski does, the theory of unswerving, automatic, "slavish, fascinated, passive" obedience to social codes' (1939: 208). This theme of individual freedom is repeated by Wallwork: 'Durkheim was quite willing to accept Kant's claim that the self is free in some sense to choose ... "it is not necessary to believe that the human personality is totally absorbed in the bosom of the collective being"' (1972: 36). Finally, Pope (1975: 363) also stresses the microscopic level in Durkheim's work, but in a slightly different way by focusing on the conflict between the unsocialized individual and society: 'The force opposing society is the nonsocial (unsocialized) individual ... an opposition that constitutes the central dynamic of his theory.' Thus, there seem to be enough claims (although there are certainly many counterclaims) to lead one to believe that Durkheim has some insights into the microscopic level and these, in concert with his elaborate analyses of the macroscopic levels, might well make it useful to analyze his perspective from the vantage point of an integrated paradigm.

Also leading one to look to Durkheim from this viewpoint is the fact that he had a sense of 'levels' of social analysis, although he did not spell them out in precise detail. However, Lukes (1973: 9–10) made Durkheim's interest in levels of social analysis very explicit. Translating Durkheim's (and Lukes's) terms into those used in the preceding chapter, it is clear that he was aware of a continuum of social reality encompassing the macro-objective (anatomical or morphological social facts), macro-subjective (norms, beliefs and practices, and stable social currents), and micro-subjective and micro-objective (the transitory outbreaks in an assembly of people) dimensions. Durkheim had a far clearer conception of the microscopic levels, particularly the micro-subjective, than he is usually given credit for; they will be dealt with later in this chapter along with an analysis of the weaknesses of Durkheim's work in this realm.

The fact that Durkheim views social reality as a continuum rather than as a discrete set of levels is an essential insight, and one that is accepted here wholeheartedly, even though it is often necessary for heuristic purposes to divide social reality into levels. Durkheim's conception of a continuum leads him (and me) to be imprecise on where one level ends and another begins. They all meld imperceptibly into each other.

For example, Durkheim is not precise on where macro-subjective phenomena like norms end and macro-objective phenomena like morphological factors begin. Norms and social currents are certainly macro-subjective, but we begin to move to the micro-subjective level in talking about currents of opinion and transitory outbreaks. The lack of a clear dividing line between the macro-subjective and the micro-subjective is highlighted by Durkheim's use of the French word *conscience* in his early and crucial concept of the collective conscience. According to Lukes (1973: 4), 'the beliefs and sentiments comprising the *conscience collective* are, on the one hand, moral and religious and, on the other, cognitive'. The collective conscience encompasses *both* macro-subjective ('moral and religious') and micro-subjective ('cognitive') phenomena, although Durkheim almost always used the term to refer to macroscopic phenomena (see also Wallwork, 1972: 37).

The fact that Durkheim did not in general clearly separate the macro-subjective from the micro-subjective is also found in his work on primitive classification where Durkheim (and Mauss) try to show the roots in the social world of the classification system used in the mind. Needham (1963: xxvi), in his introduction to *Primitive Classification*, points out how it is impossible to clearly separate the two levels in their work: 'They aptly call their essay a "contribution to the study of collective representations", but their real concern throughout is to study a faculty of the human mind. They make no explicit distinction between the two topics ... so that conclusions derived from a study of collective representations are taken to apply directly to cognitive operations.' Thus, the following discussion of Durkheim's work begins at the macro-subjective level with the clear sense that he systematically refused to clearly differentiate this level from at least some of the others; indeed, his commitment to the idea of levels of social analysis as part of a social continuum made such clear-cut differentiations impossible.

Macro-Subjectivity

Collective Conscience As I have already pointed out, Durkheim's richest insights lie at the macro-subjective level. In fact, when Durkheim talked of social facts, he most often had in mind moral facts, or macro-subjective phenomena. In his early efforts at dealing with morality, Durkheim developed the idea of the collective conscience. Durkheim (1893/1964: 79–80) defined this basic concept in *The Division of Labor in Society*: 'The totality of beliefs and sentiments common to average citizens of the society forms a determinate system which has its own life ... It is, thus, an entirely different thing from particular consciences, although it can only be realized through them.' Several points are worth underscoring about this definition in terms of our interest in macro-subjectivity. First, it is clear that Durkheim conceives the collective conscience as being societal-wide when he speaks of the 'totality' of people's beliefs and sentiments. Second, Durkheim clearly views the collective conscience as being an independent, determinate, macro-subjective system. But, third, he is also aware of its ties to the micro-subjective level when he speaks of it being 'realized' through individual consciousness.

That the collective conscience is also related to the macro-objective form of society is made clear by the fact that Durkheim relates the collective conscience to the type of society in which it is found. Societies are dichotomized into those characterized by mechanical and organic solidarity. In societies characterized by mechanical solidarity the collective conscience covers virtually the entire society and its members, is believed in with great intensity (as reflected, for one thing, by the use of repressive sanctions when it is violated), is extremely rigid, and has a content that is highly religious in character. In societies with organic solidarity the collective conscience is much more limited in its domain and in the number of people enveloped by it, is adhered to with much less intensity (as reflected by the substitution of restitutive for repressive laws), is not very rigid, and has a content marked by 'moral individualism', or the elevation of the importance of the individual, the human being, to a moral precept.

Collective Representations As we have seen, the collective conscience is very general. Durkheim's dissatisfaction with its amorphous character led him to abandon it progressively in favor of the much more specific, but still macro-subjective, notion of collective representation. Collective representations may be viewed as specific states, or substrata, of the collective conscience (Lukes, 1973). Although they are more specific than the collective conscience, collective representations are not reducible to the micro-subjective realm: 'they have *sui generis* characteristics' (1973: 7). It is the *sui generis* character of collective representations (as well as the collective conscience) that places them generally within the macro-subjective realm. They transcend the individual because they do not depend on any particular individual for their reality. In addition, they have independent existence because their temporal span is greater than the lifetime of any individual.[4]

Social Currents Durkheim became even more specific (and more dynamic) in his analysis of macro-subjectivity in his discussion of 'social currents':

> But there are other facts without such crystallized form which have the same objectivity and the same ascendancy over the individual. These are called 'social currents'. Thus the great movements of enthusiasm, indignation, and pity in a crowd do not originate in any of the particular individual consciousness. They come to us from without and can carry us away in spite of ourselves. (1895/1964: 8)

While Durkheim explicated the idea of social currents in *The Rules of Sociological Method* (1895/1964), he used it as a major explanatory variable in *Suicide* (1897/1951). In brief, his argument there was that suicide rates change as a result of changes in social currents. At the most basic level this means that a greater or lesser number of people commit suicide as a result of what happens at the macro-subjective level of social currents. Here is the way Durkheim describes his thinking on the relationship between social currents and suicide:

> Every social group has a collective inclination for the act, quite its own, and the source of all individual inclination, rather than their result. It is made up of currents of egoism, altruism or anomy[5] running through the society under consideration with the tendencies to languorous melancholy, active renunciation or exasperated weariness derivative from these currents. These tendencies of the whole social body, by affecting individuals, cause them to commit suicide. (1897/1951: 299–300)

It is difficult to think of a clearer or more explicit statement of Durkheim's conception of social currents and their impact on the thoughts (e.g. 'languorous melancholy') and actions (suicide) of individuals.

Religion Durkheim devoted an increasing amount of attention over the course of his work to religion as a macro-subjective phenomenon. This increasing concern is best seen in *The Elementary Forms of Religious Life* (1912/1965), which can be interpreted as focusing almost exclusively on macro-subjectivity. Religion, itself, may be seen as a macro-subjective phenomenon, and Durkheim defines this aspect of macro-subjectivity very broadly as 'systems of ideas which tend to embrace the universality of things and to give us a complete representation of the world' (1912/1965: 165).

One of Durkheim's concerns in *The Elementary Forms of Religious Life* was the source of religion in earlier forms of macro-subjectivity. Durkheim argued that the roots of modern religion lay in primitive totemism and he made it clear that totemism too was part of the macro-subjective domain:

> Totemism is the religion, not of such and such animals or men or images, but of an anonymous and impersonal force, found in each of these beings but not to be confounded with any of them. No one possesses it entirely and all participate in it. It is so completely independent of the particular subjects in whom it incarnated itself, that it precedes them and survives them. Individuals die, generations pass and are replaced by others; but this force always remains actual, living and the same. It animates the generations of today as it animated those of yesterday and as it will animate those of tomorrow. (1912/1965: 217)

Not only does Durkheim make clear the macro-subjective character of totemism, and the roots of religion in totemism, but he also underscores an essential focus of an integrated paradigm: the *historical analysis* of social forms. On the issue of history, Durkheim is not only making clear the historic roots of religion, but also the fact that people in the past, present, and future are, and will be, faced with macro-subjective forms that shape their lives.

But there is even more to Durkheim's analysis of religion that is of significance for understanding macro-subjectivity. For one thing, Durkheim also demonstrates the degree to which primitive religion is at the root of other forms of macro-subjectivity, including morality and systems of scientific thought. Beyond linking religion to other macro-subjective forms, Durkheim also links it to the micro-subjective level: 'we have established the fact that the fundamental categories of thought ... are of religious origin' (1912/1965: 466).

By way of summarizing this discussion it can be said that Durkheim made the macro-subjective level the focus of his analysis and offered a number of insights including his unwillingness to completely and arbitrarily separate this level from the others, his sense of the multidimensionality of macro-subjectivity as a level of social reality composed of a number of sublevels, and his sense of the historicity of the macro-subjective level as well as of its historical impact on the other levels of social reality. Furthermore, and perhaps most importantly, there are the ways in which the various levels of social reality interpenetrate in Durkheim's work. Although the focus in this section was on macro-subjectivity, there has been much discussion of the other levels as they relate to macro-subjectivity. More of Durkheim's insights into macro-subjectivity will be encountered as we proceed, for Durkheim was ever aware of the way it affects, and is affected by, the other levels.

Macro-Objectivity

The macro-objective level in conjunction with the macro-subjective level are what Durkheim (1895/1964: 13) means when he talks about social facts, or 'every way of acting, fixed or not, capable of exercising on the individual an external constraint'. All of the elements of macro-subjectivity discussed above fit this definition, as do the macro-objective phenomena that are about to be discussed. Macro-objective phenomena occupy a curious role in Durkheim's thinking. They often occupy a position of causal priority, but in spite of this priority they seem to interest Durkheim far less than macro-subjective entities. At other times macro-objective phenomena are treated as dependent variables determined by macro-subjective forces.

At the most general level, Durkheim discusses society as a macro-objective phenomenon, but he is not always consistent in the way he deals with society. As Lukes (1973: 12) points out, society was sometimes 'real concrete society, e.g. France or the State'. At other times Durkheim tended to talk about more microscopic phenomena, such as the family or an occupation, as society. This tendency to identify disparate phenomena as society is underscored by Pope: 'Durkheim's conception exhibits great "displacement of scope" ... He treated France as a society; he also referred to a married couple as a society' (1976: 192). Although this is a problem, the situation is made even worse by the fact that Durkheim sometimes wrote about society as if it was the same as common morality. In this case, his refusal to differentiate the macro-objective and macro-subjective levels becomes a serious problem.[6] A society is best thought of as a structural reality that encompasses a common morality, but for heuristic purposes it is useful to think of society as a macro-objective (structural) phenomenon. More generally, while it is desirable to view the real world as a series of interpenetrating levels, it is best to keep them conceptually distinct for analytic purposes.

Durkheim's overwhelming interest in macro-subjectivity often led him to think of macro-objective phenomena as of secondary significance. For example, Durkheim clearly identifies the church as a macro-objective phenomenon.[7] A church is seen as a structure whose major function is to translate the common ideas of a religion into common practices (1912/1965: 59). But Durkheim is not interested in the church *per se*, but more in its functions for the macro-subjective religion. Thus, Durkheim defined the church as the structure that serves to differentiate one form of macro-subjectivity (religion) from another (magic). In politics, Durkheim saw the state performing a variety of macro-subjective functions including the maintenance of the common morality and, more specifically in modern society, the cult of the individual (Giddens, 1972: 18; Lukes, 1973: 272). A similar argument can be made about occupational associations. Durkheim conceived of these associations as a means of coping with the pathological moral (macro-subjective) problems that he saw as part of the transition from mechanical to organic solidarity. Anomie is seen as the most important of these moral pathologies, and the occupational association and its system of rules was to be designed to help resolve it (Durkheim, 1893/1964: 5).

In addition to structural phenomena like society and occupational associations, Durkheim also makes much of what he calls morphological factors. Durkheim sometimes uses these morphological factors as the cause of important social changes; on other occasions he treats them as outcomes of these changes, or even as indexes to these outcomes. Perhaps the best known of the former type of morphological factor in Durkheim's work is 'dynamic density'. It is the main causal factor in the increasing division of labor. Key factors in dynamic density are the increasing number of people, and their increasing interaction, which, in turn, led to the transition from mechanical to organic solidarity, or more generally from a society characterized by one form of macro-subjectivity to a society characterized by another form. Thus, somewhat ironically, given Durkheim's focus on macro-subjectivity, the central causal factor in his theory of social change is a macro-objective force (Tiryakian, 1962: 17).[8] He is not focally interested in these morphological factors *per se*, but rather in their impact on macro-subjectivity.

Micro-Subjectivity

It was Durkheim's overly zealous position for sociology and against psychology that led many (e.g. Lukes, 1973: 228; Nisbet, 1974: 32; Pope, 1975: 368, 374) to assume that Durkheim's work was weak on consciousness (the micro-subjective level). As Pope (see also Nisbet, 1974: 52) points out, a major reason that Durkheim is supposed to have ruled out concern for the micro-subjective is his concern for science. Pope makes this point in discussing why Durkheim did not deal with intent in his study of suicide: 'In so far as intent is employed, though, it will, in Durkheim's estimation, lack the objectivity that is the *sine qua non* for scientific definitions' (1976: 10–11).

Although there is some truth to these claims, they grossly exaggerate the reality to be found in Durkheim's work. While Durkheim may have made statements against the study of micro-subjectivity, the fact remains that he did deal with this level in many places and in a variety of ways. However, it is also true that he treats micro-subjectivity as a secondary, or residual, factor, or more commonly as a dependent variable to be explained by social facts.

Although one can cite many places where Durkheim was critical of dealing with the micro-subjective level, one can also cite a number of locations in which he demonstrated his awareness of the significance of micro-subjectivity and he even integrated it directly into his work. Although he makes a similar point in several places (e.g. *Suicide*, 1897/ 1951: 315), the following is Durkheim's clearest statement on his ultimate interest in micro-subjectivity: 'In general, we hold that sociology has not completely achieved its task so long as it has not penetrated into the mind … of the individual in order to relate the institutions it seeks to explain to their psychological conditions … man is for us less a point of departure than a point of arrival' (cited in Lukes, 1973: 498–9). It appears that Durkheim focused on 'external' facts (e.g. suicide rates, laws, etc.) because they were amenable to scientific analysis, but he did not integrate an understanding of micro-subjectivity into his theoretical system. Even though he never quite achieved an adequate integration, he did address the issue of micro-subjectivity in several different ways.

Assumptions about Human Nature One of his assumptions about human nature may be viewed as the basis of his entire sociology. That assumption is that people are endowed with a variety of egoistic drives[9] which, if unbridled, constitute a threat to people as well as to the larger society. To Durkheim, people were characterized by an array of passions. If these passions were unconstrained, they would grow and multiply to the point where the individual would be enslaved by them. This leads Durkheim to his curious (on the surface) definition of freedom as external control over passions. People are free when their passions are constrained by external forces and the most general and most important of these forces is the collective conscience. It can be argued that Durkheim's entire theoretical edifice, especially his emphasis on macro-subjectivity, is erected on this basic assumption about people's passions. As Durkheim puts it, 'Passion individualizes, yet it also enslaves. Our sensations are essentially individual; yet we are more personal the more we are freed from our senses and able to think and act with concepts' (1912/1965: 307–8).

To return to an issue raised earlier, freedom for Durkheim comes from without rather than from within and this requires a morality to constrain the passions. But freedom, or autonomy, has another sense in Durkheim's work. That is, that freedom does not come from within, but rather is a characteristic of the common morality that is internalized in the actor. Individual autonomy is derived from the internalization of common morality that emphasizes the significance and independence of the individual (Lukes, 1973: 115, 131). Thus freedom is a characteristic of society, not of individuals. Here, as elsewhere, we see the degree to which Durkheim emphasizes the macro-subjective (in this case 'moral individualism') over the micro-subjective.

Socialization   Given his views on innate human passions and the need to constrain them by common morality, it should come as no surprise that Durkheim was very much interested in the internalization of social morality through education and more generally through socialization. Social morality is simultaneously both inside and outside of us; common morality 'penetrates us' and 'forms part of us' (Durkheim, cited in Lukes, 1973: 131). Although he based much of his work on it, Durkheim, in Pope's (1976: 195) view of *Suicide*, had 'a primitive notion of internalization', one that lacked an adequate 'social psychology of internalization'. Thus despite the fact that it is basic to his sociology, Durkheim did not explain the process of internalization in any detail.

Durkheim is not focally interested in the issue of internalization, but rather in how it bears on his interest in the macroscopic problems of his day. The essence of the problem for Durkheim is the decline in the degree to which macro-subjectivity exercises constraint over consciousness (Nisbet, 1974: 192). Durkheim's interest in anomie in both *Suicide* and *The Division of Labor in Society* can be seen as manifestations of this concern.

Not only was Durkheim interested in this problem, he was also interested in suggesting reforms aimed at coping with the problem of inadequate socialization. Much of Durkheim's work on education, and socialization in general, can be seen in this context. Education and socialization were defined by Durkheim as processes by which the individual learns the ways of a given group or society. Learned in the process are necessary physical, intellectual, and, most importantly to Durkheim (1922/1956: 71), moral tools to function in society. Moral education has three important aspects (Wallwork, 1972). First, its goal is to provide individuals with the discipline they need to restrain the passions that threaten to engulf them. Second, individuals are instilled with a sense of autonomy, but it is a characteristically atypical kind of autonomy in which children understand that they must freely accept constraint (Wallwork, 1972: 127). Finally, the process of socialization is aimed at developing a sense of devotion to society as well as to its moral system. All of these aspects of moral education can be seen as efforts to combat the pathological loosening of the grip of macro-subjectivity on micro-subjectivity in modern society. At the most general level, Durkheim is concerned with the way in which collective morality constrains micro-subjectivity, the way it stands 'outside' people and shapes their thoughts (and actions). Of course, macro-subjectivity cannot act on its own, but only through agents. Of greater importance, however, is the degree to which the individual constrains himself by internalizing social morality: 'For the collective force is not entirely outside us; it does not act upon us wholly from without; but rather, since society cannot exist except in and through individual consciousness, this force must also penetrate us and organize itself within us' (Durkheim, 1912/1965: 240). Wallwork does an excellent job of clarifying the importance of the internalization of morality in Durkheim's system:

> A normal mind, Durkheim observes, cannot consider moral maxims without considering them as obligatory. Moral rules have an 'imperative character'; they exercise a sort of ascendancy over the will which feels constrained to conform to them ... Moral 'constraint does not consist in an exterior and mechanical pressure; it has a more intimate and psychological character' ... this ... is ... none other than the authority of public opinion which penetrates, like the air we breathe, into the deepest recesses of our being. (1972: 38)

Durkheim offers a specific example of this process of internal constraint in his study on religion: 'if he acts in a certain way towards the totemic beings, it is not only because the forces resident in them are physically redoubtable, but because he feels himself morally obligated to act thus; he has the feeling that he is obeying an imperative, that he is fulfilling duty' (1912/1965: 218).

These concerns with internalization, socialization, and education can all be seen in the context of the constraining effect of macro-subjectivity on micro-subjectivity. Whether the constraint is external, or internalized, it still comes down to external morality controlling the thoughts and actions of people.

Durkheim's limited thoughts on the micro-subjective level led many to assume that his ideal actor was one who was almost wholly controlled from without. His ideal actor would seem to be a total conformist. Although there is much to recommend this view, and some modern sociologists in following Durkheim seem to have adopted this position, Durkheim (cited in Giddens, 1972: 113) himself did not subscribe to a view of the actor as a total conformist: 'conformity must not be pushed to the point where it completely subjugates the intellect'. Although Durkheim left open the possibility of individual freedom, the thrust of his work was in the direction of outlining external constraints on actors and furthermore the desirability of such constraints.[10]

Dependent Variables   Micro-subjectivity most often occupies the position of dependent variable in Durkheim's works, determined by various macro-objective and especially macro-subjective phenomena (Pope et al., 1975: 419). Although several examples of micro-subjective dependent variables will be discussed, it should be made clear that although

Durkheim deals with them, it is often only in a vague and cursory sense. In *Suicide*, for example, Durkheim is quite uncertain how social currents affect individual consciousness and how changed consciousness in turn leads to a heightened likelihood of suicide (Pope, 1976).

In *The Division of Labor* micro-subjectivity is dealt with in a most indirect sense, but it is clear that it is a dependent variable. That is, the sense of the argument there is that changes at the macroscopic level lead to changes in micro-subjective processes. In mechanical solidarity, individual consciousness is limited and highly constrained by a powerful collective conscience. In organic solidarity, individual potentialities expand as does individual freedom. But again, although this sense of micro-subjectivity as a dependent variable is certainly there, it is largely unexplored by Durkheim and is left largely implicit. In *Suicide*, however, the status of micro-subjectivity as a dependent variable is much clearer. Schematically, the main independent variable is collective morality and the ultimate dependent variable is suicide rates, but intervening is another set of dependent variables that can only be micro-subjective states. Lukes's point about 'weak points' in the individual implies the micro-subjective level: 'The currents impinge from the outside on suicide-prone individuals at their "weak points"' (1973: 214).

Lukes (1973: 216–17) goes further on this issue and argues that there is a social-psychological theory hidden beneath the aggressively sociologistic language found in *Suicide*. One part of that theory is the belief that individuals need to be attached to social goals. Another aspect is that individuals cannot become so committed to such goals that they lose all personal autonomy. Finally, as has been discussed before, Durkheim believed that individuals possess passions and people can only be contented and free if these passions are constrained from without. One can find in *Suicide* specific micro-subjective states associated with each of the three main types of suicide.

> These subjective states, themselves effects of given social conditions, impel the individual to suicide ... 'the egoistic suicide is characterized by a general depression in the form either of melancholic languor or Epicurean indifference' ... Anomic suicide is accompanied by anger, disappointment, irritation, and exasperated weariness ... while the altruistic suicide may experience a calm feeling of duty, the mystic's enthusiasm, or peaceful courage. (Durkheim, 1897/1951: 277–94, cited in Pope, 1976: 197)

Thus Durkheim saw well-defined micro-subjective states accompanying each form of suicide. Just as clear is the fact that these are peripheral interests to Durkheim who maintained a steady focus on the macroscopic level (Lukes, 1973: 35; Nisbet, 1974: 115).

We can find a specific example of this in Durkheim and Mauss's (1903/1963) work on the impact of the structure of society on the form of individual thought. Basically, Durkheim and Mauss argued that the form that society took affected the form of thought patterns. They were contesting those who believed that mental categories shape the social world. Their view is that it is the social world that shapes mental categories (1903/1963: 82). While specific components of macro-objectivity (e.g. family structure, economic or political systems) played a role in shaping logical categories, Durkheim and Mauss devoted most of their attention to the effect of society as a whole:

> Society was not simply a model which classificatory thought followed; it was its own divisions which served as divisions for the system of classification. The first logical categories were social categories; the first classes of things were classes of men ... It was because men were grouped, and thought of themselves in the form of groups, that in their ideas they grouped other things. (1903/1963: 82-3)

Durkheim's emphasis on the macroscopic level is well illustrated by this discussion of the impact of society on logical categories. An essential problem is that Durkheim does not analyze the corresponding process – the way in which the operation of mental categories in turn shapes the structure of society.

To do a more adequate sociology, Durkheim had to do more with the micro-subjective level than treat it as an unexplored dependent variable. An almost total focus on the macroscopic level leaves out important elements of an adequate sociological model. Lukes (1973) makes some telling points here in his discussion of *Suicide*. He argues, quite rightly, that an adequate explanation of suicide cannot stop with an examination of social currents. In his view, 'explaining suicide – and explaining suicide rates – *must* involve explaining why people commit it' (1973: 221, emphasis added). Second, Durkheim was wrong in assuming that micro-subjectivity was not amenable to scientific inquiry and explanation. It can be done and furthermore must be done if we are to go beyond partial theories of social life. Nothing is solved by simply acknowledging the existence of the micro-subjective, but then refusing to examine it. Durkheim's commitment to a narrow view of science led him awry as did his tendency to make radically sociologistic statements that ruled out recourse to the micro-subjective:

> He need only have claimed that 'social' facts cannot be wholly explained in terms of 'individual' facts; instead he claimed that they can only be explained in terms of social facts ... it would have been enough to have claimed that no social phenomenon, indeed few human activities, can be either identified or satisfactorily explained without reference, explicit or implicit, to social factors. (1973: 20)

In addition to not dealing with micro-subjectivity in any detail, Durkheim also failed to give it an active role in the social process. Despite his disclaimer mentioned above, people are in general controlled by social forces in his system; they do not actively control those systems. This led Wallwork (1972: 65, emphasis added) to contend that 'the principal weakness ... is Durkheim's failure to consider *active* moral judgment'. Durkheim gave too little independence to actors (Pope and Cohen, 1978: 1364). When Durkheim did talk of autonomy, it was in terms of the acceptance of moral norms of autonomy. Individuals only seemed capable of accepting these norms and of controlling themselves through their internalization. But as Wallwork (1972: 148) points out, autonomy has a much more active component: 'Autonomy also involves willful exploration, spontaneous initiative, competent mastery, and creative self-actualization.' Indeed, research into cognitive processes, in part done by Piaget who was working in the Durkheimian tradition, indicates that this micro-subjective creativity is an important component of social life (1972: 67). In other words, a more complete sociology requires a more creative actor and insight into the creative processes.

In summary, we have seen that contrary to the view of many, Durkheim *does* have a variety of things to say about micro-subjectivity. However, its residual character in his theoretical system makes his insight vague and amorphous. More damning is the fact that the thrust of this work leads to a passive image of the actor while an active actor is an essential component of an integrated sociological paradigm.

Micro-Objectivity

Given his primary orientations to macroscopic and subjective factors in general, Durkheim is weakest on the micro-objective level. He has little or nothing to say directly on individual action and interaction. Implied in his system are various changes at this level as a result of changes at the macroscopic level, but they are not detailed. For example, it seems clear that the nature of action and interaction is quite different in mechanical and organic solidarity. The individual in mechanical solidarity is likely to be enraged at a violation of the collective conscience and to act quickly and aggressively toward the violator. In contrast, an individual in organic solidarity is likely to take a more measured approach such as calling a police officer or suing in the courts. Similarly, in *Suicide* the assumption behind changes in suicide rates is that the nature of individual action and interaction changes as a result of changes in social currents. People may be more or less likely to interact with peers; they would be more or less likely to kill themselves. Suicide rates are used as cumulative measures of changes at the individual level, but the nature of these changes is not explored, at least in any detail. Similar points could be made about Durkheim's other works, but the critical point is that micro-objectivity is left unanalyzed in Durkheim's work.

Conclusion

Does Durkheim offer us an integrated theory of social reality? The answer, given the preceding discussion, must be yes, but it is an integrated theory with a number of serious liabilities. These liabilities would tend to indicate that Durkheim would *not* be an adequate exemplar for an integrated paradigm, but he does offer insights that would be useful in the development of that paradigm. We can close this discussion with an enumeration of the strengths of Durkheim's work and then turn to the problems that prevent his work from being an adequate exemplar.

On the positive side, Durkheim has a number of things to offer to an integrated paradigm:

1 A sense of the multiple levels of social analysis.
2 Some insight into the interrelationships among these levels; indeed into the fact that in the real world they meld imperceptibly into each other.
3 A schema that makes it clear that there are not only major levels of social analysis, but also a number of sublevels within each. For example, there is his identification of collective conscience, collective representations, and social currents within the macro-subjective level.
4 A powerful theory of the macro-subjective level and its significance in the social world.
5 A sense of the importance of historicity and the need to study the multiple levels of social analysis historically.

However, a number of problems point to the fact that Durkheim would not be an adequate exemplar for an integrated paradigm:

1 His overemphasis on the macro-subjective level.
2 His corresponding tendency to downplay the significance of the other levels.
   (a) Macro-objective forces tend to be comparatively unexplored causes or results in his theoretical system.[11]
   (b) Micro-subjectivity, although there, tends to be underdeveloped. More importantly, it is viewed as a passive force, a dependent variable, that cannot play a dynamic role in his system.
   (c) Micro-objectivity is almost entirely unexplored.

3 Although his lack of clear dividing lines is laudable, it sometimes led him to confuse phenomena that need to be kept distinct, at least heuristically (e.g. using collective conscience to refer to both macro- and micro-subjective phenomena simultaneously).

4 Although he has clear assumptions about human nature, they are comparatively unexplored in his work.
5 Durkheim's narrow sense of the nature of science and the scientific method led him to downplay the significance of factors, especially the micro-subjective, which need to be examined more fully in a more integrated paradigm.
6 His conservative politics led him to focus too much attention on the macroscopic level and on reforms that needed to be made at that level. [12]
7 Finally, and most importantly, Durkheim had a tendency to think in one-way causal terms. Although he often addressed feedbacks among various levels, he did not have an overall model that allowed the microscopic levels a dynamic role in shaping the macroscopic levels.

In sum, it should come as little surprise that Durkheim is *not* a suitable exemplar for an integrated paradigm, but his work is not without fruitful insights for those who are interested in developing such a paradigm. More importantly, from an M_u point of view, an analysis of his work as a potential exemplar for an integrated paradigm offers new insight into Durkheimian theory.

Karl Marx

The situation, of course, is quite different in the case of the work of Karl Marx. Given the dialectical image of the subject matter of the integrated paradigm, it is clear that Marx's work would be a likely candidate for exemplary status. Here I am not simply using the integrated paradigm as an M_u tool, but also seriously looking for an exemplar for that paradigm.

As was true of Durkheim, some important interpretations of Marx's work would lead one to doubt that his work could serve as an exemplar for an integrated paradigm. Marx has often been seen as a determinist, and not as someone who gives relatively equal weight to all aspects of the social world. An early (Kautsky, 1927/1978) and to some degree continuing interpretation of Marx was as an economic determinist. More recently, Marx has been seen as a structural determinist (Althusser and Balibar, 1970; Althusser, 1977). While evidence to make such cases can be drawn from Marx's diverse and complicated body of work, it is also possible to see his work in such a way that it would be consistent with the integrated sociological paradigm. For example, Meszaros argues that 'The Marxian system ... is organized in terms of an inherently historical – "open" – teleology which cannot admit "fixity" at any stage whatsoever' (1970: 118). More importantly, Gramsci explicitly rejects deterministic views of Marx's theory and argues that based on Marx's theory we must deal with the relationship between the structure of society and the actor, 'the consciousness of the individual who knows, wishes, admires, creates' (1971: 353–4). As was the case with Durkheim, there is at least enough opposition to the macrodeterminist position to encourage us to look further in Marx's work for the elements of an integrated paradigm. While with Durkheim we began at the macro levels and worked 'down', with Marx we will begin at the micro levels and move 'up' to the macro levels.[13]

Micro-Subjectivity

Species Being   I begin here (as I did in Chapter 2) with Marx's work or the (largely) micro-subjective level because it is, in my view, the basis of his entire theoretical system. The key concept in Marx's work on micro-subjectivity is species being. Marx's thoughts on species being essentially involve a set of ideas about human nature (his philosophical anthropology), although his concepts posit a human nature that is radically altered by the character of the environment. Furthermore, species being is not something that people have had in the past, or have now, but is something that they have the potential to attain. People always have some level, some elements, of species being, but the full expression of species being can only be attained in communism.

The basis of Marx's conception of species being is his ideas on powers and needs (Ollman, 1976). Powers are faculties, abilities, functions, and capacities. Needs are the desires people feel for things that are not immediately available. Both powers and needs are greatly affected by the nature of the social setting. People have natural powers and needs that they share with lower animals, but what interests Marx most are species powers and needs, those that set people apart from lower animals.

The heart of the notion of species being lies in Marx's view that people differ from animals in their possession of self-consciousness as well as in their ability to link thought to action. Marx borrowed these ideas from Hegel, but Marx is critical of Hegel for discussing self-consciousness as if it exists independently of people rather than focusing on the consciousness of real, sentient human beings: 'Hegel makes man *the man of self-consciousness* instead of making self-consciousness the *self-consciousness of man*, of real man, man living in a real objective world and determined by that world' (Marx and Engels, 1845/1956: 254).

Marx does much more than simply assert that the consciousness of people is different from that of lower animals: he pinpoints some of the key differences. First, people unlike animals do not simply act mindlessly, but separate themselves mentally from what they are doing.

Second, people choose to act or not to act; if they opt to act, they can choose which course of action to follow. Third, people can plan beforehand what they intend to do. Fourth, people are flexible mentally (and physically). Fifth, people can give close attention to what they are doing over long periods of time. Finally, people's mental capacities lead them to be highly social (Ollman, 1976).

These mental capacities allow people to engage in activity of a distinctive kind, quality, and pace. People, unlike lower animals, can control their activities through consciousness.

> The animal is immediately one with its life activity. It does not distinguish itself from it. It is *its life activity*. Man makes his life activity the object of his will and of his consciousness ... Conscious life activity distinguishes man immediately from animal life activity. It is just because of this that he is a species-being. (Marx, 1932/1964: 113)

Marx's abstract sense of human consciousness and activity had to be linked to the real world of other people and nature. Ollman (1976) details three aspects of that linkage. First, people perceive, in a rather unorganized way, nature and other people. Second, by a process of orientation people organize this array of perceptions. Finally, through appropriation people, often in concert with other people, use their creative powers or nature in order to satisfy their needs. People thus shape their settings, but the nature of perception, orientation, and appropriation is also affected by those settings.

We can generally distinguish among three broad, historically situated types of social settings. Primitive society provides people with a 'narrow satisfaction' (Marx, 1857–8/1964: 85). Life is so difficult that people are only able to use a small portion of their creative potential in the act of appropriation. Capitalism 'leaves us unsatisfied, or, where it appears to be satisfied with itself, is *vulgar* and *mean*' (1857–8/1964: 85). Although in many ways life is not as hard as it was in primitive society because of organizational and technological advances, the nature of capitalism prevents people from expressing their species being. Instead of expressing their creative capacities in the act of appropriation, they are reduced to focusing on earning enough money so that they can afford the commodities that result from the collective acts of appropriation. However, in communism the structural forces leading to the distortion of human nature in capitalism are overthrown, useful organizational and technological advances are retained, and people are for the first time able to fully express their species being. As Marx puts it, communism is an epoch in which man 'brings his species powers out of himself' (1932/1964: 151). Or, with slightly different emphasis, Ollman contends that 'Communism is the time of full, personal appropriation' (1976: 93).

It is important to note that in discussing Marx's thoughts on species being, and especially consciousness, we are focusing on micro-subjectivity, but it is in the nature of Marx's dialectical thinking that we also must deal with micro-objectivity (the activity involved in appropriation) and macro-objectivity (the structures of the various social settings). Marx's characteristic of often engaging multiple levels simultaneously is one of the factors that makes Marx's work an attractive possibility for an exemplar for the integrated paradigm.

Marx's notion of work also links micro-subjectivity and micro-objectivity. Work may be defined as 'conscious, purposive activity in the production process' (Ollman, 1976: 98). Work therefore involves *both* consciousness (micro-subjectivity) and activity (micro-objectivity). Most generally for Marx, work involves creativity, but in capitalism people are prevented from expressing their creativity in their work.

In the activity involved in appropriating the natural world, people always objectify: that is, they engage in the process of *objectification*[14]; they produce objects. This process of objectification is normal and expresses species being, if it involves several characteristics (Israel, 1971: 39). First, the activity must involve the consciousness of the actors. Second, the actors must be able to fully express their capabilities. Third, the actors must be able to express their sociality in the process of objectification. Fourth, the process of objectification must not merely be a means to some other end (e.g. earning money). In its most general sense, objectification must involve the creative capacities of individuals.

The process of objectification in capitalism clearly does not engage those creative capacities. In producing objects in capitalism, the consciousness of people is minimally involved; only a small proportion of their capabilities are required by their work; people often work in an isolated manner or even in competition with fellow workers; and objectification is often reduced to simply a means to an end. As Marx put it in terms of the last point: 'Indeed, labor, *life-activity, productive life* itself, appears ... merely as a *means* of satisfying a need – the need to maintain physical existence' (1932/1964: 113).

Implied in the discussion of objectification is still another aspect of species being, the fact that people are inherently social. At a micro-subjective level this means that people are oriented to relate to other people, but of course, this also manifests itself at the micro-objective level in terms of people's actual relationships with one another. People need to relate to other people both because they need human relationships and in order to be able to appropriate nature adequately. Meszaros underscores the significance of sociality to Marx: 'the "essence of human nature" is ... *sociality* ... "Sociality" as the defining character of human nature can only exist in the relations of individuals to each other' (1970: 149).

Alienation   If species being expresses Marx's ideal of what people ought to be like, and what they ultimately will be like in communism, alienation deals with what happens to species being in capitalism. One could say that alienation is the state of species being in capitalism and that species being, from Marx's viewpoint, is in an abysmal state. In ideal species being everything is in harmony, everything is interconnected: people, thoughts, actions, other people, products, nature, etc. However, in capitalism that natural interconnectedness is broken by the basic macrostructures of capitalistic society. Thus, alienation is not itself a micro-level concept, but it does imply a breakdown in the most important aspect of micro-subjectivity in Marx's work, species being. As a result of alienation the individual at work in capitalism does not affirm himself but denies himself, 'does not feel content but unhappy, does not develop freely his physical and mental energy but mortifies his body and ruins his mind' (1932/1964: 110).

The distortions of species being caused by capitalism are numerous. While living in species being, people can be no more or less than they actually are; but in capitalism money has the power to bestow on people powers and abilities that they do not possess (1932/1964: 167). The structure of manufacturing turns the worker into a 'crippled monstrosity' by forcing him/her to work on minute details rather than utilizing the whole of his or her capacities (1867/1967: 360). The worker also suffers the monotony of doing the same thing over and over again. Engels (cited in Venable, 1945: 137) underscores this problem: 'Nothing is more terrible than being constrained to do alone one thing every day from morning to night against one's will ... in such unbroken monotony, that this alone must make his work a torture ... if he has the least human feeling left.' Capitalism makes people so 'stupid and one-sided' that they feel an object is only theirs when they possess it, that is, when it is 'eaten, drunk, worn, inhabited'. For all of these reasons (and many more) work in capitalism is not an expression of species being. In fact, in many ways it is the opposite of species being. With their human functions so highly alienated, people are no longer able to express their species powers and needs and are forced to concentrate on natural powers and needs. 'As a result, therefore, man (the worker) only feels himself freely active in his animal functions – eating, drinking, procreating ... and in his human functions he no longer feels himself to be anything but an animal. What is animal becomes human and what is human becomes animal' (Marx, 1932/1964: 111).

Of course, Marx not only describes and critiques capitalism, but wants to see it overthrown. Species being needs to be emancipated from capitalism: 'Human emancipation will only be complete when the real, individual man ... has become a *species-being*' (Marx, quoted in Bender, 1970: 66). Thus, Marx's work on species being, largely on the micro-subjective level, leads him to a critique of capitalist society and to a political program oriented to overcoming the structures of capitalism so that people will be able to fully express their species being for the first time.

Micro-Objectivity

Production   The micro-objective level is probably the least developed in Marx's work. However, much of his work is premised on its existence and significance. That is, Marx's materialism, and his rejection of Hegelian idealism, led him to focus on material, in our terms, objective (micro and macro) phenomena. As Marx and Engels put it: 'The premises from which we begin – are the real individuals, their activity and the material conditions under which they live' (1845–6/1970: 42). While a focus on 'real individuals' provided the basis of Marx's interest in micro-objectivity, activity, especially productive activity, lay at the heart of this interest.

While the form of their consciousness may abstractly differentiate people from animals, it is only when the creativity inherent in human consciousness is transformed into productive activity that people are actually distinguished from lower animals. People 'begin to distinguish themselves from animals as soon as they *produce* their means of subsistence, a step which is conditioned by their physical organization. By producing their means of subsistence men are indirectly producing their actual material life' (1845–6/1970: 42). What they are is not what they think, but rather what they actually do. 'As individuals express their life so they are. What they are, therefore, coincides with their production, both of *what* they produce and with *how* they produce' (1845–6/1970: 42).

Thus, a central focus for Marx at the micro-objective level is the act of production. But it is important to remember that Marx is a materialist and not an economic determinist. Thus, he is not restricting himself to economic production, but would also include artistic, religious, and political production, among other kinds of production.

Social Relationships   A second component of Marx's interest in micro-objectivity is the social relationships between people. Marx talks of 'the need, the necessity, of intercourse with other men' (Marx and Engels, 1845–6/1970: 51). Or, 'Man is in the most literal sense of the word a *zoon politikon*, not only a social animal, but an animal which can develop into an individual only in society' (Marx, 1857–8/1973: 84). These patterns of social relationships, as well as the pattern of productive activity (which, of course, cannot be done without relating to other people), are the core of a sociological interest in micro-objectivity. Marx does not offer us a great deal on micro-objectivity, but to his credit he is aware of it and the degree to which it (along with the micro-subjective level) provides the basis for the analysis of the macroscopic levels. It is these linkages that are far more insightful than Marx's work on the micro-objective level *per se*.

Macro-Subjectivity

Class and False Consciousness   Marx's discussion of class and false consciousness leads to insight into his thinking at the macro-subjective level. Marx's thoughts on macro-subjectivity in general were affected by his efforts to distance himself from Hegel and the Hegelians who focused on macro-subjective phenomena such as the Spirit, the Geist. The idealism of such an orientation led Marx in the direction of materialism. At some points (e.g. Marx, 1859/1970: 20–1) it seems as if Marx goes too far and argues that macro-subjectivity is determined by macro-objective structures. However, this *does* go too far because, as I have already discussed, Marx does *not* offer a deterministic perspective. Thus, while Marx is led at the macro level to focus on objective phenomena, he does not lose sight of macro-subjectivity or reduce it to the status of an epiphenomenon.

The ideas of class consciousness and false consciousness are intimately related in Marx's work. What is characteristic of capitalism, for both the proletariat and the capitalist, is *false* consciousness. The idea systems of both contain erroneous conceptions of how the capitalist system works and their role and interest in it. We are not surprised to learn that the proletariat has false consciousness, but the capitalist is another matter. But the fact is that the capitalists have a number of elements of false consciousness. For example, they believe that profits come from their expertise rather than from the exploitation of the proletariat. Moreover, capitalists are unaware of the contradictions that exist within capitalism and the fact that their actions are contributing to the contradictions that will ultimately lead to their downfall as well as to the collapse of the capitalist system.

But there is a crucial difference between the two classes. The capitalists can never transform their false consciousness into true class consciousness; this transformation is *only* possible for the proletariat. Proletarians can gain a true sense of capitalism because they are at the bottom of the system, a propertyless class, basically excluded from the system. Capitalists, on the other hand, are so deeply enmeshed in the system that they can never attain the distance needed to see the system for what it really is.

But what exactly are class and false consciousness? Are they micro-subjective characteristics of individual consciousness? Or macro-subjective characteristics of social classes? Lukács (1922/1968) makes it clear that class consciousness is not reducible to micro-subjectivity. There is a separable macro-subjective realm in Marx's thinking and it has a coercive effect on individual thought and action:

> Now class consciousness consists … of the appropriate and rational reactions 'imputed' … to a *particular typical position* in the process of production. This

consciousness is, therefore, *neither the sum* nor *the average* of what is thought or felt by the single individuals who make up the class. And yet the historically significant actions of the class as a whole are determined in the last resort *not* by the thought of the *individual* and those actions can be understood only by reference to this consciousness. (1922/1968: 51)

Thus, in talking about class (and false) consciousness, Marx is not talking about individual consciousness, but the consciousness of the class as a whole. In other words, he is operating on the macro-subjective level.

Ideology   The other major dimension of Marx's analysis at the macro-subjective level is ideology. An ideology can be defined as an integrated system of ideas that is external to, and coercive over, the individual. Ideologies clearly take on an independent, macro-subjective existence in Marx's theoretical system.

At least two basic, interrelated ideas are involved in Marx's conception of ideology. First, ideologies represent the material interests of the ruling class, but they in turn have an impact on those interests. Second, and relatedly, these ideas constitute an 'inverted, truncated reflection of reality' (Lefebvre, 1968: 64). However, what is centrally important to our interest in an integrated paradigm is that these ideologies have an existence independent of individual actors. Lefebvre (1968: 76) catches the essential point for us here in discussing the effect of ideologies on members of oppressed classes: 'It is the role of ideologies to secure the assent of the oppressed and exploited. Ideologies represent the latter to themselves in such a way as to wrest from them, in addition to material wealth, their spiritual acceptance of this situation, even their support.'

An ideological system functions to alter the thoughts and actions of members of the oppressed class. Of course, ideologies do not function in a vacuum; they operate through agents who carry out their dictates. Thus, ideologies affect the actions of agents of the ruling class who, in turn, affect the thoughts and actions of the proletariat. In this way, macro-subjective ideologies are linked to the macro-objective structure of society. And they, in turn, are linked to the thoughts and actions of individual capitalists and members of the proletariat. Thus, as usual in Marx's work, each level is tied into every other level.

Macro-Objectivity

Although Marx certainly dealt with all major levels of social reality, his richest ideas deal with the macro-objective structures of capitalist society. While Marx recognizes the independent and coercive existence of macro-objective structures (particularly economic structures), he is also aware that these structures are created by actors both historically and by their daily thoughts and actions. It is also important to note that Marx focused on macro-objective structures not because they are always centrally important, but because they had become centrally important in capitalism. The structures of capitalism had become reified and were exerting control over people's thoughts and actions; they were the cause of alienation. These structures needed to be understood both because of their central importance and because such an understanding would aid in their eventual overthrow.

Commodities   The basis of all of Marx's work on the macro-objective level, as well as the place that it is most clearly tied to the microscopic realms, is his analysis of commodities. As Lukács puts it: 'the problem of commodities is ... the central *structural* problem of capitalist society' (1922/1968: 83). While a commodity is not itself a macro-objective structure, it lies, as we will see, at the base of the development of such structures.

Production of commodities is related to the natural process of objectification. As long as people produce for themselves, or for those immediately around them, they are able to control the objects; the objects cannot achieve an independent existence. However, in capitalism this process of objectification takes on a new and dangerous form. Instead of producing for one's self, or for one's immediate associates, the actor produces for someone else (the capitalist) and the products, instead of being used immediately, are exchanged in the open market for money. While people produce objects, in capitalism their role in, and control over, commodities becomes mystified. The commodities, and the market for them, come to be separated from the individuals. As Marx puts it, 'a commodity is ... an object outside us' (1867/1967: 35).

Once we have commodities and a market for them, we have the development of the *fetishism of commodities*. This involves the process by which people lose sight of the fact that it is their labor that gives commodities their value. They come to believe that value arises from the natural properties of things, or that value is conferred through the impersonal operation of the market. Thus, the market takes a place in the eyes of the actors that in Marx's view only actors could perform: production of value. In Marx's terms, 'a definite social relation between men ... assume[s], in their eyes, the fantastic form of a relation between things' (1867/1967: 72). According reality to commodities and the market for them, people in capitalism progressively lose control over them.

The beauty of Marx's discussion of commodities and their fetishism is that it takes us integratively from the micro-subjective and micro-objective levels to the macro-objective level. That is, people endowed with creative minds interact with other people and nature to produce objects but this natural process is subverted and leads to the creation of a macro-objective level of commodities and the market that is external and coercive.

As pointed out earlier, this economic process can be extended to a variety of other realms because Marx conceives of production as something much broader than simply economic production. It is this ability to think of this process that brings us to the concept of reification which (as we saw in Chapter 2) can be seen as similar to the fetishism of commodities, but is applicable to a number of social institutions and not just the economy. That is, when people believe that a range of social structures are beyond their control and unchangeable, this belief often comes to be a self-fulfilling prophecy: the structures actually *do* acquire a life their own.

Economic Structures   The most general economic, macro-objective structure in Marx's work is *capital*. As an independent, macro-objective structure, capital (through the actors who work on its behalf, the capitalists) became coercive on, and exploitative of, the actors who were responsible for its creation. Thus, Marx talks of the power of capital as appearing 'as a power endowed by Nature – a productive power that is immanent in Capital' (1867/1967: 333). Workers are exploited by a system that they have forgotten that they produced and continue to produce through their labor *and* that they have the capacity to change. 'By means of its conversion into an automaton, the instrument of labour confronts the labourer, during the labour-process, in the shape of capital, of dead labour, that dominates, and pumps away, living labour-power' (1867/1967: 423).

Marx also analyzes the process by which private property becomes fetishized in capitalism. In his view, of course, private property, like the other macro-objective components of capitalism, is derived from the labor of workers. '*Private property* is thus the product, the result, the necessary consequence of *alienated labour*, of the external relation of the worker to nature and to himself' (1867/1967: 117). But people lose sight of this fact and ultimately control over it. Private property, like all reified structures, will need to be destroyed in order for communism to arise. In fact, Marx sees communism as the '*positive* transcendence of *private property*' (1932/1964: 135).

Division of Labor   The division of labor is another macro-objective component of capitalism that comes under Marx's scrutiny. As usual, Marx links his critique of this macrostructure to his sense of micro-subjectivity: 'The examination of *division of labor* and *exchange* is of extreme interest because these are *perceptively alienated* expressions of human *activity* and of *essential human power* as a *species* activity and power' (1932/1964: 163). Ollman goes even further in linking the division of labor not only to Marx's early interest in species being, but also to his later work on the structure of capitalism:

> the division of labor occurs and ... it brings alienation in its wake. The further it develops, that is the smaller the task assigned to each individual, the more alienation approximates the full-blown form it assumes in capitalism. Even at its origins, however, Marx could speak of the division of labor affording us the first example in history of how man's own deed becomes an alien power opposed to him, which enslaves him instead of being controlled by him. (1976: 159)

In its most general sense, the division of labor in capitalism refers to the division between the owners of the means of production and those who must sell their labor time to the owners in order to survive. But in a more specific sense, Marx is interested in the tendency to structure work so that people are forced to specialize in ever more minute areas. Such specialization prevents people from expressing all but a few of the aspects of their species being. The specialization of labor develops 'at the expense of the whole of man's working capacity' (Marx, 1867/1967: 350). For example, narrow specialization has the effect of 'stunting him, dehumanizing him, reducing him to a mere fragment of a man, a crippled monstrosity, an appendage to a machine' (Venable, 1945: 124).

Social Class   Marx did not devote a lot of explicit attention to social classes, but his isolated statements make it clear that social classes are macro-objective structures that are external to, and coercive on, people. For example, he says: 'The social character of activity appears here as an alien object in relation to the individuals ... Their mutual relationship appears to the individuals themselves as something alien and auto-nomous, as an object' (Marx, cited in Ollman, 1976: 204). Ollman (1976: 204–5) is explicit that social classes are 'reified social relations' or 'the relations between men have taken on an independent existence'. Ollman also links classes to the prototypical macro-objective phenomena in Marx's work commodities: '*Class and commodity are brothers under the skin*' (1976: 205, emphasis added). Social classes arise out of the acts of production, people come to fetishize these classes, and as a result they come to have an independent life of their own that is coercive over people.

Conclusion

The preceding discussion makes Marx's multileveled theory much too static. Marx, of course, offered a very dynamic theory of the social world. At one level this is manifested in his general law of capitalist accumulation. But more generally, the dynamism in Marxian theory is provided by his dialectical orientation. It is the *dialectic* that is the key to understanding the interrelationship among the levels discussed above.

Thus, Marx's work, unlike Durkheim's, does provide a viable exemplar for those who wish to work within an integrated sociological paradigm. This is not to say that Marx's work offers anything close to all of the answers required by an integrated paradigm, but it is the place to begin in the development of such a paradigm.

Notes

The material covered in this chapter is derived from *Toward an Integrated Sociological Paradigm: The Search for an Exemplar and an Image of the Subject Matter* (1981b: 31–69, 107–29) and (with Richard Bell) 'Emile Durkheim: Exemplar for an Integrated Sociological Paradigm?' (1981).

1   To repeat once again, the exemplar concept is used here differently from Kuhn (from whom it is being borrowed). Kuhn, at least in his later work, sees an exemplar as a concrete piece of research that serves as a model for groups of scientists. In my view, there are no such exemplars in sociology. Instead, our exemplars tend to be bodies of work done by particular sociologists that serve as models for groups of sociologists (see Chapter 3).

2   In *Toward an Integrated Sociological Paradigm* (Ritzer, 1981b) I review the work of a number of potential exemplars. To make the discussion manageable in this chapter, I focus on Durkheim and Marx.

3   Although Durkheim is careful to point out that he is dealing with suicide rates, and not individual suicides, it seems clear that the basis of suicide rates is the individual suicide. Furthermore, a suicide rate is no more than the sum of individual suicides.

4   Although collective representations exist outside actors, it is also true that they may extend into the individual and be manifest in cognitive and affective states. This is similar to the contemporary view on norms and values and the degree to which they become internalized.

5   As well as fatalism.

6   Among those who also make this point are Gouldner (1958: xxi), Tiryakian (1962: 17), and Wallwork (1972: 75, 19).

7   Of course, a church also has a macro-subjective component.

8   One possible exception to his tendency to accord causal priority to morphological factors is Durkheim's macro-subjective notion of collective effervescence. The idea appears in several places in Durkheim's work, but is never spelled out in great detail. These are the great moments in history when a collectivity is able to achieve a new level of collective mental exaltation which in turn can lead to great changes in the structure of society such as happened during the Reformation and Renaissance. Although potentially very important, Durkheim never spells out collective effervescence with the result that it plays a negligible role in his sociology.

9   Which were no doubt stimulated by society.

10   In an interesting paper, Mulligan and Lederman (1977: 539) argue that Durkheim could have conceived of a more creative actor had he adequately differentiated between rules that regulate social life (his focus) and rules 'which bring into being *novel* forms of behavior'. They argue, in effect, that had Durkheim analyzed these 'rules of practice' he

would have been able to account for creativity macroscopically. While this may be true, it does not negate the fact that Durkheim also needed a more creative conception of the actor.

11   His work in *The Division of Labor* (1893/1964) is something of an exception to this.

12   While he is conservative in terms of our present political views, Durkheim was in the French politics of his day more of a liberal and he thought of himself as such.

13   This is no accident since in a very real sense Durkheim operates with 'top-down' model and Marx with a 'bottom-up' model. Furthermore, as we saw in Chapter 2, Marx utilizes an architectonic that begins at the 'bottom' with a micro-level philosophical anthropology.

14   We have already seen (Chapter 2) the importance of this idea not only in Marx's work, but also in that of Weber, Simmel, and Berger.

6

METHODOLOGICAL RELATIONISM: LESSONS FOR AND FROM SOCIAL PSYCHOLOGY

This chapter has three objectives. The first is to delineate a new metatheory[1] – methodological relationism – designed to take its place beside methodological individualism and methodological holism as a perspective that overarches the social sciences. We will review thinking on methodological individualism and holism and then will outline the parameters of methodological relationism.[2] We also will discuss anticipations of methodological relationism in the philosophical literature.

The second goal is to demonstrate that social psychology (and sociology more generally) always has been relational; had philosophers paid serious attention to work in that field, they would have developed methodological relationism long ago. This belated delineation of methodological relationism allows social psychologists to clarify their metatheoretical base. At the minimum, it eliminates the anomaly posed by the disparity between the relationism of social psychology and its need to choose between individualism and holism, metatheories that never comfortably described the nature of the field. Although some social psychologists may have been individualists and a few may have been holists, the great majority have been and are relationists.[3] An examination of what social psychologists actually do can aid in refining further the new metatheoretical position that we are labeling relationism.

Whereas the preceding objectives concern what social psychology has to offer to metatheory, the third objective in this chapter is to show what metatheoretical work can do for social psychology. More specifically, the goal is to use the idea of relationism to reflect on what was described in the 1970s as the 'crisis' in social psychology (Archibald, 1977; Boutilier et al., 1980; Burgess, 1977; Georgoudi and Rosnow, 1985; Hewitt, 1977; House, 1977; Liska, 1977; Stryker, 1989; Turner, 1988) and is described today, in less superheated terms, as a concern about the field's fragmentation. For example, social psychologists debate continually over whether there are two social psychologies (Boutilier et al., 1980; Stryker, 1989) or three (House, 1977) (to complicate matters further, Rosenberg and Turner, 1981 argue there is only one), as well as over the appropriate subject matter for each.

We will argue that there are many different social psychologies, arrayed on a continuum ranging from individualism to holism. The great majority of works in social psychology, however, are dispersed around the middle of this continuum, which is defined by its relationism. Even in this middle ground, social psychological positions show important differences. In discussing this continuum, especially as it is defined by relationism, we hope to cast new, or at least different, light on the fragmentation in social psychology. On the one hand, we will argue that because we are merely dealing with different types of relationism, social psychology is less fragmented than is often supposed to be the case. On the other, we will contend that examining the various approaches in social psychology in terms of relationism gives us a clearer sense of the possibility of a more integrative approach to social psychology.

Relationism, Holism, and Individualism

The work of sociologists and other social scientists, especially economists, played a key role in the emergence of the long-running and pivotal concern of philosophers of social science with individualism and holism. In turn, social scientists have come to be influenced by the work of philosophers on this topic.

Within sociology[4] a major resource for the philosophical work on individualism was Max Weber's analysis of social action; Emile Durkheim's work on social facts was a significant source of the holistic perspective.[5] Within economics, Weber's ideas influenced the individualistic perspective of Mises (1976), which in turn had an important impact on the more elaborate individualistic perspective of Hayek (1955), one of Mises's students. In fact an economist, Schumpeter, is credited with 'inventing' the concept of methodological individualism (Mandelbaum, 1957).

The roots of the individualism–holism debate can be traced to the social sciences (especially sociology, economics, and psychology), but it has come to be usurped largely by philosophers. Although philosophers often are interested in the implication of this issue for the social sciences, they have largely ceased to look to the social sciences for input into the debate (A. Rosenberg, 1988: 206). Thus, although the individualism–holism debate originated largely in the social sciences and continues to be highly relevant to them, the literature has come to be dominated by philosophers of social science who debate the issue among themselves with little or no input from the social sciences, to say nothing of the social world. The major works and positions on individualism–holism are the products of noted philosophers, or a least of thinkers who are known best in philosophy. The major contributors to this literature include Agassi (1960), Brodbeck (1954), Elster (1982),

Gellner (1956/1973), Goldstein (1956; 1958), Jarvie (1964; 1972), Mandelbaum (1955; 1957), Popper (1950; 1961), and Watkins (1952b; 1957).

Relationism represents a challenge to many of the philosophers who have dealt with these issues and have presumed, if they have not stated explicitly, that the individualistic and the holistic positions exhaust the range of possibilities. For example, Watkins (1968: 270, emphasis added) argued: 'If methodological individualism means that human beings are supposed to be the only moving agents in history, and if sociological holism means that some superhuman agents or factors are supposed to be at work in history, then *these two alternatives are exhaustive.*' Not only do scholars regard these two positions as exhaustive, but many also view them as incompatible:

> But if 'methodological individualism' and 'methodological holism' are given the meanings I gave them in my paper, then an eclectic belief in both becomes hardly possible. If you become persuaded that the metaphysical assumption on which methodological holism is based is true, then … You would believe that the things we do because we want to do them are really done because our society requires us to do them. This is not the sort of idea with which an individualist can come to a comfortable compromise. (1968: 271)

Watkins reflects the general philosophical perspective that individualism and holism are both exhaustive and mutually exclusive.

Our view is that Watkins and most other philosophers neglected a third alternative, *methodological relationism*. This metatheory is not only possible; it has been employed already, at least implicitly, by a range of social psychologists (and sociologists). Furthermore, this new perspective includes, at least in part, elements of holism and individualism. In short, social psychologists already have demonstrated that individualism and holism are *not* exhaustive and that they *are* compatible.

In the ensuing pages we will not only discuss the issue of individualism and holism, but also argue that relationism deserves a conceptual place beside them and ought to be added, if not become central, to the metatheoretical and philosophical literature on this issue. This statement suggests that philosophers of the social sciences need to spend more time studying developments in them and less time trying to impose their perspectives on them. Because of their prior commitments to either individualism or holism, philosophers have been blind to the possibility of relationism. Exposure to both classic and recent work in social psychology would open their eyes to this alternative. Indeed, it is hard to understand how philosophers of science in general, and particularly of social science, have missed the idea of relationism because it goes not only to the heart of social psychology, but also to the essence of the social world. Similarly, it is hard to understand how social psychologists have struggled with individualism–holism so long without balking at the incompatibility between those metatheories and their own work. In the following discussion we will focus on *methodological* individualism, holism, and relationism. The focus on methodological issues is based on our view that this is the most important concern in the social sciences, and of the greatest relevance.

The problem with defining methodological individualism and, to an even greater degree, methodological holism is that scholars who have worked with these concepts have not reached a consensus on a definition.[6] If one traces the way in which individualism has been used, from one of its earliest sources in Mill (1843/1950), through the works of Dilthey, Weber, Mises, Hayek, Schumpeter, Popper, and Watkins (to name only a few of the major figures in this tradition), one finds substantial disagreement and much internal debate.

First, and most important, methodological individualism involves the idea that all *explanations* of social phenomena must be rendered in terms of individuals and their thoughts and actions. This perspective contains subjective and objective branches. The subjectivists seek to explain all social phenomena in terms of the mental processes of individuals. Weber usually is regarded as the paradigmatic subjectivist among methodological individualists (Mises and Hayek also are important) because of his view that 'for the subjective interpretation of action in sociological work these collectivities must be treated as *solely* the resultants and modes of organization of the particular acts of individual persons, since these alone can be treated as agents in a course of subjectively understandable action' (1921/1968: 13). Action, as Weber defines it, is the subjective meaning that an individual attaches to his or her behavior; social action exists when its 'subjective meaning takes account of the behavior of others and is thereby oriented in its course' (1921/1968: 4). The main representatives of a more objectivistic individualism are Popper and Watkins, who accept the explanatory importance of such subjective motives but argue that to such phenomena must be added a concern for more objective actions, social relationships, and the situations in which they occur.[7]

Second, methodological individualists do not deny the existence of macro-level social concepts or phenomena, but they contend that all social concepts and/or phenomena must be *defined* in terms of individuals. In other words, definitions must refer to some or all of the following characteristics: individuals, their psychic states, physical states, actions, and interaction (Udehn, 1987: 43).[8]

Third, methodological individualists do not deny the utility of macrosocial concepts in *understanding* social phenomena or action. They have difficulty, however, with the use of macrosocial concepts in *explanations* of social phenomena or action. They argue that explanations must be rendered *only* in terms of individuals and the aforementioned characteristics. Therefore methodological individualists see a place for macrosocial concepts; such concepts, however, do not belong in the realm of explanation.[9]

One of the major distinctions between methodological holism and methodological individualism is their position on the issue of reducibility and irreducibility. Methodological individualists believe that social phenomena are reducible to statements about individuals, whereas holists believe that some societal concepts are not reducible to individual facts without a remainder (Mandelbaum, 1955). Methodological holism is based on the premise that the properties of wholes or systems cannot be *explained* in terms of the properties of their parts (Phillips, 1976: 34). According to Phillips (1976: 41), this type of holism is directly opposed to the doctrine of methodological individualism.[10] In order to properly analyze and explain complex social phenomena or systems, it is necessary to study the whole, because the parts do not explain such phenomena.

Several basic premises of *methodological* holism[11] parallel the basic assumptions of methodological individualism. First, explanations of macro-level (*not* micro-level) social phenomena must be rendered in terms of other macro-level phenomena. Within holism, as within individualism, there are subjectivists and objectivists. The subjectivists seek to explain all social phenomena in terms of macro-level subjective phenomena such as ideas, culture, norms and values, social institutions, and nonmaterial social facts. The objectivists seek to explain social phenomena in terms of material social facts, social structures, social positions, and the like.

Second, holists do not deny the existence of micro-level concepts and social phenomena. They insist, however, that all social phenomena must be defined in terms of social wholes.

Finally, no holist denies the utility of employing micro-level social phenomena to understand social phenomena, but holists have difficulty with the idea that explanations can be rendered in terms of such individual phenomena. Micro-level concepts have a place in holism for an understanding of social phenomena, but they do not have a place in the realm of explanation.

Extrapolating from the basic premises of methodological individualism and holism, we can delineate, at least in a preliminary way, the fundamental assumptions of *methodological* relationism. Before we begin that delineation, however, we must mention the position of relationism on the issue of reducibility. Relationists accept both points of view on this issue, thereby demonstrating once again that individualism and holism are *not* incompatible. Methodological relationism takes the position that individuals *are* the basic components of social wholes such as groups and society. Relationism, however, also accepts the idea of emergence and therefore acknowledges that social wholes *are* more than the sum of the individual parts. The existence of both social wholes and social individuals poses no major difficulties for relationists.

The first basic assumption of relationism is that explanations of the social world must involve the relationships among individuals, groups, and society.[12] According to this view, social individuals, groups, and larger social wholes cannot be explained without analyzing the social relationships among and between them. Thus, for example, if individual action is truly to be explained, it must be related to the actions of other relevant individuals and embedded in the context of the groups and larger social settings in which it takes place. To explain the group, we must concern ourselves with individual relationships within the group as well as with the links between groups and to the larger society. An explanation of the larger society requires that we take into account relationships among and between individuals and groups within society, as well as the relationship of that society to other societies. Furthermore, individuals, groups, or social wholes, taken alone, cannot explain relational phenomena adequately. Relationists can be concerned with either subjective (e.g. mind and culture) or objective (e.g. behavior and structure) relationships, as well as with those which involve a mix of subjective and objective elements.

Second, relationists do not deny the existence of either individuals or wholes. Concepts can be developed to deal with both individuals and wholes, but those concepts must be defined to include the relations between them. Thus our conceptualization of individuals, groups, and societies must take into account the relationships that exist within and between each. For example, a group must be defined as a set of individual relationships. This conceptualization also must make clear that the group is defined not only by a set of individual relationships, but also by its relationship to the larger social whole in which it is found. Similar conceptualizations of individuals and societies must be offered.

Third, individualistic and holistic concepts may be useful for gaining an understanding of social phenomena, but relational concepts must be employed if explanation is our goal. Thus we can use the individual-level concepts derived from methodological individualism and the societal-level concepts borrowed from methodological holism to understand the social world more fully. Yet, if we truly want to explain what is occurring in the social world, we must employ relational concepts. For example, a relational sense of the group, which leaves it open to individual and societal relationships, would permit us to explain a wide range of social phenomena. The same point can be made about the need for a relational sense of individuals and of the society.

In view of this brief outline of relationism, philosophers of social science now should develop a far more detailed delineation of relationism and its relationship to individualism and holism, based on traditional and recent sociological literature as well as on some of the anticipatory work in philosophy (to be discussed below). In doing so, they must immerse themselves in the work of social psychologists (and other social scientists), just as the earlier philosophers of holism and individualism based their ideas on the work of social theorists such as Weber and Durkheim. We contend that historically this more general metatheoretical position of relationism has been suggested, and its outlines have been delineated, by the work of social psychologists. More recently and more specifically, it has been outlined in the work on the links between micro and macro and between agency and structure.

Philosophical Anticipations of Methodological Relationism

Although so far we have been harsh on philosophers, we would like to suggest in this section that at least some philosophers within the individualism–holism tradition can be viewed as having anticipated relationism, at least in part.

We can begin with the thoughts of Karl Popper, who is associated with individualism. Popper (1961: 85–6, emphasis added) writes of 'the quite unassailable doctrine that we must try to understand all collective phenomena as due to the actions, interactions, aims, hopes and thoughts of individual men, *and* as due to *traditions* created and preserved by individual men'. The addition of the idea of 'traditions' may be regarded as part of Popper's more general effort to argue that individualism does not necessarily imply psychologism. Along the same lines, Popper also adds the term 'institutions'; according to Udehn (1987: 25), this term, as used by Popper, may be defined 'in a broad sense to cover every manmade social arrangement, from organizations such as universities and other schools, to language and writing'. The use of the idea of institutions, which implies some elements of holism, within methodological individualism, is a crucial equivocation that would seem to make Popper's position partially compatible with what we call relationism.

Agassi (1960: 244, emphasis added) seeks quite explicitly to develop Popper's ideas on institutions: 'My aim in the present essay is to argue that individualism need not be psychologistic, and to defend *institutionalistic individualism*, which I consider to be Popper's great contribution to the philosophy of the social sciences.' Agassi defines institutionalistic individualism[13] as the view that 'society is the *conventional means of co-ordination* between individual actions' (1960: 244). This statement seems to be a strong move toward holism and relationism, but Agassi continues to consider it as within the tradition of individualism:

[I]nstitutions can be explained as inter-personal means of co-ordination, as attitudes which are accepted conventionally or by agreement. Not that an agreement was signed by those who have the attitude, but the attitude is maintained by one largely because it is maintained by many and yet everyone is always at liberty to reconsider his attitude and change it ... It accords with the classical individualistic idea that social phenomena are but the interactions between individuals. Yet it does not accord with the classical individualistic-psychologistic idea that this interaction depends on individual aims and material circumstances alone; rather it adds to these factors of interaction the existing inter-personal means of co-ordination. (1960: 267)

Although Agassi is striving to fit his institutionalistic individualism into individualism, we believe that it anticipates and fits more comfortably into relationism.

Jarvie (1964; 1972) also offers a perspective on individualism–holism that demonstrates a move toward relationism. In his view, action is the only phenomenon that must be addressed in terms of individualistic concepts; all other social phenomena require holistic concepts (Udehn, 1987: 36). More important for our purposes is Jarvie's model of *situational logic*, which he regards as

a very simple and intuitive notion. We assume that people have certain aims, that they also have certain means (restricted by their physical nature and by the social set-up of institutions and traditions), and certain knowledge and beliefs about means and about the set-up. Armed with all this they act to achieve their aims within the social situation created by traditions, institutions, and the aims and actions of other people. Such a model, of an actor facing a social set-up, equipped with certain knowledge and beliefs, and striving to attain certain ends, strikes me as being *the* explanation form of the social sciences. (1964: 71)

Jarvie's notion of situational logic anticipates and comes very close to what we mean by relationism. Yet Jarvie, like all other philosophers who deal with this issue, remains confined within the parameters of the individualism–holism debate. He says, however, that the 'doctrine of methodological individualism ... is not identical with situational logic, but is part of it' (1972: 32). This statement could be read to imply that the other 'part' of situational logic is holism. Taken in this way, Jarvie can be viewed as combining individualism with holism and as moving toward relationism.

One also finds movement toward relationism among holists. Mandelbaum (1955: 317), for example, in his essay on societal facts, contends: 'There are societal facts which exercise external constraints over individuals no less than there are facts concerning individual volition which often come into conflict with these constraints.' Similarly, in an essay on societal laws, Mandelbaum (1957: 222) argues that 'one might hold that an adequate explanation of social phenomena would have to use *both* psychological laws and societal laws, and that neither of these types of laws is reducible to the other'.

Other ideas in the philosophical literature on individualism–holism also indicate movement toward relationism. Goldstein (1956: 811) suggests the idea of 'methodological collectivism' to deal with 'problems confronting social science that require solutions not amenable to individualistic analysis and yet not holistic or historistic'. Udehn (1987) surveys a number of 'weak' versions of methodological individualism (ideas of the collective actor, institutional individualism, structural individualism, Marxist methodological individualism) that imply a relationist orientation. Udehn (1987: 202) himself suggests such a position when he argues that methodological individualism is practically impossible and is productive of trivial theories, and that social science 'cannot do without reference to social institutions and social structure in its explanations'.

In addition, a variety of ideas within the social sciences suggest relationism. These include Piaget's (1970: 8–9) relational alternative to individualism and holism, namely 'operational structuralism', Ollman's (1971) discussion of the importance of relations in Marx's work, and Szmatka's (1989) case for 'multilevel' explanations.

Thus an array of relationistic ideas have existed within philosophy (and sociology), but these have been subsumed under the broader heading of individualism or holism. When these hints are combined with the fact that the great majority of social psychologists and sociologists have been concerned with relations of one kind or another, we have a broad base upon which to build a methodological relationism that at least can parallel methodological holism and methodological individualism in importance and significance.

The idea of relationism is likely to be met with coolness, if not hostility, from both individualists and holists. Because relationism often accepts the idea of emergent social realities, it is apt to be rejected by individualists. Holists are less liable to be hostile to relationism, but they will be uncomfortable with the frequent emphasis on individualism.

Relationism in Social Psychology

As we have made clear thus far, most of sociology in general, and certainly most of the work in social psychology, has been neither individualistic nor holistic, but rather has been concerned with a wide range of *relationships* among individuals, groups, and societal-level phenomena, or, to put it more abstractly, with the interrelationship among and between micro-, meso-, and macro-level phenomena.[14] Mead's (1934/ 1962) *Mind, Self, and Society*, Gerth and Mills's (1953) *Character and Social Structure*, and Berger and Luckmann's (1967) *The Social Construction of Reality*, to name only a few of the classics in social psychology, are clearly relational. Furthermore, social psychology itself is defined most often in relational terms. House (1977: 162, emphasis added) defines social psychology as the study of 'the *relationship* between individual psychological attributes and social structure, situations, and/or environments'. Similarly, Rosenberg and Turner (1981: xv, emphasis added) accept the definition of social psychology as the 'study of the primary *relations* of individuals to one another, or to groups, collectivities, or institutions, and also the study of intraindividual processes in so far as they substantially *influence, or are influenced by*, social forces'.

The most dramatic recent developments in sociology, in which social psychologists are deeply involved, are not captured by the ideas of either individualism or holism. In the 1980s and the early 1990s one finds a strong focus in sociology and social psychology on the *relationships* between social wholes and social individuals. In the United States this focus has taken the form of concern about the micro–macro link (Liska, 1990; Ritzer, 1990b); in Europe it is found in the literature on agency–structure integration. Cognizance of this development, as well as of the inherently relational character of social psychology, leads us once again to the fact that a new metatheoretical orientation must be articulated on this issue: *methodological relationism* must take its place beside methodological holism and methodological individualism as a central metatheoretical position within social psychology.

Various social psychologies deal with various kinds of relationships, but all social psychologies are relational. Stryker (1989: 45, emphasis added) differentiates between psychological social psychology (PSP) and sociological social psychology (SSP), but defines *both* relationally: 'Psychological social psychology is presumably defined by a focus on individual behavioral, cognitive and affective processes, its central task is *the comprehension of the impact of social stimuli on those individual processes* ... Sociological social psychology is ... defined by the *reciprocity of society and individual*, its fundamental task the explanation of social interaction as the medium through which that reciprocity is expressed' (1989: 46).

Within each of these broad types of social psychology can be found more specific social psychologies dealing with specific relations. For example, within psychological social psychology we find social learning theory addressing the way in which people acquire effective responses (Bandura, 1969; 1971; 1977), exchange theory discussing rewards and costs in interpersonal relationships (Homans, 1958; 1961/1974), and equity theory addressing the issue of fairness in interpersonal transactions (Adams, 1963).

Within sociological social psychology, House (1977) identified six different approaches, all of which are relational in one way or another. The first concerns the impact of social class on self-image, personality, and values (Kohn, 1969; 1989; M. Rosenberg, 1965; 1989). A second approach addresses the 'reciprocal relation of "modernization" to individual personality and behavior' (House, 1977: 171). Contributors to the second approach include Inkeles (1969) and Portes (1973). Third is an orientation that approaches the relationship between urban residence and individual personality and behavior (Fischer, 1976). A fourth body of literature deals with the role of individual motivations in the process of status attainment (Featherman, 1972; Majoribanks, 1989; Sewell and Hauser, 1974). Fifth is a concern for the relationship between personality and performance in organizational roles (Kohn, 1969; Merton, 1968). Finally, scholars have studied the role of psychological factors in the political process (Sears, 1969). Other sociological social psychological approaches exist in addition to the six that House identified. One example is a concern with the relationship between American values and personal attitudes toward others (Katz and Hass, 1988). In another, Hegtvedt (1988) studied the influence of social factors, such as structural power and status, on self-perceptions and the perception of others.

The key point is that in the two major varieties of social psychology, as well as in each of the subtypes, social psychologists are concerned with relationships. Had philosophers been knowledgeable about this literature, they might have found it difficult to adhere to the idea that individualism and holism are exhaustive metatheories. The literature in social psychology clearly provides the basis for delineating relationism.

A gap always has existed between what social psychologists *do* and the metatheoretical underpinnings of their work. This would not be a problem except that social psychologists seem to take individualism–holism seriously and often try to position themselves as either individualists or holists. Thus the fit between their metatheory and their actual practice is usually uncomfortable. The explication of relationism should allow many social psychologists to employ, for the first time, a metatheory that is appropriate to their work. Although the nature of most work is not likely to change (after all, it is largely relational), the relational aspects may become more explicit. Practitioners then will be relieved of the uncomfortable and perhaps distorting need to interpret their findings in terms of an inappropriate metatheory.

Methodological Relationism and the Various 'Faces' of Social Psychology

Having discussed what social psychology might have contributed to the development of relationism as a metatheory, we now change our focus and address the contribution that an understanding of that metatheory can make to social psychology. We hope to show that although relationism may not deal explicitly with the fragmentation in social psychology, at least it may lead to a better understanding of that fragmentation.

We postulate a continuum of metatheoretical positions, on which individualism and holism occupy the poles and relationism holds the middle ground. We believe that although some work in social psychology is based on individualism (e.g. rational choice theory, behaviorism) and some on holism (Blau's macro-level exchange theory and his later move to structural sociology), by far the majority of social psychologies fall somewhere in the middle; that is, they constitute some variety of relationism. In itself, however, such a differentiation does not help us much in examining the splintering of social psychology.

We are aided further in this task when we make distinctions *within* relationism: that is, when we identify *types* of relationism. Toward the individualism end of the continuum, but still within relationism, we can identify a body of work in social psychology that deals with the micro-to-macro relationship: that is, work that begins at the micro level and moves toward the macro level; work that originates near the individualism pole, but still is part of relationism. Coleman's (1986) expression of interest in this relationship is only one example. Among the six varieties of sociological social psychology discussed by House and mentioned earlier in this chapter, the last three (individual motivations and status attainment; personality and performance of organizational roles; psychological factors in the political process) are concerned with the micro-to-macro relationship. Similarly, when we focus on work that originates near the holistic end of the continuum but still remains within relationism, we encounter a variety of approaches concerned with the macro-to-micro relationship. The first three of House's types of sociological social psychology (effect of social class on self-image, personality, and values; modernization in relation to personality and behavior;[15] urban residence in relation to individual personality and behavior) share an interest in the macro-to-micro relationship.

At the center of the continuum, however, and at the heart of relationism, are perspectives that give relatively equal weight and attention to micro- and macro-level phenomena and to the relationships between them. In addition, these perspectives tend to examine the reciprocal (dialectical) relationships between micro and macro phenomena. Turner (1988: 1) offers a useful example of such an approach. He begins with the contention that 'our finest investigators [Inkeles, Kohn, Rosenberg, Seeman, Elder] have convincingly traced the influence of structural variables on individual personality. Yet, we apologize constantly for our one-sided neglect of individuals' effects on society.' Turner is dedicated to developing what he calls a 'circular' approach that does not neglect the individual, but deals with the dialectical relationship between the individual personality and macro-level culture and social structure.

Stryker (1980: 53) articulated a similar perspective more than a decade ago: 'A satisfactory theoretical framework must bridge social structure and person, must be able to move from the level of the person to that of large-scale social structure and back again ... There must exist a conceptual framework facilitating movement across the levels of organization and person.' A more recent variety of this approach is Liska's (1990) effort to cope with the limitations of Coleman's micro-to-macro approach by addressing both that link and the macro-to-micro link. Liska's approach, however, is limited by the fact that he discusses a series of one-way relationships and fails to treat them in a 'circular' or 'dialectical' fashion.

In symbolic interactionism we find evidence of a movement toward this more integrative, micro–macro orientation. Fine (1990), for example, argues that a 'new' symbolic interactionism has been formed by the integration of traditional ideas of symbolic interactionism with ideas drawn from such microtheories as behaviorism and phenomenology as well as from such macrotheories as structural functionalism and neo-Marxian theory. Similarly, Baldwin (1986: 156) reinterprets Mead as offering a more integrative theoretical perspective: 'Mead succeeded more than most social theorists have at creating a nondualistic theory that unifies ... micro and macro society.'

Within exchange theory, Emerson and Cook have taken the lead in developing a version of that theory which approaches the micro–macro relationship in a more integrated manner. Crucially important is the integration of the idea of networks into exchange theory. As Cook (1987a: 219) argues, 'The notion, exchange networks, allows for the development of theory that bridges the conceptual gap between isolated individuals or dyads and larger aggregates or collections of individuals (e.g. formal groups or associations, organizations, neighborhoods, political parties, etc.).' More recently, Cook et al. (1990: 175) have seen the strength of exchange theory as residing in micro–macro integration because 'it includes within a single theoretical framework propositions that apply to individual actors as well as to the macro-level (or systemic level) and it attempts to formulate explicitly the consequences of changes at one level for other levels of analysis'.[16]

Thus social psychology contains three broad types of relationism, with significant differences within each type. The first concerns micro-to-macro relationships, gives priority to micro-level phenomena, tends to coincide with what is usually called psychological social psychology, and falls toward the individualist end of the continuum. The second addresses macro-to-micro relationships, accords priority to macro-level phenomena, tends to be identified with sociological social psychology, and falls toward the holist end of the continuum. Finally, in the middle of the continuum can be found the type of social psychology that deals with the dialectical relationship between micro and macro, refuses to give priority to either micro or macro, and seems to be consistent with newly emerging perspectives in sociology and social psychology.

Given this distinction, what can we say about the fragmentation of social psychology? For one thing, the degree of fragmentation is reduced somewhat by ruling out of social psychology the individualistic and holistic theoretical perspectives. The former can be viewed as psychologism, the latter as sociologism. In light of the inherently integrative and interdisciplinary character of social psychology, individualistic and holistic perspectives would seem to have only a limited role in such a field.[17]

Excluding psychologism and sociologism and regarding social psychological perspectives as existing on a continuum, we can conclude that the proper province of social psychology is relationism. Granted, this continuum can accommodate perspectives based on various types of relations (micro-to-macro, macro-to-micro, micro–macro), but these perspectives, as well as the numerous subtypes within each, vary in degree rather than in kind. That is, they are *all* concerned with the micro–(meso)–macro relationship, although they emphasize different aspects. Viewed in this way, social psychology does *not* contain a great deal of fragmentation. Whether to give priority to the micro or to the macro, or to give equal weight to each, hardly seems an adequate basis for regarding the field as fragmented. These differences in emphasis should not cause apoplexy in social psychologists.

The view expressed here about social psychology permits an even stronger position on the issue of fragmentation in the field. Because the various social psychologies merely represent different types of relationism, it should be possible to consider the development of a more integrated social psychological paradigm. Such an integration is made more possible by the fact that social psychologists are drawing, at least implicitly, on only one metatheory rather than on several different metatheories. I have long argued for the need for greater integration (Ritzer, 1981b) and synthesis (Ritzer, 1990a) in sociology. We will leave it to social psychologists to develop such an integrated approach. We argue that because much of social psychology draws upon the same metatheory, such an integrative perspective is not only possible but attainable. At least it is clear that there are no metatheoretical barriers to the construction of an integrated social psychological theory. If barriers exist, they are more likely to be traceable to the politics of the field than to underlying theoretical assumptions.

Conclusion

The delineation of methodological relationism is, in our view, of great importance to social psychology, sociology, the social sciences, and the philosophy of social science. It would begin to fill a major gap in the philosophy of social science, would permit the development of an orientation that concerns itself with basic tensions and weaknesses in the history of the work on individualism–holism, and would bring thinking in philosophy on this issue into line with the realities of work in the social sciences, especially social psychology. The exposure of philosophers of social science to these bodies of sociological and social psychological work would restore a better balance to the relationship between the philosophy of social science and the social sciences. All too often philosophers have explicated their ideas in isolation from developments in the social sciences. A philosophy of social science more closely attuned to developments in the social sciences would be an improved philosophy more relevant to contemporary realities in the social sciences and more in harmony with the workings of the social world.

The proposal of this new idea of methodological relationism promises to inject new life and renewed relevance into the long-running and (by now) quite stale debate over methodological individualism and methodological holism. Individualism–holism has long been marginal, if not irrelevant, to the relational work that has dominated social psychology. Philosophers, taking their lead from this work in social psychology, now are in a position to delineate and explicate the idea of methodological relationism and to compare and contrast it with methodological individualism and methodological holism. In doing so, they will refine a philosophical position that should, in turn, provide social psychologists with a more appropriate metatheoretical underpinning for their work.

Sociologists in general, especially social psychologists, have been studying relations without a clear metatheoretical base. At some level they must have been discomfited for a long time by the lack of fit between their work and the tenets of methodological individualism and methodological holism. The systematic development of methodological relationism will provide the needed base. It will remove the discontinuity between social psychology and its metatheories.

Methodological relationism has two additional specific implications for social psychology. First, most social psychologists always have practiced relationism. If philosophers had carefully studied work in social psychology, they would have developed a sense of methodological relationism long ago. Even now, philosophers have much to learn from social psychology, and those who delineate methodological relationism need to study it carefully. Second, the supposed fragmentation of social psychology seems less problematic when we recognize that the great majority of work in social psychology involves little more than varieties of relationism. Furthermore, the possibility of an integrated social psychological approach seems far more likely when we view social psychology in this way.

Notes

The source for this chapter is (with Pamela Gindoff) 'Methodological Relationism: Lessons for and from Social Psychology' (1992).

1 A perspective that overarches a scientific field (Ritzer, 1991b).

2 To simplify matters, we will use the terms *individualism* and *holism* throughout much of this discussion to mean methodological individualism and methodological holism. (We will also use *relationism* for methodological relationism.) As Goldstein (1958), Scott (1961), and Udehn (1987) demonstrate, methodological issues are only one of several concerns (the others are ontological and epistemological) that often are discussed (and confused) in the individualism–holism literature. We will touch on the ontological and epistemological variants in notes.

3 Here we are thinking of sociologists engaged in social psychology.

4 House (1977), however, considers Weber and Durkheim to be social psychologists.

5 In fact, in her anthology *Readings in the Philosophy of the Social Sciences*, Brodbeck (1968) begins the section devoted to holism–individualism with an excerpt from Durkheim's work on social facts.

6 Among the individualists, Mises believes that social phenomena must be explained in terms of human action; Weber focuses on the interpretive understanding of social action; Hayek concentrates on attitudes, opinions, and beliefs; Popper examines attitudes, expectations, and relations; and Watkins is concerned with dispositions, beliefs, and individual relationships. While these perspectives overlap, they also reveal differences in the ways these philosophers (and others) define 'individualism'. Among the holists, Durkheim wishes to emphasize social facts, which are to be treated as external to and coercive over individuals; to Watkins, methodological holism suggests that explanations of social phenomena must be rendered in terms of superhuman agents or factors; Mandelbaum focuses on irreducible societal concepts; Udehn writes about holism in terms of social wholes, social structures or positions that have an existence independent of individuals; and Phillips concentrates on social wholes because parts (e.g. individuals) cannot explain social wholes.

7 Such a viewpoint seems to indicate a tendency toward relationism. We will discuss this point later in this chapter.

8 Udehn, drawing on Watkins, also includes social situation and physical environment in this list, but we exclude them here because they clearly move us away from individualism and toward holism and relationism. (The inclusion of interaction here already moves us in that direction.)

9 Methodological individualism can be distinguished from ontological and epistemological individualism. Ontological individualism is the doctrine that *only* individuals are real in the social world. Within the subjectivist camp, only Weber gives a truly methodological meaning to individualism with his notion of an interpretive sociology. Mises took Weber's subjectivist method and changed it into a subjectivistic ontology (Udehn, 1987: 15). His ontological thesis is that only human beings are real and that collectivities exist only in the actions of individuals (1987: 16). In addition, Mises believes that social reality is the only reality, whereas according to Weber, it is the subject matter of sociology (Udehn, 1987: 18). Still within the subjectivist camp, Hayek also offers an ontological position on individualism: he denies the existence of social wholes as definite objects. According to Hayek, neither the collective concepts of everyday life (e.g. society) nor those of the social sciences (e.g. government) are real. Rather, they are theoretical constructions that are not real apart from the theories about them. Therefore the thesis of ontological individualism is that only individuals are real, and their actions and interactions are what constitute social reality. Epistemological individualism subscribes to the notion that what we know about social phenomena stems from our knowledge about individuals,

their actions, and their interactions. Whereas Goldstein (1958) distinguishes between methodological and ontological individualism, Scott (1961) distinguishes between methodological and epistemological individualism. Scott views Hayek as a methodological individualist (which is at least partially true) and Popper as an epistemological individualist. According to Scott, Hayek is concerned with the methods that are employed in gathering information and formulating theories, whereas Popper is concerned mainly that our explanations and knowledge of social phenomena be in terms of individuals, not collectivities (1961: 331). Popper, according to Scott, demonstrates his epistemological individualism when he contends that what social scientists know about collective phenomena is based on what they know about the individual's actions, interactions, aims, and so on (1961: 333).

10   Phillips (1976) distinguishes among three types of holism (holism I, II, and III) that parallel the ontological, methodological, and epistemological distinction, although he does not use those terms. We focus here on methodological holism (Phillips's holism II).

11   In spite of the priority of methodological holism in this area, most scholars argue for or against ontological holism. Within ontological holism we find most of its premises with which we are familiar and that we commonly associate with holism. Phillips (1976) concluded that ontological holism (holism I) contains a number of interrelated ideas. First, the analytic approach to study is inappropriate for the study of society as a whole. Second, the whole is more than the sum of its parts. That is, the whole cannot be understood by a study of the parts because the whole is an emergent phenomenon. Third, the whole determines the nature of the parts; therefore the parts cannot be understood in isolation from the whole. Finally, the parts are dynamically interrelated and interdependent (1976: 6). These ideas describe the way wholes are; therefore, they exemplify ontological holism. Epistemological holism (holism III, according to Phillips) involves the idea that there exist some social phenomena which can be known and understood only in terms of social wholes (Udehn, 1987: 95). For Phillips, the basic premise is that science has an important place for concepts which refer to the properties of wholes. This is the one type of holism with which the individualists have no real problems. The terminology of social wholes is acceptable to the individualists as long as the explanations of phenomena are rendered in terms of individuals (Phillips, 1976: 44).

12   Ontological relationism is based on the premise that what is real are the relationships among individuals, groups, and society. Individuals, groups, or society cannot exist without social relationships. Epistemological relationism contends that our knowledge of the social world and the concepts that we fashion to know that world must be formulated in terms of the relationship between individuals, groups, and society.

13   Udehn (1987: 33), operating with a conventional sense of the split between holism and individualism, regards these paired elements as incompatible and irreconcilable.

14   Despite the difficulties involved in equating micro–meso–macro terminology with individual–group–society, we will often use the two sets of terms interchangeably in the remainder of this chapter.

15   This type, however, might be more like the type of social psychology to be discussed below.

16   Even Hilbert's (1990) effort within the ethnomethodological tradition to transcend the micro–macro relationship can be included under relationism. His position is relational in the sense that conversation (micro) and structures (macro) are generated simultaneously in interaction.

17   Although those relations are different from those of concern, individualism and holism deal with relations. Individualism includes interest in intraindividual as well as interindividual relations. Holism includes concern for relations among social wholes. Neither however, deals with the micro–meso–macro relationship.

FROM EXCLUSION TO INCLUSION TO CHAOS (?) IN SOCIOLOGICAL THEORY

It was not that many years ago that American sociological theory[1] was dominated by a single perspective – structural functionalism (Davis, 1959; Gouldner, 1970). There were other theoretical orientations (most notably, symbolic interactionism), but they and their adherents tended to be marginalized and excluded from both the intellectual center of sociology and positions of power within the discipline.

Famously, structural functionalism came under siege in the 1950s and 1960s and its decline created space for the emergence of a number of other theoretical perspectives and, eventually, their inclusion within the mainstream of the discipline. By the 1970s a number of theories dotted the landscape of sociology. Yet, it was possible to identify a few well-defined paradigms, each with two or more theoretical components, that defined the discipline (see Chapter 3). The comparative openness of a multiple paradigm science was welcomed by many after years of hegemony by a single perspective. However, it is important to remember that this was still a period of limited theoretical options. And theorists were still constrained, at least after they had opted into one of the extant theoretical orientations. There was still great pressure on a theorist to choose a perspective and, once having chosen one, to remain within its confines. In the ensuing decade other theories came of age, but it was still possible to define a limited number of perspectives within sociological theory (and paradigms within sociology).

However, in the last decade, or so, all of what came before in sociological theory has been called into question with, among other things, the increasing influence of several intertwined perspectives including feminist social theory, multicultural theory, and postmodern social theory. At the minimum, these orientations add innumerable new theorists (Gilman, DuBois, and Baudrillard, to mention just one example from each) and theoretical perspectives (radical feminism, queer theory, Foucauldian theory, for example), creating a much more variegated theoretical landscape. More importantly, the positions adopted by these theories have led to much more openness in sociological theory. We have gone from a field dominated by exclusion to one in which inclusion is the watchword. As a result, theorists have many more options, and there is less need to choose a single perspective as one's own, but it is also a confusing world with what, to many, looks like far too many choices. Furthermore, feminist and multicultural theory call into question what we have previously considered to be important theoretical positions by reinterpreting them as the products of white male power politics. And all of them, but especially postmodern social theory, lead to a questioning of what have long been considered the basic premises of sociological theory. The result is a wide open theoretical world – one that is so open and contested that it borders on, if it has not already descended into, chaos.

This issue is of special interest to me since I have spent a good portion of my academic life seeking to map and remap social theory. It is clearly increasingly difficult to do such a survey. The old signposts are fading and need to be relegated to a map of a bygone world. Complicating matters is the fact that many of the perspectives that have the potential to be the new signposts refuse to be recognized as such, are difficult to locate with any precision, and, in any case, contest the whole idea of social theory, let alone the mapping of it. Paradigmatic here is Michel Foucault who wrote, in a now-famous quotation, 'Do not ask who I am and do not ask me to remain the same ... More than one person, doubtless like me, writes in order to have no face' (in Miller, 1993: 19). These constitute problems for those of us interested in such maps, and in mapping more generally. And the inability to offer a map does constitute problems for theorists, especially those who are just starting out in the field. But, the real problem is not the lack of a map, but the disorder, if not chaos, in sociological theory. It has created either a crisis, a unique opportunity, or some combination of the two, but whatever it turns out to be from the vantage point of the future, it means even bigger changes are in store for sociological theory and sociology more generally.

We should not be surprised by the current state of sociological theory since it, and sociology more generally, is always a reflection of the larger society. For example, George Huaco (1986) linked the hegemony and later decline of structural functionalism to the changing fortunes of the United States in the world order. The later multiparadigmatic state of sociology could be seen as a reflection of the emergence of multiple power centers on the world stage. Today, it is clear that feminism and multiculturalism are powerful forces within American society and it is not surprising that they are reflected in the changing structure of sociological theory. More generally, a convincing case could be made[2] that we are moving beyond modern society into a postmodern age and, again, it is no surprise that sociological theory is reflecting this change with the growing importance of postmodern social theories.

In seeking to better understand theoretical perspectives metatheoretically, we always need to consider both the external-social and external-intellectual contexts. In this case, the current state of sociological theory is a result of changes, as we have seen, in society (the coming of a postindustrial, postmodern social world) as well as in surrounding intellectual fields (postmodernism, feminism, and multiculturalism developed largely, at least at first, in neighboring disciplines). The other two major sets of factors to take into account in a metatheoretical analysis of the current state of social theory are the internal-social (e.g. the entry of many more women and other minority group members into sociology; the resulting decline in the importance of elite invisible colleges, schools, and networks; the reduced importance of having degrees from elite schools, and so on) and the internal-intellectual (e.g. the declining importance of schools of thought in sociological theory) (see Chapter 1).

It is easy to criticize sociological theory as it existed in 1950, or even 1975, but theory in those days had many attractions. It was relatively easy for a newcomer to sociological theory, or an observer of the theoretical scene, to get a sense of the landscape and of its single predominant theory, or of the relatively few important theories that dotted the terrain. If one wanted to choose a particular theoretical orientation, it was a relatively uncomplicated process. In fact, it may have been preordained by one's choice of a graduate school and a mentor. Having chosen, or stumbled into, a particular perspective, it was a simple matter to pick out the competitors (if any existed) and to position oneself *vis-à-vis* each of them. Most importantly, working within the relative safety of a given theory, it was possible to flesh out and expand that orientation. Theory-building was relatively easy in such an environment.

However, there are also many liabilities associated with such a theoretical world. In a field dominated by one theory there is virtually no choice, and even with multiple paradigms there is great pressure to choose one theoretical perspective over all of the others. It is difficult to adhere to, or even work with, two or more perspectives, or to 'leap' from one to another as the need arises (see Chapter 3). And, it is even more difficult to eschew all of the alternatives and adopt an independent theoretical stance. Having chosen a given perspective, one is led to work within it and to defend it from adherents of other perspectives. A competition emerges among the supporters of each of the perspectives and much effort is devoted to, or wasted on, gaining a position of preeminence within sociological theory. This leads to warfare between theories, most of it unproductive if not counterproductive. Perhaps the most important point to be made about such a theoretical universe, from the point of view of this chapter, is that it is inherently constraining of the individual theorist who is under pressure to choose a theory, work within it, defend it from external attack and, in turn, attack competing perspectives.

In contrast to the situation in the past, today's theorists need not be constrained by *any* theoretical perspective. The old schools of social theory are disappearing and departments that trained people in a particular perspective are all but gone. Most students today are taught the fundamentals of a range of theories. As a result, few emerge from graduate training with a specific theoretical identity and those who do are likely to shuck it very quickly. It's an open field for today's theorists who are free to pick and choose ideas from the entire field of social theory. They can put together a perspective of their own based on ideas drawn eclectically from many different theories (this is a good description of what Anthony Giddens, among others, has done). Or, as they move from issue to issue, they can utilize different theoretical perspectives (I have tended to do this in my work, drawing on Marx, Weber, Simmel, the postmodernists, and so on). And, one can still even choose to identify with, and work within, a single theoretical perspective. Unlike in the past, however, there is little or no pressure to do so and thinkers are free to move in and out of such a perspective as they see fit. There is also no need to blindly defend it or to mindlessly attack competing perspectives.

One by-product of this situation is that today's theorists have an unprecedented number of theoretical ideas from which to choose. Previously, one was largely limited to the ideas internal to the perspective one had opted into. Now, the entire range of theoretical perspectives is open to everyone. This means that theorists simply have a lot more lenses at their disposal and with which to examine the social world. They are going to see a lot more things and they are going to be able to look at those things in many different ways and from many different angles. This means that we are going to have much more powerful theories which yield far greater insight into the social world.

Yet this is not a comfortable world, and while that discomfort can be a strength (it can be seen as a kind of 'energizing disarray'; among other things, it serves to prevent theoretical complacency), it can also be a serious problem. It is becoming increasingly difficult for theorists to know precisely where they stand, to say nothing of where all other theorists stand. Those who seem to be in one place at a given point in time are likely to be somewhere else the next time one looks (think of Jeffrey Alexander's theoretical gyrations into and out of neofunctionalism). No one, including oneself, seems to stand for anything theoretically, at least not for long. More generally, a theorist no longer can rely on a stable set of like-minded thinkers. There is no comfortable theoretical home in which one can embed oneself. At the same time, there is also no stable set of theoretical antagonists in opposition to which one can define oneself. The 'we' and 'they', the insiders and the outsiders, in sociological theory are no longer so clear-cut.[3] Theorists are being asked to operate in a highly ambiguous world.

Further complicating matters for today's social theorist is the fact that feminist theory, multiculturalism, and postmodern social theory are questioning all of the extant theoretical perspectives and even the enterprise of theory itself. Feminists argue that important feminist theorists have been ignored and that women have not been taken into account in extant theories (Lengermann and Niebrugge-Brantley, 1998). Not only has feminist theory been legitimated, but an extraordinary number and variety of feminist social theories have come to the fore. Similarly, the multiculturalists argue that the work of theorists from many different groups has been ignored or dismissed and that representatives of these groups have not heretofore been integrated into sociological theory. The result has been a flowering of multicultural theories from the black, Chicano, and gay communities, among many others. Works that would never have been thought of as theory are now readily accepted as such. As a result, whole new styles of theoretical work have been legitimated. Many of those associated with feminist and multicultural theory have been heavily influenced by postmodern theory, but the latter has also had a powerful impact of its own on sociological theory (Rogers, 1996).

Postmodernists, too, challenge not only specific sociological theories, but sociological theory more generally, as well as sociology itself. The reasons for these challenges are well known and get to the heart of postmodern theory. Many sociological theories (for example, Marxian theories of capitalism; Weberian theories of increasing rationalization) are attacked for offering grand narratives of, say, the history of the Western world with the result that alternative stories of that development have been stifled. Similarly, other types of narratives have also been muffled. Traditional sociological theories (e.g. structural functionalism and symbolic interactionism) are also attacked for being totalizations purporting to be able to explain all there is to know about the social world. Sociological theories are seen as often based on essentialistic views of human nature (the rational choice that lies at the heart of rational choice theory) that are of dubious legitimacy and in any case serve to exclude other types of human beings. Then there are attacks on sociological theory for its tendency toward scientism (especially in perspectives like rational choice and exchange theory) which also tends to be exclusionary and, in any case, does not seem to have led to any great advances, let alone breakthroughs, in knowledge. Finally, sociological theories are seen as insular and not being open to other sociological perspectives, to say nothing of theories in other disciplines. Ultimately, the postmodernists would reject the whole idea of a sociological theory, not only for the reasons listed above, but also because they would question both the idea of theory as a distinctive undertaking (even though that is what they usually do themselves) as well as the idea that there is anything that can clearly be delineated as sociological and differentiated from neighboring disciplines.

If one were to accept all of these critiques, then little or nothing would be left of sociological theory; there would be nothing but a void where sociological theories once thrived. However, those theories, such as they are, are still (perhaps dimly) there and new ones have been, and are being, added. The flowering of feminist and multicultural social theories is supplemented by the fact that the postmodernists are explicitly and implicitly adding their own perspectives to the burgeoning list of theories. Foucault, Baudrillard, Derrida, Virilio, and many others have, perhaps inadvertently, created perspectives that look to many observers a lot like social theories. Indeed, it could be argued that these critics of all theory, perhaps especially sociological theory, have done more than any others in recent years to revive social theory and to contribute whole new ways of thinking about the social world.

Take Baudrillard, for example. This arch-critic of theory and of sociology has worked with, and popularized, a series of ideas that a number of sociological theorists have found quite intriguing, including fatal strategies, political economy of the sign, the code, seduction, implosion, symbolic exchange, and simulations. We would anticipate much theorizing on these and other ideas[4] and the development of something like a Baudrillardian paradigm with multiple theories emerging under that heading.

So we have a perspective that is pronouncing the death of theory, but is itself giving birth to a set of theories that show every sign of developing further in the future. All of the extant theories that have been attacked by postmodern theory continue to exist, although their underpinnings have been severely shaken by that critique. Multiculturalism and feminist theory have similarly shaken existing theories and produced a profusion of their own ideas and perspectives. The net result is a confusing, even chaotic, domain of social and sociological theory in which all theories seem to be built on beds of sand and every theory is contested, as is theory itself. Nevertheless, theories persist and even increase in number and diversity.

We no longer exclude very much from social theory. To put it another way, we have moved from an exclusionary world to one which is willing to include almost anyone, almost any set of ideas. Any examination of overviews of multicultural, feminist, and postmodern theories yields innumerable works that not only would not have been considered theories not too long ago, but would have been seen as antitheoretical. This is a very different, much more democratic world and it is one with a plethora of fresh ideas and perspectives. The trick will be to be able to revel in the chaos rather than being put off or overwhelmed by it. Many older theorists may find themselves in the latter categories, but the younger generations have been socialized in such a way that they will be better able to use the chaos to their advantage. Like it or not, we are not going back to a safe world of a single dominant paradigm or even of a limited number of paradigms. Multiculturalism, feminism, and postmodernism have opened a Pandora's box that, once open, cannot be shut again.

So, what we have is a new world of theory which is free, confusing, chaotic, and lacking in anything that a thinker can hold on to as a base or as an incontrovertible truth. Even the idea of truth itself is hotly contested. In fact, given this description, it could be argued that whatever we think of postmodern social theory, we have entered the postmodern era in sociological theory. If this is an accurate description, then the implications for the practice of sociological theory are obviously enormous.

What can theorists accomplish in such an environment? One thing they clearly cannot do is 'advance' a theoretical perspective. Such a notion is based on the dubious idea of the existence of a well-defined theoretical perspective. And it is based on the even more dubious idea that there is such a thing as progress toward some ultimate goal of full knowledge or a fully elaborated theoretical perspective. But if today's theorists cannot advance knowledge, they can gain new insights into the social world and they can create new theoretical ideas. On the one hand, they can use any theoretical idea to analyze heretofore unanalyzed aspects of the social world. Similarly, they can use two or more such ideas, in combinations not employed previously, to yield new insights. On the other hand, immersion in a wide range of theoretical ideas, as well as analysis of their applicability to the social world, could well yield new theoretical ideas. The measure of theory today must be the creation of new insights and new ideas rather than advancing some theoretical perspective. These new insights and ideas do *not* necessarily represent advancement. They are simply new, different, useful for a time, and ultimately to be altered or discarded for newer and more useful ideas and insights.

In many ways this is a much tougher theoretical world in which to operate. It was much easier to adopt a theoretical perspective, learn all there was to know about it, and then seek to extend it in various directions. This was reasonably close to what Kuhn (1962; 1970b) called 'normal science' as that notion is applied to theoretical work. Today, however, few of us have, or even want, the safe haven of a theoretical paradigm whose frontiers we can explore and develop further. Rather, we are more or less on our own in theory, working and reworking a set of theoretical ideas in order to come up with something new and useful. Clearly, it is far more difficult to labor on one's own in an effort to produce something new than it was to work within a well-defined group of theorists (school, invisible college, and the like) in order to flesh out an extant theoretical paradigm. We are largely out there on the tightrope on our own and we are working without a net. It is a risky, uncomfortable world, but it is a world that offers the theorist some unprecedented opportunities to create new ideas and new insights into the social world in exchange for the risks.

While there is an openness and a diversity that most would welcome, the big danger is that such fluidity will end with it being impossible to define sociological theory, as well as any specific theories. Do we need a distinctive domain known as sociological theory? Do we need specific theories?

In some senses we need neither. The idea of a theory is derived from the natural sciences and the notion that it would be possible to create a perspective, like Einstein's theory of relativity, that explained a large portion of social reality and could be used to make predictions about the future. While a few contemporary sociologists adhere to such a view, in the main our failure, after almost two centuries of trying (assuming we take as our starting point Comte's definition of sociology in the early part of the nineteenth century and his subsequent effort to develop such a theory), has led most social theorists to recognize the futility of such an effort (Halfpenny, forthcoming). The critiques mounted by supporters of multiculturalism, feminism, and postmodernism led many others to this view. If such explanation and prediction is not the goal, then for what do we need theory? It could be argued that the whole idea of theory has led to an artificial and largely dysfunctional distinction between theoretical and empirical sociology; between theorists and other types of social analysts. In fact, of course, none of these can function without the others. Thus, the 'end of theory' would represent the recognition of the historic failure of the scientific base upon which our most basic notions of theory were based, as well as of the dysfunctions associated with such a separable enterprise.

Yet, whatever its liabilities, the existence of something called theory has contributed importantly to sociology. From my perspective, one of the most important of those contributions has been the generation of new ideas. There is something about working within theory in general, and a given theory in particular, and differentiating one's perspective from those of competitors, that leads to the generation of new ideas. There is an analogy, once again, to some aspects of Kuhnian theory in the sense that there are advantages to working within the confines of a (theoretical) paradigm, most importantly inhabiting a safe and comfortable base from which to generate new ideas. Furthermore, the Kuhnian perspective also recognizes the dynamism associated with multiple paradigmatic perspectives and the need to strengthen one's perspective while defending it from the assault of others. All of that, as well as the new theoretical ideas that sprung from it, would be lost were we to witness the end of theory.

The fact that we are even entertaining the possibility of the end of theory is reflective of the chaotic situation in which sociological theory finds itself. Many observers in the past have discussed a state of 'crisis' in sociological theory (Gouldner, 1970), but whether or not those were genuine crises, it seems clear that we are in the midst of one now. It is not likely that theory as we have known it will survive this crisis, and it may even be that theory itself will succumb. Turmoil can either prevent meaningful work in theory, or be a unique opportunity to create some exciting new perspectives. My guess is that once this particular crisis is over (and there will be others), we will look back on it from a very different intellectual landscape and view it as a period in which crisis proved to be more constructive than destructive. But, that may be little consolation for those of us who are trying to get our theoretical bearings, and to do theoretical work, at the beginning of a new millennium.

Notes

This chapter appears for the first time in this volume. I would like thank Doug Goodman for his assistance with it.

1 This chapter falls within the domain of sociological metatheorizing, specifically M_u, that is metatheorizing in order to gain a better understanding of sociological theory.

2 A good case can also be made that modernity is still with us, or that modernity and postmodernity coexist, and have done so for some time.

3 There is a long tradition of theoretical work on this issue including Simmel on the stranger, Elias on the established and outsiders, and Bauman on various types of insiders and outsiders.

4 Works already in existence that have been strongly affected by Baudrillard's ideas are Gottdiener (1997) and Ritzer (1999).

8

THE IMPLICATIONS
OF POSTMODERN SOCIAL
THEORY FOR METATHEORIZING
IN SOCIOLOGY

There exists an implicit tension or ambivalence in postmodern (and the closely related poststructuralist) thought concerning the status of metatheorizing. On the one hand, many scholars we associate with postmodern and poststructuralist theory practice a form of metatheorizing since they theorize about theory. For example, Michel Foucault (1966/1973), mainly in his archaeological phase, advocated studying the rules that govern and construct theoretical and scientific discourse within specific historical and social contexts. Certainly such works as *Madness and Civilization* (Foucault, 1965) and *The Birth of the Clinic* (1975) exemplify this orientation toward discourse. Indeed, even in his genealogical work Foucault (1969, 1971/1976) focused on the historical struggles over the systems of rules that govern discourse.

On the other hand, much of postmodern social theory stands in opposition to metatheorizing in sociology. For one thing, most postmodernists have a disinclination to even mention their theoretical precursors, let alone analyze their work in a systematic fashion. The demand that metatheorizing be done systematically would seem far too constraining to the generally freewheeling postmodern thinkers. Thus, Baudrillard's (1983/1990) 'pataphysics' ('science' of imaginary solutions), his orientation to what has been described as science fiction (Best and Kellner, 1997), and his propensity in later work to write books composed of seemingly unrelated aphorisms, all have little or nothing of a systematic character about them. For another, metatheorizing, as we will see, involves disciplinary and epistemological distinctions that postmodernists eschew. And, metatheorizing has at least some associations with the kind of scientific perspective that postmodernists reject as being related to a modernist perspective. For example, one of the founders of metatheorizing, Paul Furfey (1953/1965), defined metasociology (of which metatheory is a part) as an 'auxiliary science which furnishes the methodological principles presupposed by sociology'.

Nonetheless, postmodern social theory offers an array of new tools and perspectives to those interested in doing metatheoretical work. Metatheorists do not need to buy into the entire perspective to find ideas that would be of utility to them. Nor do they have to take postmodernism's ambivalence toward their approach to mean that they cannot borrow ideas from it or learn from its critical perspectives. Thus, the goal in this chapter is to ransack postmodern social theories for ideas that should prove useful to those interested in new approaches to doing metatheorizing in sociology. This parallels the case in social theory where one need not necessarily buy into the entire perspective in order to see the utility of a variety of specific postmodern ideas and insights.[1] Thus, one does not have to accept the Baudrillardian perspective, especially in its late, mad form, in order to see the utility of thinking about the social world from the point of view of ideas like simulacrum, hyperreality, and implosion.

We can divide this chapter into three sections. In the first we look to postmodern theory for a series of conceptual tools that can help metatheorists in their study of theoretical work. In the second, we turn to a related set of ideas that are useful in doing more critical analyses of theory. Finally, while we address metatheorizing in general in the first two sections, in the last section we take a more focused, albeit brief, look at the implications of postmodern social theory for the three specific types of metatheoretical work.

Conceptual Tools

Text

Postmodernists accord great importance to the notion of 'texts'. This is seemingly not problematic from the point of view of metatheoretical work since metatheorists would certainly acknowledge that they study theoretical texts. Nevertheless, postmodernists and poststructuralists tend to write about texts in a very specific way. For example, Roland Barthes (1977: 155–64; see also Mowitt, 1992), in his essay 'From Work to Text', formulates a seven-point manifesto in which he distinguishes 'the work' from 'the Text'.

First of all, Barthes points out that while other critics posit the onto-logical reality of the work (see below for a discussion of the work and metatheorists' traditional concern with it) as an object of consumption by the reader, the perspective of textuality consists of a methodological imperative that encourages the role of the active, productive reader. According to Barthes, 'the work is a fragment of substance, occupying part of the space of books (in a library, for example), the Text is a methodological field ... or again, *the Text is experienced in an activity of production*' (1977: 157) while 'the work is normally the object of a consumption' (1977: 161). Metatheorists have tended to consume theoretical works, but this orientation accords the metatheorist (and other readers) a much more active role in the production of the text. In the main this implies that metatheorizing can be a much more active and creative enterprise.

Second, for Barthes 'the Text is that which goes to the limit of the rules of enunciation (rationality, readability, etc.) ... the Text tries to place itself very exactly *behind* the limit of the *doxa*' (1977: 157–8). In other words, embracing textuality entails pushing metatheorizing to the limits of rationality and readability in order to gain a new, often critical, perspective on prevailing opinion. A critical orientation would not be new to metatheoretical work, but pushing the limits of rationality and readability would. Metatheorists, like most social theorists, have tended to be slavish in their efforts to make rational arguments and to put them in as readable a form as possible. Playing with the limits of rationality and readability might lead to some creative new metatheoretical work.

Third, '*the Text' plays* with the '*infinity* of the signifier' while 'the work closes on a signified' (1977: 158). In this passage, Barthes shifts the emphasis of criticism from the signified, or the idea or concept to which words purportedly refer, to the signifier – the 'sound-image' or the word itself. Barthes here opposes the referentiality of the work (and metatheorists' traditional analysis of it) to the poetics of textuality. Metatheoretical work has been notably short on such 'poetics' and more poetic metatheorizing might be refreshing, to say nothing of offering the possibility of novel insights.

Fourth, according to Barthes, 'The Text is plural ... it answers not to an interpretation, not even a liberal one, but to an explosion, a dissemination' (1977: 159). Here Barthes argues that, in his version of textual criticism, the productive activity of the reader and the emphasis on the signifier lead to proliferation of meaning, rather than to a consensus on the essential meaning of a work. This would mark a significant shift for metatheorists who have traditionally been oriented to finding the 'essence' of a work or theorist under study, as well as coming to a consensus about that essence. Instead, Barthes's position here implies the search for many different views on the essence or meaning of a text.

Fifth, Barthes contends that his orientation toward 'the Text' deposes the authority of the author in favor of the creativity of the reader. 'The author is the reputed father and the owner of his work' while 'As for the Text, it reads without the inscription of the Father' (1977: 160–1). This has implications similar to those of Barthes's first point. Metatheorists, as readers, would accord much less importance to what the author of a theoretical text intended and this would serve to free their own interpretive skills.

Sixth, Barthes brings together the above points: 'The Text (if only by its frequent "unreadability") decants the work (the work permitting) from its consumption and gathers it up as play, activity, production, practice' (1977: 162). Closely related to previous points, metatheorists are freed not only to do their interpretations, but also to do them more actively, even playfully. Playfulness has been something virtually completely absent from metatheoretical work and freeing the analyst to deal with texts under study more playfully might yield unusual and useful insights.

Finally, Barthes suggests that his orientation toward 'the Text' enables the reader to experience *jouissance*, an erotic enjoyment, both 'extreme and disconcerting' (Sturrock, 1979: 72). 'As for the Text, it is bound to *jouissance*, that is to a pleasure without separation' (1977: 164). It is hard to think of the kinds of texts studied by metatheorists as yielding 'erotic enjoyment', but nonetheless metatheorizing that reflects more enjoyment, more pleasure would at least be welcome and perhaps produce some interesting new perspectives.

In short, 'the Text', as a methodological orientation to reading and writing, rather than an ontological reality, encourages action, productivity, and play, while the work exists as authority, consumption, and closure. Metatheorists, however, have tended to focus on 'works', especially 'masterworks': that is, important pieces authored by specific social thinkers. The latter often lead to metatheoretical work that focuses on specific works and how they relate to the biographical characteristics of the author (see the 25 essays on theorists and their theories in Ritzer, 2000a; Pampel, 2000). Thus, one might seek to relate Weber's interest in bureaucracy, Calvinism and the conflict between them to the orientations of his parents and their fundamental disagreements (Mitzman, 1969). This involves an effort to find the fundamental 'meaning' or explanation of a work in the essential character and experiences of the author. Postmodernism generally points us away from the idea that a work has an essential meaning. If we take Barthes's notion of 'Text' seriously, this would lead metatheorists to write about sociological theory in a way that would highlight the plurality of the classics, for example. This might provide a fruitful way of pursuing metatheory as a prelude to the development of new theories, or Ritzer's M_p (1991b). In addition, the notion of textuality leads us away from a focus on the author and to the text and its relationship to other texts (*intertextuality*; see below). As Jameson (1991: 77) puts it, 'the autonomous work … along with the old autonomous subject or ego – seems to have vanished, to have been volatized'. The notion of 'the Text' encourages theorists to view instances of theory as a tissue or woven fabric in which many 'quotations without inverted commas' form layers of signification and in which many 'influences' interpenetrate (Barthes, 1977: 160). In this view, the interweaving of many threads of theory recombines signifiers in such a way that 'the Text' allows for infinite rereading and rewriting.

Intertextuality

While textuality and intertextuality are not new to metatheorists, what is new to them is the idea that they ought *not* to search for the under-lying meaning of a work, especially through a greater understanding of the author of that work. After all, virtually all metatheorists have been modernists committed to a search for just such an underlying meaning. A good example of someone who devoted much attention to the thinker as a way of getting at the hidden meaning of a text is Alvin Gouldner (1965: 170–1) who argued, 'Some social scientists are interes-ted in studying industrial workers; some study physicians; and still others, drug addicts and prostitutes. I happen to be curious about social theorists, as part of a sociology of social science.' More specifi-cally, Gouldner looks at such things as a sociological theorist's training, institutional affiliations, career patterns, and positions within sociology. Gouldner believes that it is important to understand the theorist if we want to understand the theory since 'much of theory-work begins with an effort to make sense of one's experience' (1970: 484). This is the kind of perspective that postmodernists would say is badly in need of 'decentering' (see the discussion of decentering below).

Although not to this point done to any great extent by post-modernists, there have been many intertextual analyses in metatheory. Thus, in the volume mentioned above (Ritzer, 2000a), the authors also relate theorists' work to their intellectual context, including related works. More generally, some metatheorists (e.g. Sorokin, 1928; Tiryakian, 1979; 1986) have looked at 'schools of thought' within social theory and that implies, among other things, a concern with what serves to unify various works associated with specific theoretical approaches as well as what differentiates them as a set from other theoretical schools. Similarly, the various paradigmatic analyses of sociology have tended to focus on commonalities among sets of theoretical works as well as what serves to differentiate one set from other sets of such work. Let us use Ritzer's work on sociology's multiple paradigms (Chapter 3) and architectonics (Chapter 2) to illustrate this point.

Ritzer argued that sociology is a multiple paradigm science com-posed of three major paradigms – social facts, social definition, and social behavior. Each paradigm is characterized by, among other things, a distinctive set of theories. Thus, the social facts paradigm, given its focus on Durkheimian social facts, encompasses structural functional-ism, conflict theory, and systems theory. An intertextual analysis of these theories reveals a number of commonalities, especially the fact that they all take social facts as their focal concern. The social definition paradigm encompasses such theories as action theory, symbolic interactionism, phenomenological sociology, and ethnomethodology. Intertextual analysis of these theories indicates that they share a concern for the definition of the situation and resulting action. Finally, the social behavior paradigm focuses on relatively automatic behavior and intertextual analysis reveals that exchange theory and behavioral sociology (and perhaps now rational choice theory) share such an orientation. Thus, intertextual analysis reveals three theory clusters, the components of each of which have a number of important things in common. Furthermore, this intertextual analysis reveals fundamental differences among the three clusters of theory and these differences are at least as consequential as the similarities within clusters.

Similarly, in Ritzer's work on architectonics he sought to outline the six basic elements of one basic architectonic through an intertextual analysis of the work of Marx, Weber, Simmel, and Berger and Luckmann. This revealed a basic underlying commonality in their work. At the same time, it is suggested at the end of Chapter 2 that there are other architectonics in social theory that serve to distinguish among groups of social theorists. This work on paradigms and architectonics illustrates the point that metatheorists have long been practitioners of intertextual analysis.

However, while metatheorists have done a great deal of intertextual work, it is usually with the objective of finding the deeper meaning underlying the texts being studied. The notions of a paradigm and an architectonic carry with them that sort of implication. In uncovering sociology's basic paradigms one is seeking to get at some hidden but essential meanings that are crucial to understanding the commonalities among theories and differences between sets of theories. More generally, the overall structure of sociology's paradigms reveals essential characteristics of the field as a whole such as the fact that because there are multiple paradigms, there is no single dominant paradigm and therefore normal science is all but impossible. In getting at the architectonic that undergirds the work of a group of theorists, the metatheorist is similarly getting at the idea that there is a hidden but essential commonality that helps to unify their contributions and to account for similarities in their substantive work.

Discourse

Most scholars associate the analysis of discourse with the work of Michel Foucault. Metatheorists interested in the analysis of discourse would likely find Foucault's (1969, 1971/1976) ideas quite useful. In *The Archaeology of Knowledge*, Foucault discusses discourse in many different ways, and eventually settles on a rather cryptic definition: 'We shall call discourse a group of statements in so far as they belong to the same discursive formation ... it is made up of a limited number of statements for which a group of conditions of existence can be defined' (1969, 1971/1976: 117). And again, 'the term discourse can be defined as the group of statements that belong to a single system of formation' (1969, 1971/1976: 107). At another point in the same book, Foucault discusses discourse as a way of organizing concepts, regrouping objects of study, and types of enunciation, the combination of which produces themes or theories, which he also calls 'strategies' (1969, 1971/1976: 64). In contrast to Roland Barthes's ideas about 'the Text', the analysis of discourse, while possibly employing the strategies of textuality and intertextuality, raises the level of analysis. The analysis of discourse leads scholars to examine the complex constellations of discourse that emerge under specific social and historical conditions of existence. As such, the analysis of discourse studies 'texts' as artifacts and 'monuments' (1969, 1971/1976) and as evidence of particular historical discursive formations. In other words, Foucault's emphasis was on 'the text' as evidence, rather than on 'the Text' as the site of 'collaboration' between writers and readers (see Barthes, 1977: 163).

Foucault's work would lead metatheorists to focus on the statements, relationships among statements, discursive formations and the rules by which they are formed, the contradictions which exist within discursive formations, and the changing nature of discourse (especially its discontinuities) over time. This, of course, leads the metatheorist away from looking at the relationship between author and work and in the direction of looking at theories as social and linguistic formations.

Foucault's later method of genealogy is famously concerned with the relationship between knowledge and power and would clearly lead metatheorists in the direction of a greater concern for the relationship between power in the field of sociology and the fate of paradigms, theories, and the like. It would also relate the fate and notoriety of theories to issues of power in the larger society. Thus, for example, Huaco (1986) has linked the rise and fall of structural functionalism to the changing nature of the position of the United States in the world order.

Deconstruction

At bottom, deconstruction, as practiced by Jacques Derrida (1974; 1978) and others (e.g. Paul de Man, Gayatri Spivak), is a form of textual criticism that scrutinizes the ways in which texts are constructed. In other words, one can think of deconstruction as the 'reverse engineering' of texts. A deconstructionist critic begins with the finished product, a text or constellation of texts, and proceeds by studying the ways in which various literary devices and strategies of argumentation give the text the impression of working toward a unified coherent whole (as well as working against itself) (Hoy, 1985: 44). Several aspects of deconstruction can be linked to metatheorizing, as follows.[2]

Decentering The operation known as 'decentering' has many fruitful applications in postmodern and poststructuralist thought. First of all, decentering consists of the effort to dislodge the Cartesian fully conscious, knowable, and knowing self from its position of authority in Western thought. 'I think, therefore I am' entrenches an autonomous subject as the center of both knowledge and being. Postmodern and poststructuralist theory is only the most recent attempt to decenter the rational, autonomous subject. Derrida, in his lecture 'Structure, Sign, and Play in the Discourse of the Human Sciences', sees precursors to his own deconstructionist project in 'the Nietzchean critique of metaphysics', 'the Freudian critique of self-presence', and 'the Heideggerean destruction of metaphysics' (1978: 280). To this list others might add Saussure's reformulation of linguistics, which influenced Claude Lévi-Strauss's statement to the effect that 'I believe the ultimate goal of the human sciences to be not to constitute, but to dissolve man' (1966: 247), and Foucault's 'wager that man would be erased, like a face drawn in the sand at the edge of the sea' (1970: 387). Moreover, we can find this theme in other high structuralist texts, such as Roland Barthes's essay 'The Death of the Author' (1977: 142–8). 'To give a text an Author is to impose a limit on that text, to furnish it with a final signified, to close the writing', but to remove the author as the autonomous subject behind the text is to 'liberate what may be called an anti-theological activity, an activity that is truly revolutionary since to refuse to fix meaning is, in the end, to refuse God and his hypostases – reason, science, law' (1977: 147). Louis Althusser's structuralist Marxism adopts a somewhat similar position. Decentering forces such ultimate *author*-ities as God, the Author, Consciousness, and Man into a field of mutually constitutive relationships rather than leaving them at the apex of a hierarchy of knowledge.

Michel Foucault's work elaborates a slightly different type of decentering. In the introduction to his methodological work, *The Archaeology of Knowledge*, Foucault distinguishes his project from that of previous historians and philosophers by arguing: 'A total description draws all phenomena around a single centre – a principle, a meaning, a spirit, a world-view, an overall shape; a general history, on the contrary, would deploy the space of dispersion' (1969, 1971/1976: 10). Foucault replaces 'drawing in to the center' with a 'space of dispersion', and in doing so, he initiates a shift of perspective from centers to fields of relationships in which the margins play an important role.

This would lead metatheorists, among other things, to question the centrality of the thinkers most often included in the canon and to seek out important theorists largely if not completely ignored by the discipline. One sees this most commonly among minority groups where there are ongoing efforts to resuscitate thinkers ignored in their time and to this day because of their minority group status. This is especially notable in feminist theory where efforts are being made to make the case for the central importance of such thinkers as Harriet Martineau (Hoecker-Drysdale, 2000), Charlotte Perkins Gilman (Lemert, 2000), and Marianne Weber (Lengermann and Niebrugge-Brantley, 1998). But efforts to reassess the centrality of long-ignored theorists is not restricted to minority group members; one often sees efforts to bring to the fore heretofore ignored white male thinkers. For example, with the increase in interest in the sociology of consumption there is a resurgence of interest in Thorstein Veblen (Ritzer, 2000b; Ritzer et al., forthcoming; Diggins, 1999). All such efforts are useful, if for no other reason than they prevent us from falling into the habit of trotting out the same old theorists and theories on all occasions. Maximally, we often do find that a forgotten thinker really deserves a more detailed second look.

Locating the Promising Marginal Text   This is obviously related to the notion of decentering. Traditionally, metatheorists would seek out a *central* text and argue that it best exemplifies the thinking of a theorist or of a school of thought. Thus, one might identify *Economy and Society* (Weber, 1921/1968) or *The Protestant Ethic and the Spirit of Capitalism* (Weber, 1904–5/1958) as the text which best gets at the essence (a notion postmodernists would reject) of Weber's thinking. However, the logic of deconstructionism would lead the analyst away from such canonical works and in the direction of more marginal works that might prove more revealing. Thus, it might turn out that a letter written by Weber, or a book review, or even a secondary work (say, *The Agrarian Sociology of Ancient Civilizations*: Weber, 1896–1906/1976) offers unparalleled insights into, or unearths contradictions within, Weber's *oeuvre*.

Many of the same kinds of things can be done in reinterpreting schools of thought. In any school, there are always key texts that are defined as standing at the core of a given theoretical perspective. A good example is Merton's (1949/1968) essay 'Manifest and Latent Functions', which is usually viewed as the central document in structural-functional theory. However, great dividends, including a better understanding of that theory, might result if a metatheorist looked at less well-known pieces by Merton or, better yet, positioned Merton's work in a field of discourse or space of dispersion that included the marginal texts and perspectives against which structural functionalism defined itself. Even more might be gained by the study of long-ignored texts in the structural-functional tradition.

And of course, there are the theories that never made it, or were central at one time but have lost their following. Among the latter, as mentioned above, action theory comes to mind as a theory that was of some significance in the early twentieth century, but is all but forgotten today. Revisiting that theory and some of the major thinkers associated with it (e.g. Florian Znaniecki) might pay enormous dividends.

This form of decentering could also be practiced more microscopically. Certain passages of specific works are often presented by the authors in such a way that they are made to seem of central importance. Over the years, secondary analysts have tended to emphasize those passages, or to enshrine other passages, as being of key importance. In this context, deconstructionism leads one away from the familiar passages and into ignored portions of the text or perhaps rarely read footnotes. A similar implication applies to the secondary literature on a theory or theorist. Certain pieces (e.g. Parsons's *The Structure of Social Action*, 1937) achieve their own canonical status and are almost always cited by later analysts. However, the secondary literature on the most important theorists is vast and a systematic search of it may well turn up some interpretive gems in out-of-the-way places. It can also reveal weaknesses and distortions in the canonical interpretive work.

Disclosing the Undecidable Moment   This takes us more into the history of social theory and an analysis of some of the courses taken and, more importantly from the point of view of deconstructionism, *not* taken by social theory. At the micro level this might lead us into the biographies of specific theorists and why they chose one direction rather than another. For example, we might want to study why Talcott Parsons chose to move in the direction of the macro-oriented structural functionalism rather than pursuing the micro-implications of his early analysis of the unit act and of action theory. At a more macro level we might be led to wonder why symbolic interactionism in the 1930s and 1940s moved in the more interpretive direction championed by Blumer rather than following Mead's propensity toward a more realist orientation. There are clearly many key moments in this history of social theory and, while we may never be able to 'decide' issues unequivocally, it is useful to plumb these periods for insights into directions chosen and perhaps more importantly those not taken.

Reversing the Resident Hierarchy, only to Displace it   This idea, which as we will see, is a specific form of decentering, has at least four implications for metatheoretical work. First, the reversal of hierarchies in theoretical vocabularies can be taken as an ironic intervention in sociological theory in which theorists realize the inadequacy or fatuity of their characterizations (White, 1978: 1–25). Richard Rorty (1989: 73–95), for example, exalts the reversals and negations of the ironist because they lead us to doubt received theoretical vocabularies and they remind us that things can always be seen in different ways. Clearly the leading schools of thought or theoretical vocabularies are not dominant because they are somehow the 'best' or most representative of social reality. A great deal of social labor goes into producing a dominant way of theorizing, and the reversals recommended by deconstructionists help us to see that the received hierarchies are in many ways inadequate or distorted.

Second, there is clearly a hierarchy of schools of sociological theory and there is a tendency to devote most attention to the leading schools. This suggests that what metatheorists need to do is focus more attention on the most marginal of schools (this is another version of decentering) for their marginality may tell us a great deal about the theoretical system in which they exist. Furthermore, their very marginality may make them far easier to study than high-ranking theoretical perspectives. This is traceable to the fact that those associated with low-ranking perspectives have little to hide while thinkers linked with the premier schools have a vested interest in concealing things that may adversely affect their exalted status.

Third, within every school, even those lowest in the hierarchy, there is a hierarchy of thinkers associated with the perspective. Instead of focusing on the leading thinkers associated with such a perspective, the goal would be to devote more attention to the work of those with little or no status in the area (again, a decentering move).

Fourth, and similarly, specific ideas have come to be seen as of central importance in every theoretical perspective. These specific ideas, for example those associated with Merton's functional paradigm, tend to come to the fore any time a given theory is examined or discussed. However, it is entirely possible that important ideas have been lost and a search for those marginal ideas could pay huge dividends. There is an unfortunate tendency to trot out the same old ideas (and theorists) any time a theoretical perspective is examined. This tendency can be counteracted by a continual effort to unearth ideas that have been shuffled to the bottom of the hierarchy or even lost to history (decentering, yet again).

All of this, as well as much else that involves decentering, relates to the idea of the 'strength of the weak' associated with postmodern social theory (Genosko, 1994). This is usually applied to the 'social' world (although Baudrillard proclaims the death of the social) and the idea that the masses, while lacking in power, actually exert their strength by luring (albeit not consciously) those in power into self-destructive acts.

In de Certeau's (1984) work it involves the view that actors, especially consumers, while seemingly weak, actually have great power. In meta-theorizing, this idea can be taken to mean that it is the seemingly weak theorists, theoretical perspectives, or concepts that actually exercise great power in social theory. Perhaps it is they and their weaknesses that play a greater role (in heretofore unexplored ways) in defining theory than obvious, more powerful candidates that always end up the focus of great attention.

However, the search for low-ranking schools, theorists, or ideas should not be turned into a routine or into a new reverse hierarchy. Deconstructionism leads to the idea that all such routines or hierarchies need to be continually displaced. Such an injunction prevents meta-theoretical work from settling into any comfortable routines; any new construction must immediately be deconstructed.

It is this aspect of deconstructionism that has the most implications for metatheorizing. As modernists, most metatheorists have implicitly engaged in deconstruction, but almost always with the objective that they and/or those influenced by their work would engage in a process of reconstruction. This could involve the rebuilding of the theory they have just deconstructed or the use of the lessons learned to create an entirely new theoretical perspective. As modernists, most metatheorists would reject the idea of deconstruction in order to further deconstruct. Rather, they would be oriented to the modern view of progress toward the goal of the ultimate theoretical perspective. However, as with all modern notions, this seeks an end or closure of the theoretical 'conver-sation' in the creation of that ultimate theory. The postmodern view is that the goal is not to end the conversation in some ultimate truth (since there is none), but rather to continually deconstruct in order to keep the conversation going (Rorty, 1979). Such an objective makes sense for metatheoretical work, in fact it may be the *raison d'être* for such work. One round of metatheoretical work may be seen as merely the basis for the next round of such work and not as aimed at some ultimate and conclusive objective. In these terms metatheorizing may be seen as the exercise *par excellence* in keeping the theoretical conversation going. As we will see below, however, this has similar but slightly different impli-cations for the three varieties of metatheoretical work.

Dismantling in Order to Reconstitute what is Already Inscribed Since postmodern social theory is inherently poststructuralist, this idea is not meant to imply that the already inscribed idea is the 'essence' of a theoretical perspec-tive and once it is uncovered our task as metatheorists is completed. Once that which is already inscribed is reconstituted, the 'goal' (if one can think in terms of a 'goal' from the point of view of deconstruction-ism) would be to seek to reconstitute that which is inscribed in what we have recently reconstituted. Again, there is a sense of metatheorizing as a never-ending process of deconstructing that which we have just deconstructed.

This encourages the metatheorist to see to it that the dismantling of a text in the practice of deconstruction leads to novel translations (or reconstitutions) of that text. In other words, it contributes to the post-structuralist view of the reading of texts as a process in which readers actively *construct* meanings rather than simply discover an intended meaning in a text.

Tools with which to Critically Analyze Social Theory

While all of the above ideas can be used not only analytically but criti-cally, there are a number of postmodern ideas that lead more directly to a critical orientation in metatheoretical work. We can begin with the famous ideas, most often associated with Lyotard, of postmodern social theory's incredulity of grand narratives and totalizations. On the one hand, such an admonition leads us to be wary of many metatheo-retical works that have offered either grand narratives or totalizations. Thus, some postmodernists[3] would be inclined to reject Kuhn's (1962; 1970b) grand narrative of scientific revolutions (paradigm 1, normal science, anomalies, crisis, revolution, paradigm 2) as well as Ritzer's (1975/1980) totalization that sociology was a multiple paradigm science, or in need of an integrated paradigm to supplement extant paradigms (Ritzer, 1981b). This leads us to be as critical of the grand narratives and totalizations of metatheorists as we are of those of theorists. That is to say not that there is not a role for grand narratives or totalizations in sociology, but rather that we need to be aware of their prevalence and of the problems associated with them (e.g. their tendency to exclude more local narratives and perspectives).

More importantly, admonitions like these attune metatheorists to a specific domain for their kind of work. That is, sociological theory is rife with, perhaps even dominated by, grand narratives and totalizations. For example, the grand narrative of emancipation from capitalist exploitation and alienation permeates and even drives the thought of Karl Marx. Metatheorists who take seriously the postmodern incredulity toward metanarratives might ask, to what extent does this grand narra-tive of the emancipation of the 'proletariat' drive or motivate those social theories with a Marxian orientation? And what are the consequences of such unreflective advocacy for such social theorists? Similarly, post-modernists question 'the capitalist narrative of emancipation from poverty through technoindustrial development' (Lyotard, 1988/1993: 25). Certainly a cursory reading of the graduate catalogs of any depart-ment of sociology in the United States would reveal hundreds of advo-cates, in theory and practice, of the study of development. To what extent does the grand narrative of development motivate or drive social theories, and what are the consequences of such advocacy? In fact, one might even question whether these grand narratives, which sometimes compete and sometimes collaborate, provide the ultimate legitimacy for social and sociological knowledge. Raymond Aron (1967: vii) intimated as much when he traced the heritage of sociological thought to the social and political thought of the *philosophes* and the administrative statistics of the British and French states.

In their critique of such orientations, postmodernists have called for more local narratives that avoid the dangers associated with grand narratives. Metatheorists could ascertain the degree to which such calls have been heeded and whether there has been an increase in local narratives (e.g. feminist, black, and queer) in social theory in the last few decades. Also subject to study would be the degree to which local narratives have, in fact, avoided the pitfalls associated with more general approaches. And then there is the issue of the degree to which local narratives have problems of their own.

Metatheorists are also now sensitized to look at specific theories and theoretical perspectives as grand narratives and totalizations. Thinking of specific theories as grand narratives helps us to begin thinking not only about the problems inherent in such an approach, but also about alternatives to such a narrative. For example, one way of thinking about Weber's work is that he offers a grand narrative of increasing (formal) rationalization (see Chapter 9). However, if we accept the limitations of grand narratives in general, and of this one in particular, we are then led to look for alternative formulations such as Foucault's, where a variety of different rationalities are envisioned and deployed (Smart, 2000). Furthermore, we could be led to interrogate and interpret Weber's work differently and emphasize the fact that Weber recognized and studied a number of different rationalities in a number of different domains.

Similarly useful is the idea that most of the major social theories (structural functionalism, exchange theory, conflict theory) have tended to be totalizations. This serves to alert us to the degree to which they are guilty of reaching far beyond their limitations. All social theories can be assessed in an effort to ascertain the degree to which they are totalizations. Michel Foucault (1969, 1971/1976: 10), arguing against Marxists and Hegelians, and to some extent against the historians of the *Annales* school, opposed his approach, which he labeled 'general history', to a 'total description' that 'draws all phenomena around a single centre – a principle, a meaning, a spirit, a worldview, an overall shape'. The critique of 'total history' and 'totalizations' involves a number of complex philosophical issues, but in principle it reflects Foucault's commitment to the study of the history of systems of thought over the philosophy of history. One might even argue that

Foucault at this point favored an empirical (or even empiricist) approach to the study of the history of systems of thought over the more theoretical approaches of Marxists, Hegelians, sociologists, and social historians. If the postmodernists are correct in their critique of totalizations, perhaps what we need to prize more are humbler and narrower social theories, and/or social theories that stick closer to available data. We might need to look again, even though he was far from a postmodernist, at Merton's (1949/1968) ideas on 'middle range' theories and other, similar formulations.

Postmodern social theory also attunes metatheorists to the idea that most, if not all, of the theories they study suffer from foundationalism. That is, they explicitly or implicitly seek to base their theories on a firm and quite specific philosophical foundation. A good example is rational choice theory in sociology and its effort to embed its approach in the utilitarian view of the rational actor. Metatheorists should be critical of the idea that there is one single 'right' philosophical foundation for any sociological theory, or for sociological theory more generally. Relatedly, postmodern social theory sensitizes us to the idea that such a philosophical foundation leads to the belief that there is a particular vocabulary that must be used in sociological theorizing. Thus, rational choice theory has its own terms – 'utilities', 'opportunity costs', and the like – that need to be used in doing work from this theoretical perspective. Postmodernists would oppose the idea that there is a single correct vocabulary in the same way that they would reject the idea that there is a single underlying philosophical base for a social theory.[4]

Similarly, but within the realm of their study of the social world rather than within theory itself, postmodernists critique the fact that social theories operate with an essentialist view of human beings.[5] Thus, metatheorists need to take into account the essentialism that is either explicit or implicit in social theory. For example, Marx's essentialism (see Chapters 2, 5) is quite explicit in his thinking about human actors and their 'species being', as is Coleman's (*Homo economicus*) in his rational choice theory. However, in most other cases, essentialism, while it is certainly there, is far less explicit and needs to be ferreted out by the metatheorist. Thus, Weber (see Chapter 2) certainly has an essentialist view of the actor, but it is not as explicit as that of Marx (or Coleman) and would need to be pieced together out of a number of leads in his work.

While a variety of postmodern ideas have been presented in this section for those metatheorists interested in doing critical analyses of social theory, they need not necessarily be used in this way. That is, these ideas can simply be used as sensitizing devices to alert metatheorists to key aspects of social theory that they must be sure to look at in their examinations.

However, there are other, more extreme ideas that would seem to be inseparable from a critical analysis. Most generally, there is the postmodern rejection of rationality which would lead to a similar rejection of many social theories that focus on rationality (e.g. Weber's), as well as of metatheorizing as an effort to study social theory in a rational manner. Instead, metatheorists might be urged to follow an irrational course suggested by Lyotard (1988/1993) involving anamnesis (specifically, remembering theoretical realities before the modern phase), anamorphosis (making distorted theoretical images), and anagogy (creating mystical interpretations of social theories). To the degree that one accepts such approaches, one would clearly be critical of metatheorizing as it is traditionally practiced. Furthermore, following Lyotard here would lead to a very different, to put it mildly, metatheorizing characterized by purposeful distortion and mysticism. Such a metatheoretical approach would have a hard time gaining acceptance in social scientific fields dominated by rationality and already dubious about metatheoretical work.

Then there are a number of more specific ideas associated with postmodern social theory, or with specific postmodern theorists, that would lead the metatheorist in a critical direction. Take, for example, Baudrillard's (1983) idea of a simulation. In using this idea, one could come to the realization that sociological theories are simulations of theories that exist in the 'hard sciences'. That is, they are modeled after them, but have little or none of their explanatory and predictive power. Thus, social theorists, operating in a self-interested way designed to elevate their collective status in the discipline, can be seen as having erected an edifice of social theory that is little more than a parody of social theory in the higher-status hard sciences (Ritzer, 1998: 45–8). To use another Baudrillardian term, they have created a theoretical system that exists solely in the realm of hyperreality. Such a view would, needless to say, have devastating implications for social theory.

Furthermore, it would also devastate metatheoretical work, at least as it has been generally done in the past. Metatheorists have almost always taken social theories as 'real' theories and treated them quite seriously, if not reverentially. Viewing theories as simulations might lead to a more postmodern, ludic metatheoretical approach to social theory. While it is not clear what might be gained from such a playful approach, it is clear that a less respectful examination of social theories might pay dividends. Perhaps we have been too uncritical of the ease with which we accord idea systems in the social sciences the label of social theory; maybe we need to hold those idea systems to a higher standard. Alternatively, perhaps we need to examine those ideas in a more unvarnished way as systems that do little more than pretend to be theories. Such an extreme critique might lead to the view that there are no theories in the social sciences and there could never be theories, at least in the sense that the term is used in the hard sciences. Alternatively, a debunking of what we now call theory might lead to a more clear-headed examination of what is required to create such theories.

Baudrillard (1976/1993) also makes the case for symbolic exchange and argues that the give-and-take of such an exchange has been lost in the contemporary world. For example, the dead have been ghettoized and separated from the living with the result that the symbolic exchange that characterized the relationship between the living and the dead in 'primitive' societies has been lost. Similarly, it could be argued that the ghettoization of social theory, as well as metatheoretical work, has served to eliminate the symbolic exchange between social theory and the social world, as well as between metatheoretical work and the theories that are analyzed. This would suggest that Bourdieu (see below) is right about 'socioanalysis': metatheoretical work ought to be an inherent part of theoretical work.

Application of Postmodern Social Theory to the Various Types of Metatheorizing

Throughout this chapter we have discussed metatheorizing as if it is of one piece. However, there are three major types of metatheorizing (see Chapter 1) and we need to say at least something about the applicability of postmodern ideas to each of them.

We begin with metatheorizing in order to better understand social theory (M_u). Studying social theory should not be a problem to postmodernists, although they would have serious objections to the idea of attaining a 'better' understanding of theory. This clearly implies modern notions of progress and advancement. Postmodernists might be more comfortable with M_u when the objective is simply the development of more and different perspectives on social theory. The greater the number of perspectives, the greater the understanding, at least from a postmodern view.

Beyond that, postmodernists would make a number of criticisms of specific aspects of M_u. First, in their rejection of boundaries among academic areas, postmodernists would oppose the idea that metatheorizing is somehow a separable undertaking within sociology (as well as many other fields). Of course, they are not alone in this view. Pierre Bourdieu, who practices a form of metatheorizing he calls socioanalysis, is similarly opposed to distinguishing metatheorizing from the practice of sociology. In his view, sociologists should do socioanalysis as they do their sociology (Bourdieu and Wacquant, 1992). This is a reasonable perspective. While there are gains to be made by distinguishing metatheoretical activities from other sociological practices, there is no inherent reason why the two could not be practiced in unison.

Second, postmodernists would similarly reject the idea that theory is something distinguishable from other sociological activities. They would argue that theory cannot be distinguished from other aspects of sociology. Of course, making such distinctions is precisely what has allowed for the development of modern science, but this would not be convincing to postmodernists who are highly critical of modern science. The practice of metatheorizing would be all but impossible if one did not distinguish theory from the rest of sociology; it would become an indistinguishable aspect of metasociology. However, even the latter would presumably be rejected by postmodernists for creating unnecessary boundaries between metasociology and sociology, as well as between sociology and other academic disciplines. By this logic not only metatheorizing, but also sociology itself, become impossibilities.

Third, postmodernists would reject M_u to the degree that it suggests that the study of theory somehow implies the search for some basic and underlying truth about sociological theory in general, or some specific theory or theorist. In fact, much metatheoretical work often has just such an orientation. For example, the search for sociological paradigms implies the notion that a paradigm is one such essential but hidden truth of sociology (see Chapter 3). An even better example is the search for an architectonic that undergirds the work of a number of different social theorists (see Chapter 2).

Finally, the latter implies that even if they had no general objections to metatheorizing in order to attain greater understanding, post-modernists would reject many, if not most, specific metatheoretical works of this type. For example, in the case of the idea that sociology is a multiple paradigm science, postmodernists would reject the idea of distinguishing sociology from neighboring fields, of distinguishing paradigms with sociology, of implying that paradigms are the essence of sociology, and especially the idea that sociology is a science, albeit a particular kind of science with multiple paradigms.

Metatheorizing as a prelude to developing new theory (M_p), and metatheorizing in order to create a new overarching theoretical perspective (M_o), would be criticized for many of the same reasons. Both would also be criticized for erecting boundaries around phases of metatheoretical work: a phase before developing new theory (M_p), as well as one before creating a new overarching perspective (M_o). Furthermore, both imply that M_u is a phase that comes before the other two: one cannot do either M_p or M_o without first doing M_u. M_o would also be criticized for its notion that its goal is the creation of an over-arching theoretical perspective – a metatheory. Clearly, such a goal would be regarded as an example of the kind of totalization that post-modernists reject.

Most generally, the three types of metatheorizing, taken together, suggest some sort of grand narrative. The better understanding of theory will lead to not only the creation of new theory, but also the creation of new metatheories. There is a suggestion here of progress in social theory being produced by the various activities and subgoals implied in metatheorizing in general.

Such an approach would stand in opposition to the postmodern idea that the real goal of metatheoretical work should be to keep the theoretical conversation going. However, it is possible to look at each subtype of metatheoretical work, as well as metatheorizing in general, as oriented to simply maintaining the theoretical conversation. M_u can be seen as being oriented to merely gaining additional understandings of theory, rather than the ultimate, or even a better, understanding. A range of different understandings begets still more and different understandings. The presumption is that better comprehension is associated with an increasing number of diverse understandings. Similarly, M_p can be viewed as an effort to simply add to the arsenal of available theoretical perspectives and not to the creation of *the* theoretical perspective that will come to dominate the discipline. Finally, a similar view is possible of M_o as oriented to the creation of another metatheory to supplement extant metatheories. An example would be postpositivism as a metatheory to supplement positivism, hermeneutics, and so on; or, in Ritzer's work, an integrated paradigm to supplement the social facts, social definition, and social behavior paradigms.

Conclusion

This chapter has been able to do little more than suggest a variety of the implications of postmodern social theory for metatheoretical work. There is much more of relevance within postmodern social theory and there are great differences among postmodern theorists that are worth exploring from a metatheoretical point of view. Furthermore, there are many more general and specific implications for metatheorizing than the relatively small number that we have been able to explore here. However, it is clear that postmodern social theory has a wide range of important implications for metatheorists. At its extreme, postmodern theory could be read as suggesting the abandonment of metatheoretical work (although many postmodernists do such work themselves). Less extremely, and more constructively, postmodern social theory is rich with ideas that can lead metatheoretical work in interesting new directions.

Notes

This chapter, coauthored by James M. Murphy and with the assistance of Doug Goodman, is published here for the first time. It will be published as part of a more general essay on metatheorizing (coauthored with Murphy and Shanyang Zhao) in the forthcoming *Handbook of Sociological Theory* edited by Jonathan Turner.

1   In *Enchanting a Disenchanted World* (Ritzer, 1999), I have used a number of post-modern ideas – reenchantment, implosion, simulation – in what is a highly modern work.

2   This list is derived, in part, from Spivak (1974: lxxvii).

3   Other postmodern thinkers, such as Richard Rorty (1979; 1989), while critical of grand narratives and totalizations, attempt to recover certain aspects of Kuhn's arguments, such as his criticism of positivist philosophies of science.

4   For this reason postmodernists would be critical of the architectronic discussed in Chapter 2.

5   The architectronic discussed in Chapter 2 would be vulnerable to postmodern criticism because of its essentialism.

PART TWO

RATIONALIZATION THEORY

9

RATIONALIZATION
AND DEPROFESSIONALIZATION
OF PHYSICIANS

Sociological theories are often discussed in their own terms in isolation from social changes. While these discussions can be useful, it is important that such theories be linked to the changing social world. The objective in this chapter is to take major components of the Weberian theory of rationalization and apply them to contemporary changes in and around the paradigmatic profession – physicians. As we will see, the application of rationalization theory allows us to gain new insight into what is happening to the medical profession.

The widely known and extremely important developments affecting the medical profession include antitrust decisions, corporatization, conglomeration, bureaucratization, technological change, unionization, and the rise of McDoctors (no-appointment, walk-in medical facilities modeled after fast-food restaurants), third-party payers, health maintenance organizations (HMOs), prospective payment systems based on preset diagnostic related groups (DRGs), and the like.[1] Sociologists have been interested in the nature and significance of these changes as well as how they relate to the professional status of medicine. Unfortunately, the major sociological efforts in this area have not been notably strong theoretically.[2]

In addition to theoretical weaknesses, work in this area has been characterized by conflicting and contradictory conclusions and prognostications. In *The Social Transformation of American Medicine*, Paul Starr (1982) looked at many of the changes enumerated above and forecast a weakening of the sovereignty, the deprofessionalization, of medicine.[3] In contrast, Eliot Freidson (1986) in *Professional Powers* argued that the general idea of professional decline is greatly overstated.

It is our thesis that structural changes (especially as they relate to bureaucracies and capitalism) surrounding the American medical profession are leading to greater external control over it and impelling it in the direction of absorbing many (formally) rational characteristics (Relman and Reinhardt, 1986). This greater external control and internal rationalization are crucial factors in the deprofessionalization of physicians.[4] Such changes could have profound implications for the entire professional category since physicians have for many years been the model profession.[5]

This chapter will be composed of three sections. First, we will briefly delineate those aspects of rationalization theory to be utilized in this analysis (as well as ensuing chapters). Second, we will look at the meaning of the concept of a profession as well as medicine's position as a profession. Third, we will look at the forces that are coming to control the medical profession, impelling it in the direction of increasing (formal) rationalization and, in the process, serving to deprofessionalize physicians.

A Metatheoretical Analysis of Weber's Rationalization Theory

Weber's voluminous work, especially as it relates to the issue of rationalization, is very difficult to analyze. In fact, it is tough to extract a clear definition of *rationalization* from Weber's work. He operated with a number of different definitions of the term, and he often failed to specify which definition he was using in a particular discussion (Brubaker, 1984: 1). Weber did define *rationality*; indeed, he differentiated between two types – means–ends and value rationality. However, these concepts refer to types of *action*. They are the basis of, but not coterminous with, Weber's larger-scale sense of rationalization. Weber is interested in far more than fragmented action orientations; his main concern is with regularities and patterns of action within civilizations, institutions, organizations, strata, classes, and groups. Donald Levine (1981) argues that Weber is interested in 'objectified' rationality: that is, action that is in accord with some process of external systematization.

Of great help in understanding what Weber meant by rationalization is a typology developed almost simultaneously by Kalberg (1980), Levine (1981), and Habermas (1984: 168–72), although it is buttressed, as will be shown, by an independent reading of Weber. Other typologies may be developed and supported by a review of Weber's work, but the one employed here is useful given the purposes of this chapter and accords well with Weber's own statements about rationality.

Practical rationality is to be found in mundane, day-to-day reality and involves the 'worldly interests' of the individual (Weber, 1904–5/1958: 77). The actor accepts the world as it is and seeks to deal with its difficulties in the most expedient way possible (Kalberg, 1980: 1152). In practical rationality, the actor pursues a 'practical end by means of an increasingly precise calculation of adequate means' (Weber, 1958: 293). Elsewhere, Weber contends that practical rationality involves 'the methodical attainment of a definitely given and practical end by means of an increasingly precise calculation of adequate means' (1958: 293). Practical rationality is to be found in all historical epochs and in all societal settings. While everyone is capable of practical rationality, the business classes ('merchants and artisans') have been its distinctive carriers (1958: 279). Later, Weber describes the carriers as the 'civic strata' and describes their rationality as having 'been based upon technological or economic calculations and upon mastery of nature and of man, however primitive the means at their disposal' (1958: 284). This contention about primitive means makes it clear that practical rationality has existed throughout history.

Weber draws a clear distinction between practical and theoretical rationality:

> We have to remind ourselves in advance that 'rationalism' may mean very different things. It means one thing if we think of the kind of rationalization the systematic thinker performs on the image of the world: an increasing theoretical mastery of reality by means of increasingly precise and abstract concepts. Rationalism means another thing if we think of the methodical attainment of a definitely given and practical end by means of an increasingly precise calculation of adequate means. (1958: 293)

While practical rationality is to be found in the mundane world, *theoretical rationality* involves an attempt to transcend that haphazard world by according it some sort of logical meaning. Unlike practical rationality which directly involves action, theoretical rationality involves 'an increasingly theoretical mastery of reality by means of increasingly precise and abstract concepts' (1958: 293). Logical deduction and induction, the attribution of causality, and the arrangement of symbolic meanings are all part of theoretical rationality. While practical rationality must be useful, the products of theoretical rationality need not be of any utility (1921/1978: 67). Like practical rationality, theoretical rationality is found in all epochs and in all societies, but unlike practical rationality not everyone is capable of theoretical rationality. Intellectuals 'have always been the exponents of a rationalism which in their case has been relatively theoretical' (1958: 279). While intellectuals tend to be the 'carriers' of theoretical rationality, others are capable of this type of rationality as well.

Substantive rationality involves the choice of means to ends guided by some broader set of human values. A good example is to be found in Calvinism where one feels as if one is 'fulfilling a duty' in finding the best means to an end (1904–5/1958: 177). Calvinism is a specific form of asceticism which Weber sees as an attempt 'to rationalize the world ethically in accordance with God's commandments' (1958: 291) (or as 'God-willed': 1958: 332). More specifically, Calvinism is a form of inner-worldly asceticism that is characterized by 'methodical and rationalized routine activities of workaday life in the service of the Lord' (1958: 291). Such a value system compels us from without, but it is also internalized in the actor who 'wants' to fulfill the demands of the value system (e.g. 'The Puritan *wanted* to work in a calling': Weber, 1904–5/ 1958: 181).

Focusing more specifically on *economic* substantive rationality, Weber defines this as 'the degree to which the provisioning of given groups of persons (no matter how delimited) with goods is shaped by economically oriented social action under some criterion (past, present, or potential) of ultimate values ... regardless of the nature of these ends' (1921/1978: 85).

Weber also sees substantive rationality operant in law. He discusses the substantive rationality of administration and judiciary practiced by the patrimonial prince in which utilitarian and social ethical blessings are bestowed on the prince's subject 'in the manner of the master of a large house upon the members of his household' (1958: 298). This is contrasted to formally rational law in which trained jurists 'have carried out the rule of general laws applying to all "citizens of the state"' (1958: 299). By this differentiation, Weber appears to mean, at least in part, that substantive rationality is much more arbitrary than formal rationality because the latter is codified in generally applicable laws while substantive law exists solely in the realm of unwritten values. Thus, Weber says that the bureaucracy strives for the 'removal of completely arbitrary disposition of the "chief" over the subordinate official' (1958: 242). However, the key is not its arbitrariness, but rather the fact that substantive law is dominated by values:

> But the contrast to 'substantive rationality' is sharpened, because the latter means that the decision of legal problems is influenced by norms different from those obtained through logical generalization of abstract interpretations of meaning. The norms to which substantive rationality accords predominance include ethical imperatives, utilitarian and other expediential rules, and political maxims, all of which diverge from the formalism of the 'external characteristics' variety as well as from that which uses logical abstraction. However, the peculiarly professional, legalistic, and abstract approach to law in the modern sense is possible only in the measure that the law is formal in character ... Only that abstract method which employs the logical interpretation of meaning allows the execution of the specifically systematic task, i.e. the collection and rationalization by logical means of all the several rules recognized as legally valid into an internally consistent complex of abstract legal propositions. (1921/1978: 657)

It seems clear that it is not the nature of the values that matters to Weber (they can be 'ethical, political, utilitarian, hedonistic, feudal, egalitarian, or whatever': 1921/1978: 85), but that choices are guided by a value system. What, then, differentiates a rational value system from a nonrational value system? What makes a value system rational is the fact that it involves a set of *consistent* value postulates. As with the preceding types of rationality, substantive rationality can be found in all historical epochs and in all societies.

Unlike all of the other types of rationality, formal rationality, in Weber's view, occurs only in the modern world and only in the

Occident. In *formal rationality*, the best means to an end is chosen on the basis of universally agreed-upon rules, regulations, and laws (Kalberg, 1980: 1158). Although found in a variety of settings (e.g. the capitalistic economy in general as well as in such specific aspects of capitalism as the money economy and double-entry bookkeeping, the factory, modern Western law, etc.), the paradigm case of formal rationality is the bureaucracy, in which what people do is determined by 'laws or administrative regulations' (Weber, 1958: 196). Individual choices are guided by rules rather than the values that determine action in substantive rationality. The result is action devoid of human values, such as that of the bureaucratic official who behaves in a 'spirit of formalistic impersonality ... without hatred or passion, and hence without affection or enthusiasm' (Brubaker, 1984: 21). Similarly, Weber (1921/1978: 165–6) describes the formal rationality of Weberian capitalism. Within the capitalistic economy Weber argues that 'the functionalized world of capitalism certainly offers no support for any such charitable orientation' (1921/1978: 585) and further that 'matter-of-fact considerations that are simply non-ethical determine individual behavior' (1921/1978: 1186). In modern law, issues of ultimate justice are ignored and the emphasis is placed on the application of 'definitely fixed legal concepts in the form of highly abstract rules' (1927/1981: 277). Formally rational law becomes a gapless system of legal propositions. In the private realm, we see the dominance of contracts, which are needed by formally rational businesses. Brubaker offers a good summary view of formal rationality: 'Common to the rationality of industrial capitalism, formalistic law and bureaucratic administration is its objectified, institutionalized, supra-individual form: in each sphere, rationality is embodied in the social structure and confronts individuals as something external to them' (1984: 9). Weber makes this quite clear in the specific case of bureaucratic rationalization:

> Bureaucratic rationalization ... revolutionizes with *technical means*, in principle, as does every economic reorganization, 'from without': It *first* changes the material and social orders, and *through* them the people, by changing the conditions of adaptation, and perhaps the opportunities for adaptation, through a rational determination of means and ends. (1921/1968: 1116)

Thus, while the values behind substantive rationality can be internalized in actors so that they 'want' to act in a certain way, in formal rationality they cannot be internalized so that people are 'forced' to act in the desired manner (1904–5/1958: 181).

The development of bureaucracies furthers formal rationalization in other sectors of society. For example, Weber argues that the 'modern development of full bureaucratization brings the system of rational, specialized and expert examinations irresistibly to the fore' (1958: 241). Also enhanced is the value of certificates and diplomas acquired through such examinations. Thus, the educational system is heavily affected by the advance of bureaucratization and formal rationalization.

The bureaucracy is far from the only place in which Weber saw the triumph of formal rationality. Another is the modern capitalist factory which, in turn, was heavily influenced by the formally rational military and its 'discipline'. He sees the organizational discipline in the modern factory as completely formally rational. Weber sees the height of this kind of formal rationality in the American system of scientific management:

> With the help of suitable methods of measurement, the optimum profitabi-lity of the individual worker is calculated like that of any material means of production. On this basis, the American system of 'scientific management' triumphantly proceeds with its rational conditioning and training of work performances, thus drawing the ultimate conclusions from the mechaniza-tion and discipline of the plant. The psycho-physical apparatus of man is completely adjusted to the demands of ... the tools, the machines – in short, it is functionalized, and the individual is shorn of his natural rhythm through the functional specialization of muscles and through creation of an optimal economy of physical effort. (1921/1978: 1156)

While Weber clearly has a multifaceted sense of rationality, he argues that in the West formal rationality comes to overwhelm the other three types. This is clearest in the case of the defeat of substantive rationality by formal rationality (Cohen, 1981: xxvi). For example, in his work *The Protestant Ethic and the Spirit of Capitalism*, Weber sees Calvinism as a specific example of substantive rationality that helped give birth to the formal rationality of modern capitalism. Calvinism was a substantively rational system in which a coherent set of values led the individual to behave as a nascent capitalist. However, once the formally rational system of capitalism was set in motion, it no longer needed the sub-stantive rationality of Calvinism. As Weber puts it, 'victorious capi-talism, since it rests on mechanical foundations, needs its [Calvinism's] support no longer' (1904–5/1958: 181–2). (Weber also uses machine imagery to describe the bureaucracy, 'that animated machine ... busy fabricating the shell of bondage': 1921/1978: 1402–3.) Not only did capitalism no longer need Calvinism, but it pushed it into the realm of the irrational. Furthermore, formal rationality served to destroy substantive rationality in general, and religious substantive rationality in particular. In other words, formal rationality served to demystify and disenchant the modern world. On the issue of formally rational bureaucracies, Weber argues: 'The march of bureaucracy accordingly destroyed structures of domination which were not rational in this [formally rational] sense of the term. Hence we can ask: What were these structures?' (1921/1978: 102). The structures that were destroyed were forms of domination such as patriarchalism and patrimonialism.

These can be seen as substantively rational in the sense that they are characterized by norms derived from tradition rather than the enacted norms of formally rational bureaucracies.

On a more general level, Weber sometimes talks as if formal rationality will eventually leave little room for any other type of rationality (or, for that matter, for anything else): 'Thus, discipline inexorably takes over ever larger areas as the satisfaction of political and economic needs is increasingly rationalized. This universal phenomenon more and more restricts the importance of charisma and of individually differentiated conduct' (1921/1968: 1156). While charisma is often used in Weber's work for nonrational, or even antirational, action, 'individually differentiated conduct' could apply to the other three types of rationality. That is, each of the other types exerts less control over the actor and each allows for greater differences from one individual to another than formal rationality.

While Weber is less explicit about the destruction of practical and theoretical rationality, it seems clear that his image of the iron cage of formal rationality leaves little place for either in the modern world. The rules and regulations of formally rational systems dictate what is to be done. As a result, there is little room or need for people to practically figure out the best means to an end. Similarly, there is little need for people to theoretically order situations since that order is provided by the formally rational system.

An Overarching Theory?

Although Weber had a complex, multifaceted sense of rationalization, he used it most powerfully and meaningfully in his image of the modern Western world, especially in the capitalistic economy (R. Collins, 1980; Weber, 1927/1981) and bureaucratic organizations (I. Cohen, 1981: xxxi; Weber, 1921/1968: 956–1005), as an iron cage (Mitzman, 1969; Tiryakian, 1981) of formally rational structures. Weber described capitalism and bureaucracies as 'two great rationalizing forces' (1921/1968: 698). In fact, Weber saw capitalism and bureaucracies as being derived from the same basic sources (especially inner-worldly asceticism) involving similarly rational and methodical action, reinforcing one another and in the process furthering the rationalization of the Occident. In Weber's (1921/1968: 227, 994) view, the only real rival to the bureaucrat in technical expertise and factual knowledge was the capitalist.

However, if we take Weber at his word, it is difficult to argue that he had an overarching theory of rationalization. He rejected the idea of 'general evolutionary sequence' (1927/1981: 34). He was critical of thinkers like Hegel and Marx, who he felt offered general, teleological theories of society. In his own work, he tended to shy away from studies of, or proclamations about, whole societies. Instead, he tended to focus, in turn, on social structures and institutions such as bureaucracy, stratification, law, the city, religion, the polity, and the economy. Lacking a sense of the whole, he was unlikely to make global generalizations, especially about future directions. Furthermore the rationalization process that Weber described in one social structure or institution was usually quite different from the rationalization of another structure or institution. As Weber put it, the process of rationalization assumes 'unusually varied forms' (1922–23/1958: 293; see also 1921/1958: 30; 1904–5/1958: 78), and 'the history of rationalism shows a development which by no means follows parallel lines in the various departments of life' (1904–5/1958: 77; see also Brubaker, 1984: 9; Kalberg, 1980: 1147). Weber also looked at many things other than rationalization in his various comparative-historical studies (Kalberg, 1994).

This being said, it is clear that Weber does have a deep concern for the overarching effect of the formal rationalization of the economy, bureaucracies, *and* the professions on the Western world (Brubaker, 1984). For example, in *Economy and Society*, Weber says:

> This whole process of rationalization in the factory as elsewhere, and especially in the bureaucratic state machine, parallels the centralization of the material implements of organization in the hands of the master. Thus, discipline inexorably takes over ever larger areas as the satisfaction of political and economic needs is increasingly rationalized. This universal phenomenon more and more restricts the importance of charisma and of individually differentiated conduct. (1921/1968: 1156)

Professionalization and the Medical Profession

The study of the professions has been obsessed with, and many feel distorted by, the medical profession (e.g. Arney, 1982; Berlant, 1975; Freidson, 1970; 1975; 1980; Gelfand, 1980; Larkin, 1983; Starr, 1982). After all, it was the medical profession that achieved unparalleled professional power, prestige, and income. All occupations that sought to professionalize took physicians as their model. Medicine was seen by sociologists as the paradigmatic profession and all other occupations were compared, implicitly or explicitly, to it.

Historically, sociologists have conceptualized professions and the process of professionalization in three basic ways (Ritzer and Walczak, 1986). The process (Caplow, 1954; Wilensky, 1964) and structural-functional (Goode, 1957; Greenwood, 1957)[6] views of the professions generally, and of medicine in particular, dominated until about 1970 when the dominant power perspective emerged (Forsyth and Danisiewicz, 1985;

Freidson, 1970; Hall, 1983; Jamous and Peloille, 1970; Johnson, 1972; Klegon, 1978; Larson, 1977; Ritzer, 1975a; Roth, 1974).[7] There was an almost simultaneous critique of the process and structural-functional paradigms *and* of the supposedly distinctive characteristics of the medical profession. At a general level, the power perspective rejected the idea that the professions were distinguished by any distinctive historical stages or inherent characteristics. Rather, the view emerged that what distinguishes the professions from other occupations, either wholly or most importantly, is power (McKinlay, 1973). Professions came to be seen as occupations that had the power (derived, for example, from control over uncertainty and indeterminacy: Jamous and Peloille, 1970) to win the exalted label of 'profession' and, once they did, they were seen as exploiting that situation to further enhance their power. More particularly, especially in the work of Eliot Freidson (1960; 1970; 1975; 1980), the sense emerged that what truly distinguished the medical profession was its power over clients, other occupations, and the larger society.[8]

These three approaches, especially the power orientation, led to the following definition of a *profession* as: '*an occupation that has had the power to have undergone a developmental process enabling it to acquire, or convince significant others (for example, clients, the law) that it has acquired, a constellation of characteristics we have come to accept as denoting a profession*' (Ritzer and Walczak, 1986: 62). The characteristics we have come to associate with the professions are, among others, values (altruism, autonomy, and authority over clients), general systematic knowledge (Baer, 1986), distinctive occupational culture, and community and legal recognition. Professional ideologies (Forsyth and Danisiewicz, 1985; Gieryn et al., 1985) are a major source of the view among the public that these characteristics are associated with professions.

Along with a sense of the power of the professions in general, and medicine in particular, came a sense of the *fragility* of that power. That is, while power was something that professions won for themselves, they had to work hard and continually to retain it. Clients (Rothstein, 1973), other occupations (Larkin, 1983; Zola and Miller, 1973), and the larger society (Jamous and Peloille, 1970) could bestow power, but they also had the ability to limit and even withdraw that grant (Johnson, 1972). The concern for the sources of the power of the professions was transformed, at least in part, into an interest in their loss of power, an interest in the process of *deprofessionalization* (Haug, 1973; 1975; Rothman, 1984; Toren, 1975).[9] A variety of forces seemed to be at work that were causing clients, other occupations, and the larger society to curb the power of the professions. We can define deprofessionalization as *a decline in power which results in a decline in the degree to which professions possess, or are perceived to possess, a constellation of characteristics denoting a profession*. More specifically, deprofessionalization involves a decline in the possession of, or in the perception that the professions possess, altruism, autonomy, authority over clients, general systematic knowledge, distinctive occupational culture, and community and legal recognition.

Linking professionalization/deprofessionalization with rationalization, we are arguing that physicians (and their substantive rationality) are being profoundly affected by the spread of formal rationality and that this is contributing to some degree of deprofessionalization. At one level it is simply that formally rational structures (especially capitalistic and bureaucratic) are exercising increasing control over physicians (Kerr, 1985), that more external control generally means less power, and that a decline in power is a major aspect of deprofessionalization. At another level, the distinctive substantive rationality of the medical profession (with its emphasis on values such as altruism, authority over clients, and autonomy) is being supplanted by formal rationality (with its emphasis on structures, rules, and regulations). To the degree that physicians come to be characterized by formal rationality, they will be unable to continue to lay claim effectively to the distinctive title of professional. The main thesis of this chapter, then, is that the spread of formal rationality is a major cause of the deprofessionalization of physicians.[10]

Rationalization and Deprofessionalization

In this section we examine a lengthy list of changes in large-scale structures and institutions that are exerting increasing control over physicians and impelling medicine (and its substantive rationality) in the direction of greater formal rationalization and ultimately deprofessionalization. All of these changes involve an increasing impact of capitalism and/or bureaucracy on physicians. The developments to be discussed comprise changes in governmental policies (especially at the federal level), including antitrust decisions, Medicare and Medicaid, the development of a prospective payment system, and diagnostic related groups (DRGs); structural changes in the organization of medical delivery systems, including corporatization, conglomeration, free-standing primary care centers ('McDoctors'), health maintenance organizations (HMOs), entrepreneurialism, and advertising; and changes within these organizations, including professional managers, accounting systems and an emphasis on quantifiable costs, formalization of controls, and technological advances.

As we briefly discuss each of these changes, we will focus on how they are fostering greater formal rationality in general in medicine and, more specifically, increases in the specific components of such rationality: efficiency, predictability, calculability, and control, especially through the substitution of nonhuman for human technology (Eisen, 1978; Kalberg, 1980; Ritzer, 1983). The sets of changes as well as the increases in formal rationality will, in turn, be linked to the deprofessionalization of physicians, their loss of power generally, and the erosion of their distinctive substantive values (autonomy, authority over clients, and altruism).

Changes in Government Policies

By their policies, federal (Feldstein, 1986) and state governments have exerted increasing control over medicine and played an important role in the emergence of more formally rational medicine. One key factor in the expansion of capitalism (and bureaucratization) in medicine was the birth and development in the mid-1960s of Medicare and Medicaid, both of which provided a secure source of reimbursement to those capitalists interested in investing in the medical marketplace (Michael et al., 1985). Additionally, Medicare and Medicaid helped to increase the demand for medical care.[11] Congress responded to a perceived shortage of physicians (HPEA) in 1963 (Feldstein, 1986). Increased numbers of physicians have spurred competition among physicians and one way of being more competitive is by rationalizing medical activities, that is, becoming more efficient in the delivery of medical services.

Another example of external governmental control was the 1975 Supreme Court ruling that professionals, including physicians, are subject to the provisions of the Sherman Antitrust Act. Prior to this decision, medicine (along with other professions) was seen as autonomous and self-regulating, and thus exempt from antitrust laws (Costilo, 1985; Feldstein, 1986; Havighurst, 1983). Since 1975, a number of antitrust suits have been filed challenging the anticompetitive practices of the medical profession (e.g. restraint of innovative forms of health care, price fixing). While many of these suits have been dismissed, the effect has been to help open medicine to the formally rationalizing influence of market competition.

In the early 1980s a prospective payment system emerged, by which hospitals were paid under Medicare. By using a system of diagnostic related groups (DRGs), the federal government has established the amount it will reimburse hospitals for a given medical diagnosis, no matter how long the patient is hospitalized. As a result of external control by DRGs, physicians are pressed by hospitals into becoming more efficient in their use of ancillary services and in getting patients in and out of the hospital as quickly as possible (Gray, 1986).

While the prospective payment system may help stem the rising cost of medical care, it may also have the unintended consequence of contributing to the deprofessionalization of the medical profession by threatening its autonomy and shifting authority over patients away from the doctor and into the hands of third-party bureaucrats. With discussions under way to extend the DRG payment mechanism beyond Medicare to all physician services performed during hospitalization (Mitchell, 1985), it is possible that DRGs will contribute to even more external control and deprofessionalization of medicine in the future.

Third-party payers (e.g. the government, Blue Cross) have grown increasingly concerned about spiraling medical costs and have sought to deal with the problem by limiting what they will pay for as well as how much they will pay for it (Michael et al., 1985; Vraciu, 1985). Thus, a third-party payer may have a policy of not paying for certain procedures, or not allowing hospitalization for certain procedures, or only paying a given amount for a procedure. Such policies clearly exert control over physicians and contribute to increasing formal rationality by bringing a great deal of calculability to the practice of medicine. The third-party payer's formally rational emphasis on money comes into conflict with the physician's substantive rational altruistic interest (at least, ideal typically) in the patient. As one physician-union leader put it (albeit somewhat romantically and unrealistically), doctors are 'the only ones who think of patients as individuals ... not as dollar signs' (in Colburn, 1985: 7).

Changing Nature of Medical Delivery Systems

A key development is the corporatization of medicine. The most notable element in this is the growth of investor-owned hospitals. For-profit hospitals are not new, but in the past they were primarily small, independent operations (Gray, 1986). More recently, we have seen an increasing number of for-profit hospitals owned by publicly traded health care companies that own multiple facilities. This has contributed to the continuing decline of small, independent proprietary hospitals. Medicine is coming to be increasingly characterized by formally rational, large-scale capitalistic corporations (e.g. Humana Inc., Hospital Corp. of America) that are interested in hospitals, indeed the entire medical complex, as profit-making ventures (Ermann and Gabel, 1986; Gray, 1986). As more and more physicians become employees of such hospitals, it will be difficult to maintain their altruistic values in such a profit-oriented environment. The pressure to earn profits is likely to lead such hospitals to reduce the autonomy and undermine the authority of physicians. Furthermore, not only are medical corporations likely to rationalize their own hospitals, but the competitive pressures they create are also likely to force nonprofit hospitals into taking similar actions.

Related to this is the growth of free-standing primary care centers: 'McDoctors' or 'Docs-in-the-Box,' profit-oriented chains of storefront medical outlets that are modeled after fast-food chains. These are usually drop-in, no-appointment facilities that dispense medical care in much the same efficient way that McDonald's serves hamburgers. In some cases (e.g. Humana's Medfirst medical clinics), McDoctors are owned by the large corporations that own for-profit hospitals and thereby McDoctors become simply another arena in which the corporation's principles of formal rationality can be applied. In other cases, they may be independent chains, or even single outlets opened by an enterprising physician/entrepreneur. Even in these cases, given the McDonald's model, there is a strong inclination to rationalize operations as much as possible. Fast and efficient medical service is emphasized. There is a tendency to take only those patients with simple and easily handled medical problems. Since the work is comparatively simple, and highly routinized, less well-trained technical people can often be utilized instead of the much more costly physicians. These are highly predictable settings that look and operate much the same way from one time or place to another time or place. Procedures are elaborately developed and they exert considerable control over what employees (including physicians, where present) can and cannot do.

Another significant development is the rapid growth of health maintenance organizations (HMOs) (Tarlov, 1986). While these organizations take a variety of forms, all of them are business organizations in which the objective is to work within budgetary constraints, or in some cases to turn a profit. As business organizations, HMOs are under tremendous pressure to rationalize operations in order to minimize costs and maximize income. Physicians, and their norms of autonomy, authority, and altruism, are affected by these pressures whether they control these HMOs or are employed in them.

Also significant is the 'conglomeration' of medicine. Whether it be through expanding product lines or product-line diversification, these medi-giants aim to integrate health care facilities, medical services, and insurance functions on a regional or national basis (Vraciu, 1985).[12] Large corporations are not only coming to own for-profit hospitals, McDoctors, and HMOs, but also controlling health insurance firms, buying out hospital supply companies, and generally moving in the direction of controlling as many components of the 'medical-industrial complex' as possible (e.g. nursing homes, laboratories, emergency-room services, home care: Ermann and Gable, 1986; Gray, 1986; Relman, 1980; Schlesinger, 1985). To compete, large, nonprofit organizations like Blue Cross and Blue Shield are expanding in a similar manner. In either case, ever-larger conglomerates are increasingly impelled to rationalize their operations. This means that they are going to seek ways of becoming more efficient, predictable, and calculable, of replacing more and more workers with nonhuman technologies, and of exerting increasing control over employees (including physicians).

Those physicians who resist moving into various large-scale capitalistic medical organizations are going to have to be even more entrepreneurial than they have been in the past. Physicians have, of course, always combined professionalization and entrepreneurialism, but in order to compete in today's more market-oriented medical system, physicians are going to be forced to emphasize business practices more with the result that professionalization may suffer. Further, physicians in private practice are coming to emphasize entrepreneurialism more and professionalism less by opening an array of free-standing or non-institutional health care centers including pathology labs, health promotion centers, obesity and substance abuse clinics, chains of local emergency rooms, proprietary hospitals, and nursing homes (Goldstein, 1984; Gray, 1986).

While good empirical data do not yet exist on the impact of entrepreneurialism on patient care decisions, there is suggestive evidence that 'is adequate to confirm the common sense conclusion that investments and economic arrangements that reward physicians financially for making certain patient care decisions (e.g. ordering lab tests) will bias physicians in favor of making such decisions' (Gray, 1986: 159). In any case, it is clearly harder for primarily entrepreneurial physicians to continue to claim to adhere to substantive rationality, especially the value of altruism. Furthermore, the demands of the capitalistic marketplace will exert greater control over an entrepreneurial physician.

One result of this control by the market is the expansion of advertising by the various agencies involved in the medical business, including even physicians in private practice. While there are still strong negative sentiments among some physicians toward advertising (Allen et al., 1985), there is evidence to suggest that advertising is gaining acceptance in the medical profession (Darling and Bergiel, 1983; Folland, 1985). Here is one of the clearest examples of the erosion of the distinction between professional and capitalist, between substantive and formal rationality. Again, with physicians advertising their services on television and in the newspapers, it will be harder for them to continue to put forth an altruistic image. Patients are more likely to question the authority of physicians selling their services side-by-side with used car salespeople.

Changes within Medical Delivery Systems

Within large-scale corporate hospitals, chains, HMOs, etc. we see the rise of professional managers and their power over physicians (Gray, 1986; Quintana et al., 1985). In their quest to maximize profits,[13] these managers are committed to a full-scale formal rationalization of their procedures, including those procedures that apply to the medical profession. This rationalization has a profound effect on physicians, especially if they are employed by a hospital (Battistella, 1985). As members of these rationalized hospitals, physicians are forced to work more efficiently, quantify many heretofore qualitative elements of their work (Starr, 1982), operate in a predictable manner from one time to another, utilize advanced technologies as much as possible, and, in an increasing number of domains, allow themselves to be replaced by non-human technologies, and submit to external control, often by superiors who are businesspeople rather than fellow professionals.

To Weber (1927/1981: 275), the most important presupposition of a capitalist enterprise was a rational capital accounting system.[14] Such accounting systems have become very important to medical organizations, meaning that physicians are coming to be evaluated and controlled by an array of quantitative economic measures.[15] These systems are aimed at ascertaining whether the various things that physicians do are cost-effective. The formal rationality of cost-effectiveness is likely to come into conflict with the substantive rationality of the medical profession since the main basis for a decision may shift from the welfare of the patient to the cost of an undertaking. The physician is now more likely to be a rationing agent or a gatekeeper of medical services (Agrich and Begley, 1985; Cassel, 1985).

It is feared that an emphasis on cost will tend to force medicine to abandon long-shot diagnostic techniques and treatments because they cannot be legitimized on a cost basis even though, if successful, patients might benefit from such diagnosis or treatment. Another fear is that a focus on profits will tend to prevent physicians employed in for-profit hospitals from treating low-income patients and force such patients to be sent to remaining public hospitals (Starr, 1982). These and other forces threaten the altruistic image of physicians.

While there is some evidence to suggest that for-profit hospitals may rationalize by providing less uncompensated care (bad debt and charity cases) and by treating a smaller proportion of uninsured patients, the data are weak and far from conclusive. For-profit hospitals may offer some services that differ from those offered by not-for-profit hospitals, but it has not been established that these services are necessarily the more profitable ones (Ermann and Gabel, 1986). However, for-profit hospitals do appear to rationalize operations by employing fewer people (per bed) than not-for-profit hospitals (Ermann and Gabel, 1986; Watt et al., 1986). While showing some modest increase in recent years, for-profit hospitals have not been active participants in research and teaching functions (Gray, 1986).

Another factor in the formal rationalization of medicine is the profession's increasing dependence on expensive and sophisticated medical technology. Rather than controlling simple technologies as was true in the past, physicians are finding themselves in positions whereby they are more likely to be controlled (and their autonomy reduced) by advanced technologies and the technicians who design them, control them, and interpret their results. As Reiser in his book *Medicine and the Reign of Technology* puts it: 'medicine has now evolved to a point where diagnostic judgments based on "subjective" evidence – the patient's sensations and the physician's own observations of the patient – are being supplanted by judgments based on "objective" evidence, provided by laboratory procedures and by mechanical and electronic devices' (1978: ix). Technological advance, as a component of advancing rationalization, represents a threat to the professional status of medicine. The subjective, qualitative, and autonomous judgments of physicians are beginning to be replaced by the objective, quantitative results emanating from various advanced technologies (for example, computer programs that 'help' physicians diagnose illnesses). The result of a test utilizing various advanced technologies is far more predictable, that is replicable, from one time to the next. Most importantly, these technologies are coming to exert more control over physicians.

Not only are advanced technologies coming to control physicians, they are also helping to reduce physicians' authority over patients. The patient is well aware that much of the work is being done by technologies and technicians and this serves to erode the authority of the physician in the eyes of the patient. These technologies serve to routinize, and thereby demystify, medical practice.[16,17] Furthermore, patients are increasingly able to bypass the physician altogether and go straight to the technician and in some cases even avoid the technician and go directly to the technology itself (e.g. blood pressure machines in drug stores, home pregnancy tests). All of this constitutes a threat to the ideal that professional physicians possess their own distinct body of general systematic knowledge.

In addition to being a threat to professionalization in itself, advancing technology is linked to many of the other forces serving to deprofessionalize medicine. The paradigmatic physician on his/her own in private practice is not able to afford to own most of the advanced technologies that are sweeping the field. It is the capitalist enterprises and the large bureaucracies that are able to afford these technologies. In this way, the dependence on technology is linked to the bureaucratization and capitalization of medicine. In order to gain access to these technologies, physicians must subordinate themselves to, even become employees of, these organizations. Within these organizations, the high cost of modern technologies may cause administrators to become involved in decisions that in the past had been left to the physician (Shea and Marguilies, 1985; Watts, 1985). In the past, the physician owned the (simple) technologies, or else had ready access to them in hospitals that were controlled by fellow physicians. That is now less the case, with the result that there is strong pressure in the direction of deprofessionalization.

All of the factors discussed thus far tend to put physicians increasingly in contact, and in conflict, with bureaucracies.[18] Investor-owned hospital systems, chains of McDoctors, HMOs, and third-party payers are all huge bureaucratic systems. Bureaucracies, of course, were Weber's paradigm case of formal rationality and, given our theme of the conflict between professionalization and rationalization, they become a central source of the deprofessionalization of medicine.[19] As McKinlay put it: 'The single feature that most distinguishes present-day medical practice from earlier forms – indeed has altered it almost beyond recognition – is its high degree of bureaucratization' (1982: 39). The elements of formal rationality are expressed to an extreme degree within the bureaucracy, and the physician who must work in, or deal with, bureaucracies experiences conflict over each of them. For example, the bureaucratic emphasis on efficiency often comes in conflict with what the physician feels is in the best interest of the patient. Most important is the bureaucratic notion of control from the top versus the professional norm of peer control. In huge, bureaucratic systems, those at the top of bureaucracies, and thereby those who are making decisions and issuing directives, are often nonprofessionals – bureaucrats and/or businesspeople. The control that such people are able to exercise is a profound source of deprofessionalization of physicians.[20] While at one time physicians dominated health organizations, there is now more shared authority with administrators and even subordination of physicians to administrators (Gray, 1986).

Freidson offers a somewhat different view. What Freidson (1984) emphasizes is that it is not nonprofessionals, but rather an elite group of professionals, that is coming to control other professionals. As a result, Freidson (see also, Starr, 1982) sees the emergence of a stratification system within the professions involving those who create the controls, those who impose them, and those on whom they are imposed. If we accept Freidson's view, then it is the physicians on the bottom who are most likely to be deprofessionalized – to lose their autonomy and perhaps their authority over clients. But it could also be argued that higher- or even the highest-ranking physicians will experience deprofessionalization since they will be controlled, at least to some degree, by bureaucratic rules and regulations.

In fact, although he purports to disagree with the foregoing thesis on the role of bureaucratization in deprofessionalization,[21] Freidson (1984; 1985) does tend to support it when he argues that it is not bureaucratization (and control by nonprofessionals) that is crucial, but rather the 'formalization of professional controls'. By this he means that instead of being controlled informally, professionals are being controlled by codified technical standards. What Freidson does not recognize is that this formalization of controls is part of the broader process of formal rationalization. Formalized controls serve, among other things, to make the work of professionals more predictable and to increase external control over it.[22]

Although the views expressed in the last two paragraphs see an antithesis between bureaucratization and professionalization, there is a perspective which sees the possibility of a new social form emerging out of the interrelationship of these two processes. In this view, formal rationality need not win out over substantive rationality, but the two can interpenetrate and create a new, hybrid form of rationalization. Substantively rational medical professionals and formally rational systems will *both* be transformed by their relations with one another. If this turns out to be the case, we cannot anticipate the significant deprofessionalization described in this section, but the professions will be transformed by this process and it is likely that even in this eventuality some deprofessionalization is also likely to occur.

Although he is writing about lawyers in large law firms, it is necessary to briefly address Nelson's (1981) work at this point. On the surface, Nelson's conclusions seem to contradict the basic thrust of this chapter. That is, he finds that to a large degree the large law firm has resisted bureaucratization (and formal rationalization) and retained its professionalism (and substantive rationality). However, even here, Nelson found consciousness on the part of attorneys 'of the need to rationalize their firms by identifying profit centers, formalizing data on the firms' operations, and establishing clear lines of communication and authority' (1981: 129). More importantly, he finds a clear trend toward greater formal rationalization 'in *the most rationalized form of legal services organization: the large law clinic*' and its 'computerized forms, centralized administration, advertising, and routinized procedures' (1981: 138, emphasis added). Finally, although Nelson argues against the main thesis of this chapter in the case of elite law practice, he seems to accept it in the case of medicine, at least as it is practiced in the modern hospital.

Another point worth mentioning is that modern bureaucracies are currently undergoing substantial change and are no longer so formally rational (DiMaggio and Powell, 1983; Ouchi, 1981). As the changed position of the United States in the world political economy pushes organizations in the direction of greater substantive rationality, they will link up with professionals moving into them and experiencing an increase in formal rationality. This, too, points toward lesser deprofessionalization, but deprofessionalization nevertheless.

Conclusions

The objective in this chapter has been to use the effects of contemporary social changes on medicine as a case study of the applicability of the Weberian theory of rationalization to the modern social world. Our conclusion is that these formally rational social changes are leading to greater external control over, and formal rationalization of, medicine and that these, in turn, are contributing to the deprofessionalization of medicine. The dividing line between substantively rational physicians and formally rational bureaucrats and capitalists is increasingly blurred, with the result that it is harder for physicians to claim the distinctive position of profession and to have that claim accepted by the public. Given the paucity of empirical data on this issue, and the conflicting nature of the data that exist, an adequate theoretical perspective is especially important in trying to understand what is currently happening to medicine. The theory of rationalization has allowed us to see clear linkages among a series of disparate social changes and to understand how they are changing the nature of medicine and contributing to the deprofessionalization of physicians.

While we have made the case for a specific scenario in this chapter, several other scenarios are possible. One alternative is that new forms will emerge that combine formal and substantive rationality – new professional, bureaucratic, and capitalistic structures. These new forms that combine the two types of rationality would still tend to point in the direction of deprofessionalization, but not to the degree of this chapter's main thesis. Another possibility is that rather than be controlled and changed by formal rationality, the medical profession will absorb it, control it, and emerge as powerful and as professional as ever. Still another possibility is that in the future we will witness a new form of 'hyperrationalization' (see Chapter 11) combining practical, theoretical, substantive, and formal rationality and that the medical profession will control it. In this scenario, the physicians will emerge from the current period of changes with even greater power and with an even higher degree of professionalization. Although this chapter's thesis is that significant deprofessionalization of physicians is likely, we will need to await the outcome of contemporary events to see which of these scenarios ultimately occurs. Whatever proves to be the case, Weberian theory is of great utility in helping us to understand social changes in the medical profession and generating hypotheses about the future.

A caveat is in order. Our concern has been the deprofessionalization of American medicine. We have sought to understand and explain this development with a central aspect of the theory of rationalization. A more adequate explanation would require a comparative and/or historical analysis involving medicine in other, more, less, or non-rationalizing societies. Such a comparative analysis would allow us to be on a far firmer ground in concluding that it is, indeed, rationalization that is the major causal factor in the deprofessionalization of medicine. It is hoped that this work may stimulate such cross-cultural and/or transhistorical research. More generally, it seems clear that we need more work seeking to link abstract sociological theories to what is happening in the social world.

Notes

This chapter is derived from (with David Walczak) 'Rationalization and the Deprofessionalization of Physicians' (1988) and *Metatheorizing in Sociology* (1991b: 95–104).

1 Our focus is largely on changes in medicine in the 1970s and 1980s, but some of these changes were well under way long before the 1970s, and they continue into the new millennium.

2 Starr's (1982) work is largely atheoretical. Freidson's (1986) work is stronger theoretically, but it is still not wholly satisfying from a theoretical point of view. For example, the Weberian theory of rationalization plays a central role in Freidson's (1986: 3) work (as it does in this chapter), but he has an undifferentiated sense of the concept which is not informed by the work of such important neo-Weberians as Kalberg (1980), Levine (1981), and Brubaker (1984).

3 While Starr foresaw a decline, he made it clear that such 'a trend is not necessarily fate' (1982: 449).

4 Although we are forecasting some degree of deprofessionalization of physicians, their power, status, and continuing control over a centrally important area of human existence lead us to believe that they will *not* tumble far down the professional continuum.

5 Starr makes this point in the case of physicians: 'In the twentieth century, medicine has been the heroic exception that sustained the waning tradition of independent professionalism. Physicians ... escaped from corporate and bureaucratic control ... But the exception may now be brought into line with the governing rule' (1982: 420).

6 We are combining the closely related trait and structural-functional approaches under a single heading. See Saks (1983) for an orientation that differentiates between them.

7 Just as the power approach seemed to gain preeminence, a number of analysts (e.g. Freidson, 1983; Murray et al., 1983; Saks, 1983) came to question this single-minded focus on power.

8 A possible fourth, microsociological approach (as opposed to the macrosociological orientation of the other three approaches) may be found in Dingwall (1976).

9 Since this is a Weberian analysis, we will use the concept of deprofessionalization rather than the related, and more Marxian, notion of the *proletarianization* of the professions (Derber, 1982; Oppenheimer, 1973). Proletarianization is a different and more extreme view of the loss of power of the professions. While few Marxists envision a drastic descent to the level of assembly-line workers, they do see professionals, like other proletarians, increasingly needing to sell their labor time in order to have access to the means of production.

10 As we will discuss at the conclusion of this chapter, other outcomes are also possible.

11 Also fueling this increased demand was the expansion of private sector medical insurance.

12 A related issue is the growing 'conglomerization' of the health care purchaser – for example, government or business coalitions organized to negotiate mass purchases of health care (Freedman, 1985).

13 While managers of nonprofit hospitals are also seeking to rationalize, it is the goal of profit maximization that leads the managers of for-profit hospitals to rationalize with a vengeance.

14 It is also important to look at some of the other presuppositions of capitalism enumerated by Weber since many of them also stand in opposition to professionalization. For example, Weber (1927/1981: 276) sees the freedom of the market in general, and of the labor market in particular (Begun, 1986), as one such presupposition. It could be argued that professionalization is a limitation on the labor market and therefore antithetical to capitalism. The appropriation of the means of production by the capitalist is a threat to professional power. The tendency to adopt ever more rational technologies serves to make professional activities more calculable, predictable, controllable, etc.

15 Nelson (1981) discusses how this is also occurring in the large law firm.

16 Rothman (1984) makes this point about the effect of technology, but in a study of law not medicine.

17 As a counter-position to this, Horobin (1983) argues that modern advances, while making things more determinate, have also created new areas of indeterminacy which serve to maintain the power of the medical profession.

18 See Nass (1986) for a very unusual image of this conflict from a Weberian perspective in which the professionals are viewed as leaders of one-person organizations or as organizations.

19 Rothman (1984) makes a similar point about the legal profession.

20 There are some (e.g. Schlesinger, 1985) who disagree with the view that increasing bureaucratization will reduce physician control.

21 And there are a number of conflicting studies on the issue of the relation between professionalization and bureaucratization (see Ritzer and Walczak, 1986: 205–10). Among the positions are an inherent conflict between the two, the emergence of a new organizational form that combines elements of professionalization and bureaucratization, the dominance of bureaucrats, or the dominance of professionals. More directly relevant to the thesis of this chapter, in a study of physicians in an HMO, Kerr (1985) found *both* bureaucratic restraint and professional autonomy.

22 It is also the case that lower-status physicians are more likely to be controlled by these standards than the higher-status physicians who create and enforce them. Even in this instance, however, some deprofessionalization is likely to occur.

10

THE McDONALDIZATION OF SOCIETY

While for Weber the bureaucracy was the paradigm of the rationalization process, McDonald's serves here as the major example of the more contemporary, but parallel, process I call *McDonaldization*, that is,

> *the process by which the principles of the fast-food restaurant are coming to dominate more and more sectors of American society as well as of the rest of the world.*

McDonaldization affects not only the restaurant business, but also education, work, health care, travel, leisure, dieting, politics, the family, and virtually every other aspect of society. McDonaldization has shown every sign of being an inexorable process by sweeping through seemingly impervious institutions and parts of the world.

The Dimensions of McDonaldization

Why has the McDonald's model proven so irresistible? Four alluring dimensions lie at the heart of the success of this model and, more generally, of McDonaldization. In short, McDonald's has succeeded because it offers consumers, workers, and managers efficiency, calculability, predictability, and control.[1]

Efficiency

First, McDonald's offers *efficiency*, or the optimum method for getting from one point to another. For consumers, this means that McDonald's offers the best available way to get from being hungry to being full. (Similarly, in the movie *Sleeper*, Woody Allen's orgasmatron offered an efficient method for getting people from quiescence to sexual gratification.) Other institutions, fashioned on the McDonald's model, offer similar efficiency in losing weight, lubricating cars, getting new glasses or contacts, or completing income-tax forms. In a society where both parents are likely to work, or where there may be only a single parent, efficiently satisfying the hunger and many other needs of people is very attractive. In a society where people rush, usually by car, from one spot to another, the efficiency of a fast-food meal, perhaps even without leaving their cars by wending their way along the drive-through lane, often proves impossible to resist. The fast-food model offers people, or at least appears to offer them, an efficient method for satisfying many needs.

Like their customers, workers in McDonaldized systems (holding 'McJobs': Ritzer, 1998: 59–70) function efficiently. They are trained to work this way by managers, who watch over them closely to make sure they do. Organizational rules and regulations also help ensure highly efficient work.

Calculability

Second, McDonald's offers *calculability*, or an emphasis on the quantitative aspects of products sold (portion size, cost) and service offered (the time it takes to get the product). Quantity has become equivalent to quality; a lot of something, or the quick delivery of it, means it must be good. As two observers of contemporary American culture put it, 'As a culture, we tend to believe deeply that in general "bigger is better"' (Mitroff and Bennis, 1989: 142). Thus, people order the Quarter Pounder, the Big Mac, the *large* fries. More recently, there is the lure of the 'double this' (for instance, Burger King's 'Double Whopper with Cheese') and the 'triple that'. People can quantify these things and feel that they are getting a lot of food for what appears to be a nominal sum of money. This calculation does not take into account an important point: the extraordinary profitability of fast-food outlets and other chains, which indicates that the owners, not the consumers, get the best deal.

People also tend to calculate how much time it will take to drive to McDonald's, be served the food, eat it, and return home; then, they compare that interval with the time required to prepare food at home. They often conclude, rightly or wrongly, that a trip to the fast-food restaurant will take less time than eating at home. This sort of calculation particularly supports home-delivery franchises such as Domino's, as well as other chains that emphasize time saving. A notable example of time saving in another sort of chain is Lens Crafters, which promises people 'Glasses fast, glasses in one hour.'

Some McDonaldized institutions combine the emphases on time and money. Domino's promises pizza delivery in half an hour, or the pizza is free. Pizza Hut will serve a personal pan pizza in five minutes, or it, too, will be free.

Workers at McDonaldized systems also tend to emphasize the quantitative rather than the qualitative aspects of their work. Since the quality of the work is allowed to vary little, workers focus on such things as how quickly tasks can be accomplished. In a situation analogous to that of the customer, workers are expected to do a lot of work, very quickly, for low pay.

Predictability

Third, McDonald's offers *predictability*, the assurance that their products and services will be the same over time and in all locales. The Egg McMuffin in New York will be, to all intents and purposes, identical to those in Chicago and Los Angeles. Also, those eaten next week or next year will be identical to those eaten today. There is great comfort in knowing that McDonald's offers no surprises. People know that the next Egg McMuffin they eat will taste about the same as the others they have eaten; it will not be awful, but it will not be exceptionally delicious, either. The success of the McDonald's model suggests that many people have come to prefer a world in which there are few surprises.

The workers in McDonaldized systems also behave in predictable ways. They follow corporate rules as well as the dictates of their managers. In many cases, not only what they do, but also what they say, is highly predictable. McDonaldized organizations often have scripts that employees are supposed to memorize and follow whenever the occasion arises (Leidner, 1993). This scripted behavior helps create highly predictable interactions between workers and customers. While customers do not follow scripts, they tend to develop simple recipes for dealing with the employees of McDonaldized systems (Schutz, 1932/1967). As Robin Leidner (1993: 82) argues,

> McDonald's pioneered the routinization of interactive service work and remains an exemplar of extreme standardization. Innovation is not discouraged ... at least among managers and franchisees. Ironically, though, 'the object is to look for new, innovative ways to create an experience that is exactly the same no matter what McDonald's you walk into, no matter where it is in the world'.

Control

Fourth, *control*, especially through *substitution of nonhuman for human technology*, is exerted over the people who enter the world of McDonald's. A *human technology* (a screwdriver, for example) is controlled by people; a *nonhuman technology* (the assembly line, for instance) controls people. The people who eat in fast-food restaurants are controlled, albeit (usually) subtly. Lines, limited menus, few options, and uncomfortable seats all lead diners to do what management wishes them to do: eat quickly and leave. Further, the drive-through (in some cases walk-through) window leads diners to leave before they eat. In the Domino's model, customers never come in the first place.

The people who work in McDonaldized organizations are also controlled to a high degree, usually more blatantly and directly than customers. They are trained to do a limited number of things in precisely the way they are told to do them. The technologies used and the way the organization is set up reinforce this control. Managers and inspectors make sure the workers toe the line.

McDonald's also controls employees by threatening to use, and ultimately using, nonhuman technology to replace human workers. No matter how well they are programmed and controlled, workers can foul up the system's operation. A slow worker can make the preparation and delivery of a Big Mac inefficient. A worker who refuses to follow the rules might leave the pickles or special sauce off a hamburger, thereby making for unpredictability. A distracted worker can put too few fries in the box, making an order of large fries seem skimpy. For these and other reasons, McDonald's has felt compelled to control and replace human beings with nonhuman technologies, such as the soft drink dispenser that shuts itself off when the glass is full, the French fry machine that rings and lifts itself out of the oil when the fries are crisp, the preprogrammed cash register that eliminates the need for the cashier to calculate prices and amounts, and, perhaps at some future time, the robot capable of making hamburgers.[2] Thus, McDonald's can assure customers that their employees and service will be consistent.

A Critique of McDonaldization: The Irrationality of Rationality

Though McDonaldization offers powerful advantages, it has a downside. Efficiency, predictability, calculability, and control through nonhuman technology can be thought of as the basic components of a *rational* system.[3] However, rational systems inevitably spawn irrationalities. The downside of McDonaldization is dealt with most systematically under the heading of the *irrationality of rationality*; in fact, paradoxically, the irrationality of rationality can be thought of as the fifth dimension of McDonaldization. The basic idea here is that the rational systems inevitably spawn irrational consequences. Another way of saying this is that rational systems serve to deny human reason; rational systems often are unreasonable.

For example, McDonaldization has produced a wide array of adverse effects on the environment. Take just one example: the need to grow uniform potatoes to create those predictable French fries that people have come to expect from fast-food restaurants. It turns out that the need to grow such potatoes has adversely affected the ecology of the Pacific Northwest. The huge farms that now produce such potatoes rely on the extensive use of chemicals. The need to produce a perfect fry means that much of the potato is wasted, with the remnants either fed to cattle or used for fertilizer. However, the underground water supply is now showing high levels of nitrates that may be traceable to the fertilizer and animal wastes (Egan, 1994). There are, of course, many other ecological problems associated with the McDonaldization of society: the forests felled to produce paper, the damage caused by polystyrene and other materials, the enormous amount of food needed to produce feed cattle, and so on.

Another unreasonable effect of the fast-food restaurant is that it is often a dehumanizing setting in which to eat or work. Customers lining up for a burger or waiting in the drive-through line and workers preparing the food often feel as though they are part of an assembly line. Hardly amenable to eating, assembly lines have been shown to be inhuman settings in which to work.

Of course, the criticisms of the irrationality of the fast-food restaurant will be extended to all facets of the McDonaldizing world. For example, at the opening of Euro Disney, a French politician said that it will 'bombard France with uprooted creations that are to culture what fast-food is to gastronomy' (Riding, 1992: A13). This clearly indicates an abhorrence of McDonaldization, whatever guise it may take.

There *are* great gains to be made from McDonaldization. However, the focus here is on the great costs and enormous risks of McDonaldization. McDonald's and the other purveyors of the fast-food model spend billions of dollars each year outlining the benefits of their system. However, the critics of the system have few outlets for their ideas. There are, for example, no commercials between Saturday morning cartoons warning children of the dangers associated with fast-food restaurants.

A legitimate question may be raised about this critique of McDonaldization: is it animated by a romanticism of the past and an impossible desire to return to a world that no longer exists? Some critics do base their critiques on the idea that there was a time when life was slower and less efficient, and offered more surprises; when people were freer; and when one was more likely to deal with a human being than a robot or a computer (Stauth and Turner, 1988; Turner, 1987). Although they have a point, these critics have undoubtedly exaggerated the positive aspects of a world without McDonald's, and they have certainly tended to forget the liabilities of such a world. As an example of the latter, take the following case of a visit to a pizzeria in Havana, Cuba:

> The pizza's not much to rave about – they scrimp on tomato sauce, and the dough is mushy.
>
> It was about 7:30 p.m., and as usual the place was standing-room-only, with people two deep jostling for a stool to come open and a waiting line spilling out onto the sidewalk.
>
> The menu is similarly Spartan ... to drink, there is tap water. That's it – no toppings, no soda, no beer, no coffee, no salt, no pepper. And no special orders.

A very few people are eating. Most are waiting … Fingers are drumming, flies are buzzing, the clock is ticking. The waiter wears a watch around his belt loop, but he hardly needs it; time is evidently not his chief concern. After a while, tempers begin to fray.

But right now, it's 8:45 p.m. at the pizzeria, I've been waiting an hour and a quarter for two small pies. (Hockstader, 1991: A12)

Few would prefer such irrational systems to the rationalized elements of society. More important, critics who revere the past do not seem to realize that we are not returning to such a world. In fact, fast-food restaurants have begun to appear in Havana (Farah, 1995). The increase in the number of people, the acceleration of technological change, the increasing pace of life – all this and more make it impossible to go back to the nonrationalized world, if it ever existed, of home-cooked meals, traditional restaurant dinners, high-quality foods, meals loaded with surprises, and restaurants populated only by chefs free to fully express their creativity.

While one basis for a critique of McDonaldization is the past, another is the future.[4] The future in this sense is defined as human potential, unfettered by the constraints of McDonaldized systems. This critique holds that people have the potential to be far more thoughtful, skillful, creative, and well rounded than they are now. If the world were less McDonaldized, people would be better able to live up to their human potential. This critique is based not on what people were like in the past, but on what they could be like in the future, if only the constraints of McDonaldized systems were eliminated, or at least eased substantially. The criticisms put forth here reflect the latter, future-oriented perspective rather than a romanticized past and a desire to return to it.

McDonaldization and some Alternative Perspectives: Fast Food in the Era of the 'Posts'

Because I present McDonaldization as a central process in the *modern* world, this constitutes an analysis and critique of *modernity*. However, a number of contemporary perspectives, especially postindustrialism, post-Fordism, and postmodernism, contend that we have already moved beyond the modern world and into a new, starkly different society. These views imply that this effort is retrograde because it deals with a 'modern' phenomenon (McDonaldization) that will soon disappear with the emergence of a new societal form. I contend, however, that McDonaldization and its 'modern' (as well as industrial and Fordist) characteristics not only are here for the foreseeable future, but also are influencing society at an accelerating rate. Thus, though important postindustrial, post-Fordist, and postmodernist trends are also occurring, some thinkers associated with these perspectives have been too quick to declare an end to modernity, at least in its McDonaldized form. This constitutes a critique, in whole or in part, of extreme versions of these alternative viewpoints.

Postindustrialism: McDonaldization or Sneakerization?

Of those who argue that people have moved beyond industrial society to a new, postindustrial society, the most important is Daniel Bell (1973; Waters, 2000). Among other things, Bell argues that society has moved from goods production to service provision. That is, 50 or 75 years ago the economy of the United States centered on the production of goods such as steel or automobiles. Today, however, the economy is dominated by the provision of services such as health care and fast food. Bell also points to the rise of new technologies and the growth in knowledge and information processing. He observes as well that professionals, scientists, and technicians have increased in number and importance.

However, in spite of this growth, low-status service occupations show no sign of disappearing, and, in fact, they have expanded and are central to a McDonaldized society. Above all, however, McDonaldization is built on many of the ideas and systems of industrial society, especially bureaucratization, the assembly line, and scientific management. The growth of McDonaldization at least in part contradicts Bell's idea that we have moved into a postindustrial society. Society is certainly postindustrial in many ways, but the spread of McDonaldization indicates that some aspects of industrial society will remain for some time to come.

In their book *Post-Industrial Lives*, Jerald Hage and Charles Powers (1992) have argued in favor of the postindustrial thesis. Among other things, they contend that a new postindustrial organization has arisen and that it coexists with the classic industrial organization, as well as other organizational forms. The postindustrial organization has a number of characteristics, including a leveling of hierarchical distinctions, a blurring of boundaries between organizations, a more integrated and less specialized organizational structure, an increase in behavior that is not bound by rules, and hiring policies that emphasize the creativity of potential employees.

There is no question that such organizations are on the ascent, but McDonaldized organizations are also increasing. Thus, the evidence supports *both* the postindustrial and McDonaldization theses: modern society contains contradictory organizational developments. In most cases the characteristics of McDonaldized organizations are diametrically opposed to those of postindustrial organizations. Thus,

McDonaldized organizations continue to be hierarchical, the behavior of employees and even managers is tightly bound by rules, and the last thing in the mind of those hiring for most jobs is creativity. Hage and Powers (1992: 10) see jobs involving 'tasks that are most clearly defined, technically simple, and most often repeated' being eliminated by automation. While many such jobs have been eliminated in heavy industry, they are not only alive and well, but growing, in McDonaldized organizations. Postindustrial organizations are also characterized by customized work and products, while standardized work (everyone follows the same procedures, scripts) and uniform products are the norm in McDonaldized settings.

Relatedly, a process called the 'sneakerization' of society has arisen (Goldman et al., 1994; 1995). Not quite customization, this process involves the diversification of product lines. Where there was once a single sneaker for all purposes, there are now specialized sneakers for all sorts of purposes: running, walking, aerobics, basketball, bicycling, and so on. Similar developments are everywhere: there are over 100 types of Walkman, 3000 kinds of Seiko watches, and 800 models of Phillips color televisions. These examples reflect the replacement of the mass production market by the agile marketplace.

Does sneakerization and the agile market represent a critique of, and alternative to, McDonaldization? While it is easier to McDonaldize a single type of sneaker, nothing prevents the McDonaldization of the production and sale of a wide range of sneakers. Indeed, manufacturers such as Nike and Adidas and retail chains such as The Athlete's Foot and Foot Locker have done just that. The production and sale of a wide product line represents no barrier to McDonaldization. Indeed, that is precisely where the future of McDonaldization lies.

Hage and Powers envision a broader change in society as a whole in which the emphasis has come to be on creative minds, complex selves, and communication among people who have these characteristics. Though some aspects of modern society are congruent with that image, McDonaldization demands uncreative minds, simple selves, and minimal communication dominated by scripts and routines.

In sum, the postindustrial thesis is not wrong, but is more limited than many of its adherents believe. Postindustrialization coexists with McDonaldization. The latter not only shows no sign of disappearing, but is in fact dramatically increasing in importance. This stands in contrast to the position taken by Hage and Powers (1992: 50) who argue that not rationalization but *'complexification will be the prevailing pattern of social change in post-industrial society'*. My view is that both complexification *and* rationalization will prevail but in different sectors of the economy and the larger society.

Fordism and Post-Fordism: Or, is it McDonaldization?

A similar issue concerns a number of Marxist thinkers, who claim that industry has undergone transition from Fordism to post-Fordism. Fordism, of course, refers to the ideas, principles, and systems spawned by Henry Ford.

Fordism has a number of characteristics. First, it involves the mass production of homogeneous products. To take a classic example, Model T Fords were identical down to their black color. Even today's automobiles are largely homogeneous, at least by type of automobile being produced. In fact, in the United States in 1995 Ford came out with a so-called 'world car' (i.e. the Contour), an automobile that could be sold in all world markets. Second, Fordism involves inflexible technologies, such as the assembly line. In spite of experiments with altering assembly lines, especially those undertaken by Volvo in Sweden, today's lines look much like they did in Ford's day (albeit with more nonhuman technologies such as robots). Third, Fordism involves the adoption of standardized work routines, or Taylorism. Thus, the person who puts hubcaps on cars does the same task over and over, more or less the same way each time.

Fourth, increases in productivity come from 'economies of scale as well as the deskilling, intensification, and homogenization of labor' (Clarke, 1990: 98). *Economy of scale* means simply that larger factories producing larger numbers of products can manufacture each individual product more cheaply than small factories producing goods in small numbers. *Deskilling* means that productivity increases if many workers do jobs requiring little or no skill (for example, putting hubcaps on cars) rather than, as had been the case in the past, a few workers with great skill doing all the work. *Intensification* means the more demanding and faster the production process, the greater the productivity. *Homogenization of labor* means that each worker does the same kind of highly specialized work (hubcaps, for example). This makes workers interchangeable.

Finally, Fordism involves the growth of a market for mass-produced items, which causes the homogenization of consumption patterns. In the automobile industry, Fordism led to a national market for automobiles in which similarly situated people bought similar, if not identical, automobiles.

Although Fordism grew throughout the twentieth century, especially in the United States, it reached its peak and began to decline in the 1970s, especially after the oil crisis of 1973 and the subsequent decline of the American automobile industry and the rise of its Japanese counterpart. Some argue that this indicates not only the decline of Fordism but also the rise of post-Fordism, which has a number of distinguishing characteristics.

First, interest in mass products declines, while interest in more customized and specialized products, especially those high in style and quality, grows. Rather than drab and uniform products, people want flashier goods that are easily distinguishable (Bourdieu, 1984b). Today's post-Fordist consumers are also more interested in quality and willing to pay extra for it.

Second, the more specialized products demanded in post-Fordist society require shorter production runs resulting in smaller and more productive systems. Thus, society will witness a move away from huge factories producing uniform products to smaller plants turning out a wide range of products.

Third, in the post-Fordist world, new technologies make flexible production profitable. For example, computerized equipment that can be reprogrammed to produce different products is replacing the old single-function technology. This new production process is to be controlled through more flexible systems, for example, a more flexible form of management.

Fourth, post-Fordist systems require more from workers than their predecessors. For example, workers need more diverse skills and better training to handle the new, more demanding, and more sophisticated technologies. These new technologies also mean that workers must be able to handle more responsibility and operate with greater autonomy. Thus, post-Fordism requires a new kind of worker.

Finally, as post-Fordist workers become more differentiated, they come to want more differentiated commodities, lifestyles, and cultural outlets. In other words, greater differentiation in the workplace leads to greater differentiation in the society as a whole. This in turn leads to more diverse demands and still greater differentiation in the workplace.

Though these elements of post-Fordism have emerged in the modern world, it is equally clear that elements of Fordism persist and show no signs of disappearing: there has been no clear historical break with Fordism. In fact, 'McDonaldism', a phenomenon that clearly has many things in common with Fordism, is growing at an astounding pace in contemporary society. Among the things McDonaldism shares with Fordism are homogeneous products, rigid technologies, standardized work routines, deskilling, homogenization of labor (and customer), the mass worker, and homogenization of consumption. Here is a look at each of these elements of McDonaldization from the vantage point of Fordism.

First, homogeneous products dominate a McDonaldized world. The Big Mac, the Egg McMuffin, and Chicken McNuggets are identical from one time and place to another. Second, technologies such as Burger King's conveyor system, as well as the French fry and soft drink machines throughout the fast-food industry, are as rigid as many of the technologies in Henry Ford's assembly-line system. Further, the work routines in the fast-food restaurant are highly standardized. Even what the workers say to customers is routinized. The jobs in a fast-food restaurant are deskilled; they take little or no ability. The workers are homogeneous and the actions of the customers are homogenized by the demands of the fast-food restaurant (for example, don't dare ask for a rare burger). The workers at fast-food restaurants are interchangeable. Finally, what is consumed and how it is consumed are homogenized by McDonaldization.

Thus, in these and other ways Fordism is alive and well in the modern world, although it has been transformed into McDonaldism. Furthermore, classic Fordism, for example, in the form of the assembly line, remains a significant presence in the American economy.

As you have seen, some argue that post-Fordism rather than Fordism is attuned to the production and sale of quality products. This is inconsistent with one of the fundamental tenets of McDonaldization: the emphasis on quantity and the corresponding lack of interest in quality. While this is generally the case, is it impossible to McDonaldize quality products? In some cases it is (for example, *haute cuisine* or outstanding cakes from skilled bakers), but in others, quality and McDonaldization are not inimical.

Take the boom in Starbucks coffee shops (Wichtel, 1994). Starbucks clearly sells, at high prices, high-quality coffee. A local Seattle business in 1987, by the end of 1994 Starbucks had grown to 470 company-owned stores (there are no franchises) with net sales of $285 million compared with $176 million the preceding fiscal year. The company planned to have 1500 such stores in the United States by the turn of the century, with expansion into international markets under way. Starbucks has been able to McDonaldize the coffee business without sacrificing quality. I think their secret is that they deal with a very simple product (coffee) to which they do little (brew it) or nothing (sell bags of the beans). Simple products and processes can be McDonaldized without sacrificing quality, but more complex processes and products cannot. Even burgers and fries, to say nothing of Big Macs, are far more complex than coffee.

Regarding service, which is of similar complexity in McDonald's and Starbucks, the latter has self-consciously sought to counter the problems found in McDonaldized systems, as Starbucks' founder states:

> Service is a lost art in America. I think people want to do a good job, but if they are treated poorly they get beaten down … It's not viewed as a professional job in America to work behind a counter. We don't believe that. We want to provide our people with dignity and self-esteem, and we can't do that with lip service. So we offer tangible benefits. The attrition rate in retail fast food is between 200 and 400 percent a year. At Starbucks, it's 60 percent. (Wichtel, 1994: C8)

Since service is more complex than brewing coffee, it remains to be seen whether Starbucks can offer high-quality service on a widespread and continuing basis.

Postmodernism: Are We Adrift in Hyperspace?

Then there is the more general perspective known as 'postmodernism' (Best and Kellner, 1991; Ritzer, 1997). Although there are many varieties of postmodernism, the most extreme view is that we have entered, or are entering, a new postmodern society that represents a break with modern society; postmodernity follows and supplants modernity. Among many other differences, modernity is generally thought of as highly rational and rigid, while postmodernity is seen as less rational, more irrational, and more flexible.

A number of writers, most notably Jean-François Lyotard, have explicitly viewed McDonald's as a postmodern phenomenon. Arthur Kroker et al. (1989: 119) have discussed McDonald's under the heading of 'postmodern hamburgers'. In an essay entitled 'Writing McDonald's, Eating the Past: McDonald's as Postmodern Space', Allen Shelton (forthcoming) extensively analyzes the relationship between McDonald's and postmodernism, concluding, 'I portray McDonald's as an emblem of postmodernism, a moral symbol that acts as a signpost for the times.'

To the degree that postmodernity is seen as a successor to modernity, postmodernism stands in opposition to the McDonaldization thesis: the idea that there is an increase in irrationality contradicts the view that there is an increase in rationality. Given the extreme postmodern thesis, McDonald's cannot be the symbol of both modernity and postmodernity. However, less radical postmodern orientations allow us to see phenomena like McDonald's as having *both* modern and postmodern characteristics.[5]

Thus, while Shelton associates McDonald's with postmodernism, he also links it to various phenomena that I would identify with modernism (as well as industrialism and Fordism). For example, Shelton makes the excellent point that McDonald's succeeded in automating the customer. That is, when customers enter the fast-food restaurant or wend their way along the drive-through, they enter a kind of automated system through which they are 'refueled'. In his view, McDonald's thus looks more like a factory than a restaurant. However, it is not a 'sweat shop for its customers, but a high tech factory' (Shelton, forthcoming). Therefore, from this postmodernist perspective, McDonald's is as much a modern as a postmodern phenomenon.

David Harvey (1989) also offers a moderate postmodernist argument. While Harvey sees great changes and argues that these changes lie at the base of postmodern thinking, he believes that there are many continuities between modernity and postmodernity. His major conclusion is that while 'there has certainly been a sea change in the surface appearance of capitalism since 1973 ... the underlying logic of capitalist accumulation and its crisis tendencies remain the same' (1989: 189).

Central to Harvey's approach is the idea of time–space compression. He believes that modernism served to compress both time and space and that the process has accelerated in the postmodern era, leading to 'an intense phase of time–space compression that has a disorienting and disruptive impact'. But this is not essentially different from earlier epochs in capitalism: 'We have, in short, witnessed another fierce round in that process of annihilation of space through time that has always lain at the center of capitalism's dynamic' (1989: 189, 284, 293).

As an example of space compression within the McDonaldized world, foods once available only in foreign countries or large cities are now quickly and widely available throughout the United States because of fast-food chains dispensing Italian, Mexican, or Cajun food. Similarly, as an example of time compression, foods that formerly took hours to prepare can now take seconds in a microwave oven or be purchased in minutes at a fast-food restaurant. To take a different kind of example, in the 1991 war with Iraq, television (especially CNN) transported viewers instantaneously from one place to another – from air raids in Baghdad to SCUD attacks on Tel Aviv to military briefings in Riyadh. Viewers learned about many military developments as they occurred at the same time as the generals and the President of the United States did. Thus, to Harvey, postmodernity is not discontinuous with modernity; they both reflect the same underlying dynamic.

The best-known argument that there is no discontinuity between modernity and postmodernity is made by Fredric Jameson (1984; 1991) in the essay (later, book) 'Postmodernism, or the Cultural Logic of Late Capitalism'. This title clearly indicates Jameson's Marxist position that capitalism (certainly a 'modern' phenomenon), now in its 'late' phase, continues to dominate today's world. However, it has now spawned a new cultural logic: postmodernism. In other words, though the cultural logic may have changed, the underlying economic structure remains continuous with earlier forms of capitalism, that is, it is still 'modern'. Furthermore, capitalism continues to be up to its same old tricks of spawning a cultural system to help it maintain itself.

The late phase of capitalism involves 'a prodigious expansion of capital into hitherto uncommodified areas' (1984: 78). Jameson sees this expansion not only as consistent with Marxist theory, but as creating an even purer form of capitalism. For Jameson, the key to modern capitalism is its multinational character and the fact that multinational corporations have greatly increased the range of products transformed into commodities. Even aesthetic elements that people usually associate with culture have been turned into commodities to be bought and sold in the capitalist marketplace. As a result, extremely diverse elements make up the new postmodern culture.

Jameson offers a clear image of postmodern society composed of five basic elements. Here I will present these elements and relate them to the McDonaldization of society.

First, as seen, Jameson associates postmodernity with late capitalism. There is no question that McDonaldization can be associated with earlier forms of capitalism. For example, McDonaldization is motivated by material interests, intimately associated with capitalism. But McDonaldization also exemplifies the multinationalism of late capitalism. Many McDonaldized businesses are international, with their major growth now taking place in the world marketplace.

Second, postmodern society is characterized by superficiality. Its cultural products do not delve deeply into underlying meanings. A good example is Andy Warhol's famous painting of Campbell's soup cans, which appear to be nothing more than perfect representations of those cans. To use a key term associated with postmodern theory, the painting is a *simulacrum* in which people cannot distinguish between the original and the copy. A simulacrum is also a copy of a copy; Warhol reputedly painted his soup cans not from the cans themselves, but from a photograph of them. Jameson (1984: 66) describes a simulacrum as 'the identical copy for which no original ever existed'. By definition, a simulacrum is superficial.

Clearly, a McDonaldized world is characterized by such superficiality. People pass through McDonaldized systems without being touched by them; for example, customers maintain a fleeting and superficial relation with McDonald's, its employees, and its products. McDonald's products also provide wonderful examples of simulacra. Each Chicken McNugget is a copy of a copy; no original Chicken McNugget ever existed. The original, the chicken, is hardly recognizable in the McNugget.

Third, Jameson characterizes postmodernity by a waning of emotion or affect. He contrasts another of Warhol's paintings, a near-photographic representation of Marilyn Monroe, to a classic modernist piece – Edvard Munch's *The Scream*. This surreal painting represents a person in the depth of despair, or in sociological terms, anomie or alienation. Warhol's painting of Marilyn Monroe expresses no genuine emotion. This reflects the postmodernist assertion that it was the modern world that caused the alienation depicted by Munch. In the postmodern world, however, fragmentation has tended to replace alienation. Since the world, and the people in it, have become fragmented, the affect that remains is 'free-floating and impersonal' (1984: 64).

There is also a peculiar kind of euphoria associated with these postmodern feelings, or what Jameson prefers to call 'intensities'. As an example, he presents a photorealist cityscape 'where even automobile wrecks gleam with some new hallucinatory splendour' (1984: 76).

Euphoria based on automobile disasters in the midst of urban squalor is, indeed, a peculiar kind of emotion.[6]

Clearly, the McDonaldized world is one in which the sincere expression of emotion and affect have been all but eliminated. At McDonald's, little or no emotional bond can develop among customers, employees, managers, and owners. The company strives to eliminate genuine emotion so things can operate as smoothly, as rationally, as possible. A McDonaldized world is also fragmented, as people go to McDonald's today, Denny's tomorrow, and Pizza Hut the day after. Though alienation in the McDonaldized world, especially among employees, reflects the modern world, McDonaldization also offers the free-floating affect described by Jameson. People may feel angry about, and hostile toward, the McDonaldized world, but this feeling will take a free-floating form since it is difficult to know where to direct it; after all, so many different things seem to be undergoing McDonaldization. In spite of the lack of affect in a McDonaldized society, people often feel a kind of intensity, a euphoria when they enter one of its domains. The bright lights, colors, garish signs, children's playgrounds, and so on give visitors the impression that they have entered an amusement park and are in for an exciting time.

Fourth, Jameson cites a loss of historicity in the postmodern world. Not being able to know the past has led to the 'random cannibalization of all styles of the past' and the creation of what postmodernists call *pastiches*. That is, since historians can never find the truth about the past, or even put together a coherent story about it, they must be satisfied with creating pastiches, or hodgepodges of ideas, sometimes contradictory and confused, about the past. Further, there is no clear sense of historical development, of time passing, in the postmodern world. Past and present are inextricably intertwined. For example, historical novels such as E.L. Doctorow's *Ragtime* present the 'disappearance of the historical referent. This historical novel can no longer set out to represent historical past; it can only "represent" our ideas and stereotypes about the past' (1984: 65–6, 71). Another example is the movie *Body Heat* which, while clearly about the present, creates an atmosphere reminiscent of the 1930s. To do this,

> the object world of the present-day – artifacts and appliances, even automobiles, whose styling would serve to date the image – is elaborately edited out. Everything in the film, therefore, conspires to blur its official contemporaneity and to make it possible for you to receive the narrative as though it were set in some eternal Thirties, beyond historical time. (1984: 68)

Such a movie or novel is a 'symptom of the waning of our historicity' (1984: 68). This inability to distinguish between past, present, and future shows up at the individual level in a kind of schizophrenia. For the postmodern individual, events are fragmented and discontinuous.

McDonaldized systems generally lack a sense of history. People find themselves in settings that either defy attempts to be pinpointed historically or present a pastiche of many historical epochs. The best example of the latter is Disney World (Las Vegas is another) with its hodge-podge of past, present, and future worlds. Furthermore, visitors to McDonaldized settings tend to lack a sense of the passage of time. In many cases, the designers of the system intend this. The best examples are the shopping malls and the Las Vegas casinos, both of which lack visible clocks. However, not all aspects of the McDonaldized world create such timelessness, indicating their continuing modernity. For those who choose to eat in a fast-food restaurant, time has been made important (e.g. by signs giving a twenty-minute limit on the use of tables) to prevent visitors from lingering. On the other hand, the drive-through window seems part of some timeless web as people pass through it as one link of an unending chain of destinations.

Fifth, Jameson argues that a new technology is associated with postmodern society. Instead of productive technologies such as the automobile assembly line, he cites the dominance of reproductive technologies, especially electronic media such as the television set and the computer. Rather than the 'exciting' technology of the industrial revolution, these new technologies flatten all images and make each indistinguishable from all others. These 'implosive' technologies of the postmodern era give birth to very different cultural products from the explosive technologies of the modern era.

While the McDonaldized systems do make use of some of the old-fashioned productive technologies (the assembly line, for example), they are dominated by reproductive technologies. That is, they reproduce over and over that which has been produced before; the fast-food restaurants have merely reproduced products, services, and technologies long in existence. What they produce are flattened, featureless products (the McDonald's hamburger) and services (the scripted interaction with the counterperson).

In sum, Jameson presents an image of postmodernity in which people are adrift and unable to comprehend the multinational capitalist system or the explosively growing culture and commodity market in which they live. As a paradigm of this world, and of each person's place in it, Jameson offers the example of the Los Angeles Hotel Bonaventure, designed by a famous postmodern architect, John Portman. People are unable to get their bearings in the hotel's lobby, an example of what Jameson calls *hyperspace*, an area where modern conceptions of space are useless in helping people orient themselves. This lobby is surrounded by four absolutely symmetrical towers containing the rooms. In fact, the hotel had to add color coding and directional signals because people had such difficulty getting their bearings in the hotel lobby as originally designed.

This situation in the lobby of the Bonaventure serves as a metaphor for people's inability to get their bearings in the multinational economy and cultural explosion of late capitalism. What they need now are new kinds of maps. The need for such maps reflects Jameson's view that people have moved from a world defined temporally to one defined spatially. Indeed, the idea of hyperspace, and the example of the lobby of the Hotel Bonaventure, reflect the dominance of space in the post-modern world. Thus, for Jameson, the central problem today is that people have lost their ability to position themselves within postmodern space and to map that space.

Similarly, a McDonaldized world is disorienting and difficult to map. For instance, you can be in downtown Beijing and still eat at McDonald's and Kentucky Fried Chicken. Because space and the things associated with particular places are changing dramatically, people no longer know quite where they are and they are in need of new guides. Excellent examples of hyperspace include the shopping mall, the large Las Vegas casino, and Disney World.

Thus, McDonaldization fits Jameson's five characteristics, but per-haps only because he sees postmodernity as simply a late stage of modernity. Because of this inability to draw a clear line, as well as other factors, some scholars reject the idea of a new, postmodern society. Says one, 'Now I reject all this. I do not believe that we live in "New Times", in a "postindustrial and postmodern age" fundamentally different from the capitalist mode of production globally dominant for the past two centuries' (Callinicos, 1990: 4).

Clearly, while some characteristics of today's 'postmodern' society differ dramatically from its 'modern' predecessor, great continuity exists as well. McDonaldization shows no signs of disappearing and being replaced by new, postmodern forms. It is a highly rational modern phenomenon yielding, among other things, extremely rigid structures. Thus, McDonaldization constitutes a rejection of the thesis that we have moved on to a postmodern society in which such modern phenomena are quickly disappearing. Furthermore, McDonaldized systems exhibit many postmodern characteristics side-by-side with modern elements. In other words, the McDonaldizing world demonstrates *both* modernity and postmodernity.

Globalization, or Americanization?

Yet another 'hot' theoretical issue in the social sciences these days is globalization. Globalization theorists argue that our focus should be on global processes and *not* on those stemming from any specific nation (Robertson, 1992). This, in part, is a reaction against a tendency in the past to focus on the West in general, and the United States in particular, and to see them as models for the rest of the world. Previous theorizing also tended to emphasize the impact of Western processes on the rest of the world, especially the homogenization of those cultures.

Globalization theorists argue that the nation-state in general, and the United States in particular, is not as important as it used to be. Of far greater importance are global processes that are independent of any specific nation. For example, there is a global financial world, 'finanscape', that involves the 'movement of megamonies through national turnstiles at blinding speed' (Appadurai, 1990: 298). Another example is 'ethnoscape', or the movement of large numbers of people throughout the world through tourism. In addition to such independent processes, globalization theorists also argue that exports of all sorts are moving in many different directions and not just from the West in general, and the United States in particular. Thus, they would emphasize the fact that it is not just America that is exporting McDonaldized businesses; other nations are exporting them to the United States.

While there is some truth here, and globalization is an important process, the fact remains that most McDonaldized systems have been, and are, American creations that are being exported to the rest of the world. Thus, needless to say, the McDonald's presence in, and impact on, Japan is infinitely greater than that of the Japanese chain Mos Burger on the United States. In fact, with the death of communism, and any other large-scale alternative to American-style capitalism, the world is far more open to these processes than ever before. The main opposition to these processes will come from the local level and it remains to be seen just how successful such efforts will be.

One globalization theorist argues that the 'central problem of today's global interactions is the tension between cultural homogenization and cultural heterogenization' (Appadurai, 1990: 295). Most globalization theorists contend that we are witnessing greater heterogenization (while the spread of McDonaldized systems around the world points toward homogenization). Thus, such theorists point to what they call a process of hybridization at the local level. Examples of hybridization include 'Thai boxing by Moroccan girls in Amsterdam, Asian rap in London, Irish bagels, Chinese tacos and Mardi Gras Indians in the United States' (Pieterse, 1994: 169). In fact, of course, it is possible for both things to be true. We can have the greater homogenization of some aspects of our lives (through, for example, McDonaldization) along with the greater heterogenization of other aspects.

The coexistence of homogenization and heterogenization is manifest in the idea of 'globalization' which reflects a complex interplay between the global and the local (Robertson, 1992: 173). It is certainly the case that local cultures are not crushed by processes like

McDonaldization (e.g. the resurgence of interest in betel nuts in Taipei: Wu, 1997). However, the spread of the fast-food restaurant, and other McDonaldized systems, indicates that such global processes *are* having an homogenizing effect on them. Perhaps James Watson is right in his analysis of McDonald's in Hong Kong in arguing that it 'is no longer possible to distinguish what is local and what is not. In Hong Kong ... the transnational *is* the local' (1997: 80). But, if he is, it is because McDonaldized systems have penetrated deeply into local life, and while there will be many local adaptations, there will be much homo-genization as well.

While in large part a critique of globalization theory, the McDonaldization thesis tends to be more supportive of theories of Americanization since America is the home of not only McDonald's, but so many of the other key forces in McDonaldization, and that process is being so actively exported to the rest of the world. Almost 40 years ago, Francis Williams (1962) wrote: 'The American invasion is going on all over the world: American ideas, American methods, American customs, American habits of eating, drinking and dressing, American amusements, American social patterns, American capital.' Thus, McDonald's (and McDonaldization) is, from this perspective, just one of a long line of American exports – Coca Cola, MTV, Disney, Harvard Business School techniques – that have been seen as threats to other cultures. Indeed, a furor occurred in France in the 1940s over the importation of Coca Cola to that nation; the French feared 'coca-colonization' (Kuisel, 1993).

However, there are two reasons why McDonald's and McDonaldi-zation represent a unique threat to other cultures. First, unlike previous American exports they have had an impact *both* on the way business is organized and on the culture and the way people in general lead their lives on a day-to-day basis. Second, they represent a set of principles that in both realms can be completely disengaged from their original source in McDonald's and, more broadly, American society. Once these principles have been disembedded and then reembedded in indigenous structures, it will eventually become difficult or impossible to identify these principles as originating in McDonald's or in the United States. As a result, it becomes more difficult to oppose McDonaldization as some foreign import, let alone to mount anti-American sentiment against its various manifestations. Contrast this to Coca Cola which is simply a product that retains its American identity even when it is sold and con-sumed in other cultures. While a McDonald's franchise, the Big Mac, and so on, have this quality, McDonaldization as a process is able to escape its specific material manifestations and invade any indigenous institution. Of course, it does not do this on its own. Entrepreneurs who see profits to be gained from McDonaldization are eager to apply the principles to more settings in various nations.

This brings us back to Watson's argument that it is growing impossible to distinguish the global from the local. That may be so, but it is because of the fact, at least in part, that the principles of McDonaldization have become detached from their roots and become so integral a part of local institutions and local life.

Notes

This chapter is derived from Chapters 1 and 8 of *The McDonaldization of Society* (1996: 1–16, 143–60).

1   These, of course, are the same four dimensions of Max Weber's formal rationalization theory discussed in Chapter 9; we will discuss the irrationality of rationality shortly.

2   Experimental robots of this type already exist.

3   It should be pointed out that the words *rational, rationality*, and *rationalization* are being used differently here and throughout the book from the way in which they are ordinarily employed. For one thing, people usually think of these terms as being largely positive; something that is rational is usually considered to be good. However, they are used here in a generally negative way. The positive term in this analysis is genuinely human 'reason' (for example, the ability to act and work creatively), which is seen as being denied by inhuman, rational systems such as the fast-food restaurant. For another, the term *rationalization* is usually associated with Freudian theory as a way of explaining away some behavior, but here it describes the increasing pervasiveness of rationality throughout society. Thus, in reading this book, you must be careful to interpret the terms in these ways rather than in the ways they are conventionally employed.

4   In this sense, this resembles Marx's critique of capitalism. Marx was animated not by a romanticization of precapitalist society, but rather by the desire to produce a truly human (communist) society on the base provided by capitalism. Despite this specific affinity to Marxist theory, this analysis is premised far more on the theories of Max Weber.

5   Smart (1993) argues that rather than viewing modernism and postmodernism as epochs, people can see them as engaged in a long-running and ongoing set of relationships with postmodernity continually pointing out the limitations of modernity.

6   Postmodern intensity also occurs when 'the body is plugged into the new electronic media' (see Donougho, 1989).

11

HYPERRATIONALITY: AN EXTENSION OF WEBERIAN AND NEO-WEBERIAN THEORY

The objective in this chapter is to extend the Weberian theory of rationality (and to demonstrate the utility of metatheorizing, especially M_p) by carefully analyzing and building upon the work of Weber and a number of neo-Weberians in order to push that theory in a new direction. The concept of *hyperrationality* developed in this chapter is consistent with the ideas of Weber and the neo-Weberians, although it represents a clear extension of that set of ideas.[1] In extending Weberian theory we are, following Merton (1965), 'standing on the shoulders of giants' in order to go beyond the horizons set in their own work. Weber's ideas (as well as those of his interpreters) are treated as living legacies to be expanded and to be rendered capable of addressing social realities not envisioned by Weber (and perhaps not even envisioned by more contemporary Weberians).

While we could focus on many other aspects of Weber's work, our concern is with what many consider the overarching themes in his *substantive*[2] work: rationality and the rationalization process. To adopt such an interest is to reject many of the arguments of Weber himself, as well as those of many neo-Weberians, that there is no overarching theory in Weber's work. In order for us to take the view that there *is* an overarching theory of rationality in Weber's work, we adopted some positions taken explicitly by Weber (and his followers) but rejected many others.[3] At times Weber rejected the idea of a general theory, but at other times he seemed to argue that he offered such a theory and that its focus was rationality and rationalization. We do not intend to suggest that the idea that such a theory is embedded in Weber's work is the only valid interpretation of Weberian theory, but it certainly is *one* of them. We will demonstrate this viewpoint through a metatheoretical analysis of the work of Weber and the neo-Weberians.

One source of the concept of hyperrationality, and the one that will be the focal concern of this chapter, is the Weberian and neo-Weberian theory of rationality. We will demonstrate that hyperrationality is a logical and defensible extension of that theory. There is a second source for this idea, but it will only be touched on in this chapter because of our metatheoretical focus. That second source is the contemporary social world, especially the postwar development of Japanese industry.[4]

The concept of hyperrationality flows from *both* a study of Weberian theory *and* the examination of the dramatic growth of Japanese industry.

Weber's theory of rationality focused on what he viewed as the unique characteristics of the Occident of his day. However, a new set of uniquely rational characteristics appeared in postwar Japanese industry (and Japanese society in general) that Weber did not anticipate and that is not completely described by the Weberian concept of rationality. This 'new' uniqueness requires a new theoretical concept, *hyperrationality*, to help us understand its sociological importance. It could be argued that our objective here is to create a new ideal type: hyperrationality. This is certainly acceptable, even desirable, from the point of view of Weberian methodology since new developments often require new or revised ideal types.

Why this particular ideal type? In the best Weberian tradition, the focus on hyperrationality has been chosen because of its 'value relevance'. In other words, it was selected because of its importance from the point of view of the 'evaluative ideas which dominate the investigator and his age' (Weber, 1903–17/1949: 84). Also following Weber, the focus must be on a given 'sphere of life' (or social institution) because of its value relevance as well as because it is difficult, if not impossible, to look at the society as a whole. Few issues were of greater importance from the early 1970s to the mid-1990s to the American economy (and to sociologists of the economy) than an understanding of Japan's economic success and its implications for the future of the American economy.[5]

According to Weber, 'European and American social and economic life is rationalized in a specific way and a specific sense. The explanation of this rationalization ... is one of the chief tasks of our discipline' (1903–17/1949: 34). Such an analysis remains important today, but given the rise of Japanese industry, it is also necessary to analyze the 'specific way' and 'specific sense' in which Japan's industries rationalized. That specific way and that specific sense *is* hyperrationality. In other words, Japanese industry rationalized in a manner that is different from the rationalization of Occidental industry.

This shift to a focus on Japan has some precedent in Weber's own work since Weber often analyzed rationalization processes in the Orient. In fact, Levine argues that 'he can be viewed as crediting the Orient for having developed heights of rationality in some respects superior to those reached in the Occident' (1981: 9). Along these lines, it can be argued that contemporary Japanese industry has now progressed so far that it can no longer be described by the term *rational*; a new theoretical concept – hyperrationality – is needed to adequately describe it.

While Weber made a few isolated comments specifically about Japan, he did not single Japan out for full-scale treatment as he did China and India. Thus, 'Weber did not develop a systematic analysis of

Japanese society' (Tominaga, 1989: 139). However, Tominaga, building on Weber's work and contributing his own insights into Japan, has argued that Japan provided a more favorable ground for the rationalization process than China. This favorable atmosphere allowed Japan to import, through 'cultural diffusion', Western rationality. However, as we will see, Japan did not stop with the importation of Western rationality, but went on to develop its own distinctive hyperrational system.

The ultimate objective in this chapter is to create an ideal type of hyperrationality. One route to this end, and the main concern here, is through an analysis of the major concepts in Weberian theory related to the broad idea of rationality. These concepts will be utilized, but we will put them together in a new way, to help create the concept of hyperrationality. Thus one source of hyperrationality is conceptual. This second source is empirical. That is, the concept comes not just from past conceptual work, but also from the recent historical realities of Japanese industry. In this sense, a 'historically saturated typology' is being created. The idea of hyperrationality can be judged in terms of how well it is derived from both a set of conceptual ideas and the empirical realities of Japanese industry. However, the ultimate judgment lies in the concept's utility in empirical research. As Kalberg points out, 'the formation of clear concepts [is] simply the unavoidable first step in undertaking a sociological analysis' (1980: 1177). Following Weber (1903–17/1949), the concept of hyperrationality should be used to compare, for example, American and Japanese industries, to look for divergences and similarities, to describe them, and to attempt to understand them causally.

Hyperrationality: The Conceptual Roots

While Weber does not develop a notion of hyperrationality, he does discuss the relationships among subtypes of rationality in a variety of ways. At some points he is concerned with the conflict among these subtypes, while at others he is interested in possible coexistences among these subtypes. Thus, Kalberg discusses 'the manner in which types of rationality *combine* or *struggle* against one another in history in separate rationalization processes' (1980: 1146, emphasis added). While I have some things to say about the conflicts, my main interest, given my concern with hyperrationality (which involves the coexistence of all four subtypes of rationality), is with Weber's thoughts on the various possibilities for coexistence.

Looking at substantive rationality and its conflicts first, the immediacy of practical rationality comes into conflict with the broader orientation of substantive rationality. As Weber puts it, 'the conflict between empirical reality and [substantive reality's] conception of the world as a meaningful totality, which is based on the religious postulate, produces the strongest tensions in man's inner life as well as in his external relationship to the world' (1921/1978: 451). Substantive rationality can also come into conflict with theoretical rationality, as, for example, in the case of the tendency for the substantive rationality of salvation religions to 'directly or indirectly' call for the '"sacrifice of the intellect" in the interests of a trans-intellectual, distinctive religious quality of absolute surrender and utter trust' in God (1921/1978: 567). Finally, of course, and of paramount concern to Weber, is the conflict between substantive rationality and formal rationality. Thus, Kalberg concludes, 'Formal rationalities have stood in the most direct antagonism to many substantive rationalities' (1980: 1157). For example, in discussing the relationship between a formally rational capitalist economy and the substantive rationality of Calvinism (and its ethic of brotherliness), Weber (1958: 331) argues that such an economy follows 'its own immanent laws' and grows less likely to have 'any imaginable relationship with a religious ethic of brotherliness'. Elsewhere, Weber contends that 'the people filled with the spirit of capitalism today tend to be indifferent, if not hostile, to the Church' (1904–5/1958: 70). Turning to modern politics, Weber argues that 'every ethical religion must, in similar measure and for similar reasons, experience tensions with the sphere of political behavior' (1921/1978: 590). The matter-of-factness of formally rational political behavior appears 'to an ethic of brotherliness to be estranged from brotherliness' (1958: 335). In law, Weber contends that substantive justice will inevitably conflict with the 'formalism and the rule bound and cool "matter-of-factness" of bureaucratic administration' (1921/1978: 220–1).

Most of Weber's explicit attention to conflict is devoted to a discussion of the struggles between substantive rationality and the other rationality types. However, conflicts among these other rationality types are implicit in his work. The mundaneness of practical rationality clashes with the abstraction of theoretical rationality and the creativity involved in practical rationality comes into conflict with the rule-governed character of formal rationality. The abstract search by people for answers about the world around them in theoretical rationality is likely to be stifled by the rules and regulations of formally rational systems.

Weber's thoughts on the conflicts among rationality types are important here for two very different reasons. First, they show, albeit in a negative way, that there *are* relationships among the rationality types. Second, they represent a body of ideas that need to be overcome in order to get at the idea of hyperrationality. That is, if these conflicts are inevitable and insurmountable, there can be no coexistences among subtypes of rationality and, if this is so, then there can be no such thing as hyperrationality. However, Weber himself shows that they can be overcome by offering a series of ideas on the coexistence of the various types of rationality.

Unfortunately, Weber's ideas on coexistence are neither as clear nor as explicit as his thoughts on conflict among rationality types. One exception is found in his ideas on the relationship between theoretical and practical rationality in which he concludes, in spite of the conflicts, that 'ultimately they belong inseparably together' (1958: 293). More specifically, the use of abstract ideas can help effect the 'methodical attainment of a definitely given and practical end by means of an increasingly precise calculation of adequate means' (1958: 293). In making sense of the world around them, intellectuals surely are of help in the solution of practical problems. Another exception is found in Weber's thoughts on the linkage between substantive and practical rationality where he argues that 'to the extent that an inner-worldly religion of salvation is determined by distinctly ascetical tendencies, it always demands a practical rationalism, in the sense of the maximization of rational action as such' (1921/1978: 551). On the relationship between practical and formal rationality, Weber writes that the development of economic rationalism 'though it is partly dependent on rational technique and law ... is at the same time determined by the ability and disposition of men to adopt certain types of practical rational conduct' (1904–5/1958: 21). On theoretical and substantive rationality, Weber claims that 'the destiny of religions has been influenced in a most comprehensive way by intellectualism and its various relationships to the priesthood and political authorities' (1921/1978: 500). Weber implies a linkage between theoretical and formal rationality in lawmaking and lawfinding in arguing that 'they are formally irrational when one applies in lawmaking and lawfinding means which cannot be controlled by the intellect, for instance when recourse is had to oracles or substitutes therefor' (1921/1978: 656).

Most strikingly, even formal and substantive rationality can coexist in Weberian theory. Weber writes that 'formal and substantive rationality, no matter by what standard the latter is measured, are always in principle separate things, no matter that in many (and under certain very artificial assumptions even in all) cases they may coincide empirically' (1921/1978: 108). Specifically, Weber states that substantive values can exist within formally rational capitalism if there is the 'provision of a certain minimum of subsistence for the maximum size of the population' (1921/1978: 108). When this occurs, and Weber claimed that it had within the last few decades of his lifetime, 'formal and substantive rationality coincide to a relative high degree' (1921/1978: 109). In discussing sacred law, Weber argues that the Occidental church combined formal legal technique with substantive legislation and moral ends (1921/1968: 829). Finally, Weber implies a coexistence of practical, substantive, and formal rationality when he argues that entrepreneurs must possess a 'radical concentration on God-ordained purposes; the relentless and practical rationalism of the asceticist; and methodical conception of matter-of-factness in business management' (1916/1964: 247).

Thus, while Weber does not develop a full-scale sense of the mutual interrelatedness of all four types of rationality, he clearly recognized a variety of coexistences. However, it seems clear that Weber did not foresee a future in which all four types of rationality would coexist and feed off one another to produce a level of rationality unseen in his day. It is by extending Weber's limited thoughts on coexistence that we can begin to get at the concept of hyperrationality. In doing so, the sense in Weber's work that formal rationality will ultimately and inevitably triumph over the other three types needs to be questioned (although it also informs my work on McDonaldization).

In this section, we have offered a demonstration of the roots of the idea of hyperrationality in Weberian theory. However, this new theoretical concept was created not only on the basis of a metatheoretical (M_p) study of the work of Weber and the neo-Weberians, but also out of an analysis of contemporary Japanese industry. We found that the Weberian hypothesis that formal rationality would triumph over the other types did not hold in the case of Japanese industry. Rather, the Japanese appear to have created an industrial system in which all four types of rationality coexist and feed off one another to produce a hyperrational industrial system.

Hyperrationality: The Case of Japanese Industry

Formal Rationality

While it certainly had indigenous examples of formal rationality (see below) that predated the American occupation of Japan after World War II, a number of formally rational ideas and systems were imported into Japan at the close of the war in an effort to make it more self-sufficient economically.[6] Japanese industry adopted the ideas of W. Edwards Deming and J.M. Juran, both American experts in statistical quality control, in particular through the quantification of as many factors as possible. (In fact, as we have seen, calculability is one of the crucial dimensions of a formally rational system.) Overall, the importation of Western formal rationality provided a shortcut to the modernization of industry; resulted in the saving of enormous amounts of time and money; provided a powerful incentive to set up new factories; and made it possible for these factories to be provided quickly with the most up-to-date technologies.

The late importation of these ideas (the West had been utilizing them for many decades) and systems into a society that already had strong substantive, theoretical, and practical rationality helps to explain why formal rationality did not triumph over these other forms. It was the formal rationality that was largely foreign, and while it was adopted, it was forced to accept and accommodate itself to the other types of rationality.

Japanese industry has not contented itself with the importation of Western formal rationality. It has its own indigenous forms, most of which have been developed in recent decades. One formally rational structure in existence prior to the importation of Western formal rationality, and which helped to allow it to prosper on Japanese soil, was the Ministry of International Trade and Industry (MITI) (Johnson, 1982). In brief, MITI is a formally rational bureaucratic structure that has the (formally rational) responsibility of overseeing Japan's industries in order to be sure that their individual and collective success maximizes the interest of the nation as a whole. In effect, the objective of MITI is to organize the entire structure of Japanese industry in a rational manner (Vogel, 1979: 72). Among other things MITI encourages long-range planning. Long-term thinking at MITI involves the extension of formal rationality to future planning. This gave Japan an enormous advantage over American industry in the 1970s and 1980s where formal rationality had been employed largely in the service of short-term maximization. With MITI, the Japanese created, in effect, a second formally rational system with its own bureaucratic branches, sectors, and hierarchical levels to oversee the formally rational industrial and business sector.

Another distinctively Japanese formally rational development is the 'just-in-time' (JIT) system. The JIT system involves producing and delivering finished goods just in time to be sold, subassemblies just in time to be assembled into finished products, fabricated parts just in time to go into subassemblies, and purchased materials just in time to be transformed into fabricated parts. One could say that the Japanese produced small quantities just in time, while, in contrast, industries in the United States produced large quantities 'just in case' (Schonberger, 1982: 16). The JIT system was clearly more formally rational than the Western just-in-case (JIC) system (that's why it has been adopted by so many American corporations in recent years). For example, the greater calculability associated with JIT leads to lower inventories and greater profits.

Finally, there are the bureaucratic systems that are integral to Japanese manufacturing. In many ways these systems are more bureaucratic, more formally rational, than Western bureaucracies. For example, one must have had the 'right' education, including attendance at one of the imperial universities, in order to qualify for a position within these organizations. Entry into the organizations is governed by tough entrance examinations that *all* prospective employees must take. All those who are hired in a specific job track must move through the hierarchy together as a group and at the same pace. All of these workers are regularly rotated to a variety of different positions and departments. In these and other ways, Japanese bureaucracies are more formally rational than their Western counterparts, which exercise far less control over individuals and permit much more individual variation in movement through the system.

This high degree of formal rationality paradoxically permits, and even encourages, a higher degree of substantive rationality in Japanese bureaucracies. Because the formally rational system runs so smoothly and effectively, the Japanese can allow greater flexibility in a variety of realms. For example, there are fewer status distinctions between managers and subordinates, white-collar and blue-collar workers, and so on. Responsibilities of one position are less clearly distinguished from those of other positions; there is more blending of roles and positions. Japanese workers are dominated by fewer rules and required to process far less paperwork. Workers are more likely to be viewed as people than as interchangeable bureaucratic parts. Managers and employees are far more flexible in terms of what they do and how they do it. This flexibility tends to lead to greater experimentation and openness to the generation and testing of new ideas. While in the West formal rationality tends to submerge substantive rationality, in Japan formal rationality is more likely to encourage and work hand-in-hand with substantive rationality. Given this convergence, let us turn more directly to some examples of substantive rationality within Japanese industry.

Substantive Rationality

Japan has been able to retain a consistent set of human values, which includes groupism; interdependence; *wa* (harmony); *on* (debt); and *giri* (obligation). In contrast, Western nations have tended to lose, or see a deterioration of, such a value system (Vogel, 1979: 98). This system in Japan tends *to work in concert with* formal rationality while in the West it has tended *to lose out to* formal rationality.

Japanese groupism contrasts sharply with the individualism of the West. While in individualism the individual is opposed to the group, in groupism the goal is for the individual and the group to become one. A view is encouraged in which individual interests equal group interest and group interest equals individual interests (Iwata, 1982: 39). Americans try to position themselves in a society as individuals, and they attempt to restrict mutual relations both functionally and in terms of duration of encounters. In contrast, the Japanese are inclined to position themselves in society in terms of the group(s) with which they are affiliated. The word *individualism* in Japanese denotes selfishness, isolation from others, and persons concerned only with their own advantage rather than being willing to work for the welfare of others. The person weakens the group by being individualistic, while everyone gains when all seem to make the group more efficient (Alston, 1986: 34).

There are a number of manifestations of Japanese groupism. For example, individual failure is minimized; failure is shared among the members of the work group. On the other hand, the group receives credit for any successes. There is intense group pressure to produce, and to produce high-quality goods and services. It is not unusual for workers to stay late until everyone has finished their work. Japanese companies develop an ideology (Rohlen, 1975: 208) that is similar to that of the traditional Japanese family (Alston, 1986: 27). As in their families, the Japanese are devoted to their companies and in return they receive the kind of *amae* (caring) that they receive in the family setting. For the Japanese work and play are tightly intertwined; work groups and play groups tend to be one and the same.

As a result of groupism, corporate success in Japan is seen as resulting from group effort rather than from the activities of exceptional individuals (in the United States the opposite is true). Work groups, teams, and departments are seen as the reason why the company improves productivity or exceeds quotas.

Derived from groupism, with roots in Confucianism, is the concept of *wa*, the quest for harmony, unity, and cooperation. *Wa* exists at both the cultural level and more specifically in the family, schools, clubs, and the workplace (Pegels, 1984: 67). Like groupism, *wa* operates against individualism since it demands considerable conformity. At the level of the individual organization, it is manifested in consensus-type decision making and strong respect by each individual for all others. *Wa* is maintained through a strong team spirit; members must identify with the group and be loyal to it and its goals. Because *wa* is so important, Japanese leaders often feel that they can only lead when they know where their followers want to go. The act of reaching consensus can be more important than what has been agreed to (Taylor, 1983: 115). One by-product of *wa* is that superordinates and subordinates feel responsible for one another; *wa* helps bind them together (Pegels, 1984: 73). Subordinates care about matters that in the United States are considered the sole responsibility of the supervisor. In turn, supervisors feel responsible for subordinates and their behavior both in and out of the workplace.

At one level, the substantive rationality of *wa* helps to counter the excesses of formal rationality. For example, unlike in the West, the employee is not depersonalized or treated like a machine or an appendage to one (De Vos, 1975: 218). For another, the Japanese will not use formally rational techniques if they threaten the *wa* (Alston, 1986: 124).

Groupism and *wa* (as well as the other components of this value system) have permitted the Japanese to develop their distinctive system of permanent employment,[7] a system that can be seen as being composed of both formally and substantively rational elements. It is made possible because workers feel it necessary to be loyal to the group and the members would feel they were being disloyal if they left for another employer. For their part, it would be morally reprehensible for an employer to discard a worker because he or she was no longer needed. Permanent employment reinforces, and is reinforced by, groupism and *wa*. The Japanese tend to view themselves as workers for Toyota, who happen to have a set of skills (e.g. as welders). In contrast, Americans see themselves as welders, who happen to work for Ford. The Japanese system obviously helps to engender a far greater commitment to the employing organization. The Japanese view learning a skill and then moving on to another company, a common American practice, as selfish behavior.

While it is in many ways substantively rational, permanent employment also has many formally rational attributes. For example, standardized entrance exams are used to find those employees who are most likely to contribute to the organization over the course of many years. For another, a hierarchy is employed to allow permanent employees to move up in the organization over time. For still another, periodic wage increases are based on a clearly defined seniority system so that those in whom the company has invested heavily are motivated to remain in the company. Furthermore, because pay is heavily tied to seniority, pay differences are comparatively insignificant and this reduces conflict within work groups and cohorts. All workers tend to do well together when the company is prospering and to suffer together in bad times.

Permanent employment not only is formally rational in a number of ways, but also encourages the development of a series of formally rational by-products. For example, because the company is sure that its employees will remain, it can engage in long-range planning of personnel allocation and development. For another, because it is assured of a stable pool of competent workers, the company is better able to make long-range predictions about other aspects of its operation (e.g. long-term production levels). More generally, long-term employment encourages a longer-term perspective throughout the organization. In contrast, in the United States employees and managers rarely are enthusiastic about anything but projects that get short-term results. In the United States, the likelihood that one is going to change companies operates against a long-term perspective.

Other aspects of permanent employment encourage heightened substantive rationality. For example, because they feel secure, managers are willing to take risks, to experiment, and to test out new ideas. Managers also tend to be more flexible than their American counterparts because of their greater security. For another, because they are safer from layoffs, Japanese workers will do their best even in the worst economic times. In contrast, American workers may be paralyzed by a fear of an imminent layoff and their anger may directly result in poor performance if they are told they are to be laid off. Thus here, as elsewhere, substantive rationality and formal rationality work together in Japan to produce a higher level of overall rationality.

Theoretical Rationality

Japanese society in general, and industry in particular, have also been able to maintain and develop theoretical rationality. From the national government to the individual firm, few things take precedence over the acquisition of knowledge and information (Vogel, 1979: 27). At the societal level this is manifested in widely circulated newspapers imparting highly technical information, a well-supported system of educational television, and a very active book publishing and book translation business.

For the Japanese, study and education continue well beyond the end of formal education. After they have been employed, workers are encouraged to participate in work-related study. Off the job, workers often look for opportunities to learn things that one day *may* be of use to them on the job (Vogel, 1979: 28–9). This commitment to continuing education is made possible by the existence of the formally and substantively rational system of permanent employment which makes (some) employees willing to invest the time needed to learn and (some) employers willing to pay the costs involved. This educational commitment is also supported by the substantively rational groupism and *wa* because employees are willing to do what is necessary for the welfare of the collectivity. Conversely, the collectivity, the employing organization in this case, wants to help the members improve themselves through education.

However, the major examples of the Japanese industrial emphasis on theoretical rationality are their commitment to engineering and to research and development. This commitment may be linked to Japan's high literacy rate, as well as to its people's general knowledge of mathematics, economics, and basic engineering. In terms of engineering, Japan has substantially more engineers in senior management positions than the United States and graduates more engineers each year than any other Western country. In the workplace, Japanese industries employ many more engineers and rely on them more heavily than do their Western counterparts.

The focus on research and development (R&D) is reflected in the fact that in the 1960s Japan's exports were heavily concentrated in industries (e.g. textiles, iron, steel, automobiles) with low investments in R&D, but in the 1980s the concentration shifted to those sectors (e.g. electronics, production processes, and biotechnology) that require large investments in R&D. Japanese industry has long passed the stage of being reliant on Western technology. Reflecting this reality, Japan currently registers two and a half times the number of patents as the United States, and eight times the rate of Britain.

At the national level, Japan spends 2.01 percent of its GNP on R&D. Although this figure appears to compare unfavorably to that spent by such Western nations as the United States (2.47 percent) and West Germany (2.24 percent), comparatively little of the Japanese investment goes into research related to national defense. Most of it (about three-fourths) is spent in the private sector, especially on commercial product development. In contrast, the US spends much of its research and development money on national defense and space projects that tend to produce often spectacular developments with little commercial application (McMillan, 1984: 117). Another difference between Japan and the West is that Japan's scientists are not as academically oriented as their Western counterparts. Many scientists in the West are in university settings where their focus is on publication and success in the scientific community. Many Western scientists employed in the commercial sector share these objectives. In contrast, in Japan the main rewards and career incentives for scientists lie in the corporation. Even university-based scientists work in close association with corporations, which often provide access, consultation, and research support, and may even publish research findings provided by university researchers (1984: 102).

The strong emphasis on theoretical rationality is linked to, and reinforces, the other types of rationality discussed above. For example, the substantively rational groupism and *wa* contribute to the commitment of scientists and engineers to their employers and to their eagerness to contribute their knowledge and expertise to the latter's success and well-being. The provision of this information, in turn, strengthens the collectivity and its *wa*. Permanent employment is also involved since engineers and scientists see that they will spend their entire work lives with an employer and are willing to contribute knowledge and information to the organization that will be their occupational home for life. Permanent employment also encourages engineers and scientists (and their employers) to invest the time and money in continual reeducation so that they stay abreast of the most recent developments. The long-range perspective produced by permanent employment allows engineers and scientists to work on projects that may not see tangible results, let alone profitable undertakings, for many years to come. Turning to formal rationality, MITI serves to encourage emphasis on science and engineering by its efforts to encourage technological developments within designated sectors.

Practical Rationality

While in the United States practical rationality, like substantive and theoretical rationality, has been allowed to languish, the Japanese have encouraged it to coexist with, and contribute to, the other types of rationality. One manifestation of the Japanese commitment to retain practical rationality is their 'bottom-up' management philosophy (including the *ringi* system of having documents originate with lower-level managers) which contrasts greatly with the 'top-down' approach characteristic of the United States. While American managers focus on imposing decisions on lower echelons in the organization, the Japanese are interested in allowing lower-level supervisors to define problems and then work to solve them (Pegels, 1984: 4). In many Japanese companies the key figures are lower-level department heads and division chiefs, rather than high-level executives. It is the lower-level managers who tend to work out the details of day-to-day planning. When top-down decisions do occur, Japanese executives go out of their way to disguise them and make them appear as if they resulted from bottom-up decision making (Gibney, 1982: 61). As a result of this management approach, Japanese organizations get greater contributions from managers throughout the organizational hierarchy. In other words, the organization is able to give free reign to the practical rationality of its lower-level managers and to enjoy the gains from that rationality.

This bottom-up, practical rationality is reinforced by the substantive rationality of groupism and *wa*. That is, Japanese executives can feel secure in giving lower-level managers considerable leeway because they are assured that such managers will work for the good of the company rather than slacking off or working for their own interests. Furthermore, it can safely be assumed that subordinate managers will not attack top management policies or undermine an executive's authority. Bottom-up management also contributes to the formal rationality of the organization. That is, the ideas that flow from lower-level managers help in various ways to improve the functioning of such formally rational structures as the assembly lines and bureaucracies. This is nowhere clearer than in another aspect of practical rationality in Japan: quality circles (QCs). While the bottom-up and *ringi* systems elicit the practical rationality of lower-level managers, quality circles are designed to extract and utilize the practical rationality of lower-level workers.

The QC is nothing more than a group of workers (usually led by the immediate supervisor) who meet on a regular basis to identify, analyze, and find solutions to quality problems (as well as other issues). Because of the substantive rationality of groupism and *wa*, workers are willing to voluntarily meet, often during their off hours. The idea behind this system is simple: because everyone possesses and practices practical rationality, workers often have ideas on how to improve their work process. The brainstorming sessions that occur in QCs allow people to express these ideas. Members of the QCs are encouraged not to be encumbered by the way things are currently done on the job, so that they will be more inclined to generate new, creative ideas. The Japanese have thus been able to exploit the practical rationality of those in the organization, particularly at the bottom of the organization, while in the West formally rational systems have ignored this and even tried to actively suppress it so that those at the bottom blindly conform to the demands of the formally rational system.

Like all of the other types of rationality in Japan, practical rationality reinforces, and is reinforced by, the other types of rationality. For example, the theoretically rational emphasis on knowledge and information supports the effort to utilize the skills and abilities of the lowest-ranking members of the organization. Because of the substantively rational emphasis on groupism and *wa*, it can be assumed that workers will utilize initiative without fear that they will exploit these opportunities for their own benefit. The substantively and formally rational system of permanent employment encourages participation in QC circles because such involvement assumes, and reinforces, dedication among workers to the employing organization. Further, the high-speed operations of the formally rational JIT system require that all workers be vigilant on the issue of quality.

Synergy

In the preceding discussion we have sought to demonstrate that Japanese industry is hyperrational in the sense that the four types of rationality exist simultaneously. This situation stands in contrast to the American case where the triumph of formal rationality led to the decline, or even disappearance, of the other three types of rationality. The coexistence of the four types of rationality may be seen as hyperrationality in the weak sense of the term. In a stronger sense, hyperrationality means that the four types of rationality interact with one another and out of this interaction emerges a heightened, historically unprecedented level of rationality, hyperrationality. In other words, there is a synergism among the four types of rationality so that their simultaneous interaction with one another produces a more rational system than would occur if we simply summed the effect of the four types of rationality, taken separately. Throughout the preceding discussion, a number of the synergistic aspects of hyperrationality have been underscored.

The goal in this discussion of Japanese industry has been to show how the concept of hyperrationality, derived previously from the Weberian theory of rationality, has also been derived from the case of the recent history of Japanese history. Thus, rather than being simply an abstract conceptual creation, hyperrationality is a historically saturated ideal type. Having discussed hyperrationality as it is manifest in the specific case of Japanese industry, we turn now to the creation of hyperrationality as an ideal type. The ideal type to be constructed below is a product of *both* the analysis of Japanese industry in this section and, more importantly, the conceptual analysis presented in the preceding section.

Hyperrationality: An Ideal-Typical Characterization

Consistent with its Weberian roots and its Weberian orientation, the concept of hyperrationality is discussed here in ideal-typical terms. In developing this ideal type we are following various guidelines laid down by Weber. The ideal type is to be rigorously rational and internally consistent. It involves the analytical accentuation of certain elements of reality. It resembles a utopian vision, although *not* in the sense that the social world 'ought' to operate in this manner. Thus, the ideal type is unlikely to correspond exactly with any empirical reality (even Japanese industry). It is conceptually and historically derived. It is adequate both empirically and on the level of meaning (Weber, 1921/1968: 20). It is a methodological tool that is abstracted from reality and that can be used to help us to better understand social reality. It is both transhistorical and transcultural, which means that it can be used to analyze a variety of historical periods and a variety of different societies. And, of course, the construction of an ideal type is not an end in itself, but rather a tool for empirical research.

The ideal type of hyperrationality has four elements:

1   Hyperrationality involves the simultaneous existence of practical, theoretical, substantive, and formal rationality. All of the subtypes of rationality are used here in the way they are conventionally used by Weber and neo-Weberians.
2   Each of these subtypes exists to a high degree. That is, in a hyperrational system it is important not just that all four types exist, but that each of them flourishes. There is a high degree of practical, theoretical, substantive, and formal rationality in a hyperrational system.

3 Each of the subtypes of rationality is interrelated with all of the others.
4 Out of this interaction a new level and type of rationality emerges: hyperrationality is an emergent phenomenon. This means that there is a synergism among the four types of rationality, allowing for the emergence of an extraordinarily high level of rationality.

Implications

Various issues emerge from this analysis of hyperrationality that are worth at least mentioning in this closing section. For example, there is the issue of the utilization of the ideal type of hyperrationality. While it is derived in part from Japanese industry, it can be used as a tool to analyze particular Japanese industries, to compare industries, and to analyze Japanese society as a whole. The ideal type of hyperrationality can also be used to analyze the industries of other societies, most importantly American industry. The use of this tool can allow us to pinpoint the factors that were lacking in American industry in the 1970s and 1980s from the point of view of ideal-typical hyperrationality. And it can be used to examine what aspects of Japanese hyperrationality American industry adopted in the 1990s in order to be more competitive with, and even outdo, Japanese industry. This, in effect, becomes a *sociological* and a *theoretical* way of helping one understand the failures (and more recent successes) of American industry in comparison to Japanese industry. To a similar end, one could compare ideal-typical hyperrationality to the ideal-typical formal rationality which, following Weber, is associated with American industry as well as the West in general. The isolation of differences, as well as similarities, between these two forms of rationality would be a prelude to causal analysis of why, historically, America was drawn in the direction of formal rationality while Japan moved toward hyperrationality.

Another line of analysis would be to trace out the implications of a hyperrational economy for other social institutions. Following Weber, Japan's hyperrational economy would need, among other things, a compatible political system as well as an educational system that produces the kind of people needed by such an economy.

As an ideal type, hyperrationality is a methodological utopia, but it is not an ideal in the sense that society, all societies, should move toward hyperrationality. Nor does it lead us to ignore the problems associated with hyperrationality. Just as Weber was ambivalent about formal rationality, seeing it as both liberating and enslaving, we have a similar ambivalence about hyperrationality. For example, while, as we have seen, hyperrationality as practiced in Japan has produced unparalleled growth, it has done so by enslaving people in a system that can be seen as unprecedented in its ability to exploit workers. A systematic study of Japanese-style hyperrationality would need to tease out both its liberating and its enslaving dimensions. Then there is the question of the future of Japanese and American society and industry. Given the relative success of Japanese industrial hyperrationality *vis-à-vis* American industry's formal rationality, America has sought to emulate Japanese success by importing elements of Japanese hyperrationality, just as after World War II Japan imported American formal rationality. However, the question remains: will a wholesale adoption of Japanese techniques work in the United States in the long term? More generally, as a result of Japanese successes, does the world confront an iron cage of hyperrationality that (at least in this case) dwarfs in terms of its problematic dimensions Weber's iron cage of formal rationality? Or, since Weber was wrong about an iron cage of formal rationality, is it just as unlikely that we will see an iron cage of hyperrationality? Just as Weber did not foresee hyperrationality, are we now unable to foresee the next stage in the march of rationality? Or, will the future bring with it a reversal in the direction of a less rational society? Are there viable alternatives in the modern world to rationality, be it formal rationality or hyperrationality?

Weber had deep reservations about the triumph of formal rationality. It is unlikely that the emergence and seeming supremacy of hyperrationality would ease Weber's fears. In fact, it seems likely that he would view the 'polar night of icy darkness and hardness' of hyperrationality as even darker and harder.

Conclusions

One of the things the preceding section, as well as the chapter as a whole, demonstrates is the relevance of metatheorizing, in this case the use of M_p. Specifically, a metatheoretical analysis of the Weberian theory of rationality, in concert with an empirical examination of Japanese industry, has generated a new theoretical concept: hyperrationality.

Notes

The source of this chapter is *Metatheorizing in Sociology* (1991b: 93–115); this chapter was coauthored by Terri LeMoyne.

1   This concept, as it is used here, was suggested by Ritzer and Walczak (1988). It is used in a very different way by Berger and Berger (1984: 118–20).
2   In this chapter we focus on Weber's substantive work, while in the chapter on the architectonic the focus was on the underlying structure of his work.
3   In this case the task of the neo-Weberian is much like that of the neo-Marxian. Both Marx and Weber offered vast, complex, sometimes vague, sometimes internally contradictory theories of the modern world. The result is that multiple interpretations of

these theories are possible and they can be defended by recourse to the work of the master as well as to that of the significant interpreters who have followed in his footsteps.

4   See Ritzer and LeMoyne (1990) for the details of the Japanese case.

5   In the last several years, the Japanese economy in general, and the automobile industry in particular, have endured a protracted slump. However, Japanese innovations remain important and, in fact, many of them were adopted by American automobile manufacturers (and others) and this helped them to compete better with their Japanese counterparts.

6   Because much of the focus in this book is on metatheorizing, this section on the empirical sources of the concept of hyperrationality will be presented in a greatly abbreviated fashion. For much more on this, see Ritzer and LeMoyne (1990). In addition to leaving out much detail, this discussion also omits many of the problems associated with Japanese hyperrationality. The reader should not come away from a reading of this section with the view that Japanese hyperrationality is an unmitigated success. Indeed, it can be seen as permitting an unprecedented level of exploitation.

7   It should be noted that this system covers only a small percentage of Japanese workers.

12

MANNHEIM'S THEORY OF RATIONALIZATION: AN ALTERNATIVE RESOURCE FOR THE McDONALDIZATION THESIS?

Max Weber's (1921/1958; 1921/1968) theory of rationalization lies at the base of the McDonaldization thesis (as well as the idea of hyperrationality). While that theory provides a rich resource, there are reasons why one might want to look elsewhere for additional theoretical inspiration. For one thing, Weber was far from clear about the rationalization process. One needs to extract a sense of what he meant by it from some often vague definitions of concepts, as well as from his diverse, even divergent, analyses of the various ways in which rationalization played itself out in a variety of domains (religion, polity, law, music, and so on). For another, the wealth of Weberian theory has been exploited to a large degree and further returns on one's investment are likely to diminish. Finally, explorations of other relevant theoretical resources might, at this point, prove far more fruitful in terms of deepening our understanding of rationalization and McDonaldization.

The theory that suggests itself most strongly is Karl Mannheim's thinking on rationality and rationalization. Mannheim's work is based, at least in part, on Weber's ideas (as well as on another underutilized resource, Simmel's thinking on rationality: Turner, 1986), but it also goes beyond them in certain ways. In this chapter I examine Mannheim's thinking about rationalization, contrast it to Weber's where necessary, and explore the ways in which it does or does not enrich our understanding of the McDonaldization process.

Mannheim's Early Thinking on Rationalization

In *Ideology and Utopia* (1929/1936) Mannheim offered a gross distinction between rationality and irrationality which he both refined and altered dramatically in his later work. This early thinking is reviewed here more as background to, and contrast for, what is to come in a discussion of Mannheim's later work than for its importance to our focal concerns in this chapter.

At this early stage, the rational sphere of society was defined as 'consisting of settled and routinized procedures in dealing with situations that recur in an orderly fashion' (1929/1936: 113). Such 'settled and routinized procedures' are a central component of McDonaldization: McDonaldized systems generally institute such procedures in order to control what employees, customers, and many others (e.g. suppliers) do. And those procedures exist in order to deal with recurrent situations (e.g. the ordering of goods or services by customers). To take one example, the following is the original McDonald's procedure for cooking hamburgers:

> Grill men ... *were instructed* to put hamburgers down on the grill moving from left to right, creating *six rows* of six patties each. And because the first *two rows* were farthest from the heating element, they were *instructed* (and still are) to flip the third row first, then the fourth, fifth, and sixth before flipping the first two. (Love, 1986: 141–2, emphasis added)

Employees who follow these procedures are behaving rationally, at least in terms of Mannheim's early sense of such behavior.

Mannheim defines the irrational sphere residually: the irrational must be those domains in which there is an *absence* of settled routinized procedures for dealing with recurrent situations. Again, from the contemporary perspective, McDonaldization, given its association with such procedures, serves to reduce and ultimately eliminate irrational domains. The objective is to create more and more such procedures to cover as many recurrent situations as possible. (In Weberian terms, the construction of the iron cage of rationality would be complete when all such situations are covered by procedures.) That irrationality which persists is most likely to be found in nonrecurrent situations as well as more generally in less and non-McDonaldized sectors of society.

Mannheim (1929/1936: 115) made it clear that at least in his day the irrational spheres continued to predominate over the rational sectors of society: 'rationalized as our life may seem to have become, all the rationalizations that have taken place so far are merely partial since the most important realms of our social life are even now anchored in the irrational'. While this may still be true, the progress of McDonaldization indicates that the irrational sphere has been reduced, at least to some degree, since Mannheim wrote.

Mannheim discussed several sectors in which he felt irrationality continued to predominate. The economy was still dominated by what he considered to be irrational free competition. Similarly, in the stratification system, one's place continued to be determined by irrational competition and struggle, not by rational objective tests that decided one's position within that system. And in politics, rational planning had not yet been able to eliminate the irrational struggle for dominance at the national and international levels. For Mannheim, the solution to the problem of irrationality lay in greater planning.[1] Planning would provide the routinized and settled procedures (as well as the objective tests needed in the stratification system) that would make greater rationalization possible. While Mannheim was thinking about central planning, McDonaldized systems involve much more, albeit far less centralized, planning than non-McDonaldized alternatives and thereby limit irrationality more effectively.

While the irrational continues to predominate, Mannheim seems to imply (as I do with the McDonaldization thesis) that rationalization is a process that has invaded various sectors of society and that others are likely to come under its sway in the future. In other words, the irrational is likely to retreat in the face of the forward progress of the rational. As Mannheim (1929/1936: 114) puts it, 'The chief characteristic of modern culture is the tendency to include as much as possible in the realm of the rational and to bring it under administrative control – and, on the other hand, to reduce the "irrational" element to the vanishing point.'

Mannheim was forced to back away from this optimistic view in his later work in the face of the increasing prevalence of such irrationalities as economic depression, war, and fascism. It became difficult to argue that irrationalities were disappearing. If anything, the opposite seemed to be the case. As we will see, Mannheim came to feel that rationality could not be left to advance on its own, but had to be helped along through planning. Furthermore, as he refined and even altered his sense of rationality, he saw that the progress of at least one type of rationality might in fact be a major *cause* of at least some of these irrationalities (more on this below).

At this early stage in Mannheim's work, rationalization involves behavior that is in accord with some rational structure or framework. Rational actors follow definite prescriptions 'entailing no personal decision whatsoever' (1929/1936: 115). The image is of the actor following the dictates of some larger bureaucratically organized structure (the source of the 'administrative control', the settled and routinized procedures, mentioned above) and this image is supported by the examples offered by Mannheim – petty officials, judges, and factory workers. As a result of the time in which he wrote, Mannheim (like Weber) overemphasizes the importance of bureaucracies, at least from our contemporary vantage point. McDonald's (as well as most franchisers), for example, has a minimal bureaucratic staff and structure, but it nonetheless has been able to develop and implement 'settled and routinized procedures' that it imposes on franchisees, managers, and employees. While it is not well described as a bureaucracy, McDonald's has succeeded in developing methods that leave its employees with little or no room for personal decision making.

Mannheim contrasts rational action to *conduct* which begins 'where rationalization has not yet penetrated, and where we are forced to make decisions in situations which have *as yet* not been subjected to regulation' (1929/1936: 115, emphasis added). In this early work, conduct is associated with the irrational realm and Mannheim holds the view that conduct, like irrationality more generally, will sooner or later come to be limited or even eliminated by the process of rationalization. In these terms, what McDonaldized systems have succeeded in doing is to greatly restrict 'conduct'. Rules, regulations, scripts, and the like have increased significantly the regulation of the behavior of those associated with McDonaldized systems. Thus in Mannheim's terms, at least in this early stage in his work, McDonaldization brings with it a decline in irrationality.

There is a conundrum in Mannheim's early thinking on the process of rationalization. On the one hand, he clearly favors the progressive rationalization of sectors that had hitherto been dominated by the irrational. Since they will come to be controlled by administrative dictates, irrational decisions and actions will be reduced or eliminated. On the other hand, can Mannheim really want a world in which all decisions are controlled? In which there is no personal decision making, no personal freedom, whatsoever? We will return to this issue when we discuss Mannheim's views on planning, but before we do we need to get a sense of his later analysis of the nature of rationality (and irrationality).

Mannheim's Later Thinking on Rationality

Mannheim had much more to say about rationality and irrationality, and he said it very differently, in *Man and Society in an Age of Reconstruction* (1935/1940). Mannheim's thinking on rationality had grown far more refined; he differentiated between two types of rationality and two varieties of irrationality. He argued that both rationality and irrationality can be subdivided into the 'substantial' and the 'functional' (paralleling, at least to some degree, Weber's distinction between substantive and formal rationality). Substantial rationality and irrationality deal with thinking, while functional rationality and irrationality are concerned with action. In this section we will deal with his greatly revised thoughts on rationality, while in the next section we will analyze his similarly modified thinking on irrationality.

Substantial rationality is defined as 'an act of *thought* which reveals *intelligent insight* into the inter-relations of events in a given situation' (1935/1940: 53, emphasis added). This is clearly very different from the gross definition of rationality adopted in Mannheim's earlier work. Here rationality involves intelligent thought whereas previously his more global sense of rationality (closer to what he now thinks of as functional rationality: see below) implied an almost complete lack of thought.

Substantial rationality is a micro-subjective (see Chapter 4) concept relating purely to individual thought processes (although the larger social setting is clearly implied through the notion of the situation in which the thought takes place).[2] In contrast, Weber's parallel concept of substantive rationality, or the choice of means to ends in the context of larger values, is multidimensional. It involves micro-objective action (the choice) and macro-subjective values, as well as, at least implicitly, micro-subjective thought processes leading to the choice of means to ends. Weber's conceptualization is much richer, but that very richness creates problems for those who seek to use it.

The multidimensionality of Weber's conceptualization makes it 'messy' in the sense that it combines both micro (action, and perhaps thought) and macro (values) elements within one concept. It also does not specify the nature of the relationship between its two (or three, depending on how you count them) elements, especially how much control values exercise over choices, as well as the relationship between thought and action.

Mannheim's substantial rationality is a far neater concept operating purely at the micro-subjective level in terms of individual thought and insight. As a result, there is none of the kind of ambiguity that exists in Weber's parallel concept. There is no need for Mannheim to specify micro–macro relationships, nor the linkage between thought (micro-subjectivity) and action (micro-objectivity), within the concept of substantial rationalization. The simplicity of Mannheim's conceptualization is an asset, especially if one wants to link, as both Mannheim and Weber do, substantive rationality to other concepts, especially functional (or formal) rationality. Because it encompasses several different levels of analysis, Weber's sense of substantive rationality is difficult to relate to, say, formal rationality. Is one relating thought, action, values, or some combination of the three to formal rationality? Depending on which aspect one is linking to formal rationality, one is likely to come up with very different conclusions about the nature of that relationship. On the other hand, given Mannheim's limited conceptualization, it is clear that one is concerned with the impact of substantially rational thought processes on functionally rational systems and the corresponding effect of those systems on such thinking.

The issue of the nature of this relationship is of great importance because in many ways Weber prefers substantive rationality with its human values to formal rationality in which choices are constrained by inhuman rules, regulations, and structures. However, because of the complexity of his conceptualization, it is unclear exactly what Weber prefers: substantively rational thought? action? or the larger human values that predominate in substantive rationality? For another, assuming, as most do, that it is the last, it is very difficult to come down unequivocally on the side of substantive rationality over formal rationality. The problem here is that substantive rationality, in which larger human values predominate, has the potential to lead to far greater inhumanity than formal rationality. History is rife with examples of human destruction that have been animated by so-called human values. Nazism had many such values and some of them led people to take actions that resulted in the destruction of several million people (Bauman, 1989).

While Mannheim, too, prefers substantial rationality, or at least worries about its fate in light of the growth of functional rationality, it lacks the negative possibilities that inhere in Weber's substantive rationality. Indeed, it could be argued that 'intelligent insight' would militate against such value-driven excesses as the Nazi Holocaust. Thoughtful, intelligent people would, one assumes, have been better able to see where Nazi values were taking Germany and this would have led them to oppose such a course of action.

Whatever their differences, as well as their relative strengths and weaknesses, both Weber's substantive rationality and Mannheim's substantial rationality are threatened by the development and spread of McDonaldization. We will return to this issue below.

Mannheim comes closer to his earlier, more global sense of rationality in his definition of *functional rationality* as 'a series of actions ... organized in such a way that it leads to a previously defined goal, every element in this series of actions receiving a functional position and role' (1935/1940: 53). The series of actions is functionally rational in that each has a role to play in the achievement of the ultimate goal, although the goal itself can be either rational or irrational. For example, salvation is defined as an irrational goal, but it can be sought through a series of functionally rational actions. McDonaldized systems are functionally rational with all elements occupying a functional position in a series of actions leading to the objective, say the sale of large numbers of hamburgers to the public.

Mannheim's concept of functional rationality has much in common with Weber's sense of formal rationality. For example, efficiency is a central characteristic of formal rationality from Weber's point of view, and Mannheim (1935/1940: 53) argues that a 'functional organization of a series of actions will, moreover, be at its best when, in order to attain the given goal, it coordinates the means most efficiently'.

However, Weber's concept of formal rationality has disadvantages in comparison to Mannheim's sense of functional rationality and is even messier than his (Weber's) conceptualization of substantive rationality. Like substantive rationality, formal rationality combines micro and macro elements. However, in comparison to substantive rationality which deals solely with values at the macro level, the macro level in formal rationality encompasses 'rules, laws and regulations' as well as the macro-objective structures (e.g. bureaucracies) in which they exist. This opens up the possibility of many more interrelationships between the macro and micro and therefore creates even greater ambiguity in the concept. This ambiguity is heightened by Weber's failure to specify the nature of the relationships implied in his multifaceted conceptualization of formal rationality.

As with substantial rationality, Mannheim's concept of functional rationality has advantages over Weber's parallel conceptualization, especially in its greater clarity and simplicity. Mannheim is working, at least explicitly, at the micro level, this time in terms of micro-objective actions that are arranged in a series with each action receiving a functional position and role. An organization, with rules and regulations, is implied here, but unlike Weber's definition of formal rationality (where do the rules, laws and regulations exist if not in organizations?), it is not integral to the definition.

To Mannheim, as they were to Weber, functional and substantial rationalities may be substitutes for, or even in conflict with, one another. For example, the 'grill man' described earlier may act in accord with the functional organization of the fast-food restaurant without thinking through the various steps involved in grilling a hamburger. In fact, a functional organization like the fast-food restaurant generally wants its employees to act in accord with its dictates and not to think through such steps on their own; in other words, it ordinarily does not want them to practice substantive rationality.

Mannheim argues that industrialization has led to an increase in functional rationalization, but not necessarily substantial rationalization. In fact, he goes further by arguing that functional rationalization has tended to 'paralyze' substantial rationalization by leaving people less and less room to utilize their independent judgment. This seems to be Mannheim's version of Weber's irrationality of rationality. That is, the irrational consequence of the spread of functional rationality is the decline of substantial rationality. Of course, Mannheim (like Weber) was writing before the rise of service industries like fast-food restaurants, but it can easily be argued that substantial rationality is at least as paralyzed in those settings as it is by large-scale industry. In other words, the coming of many of the service industries has exacerbated the decline of substantial rationality.

There is one other major point of resemblance between the Weberian and Mannheimian theories of the relationship between these two types of rationality: the progressive disenchantment of the world. In Mannheim's case, this means that we are seeing the disappearance of *both* utopias and ideologies: we are moving toward a world in which 'all ideas have been discredited and all utopias have been destroyed' (1929/1936: 256). In an excellent description, Mannheim depicts the movement toward the 'complete destruction of all spiritual elements, the utopian as well as the ideological ... emergence of a "matter-of-factness" ... in sexual life, art and architecture, and the expression of the natural impulses in sports' (1929/1936: 256). This progressive disenchantment of the world is, in Mannheim's view, to be regretted because people need utopias (and ideologies). As Mannheim puts it:

It is possible, therefore, that in the future, in a world in which there is never anything new, in which all is finished and each moment is a repetition of the past, there can exist a condition in which thought will be utterly devoid of all ideological and utopian elements. But the complete elimination of reality-transcending elements from our world would lead us to a 'matter-of-factness' which ultimately would mean the decay of the human will. (1929/1936: 262)

The world that Mannheim feared is now here in the fast-food restaurant and other McDonaldized systems. For example, such systems strive for a condition in which there is never anything new; that is, where everything is predictably the same.³ The objective, largely realized, is that each new visit is merely a repetition of all previous visits.

While Mannheim regrets the progressive disappearance of both ideologies and utopias, it is the demise of the latter which is the far greater problem. The reason is that while the death of an ideology would pose a crisis for the social strata espousing it, the disappearance of utopias would have a profoundly negative effect on human nature and on human development as a whole:

The disappearance of utopia brings about a static state of affairs in which man himself becomes no more than a thing. We would be faced then with the greatest paradox imaginable, namely that man, who has achieved the highest degree of rational mastery of existence, left without any ideals, becomes a mere creature of impulses. Thus, of a long tortuous, but heroic development, just at the highest stage of awareness, when history is ceasing to be blind fate, and is becoming more and more man's own creation, with the relinquishment of utopias, man would lose his will to shape history and therewith his ability to understand it. (1929/1936: 262–3)

Mannheim is obviously coming very close here to the disenchantment of the world that so interested and concerned Weber.

Weber was also highly interested in the spread of formal rationality in the West, and Mannheim has a similar level of concern for, and offers a similar hypothesis about, the spread of functional rationality.

The more industrialized a society is and the more advanced its division of labor and organization, the greater will be the number of spheres of human activity which will be functionally rational and hence also calculable in advance. Whereas the individual in earlier societies acted only occasionally and in limited spheres in a functionally rational manner, in contemporary society he is *compelled* to act in this way in more and more spheres of life. (1935/1940: 55, emphasis added)

There are two aspects of this process, as described here, that relate particularly well to McDonaldization. First, there is the spread of functional rationality (and therefore McDonaldization) to more and more sectors of society. Second, there is the compulsion to act in a functionally rational matter. (McDonaldized systems, as iron cages, in a variety of ways control all of those who find their way into them.) And it is not just the workers who are subjected to such compulsion, but also customers and clients.

While Mannheim and Weber were right to point to the expansion of functional/formal rationality in the West, it is now spreading throughout the world. One example of this is the extension of McDonald's, and the fast-food restaurant more generally, to large portions of the rest of the world.

Both Weber and Mannheim share a sense that over time formal/functional rationality is coming to dominate, squeeze out, 'paralyze' substantive/substantial rationality. Further, both accept the view that this development has a series of negative consequences. However, while in Mannheim's schema it is obvious why we should worry about the loss of the individual's ability to think, brought about by the development of functional actions, it is not as obvious why Weber's version of this should concern us. It is difficult to argue against Mannheim's view that society is adversely affected by the declining ability of people to think rationally. However, Weber's assertion that we should fret over the decline of substantive rationality is far more questionable. Again, this depends on the 'humanness' of the values in question. A formally rational system with the ability to control, or eliminate, the values associated with Nazism would clearly be preferable to one in which such values dominated formally rational systems (as was true in Nazi Germany).

Mannheim adds needed nuance to the argument by discussing the differential effect of this process on people depending upon their position in an organization. He distinguishes between those at the top of the organization and those below them. Those at the top tend to retain substantial rationality, while the substantial rationality of those below them declines as the responsibility for independent decision making is restricted to those at the top. This has disastrous consequences for a person who does not occupy a high-level, decision-making position:

> He becomes increasingly accustomed to being led by others and gradually gives up his own interpretation of events for those others give him. When the rationalized mechanism of social life collapses in times of crisis, the individual cannot repair it by his own insight. Instead his own impotence reduces him to a state of terrified helplessness. (1935/1940: 59)

This represents a huge problem if for no other reason than the fact that the vast majority of people occupy subordinate positions. Again, the description offered above applies well to a McDonaldized society, in which the majority of workers (and others) are accustomed to being told what to do and begin to lose the ability to interpret situations for themselves. Should the rationalized system collapse, we can expect such people to be comparatively helpless. However, it should be said that the further development of McDonaldization makes it more unlikely that the system will collapse.

Overall, there is a close correspondence between the Mannheimian and the Weberian approaches as they relate to McDonaldization. In Weberian terms, McDonaldization implies the spread of formal rationalization, while in (later) Mannheimian terms it involves the development, growth and spread of functional rationalization. Also similar is the idea that the spread of functional (and formal) rationalization is serving to choke off the development, even the existence, of substantial (and substantive) rationality. However, while both theorists see this as leading to a kind of disenchantment of the world, the nature of that disenchantment is quite different. For Weber, we suffer a loss of human values, while for Mannheim we suffer the loss of ideologies, utopias, and especially the ability to think.

Both of these perspectives are of utility in thinking about McDonaldization. A McDonaldized world dominated by Weber's formal rationality would be a world devoid of human values. McDonaldized systems, with their emphasis on things like efficiency and profit maximization, have little place for human values such as love or community. Mannheim's version of this is found in his analysis of the elimination of ideologies and utopias in the modern world. However, Mannheim seems more concerned with the elimination of thought than with the demise of ideologies and utopias. And it is even clearer that McDonaldized systems seek to limit, if not eliminate, individual thought. Great control through scripts (Leidner, 1993), nonhuman technologies, and the like is designed to limit the employee's, especially the lower-status employee's, need and ability to think on the job. Thus, the two theorists point to quite different implications of the McDonaldization process. Mannheim's thinking is a useful supplement to Weber's in this case because McDonaldized systems do tend to threaten not only human values, but also the individual's ability to think.

The utility of Mannheim's theorizing is enhanced in this realm because, as we have seen, he points to the fact that one's position in the organizational hierarchy affects one's ability to think. Those at the top are able to limit the effect of external constraints on them, while actively imposing such constraints on those below them in the organization. The result is that the further one descends into the McDonaldized organization, the less is the ability of employees to think through their actions on their own. Thus, Mannheim adds an important dimension of stratification to our thinking about the McDonaldized systems.

Weber sees larger structures, like bureaucracies, as the source of disenchantment. In contrast, to Mannheim disenchantment involves one type of action (functional) driving out another (substantial).

Mannheim lacks an explicit sense that macrostructures are the source of disenchantment and this allows him to propose planning, with the macrostructures that would inevitably accompany it, as the solution to the problem. However, what Mannheim fails to see is that such planning and structures would be an *increase* in McDonaldization. It is for this reason that Weber opposed socialism and the planning that accompanied it. Thus, Weber's macrostructural perspective gives him a powerful advantage, at least in this instance, over Mannheim's conceptualization.

So cases can be made, pro and con, for both Weber's and Mannheim's thinking about formal/functional and substantive/substantial rationalities, as well as the relationships between the two basic types of rationality and irrationality. Both are of utility, and pose problems, for our thinking about McDonaldization.

However, Mannheim went far beyond Weber in his conceptualization of rationalization and it is here, at least potentially, that his greatest advantage lies. The issue is whether the additional conceptual arsenal created by Mannheim furthers our understanding of McDonaldization.

Mannheim goes beyond functional rationalization to posit the intimately related phenomenon of *self-rationalization*, or 'the individual's systematic control of his impulses' (1935/1940: 55). In fact, self-rationalization is sometimes described as a type of functional rationalization and in any case the two are closely linked: 'the functional rationalization of objective activities ultimately evokes self-rationalization' (1935/1940: 56). A high level of overall rationalization occurs when functional and self-rationalization occur together. This is most likely to be found, in Mannheim's view, among the administrative staff of large-scale organizations. Here the external control of the organization's rules and regulations is supplemented by self-rationalization, especially in the case of staff members and their careers. In Mannheim's words, the career prescribes 'not only the actual processes of work but also the prescriptive regulation both of the ideas and feelings one is permitted to have and of one's leisure time' (1935/1940: 56). Self-regulation exerts control over matters (ideas, feelings, leisure time) that functional rationalization cannot reach.

Mannheim is quite correct to posit a 'deeper' level of rationalization beyond functional rationalization. The latter is designed to exercise largely external control over micro-objective actions and has little or no effect on micro-subjective cognitive processes. In a purely functional system, subordinates cannot be trusted to act on their own accord in the way they are expected to by the organization. A functionally rational system requires rules, regulations, laws, supervision, and technological control. However, external control can be extremely costly and far from totally dependable. That is, subordinates are motivated to, and often do, elude these external controls and do not perform as they are expected to by the organization.

The answer, at least in Mannheim's day, was to supplement functional rationality with self-rationalization. For example, the Human Relations movement, which was in its heyday in Mannheim's time, sought to make workers more satisfied so that they would work harder of their own accord rather than being forced to do so. In other words, the goal of such a management school was the alteration of the consciousness of workers.

Such a movement and a view seem old-fashioned today, as does Mannheim's focus on the importance of self-rationalization as a supplement to functional rationalization. In the McDonaldized world of the fast-food restaurant there is little interest in, or need for, self-rationalization; the emphasis is on honing functional rationality. That is, the goal is the better coordination of actions. As long as those actions are synchronized, there is little need for, or interest in, changing the mind-set of employees.

Why this lack of interest in self-rationalization in McDonaldized systems? For one thing, the employees in such systems are apt to be both part-time and short-term workers; the workforce may turn over two or three times a year. It is impossible to change the cognitive processes of such workers in such a short period. Furthermore, even if it could be done, there is little point in doing so since the employees are likely to be gone in relatively short order. Many chains, as well as other types of McDonaldized enterprises, have adopted, at least in part, McDonald's functionally rational approach to managing its workforce. Making this even more necessary is the fact that there has been a vast increase in temporary employees in the economy as a whole. One must rely on functional rationalization to deal with such employees since, again, there is little time for, and interest in, self-rationalization.

However, there are hierarchical differences in the need for self-rationalization. Hence, McDonald's has its Hamburger Universities designed not only to train franchisees and managers in the techniques of running a franchise, and exercising functional control over subordinates, but also to alter their mind-sets so that they can exercise self-rationalization. It is far more important for franchisees and managers to believe in the McDonald's way; they are likely to work harder for the organization when they have such beliefs. Furthermore, it is harder to control them through functional rationality than it is to control their subordinates. Nonetheless, McDonald's does utilize a high level of functional rationalization with its franchisees and managers. There are all sorts of rules, regulations, and checks by central management designed to ensure that their actions are coordinated in the way they should be.

Mannheim's point about supplementing functional rationality with self-rationality holds in the case of franchisees and managers and, more generally, for those who occupy higher-level positions in the organizational hierarchy. However, it has little applicability to the vast majority of the employees of modern McDonaldized organizations. The work world has changed dramatically since Mannheim's day, and while his thoughts on self-rationalization may have applied to large-scale productive organizations, they have little relevance to work in today's McDonaldized reproductive organizations.

Nevertheless, self-rationalization does apply, and quite well, to the customers and clients of McDonaldized systems. It is true that there are various external constraints on patrons – drive-throughs, limited menus, hard and uncomfortable seats – but these are supplemented by efforts by McDonaldized systems to 'train' consumers to control themselves and do what is expected of them. How do patrons learn what they are expected to do? Advertisements provide a kind of anticipatory social-ization so that customers know, for example, not only what to order, but how to order. Children can be counted on to teach adults (in reverse socialization) what to do (e.g. clean up their debris). Then there are signs, as well as various physical structures (e.g. visible and readily accessible garbage pails), that serve to indicate what is expected. As a result of all of these things, as well of as their own accumulated personal experiences in McDonaldized systems, the patrons of such systems can be said to be self-rationalized. Indeed, this is a key to the success of McDonaldized systems.

Self-rationalization is *not* the highest and most extreme form of rationalization in Mannheim's theoretical system. That honor goes to what Mannheim calls *self-observation*. Self-rationalization involves a

> process of mental training, subordinating my inner motives to an external aim. Self-observation, on the other hand, is more than such form of mental training. Self-observation aims primarily at inner *self-transformation*. Man reflects about himself and his actions mostly for the sake of remolding or transforming himself more radically. (1935/1940: 57)

Once again, Mannheim's thinking seems to be much more a product of his times than a generalization that is fully supportable in today's McDonaldized society. McDonaldized systems are even less interested in the self-observation (that is, self-transformation) than in the self-rationalization of the bulk of their employees. The fast-food restaurant does not and cannot expect its employees to transform themselves for the sake of a part-time or temporary job. Nor is such a McDonaldized system interested in investing the time, energy, and money needed to help ensure such self-transformation. As with self-rationalization, self-observation applies much more to managers and franchisees than it does to the vast majority of employees of McDonaldized enterprises. In Mannheimian terms, there is no need for McDonaldized organizations to seek to have the vast majority of their employees transform themselves. All that is needed is to be sure that their actions are coordinated with those of the others they work with, and then only for a few hours a week and for only the few months that their jobs are likely to last.

And what of the patrons of McDonaldized systems? It could be argued that the broader objective of those systems, and more generally of a McDonaldized society, is just such a self-transformation of those served by them. A McDonaldized system works best when customers have transformed themselves so that they are passive, pliable participants in those systems. That is, they surrender their individuality and move through McDonaldized systems smoothly, efficiently and, above all, quickly. In a sense, they agree to give up their individuality and permit themselves to be treated like, and be sold the same products as, everyone else.

Mannheim seems to envision a hierarchy, and perhaps even a historical trend, running from substantial rationalization to functional rationalization, self-rationalization, and ultimately self-observation. While in the earlier stages of modernity society may have been able to rely on functional rationalization, his view is that more complex and rapidly changing modern societies require self-rationalization and especially self-observation, which control people better and more efficiently and enable them to adapt more readily to complex new situations.

This modern grand narrative is open to question, in part because we are reexamining it in an era when it is difficult to accept grand narratives in light of the postmodern critique (Lyotard, 1984). More importantly for our purposes, it is open to question because developments in much of the work world have not followed the pattern envisioned by Mannheim. He seems to have in mind what was long ago called the 'professionalization of the labor force' (Foote, 1953). The idea was that most workers were becoming more and more like professionals. One could and should rely on self-rationalization and self-observation with such 'professional' workers, but the professionalized blue-collar workforce that Foote was describing never materialized. More importantly, the blue-collar workforce has shrunk dramatically and become less significant in the era of the downsizing of the organizations most likely to employ them. In their place has arisen a massive number of low-status, low-paid service workers like those found in the local fast-food restaurant and in McDonaldized systems more generally. It is ludicrous to think of counterpeople at the fast-food restaurant subjecting themselves to self-rationalization and self-observation for the sake of a minimum wage, part-time job.

However, returning to a theme that has arisen several times in this section, it may well be that Mannheim's grand narrative applies far better to customers and clients of McDonaldized systems than it does to employees. It is the patrons who can be seen as having lost their substantial rationality in McDonaldized systems where they are dominated by functional rationality. And it is they who can be said to have undergone both self-rationalization and self-observation in McDonaldized societies. With employees of McDonaldized systems well controlled by functional rationality, the focus shifts to customers/clients who are better able to evade such controls. In their case, functional rationality must be supplemented with self-rationalization and self-observation.

Mannheim's Later Thinking on Irrationality

We have already encountered one of Mannheim's implicit, but centrally important, views on irrationality in the discussion of the tendency over time for functional rationality to squeeze out substantial rationality. This idea is in line with Weber's thinking on the irrationality of rationality.

More explicitly, Mannheim offers the concepts of substantial and functional irrationalities to parallel substantial and functional rationalities. Both notions of irrationality are, however, residual concepts reflecting Mannheim's focal concern with rationality. Given his sense of substantial rationality as rational thought, Mannheim defines *substantial irrationality* as 'everything else which either is false or not an act of thought at all (as for example drives, impulses, wishes and feelings, both conscious and unconscious)' (1935/1940: 53).

This is a very different sense of the irrational than in his earlier work, where Mannheim had associated *rationality* with the lack of thought. Here it is substantial irrationality that involves a lack of thought. However, previously the lack of thought had been linked to administrative control (following prescriptions without any personal decision making), while in the case of substantial irrationality it is tied to drives, impulses, wishes, and feelings.

From the point of view of the employees of McDonaldized systems, it is difficult to see much utility in the notion of substantial irrationality. It is certainly the case that McDonaldized systems operate to contain such irrationality among employees, but I do not think that such containment plays much of a role in the planning associated with McDonaldization. Again, the fact that Mannheim was embedded in a world in which such irrationalities were of central importance (for example, in the rise of fascism) served to give this type of irrationality undue importance in his work, at least from the vantage point of the employees of today's McDonaldized systems.

While it is not what he had in mind for the concept, Mannheim's notion of substantial irrationality is applicable to the way in which McDonaldized systems approach their customers/clients. In a variety of ways, but especially through advertisements, McDonaldized systems seek to manipulate the needs, desires, and impulses, the substantial irrationality, of customers/clients in order to get them to become devoted, if not habitual, consumers of their products and services. For example, McDonald's utilizes its knowledge of customers' desire to have fun by offering them a carnival-like atmosphere in which to obtain their food. In another realm, malls exploit customers' fears about shopping in urban stores by offering them a crime-free (or so they would like consumers to believe) environment.

Functional *irrationality* is defined as 'everything which breaks through and disrupts functional ordering' (1935/1940: 54). In contrast to substantial irrationality, this type of irrationality is of central importance to McDonaldized systems. Such systems do want to see their function- ally rational organizations operate smoothly and, in so doing, seek to limit any outbursts of functional irrationality which threaten that smooth operation. However, I think that McDonaldized systems are far more concerned with ensuring functional rationality than with prevent- ing functional irrationality. In fact, a smoothly running, functionally rational system would tend to militate against functional irrationality.

Mannheim's view that at least one aspect of the irrationality of rationality stems from the fact that great masses of people are crowded together in large cities because of industrialization is quite dated. Mannheim seemed to be arguing that industrialization creates what used to be called 'mass society'. Thus, paradoxically, as large-scale industrial society leads to greater functional rationality, self-rationaliza- tion, and self-observation, it also creates the conditions in mass society for irrational threats to that rational system:

> it produces all the irrationalities and emotional outbreaks which are charac- teristic of amorphous human agglomerations. As an industrial society, it so refines the social mechanism that the slightest irrational disturbance can have the most far-reaching effects, and as a mass society it favors a great number of irrational impulses and suggestions and produces an accumula- tion of unsublimated psychic energies which, at every moment, threatens to smash the whole subtle machinery of social life. (1935/1940: 61)

This image appears to have little to do with what transpires in modern, McDonaldized societies. The machinery of such societies seems in little danger from the kind of emotional mass outbursts of concern to Mannheim. Once again, his thinking seems to be a product of realities that have long since passed into history, at least the history of contem- porary McDonaldized societies. Today, most people seem too busy con- suming in McDonaldized systems to engage in such outbursts.

Of far greater utility is Mannheim's sense that the functionally ratio- nal actions of those in one organization can be functionally irrational from the point of view of those in another organization. For example, when McDonaldized systems produce an abundance of low-skilled McJobs, those actions may be seen as functionally irrational from the per- spective of those in the educational system who are seeking to produce a more educated population capable of handling far more complex occupations. Thus, Mannheim (1935/1940: 55) concludes that '"functional irrationality" never characterizes an act itself but only with reference to its position in the entire complex of conduct of which it is a part'.

In Mannheim's view, the basic sources of the irrational in modern life are the *same* as the sources of the functionally rational. In other words, Mannheim offers a sociological, not a psychological, theory of the origins of both rationality and irrationality. He sees the sources of both as built into the structure of modern society.

> they are driven, now in one direction, now in another by the dual nature of social structure that certain human beings are now calculating creatures who work out their actions to the very last detail, and now volcanic ones who think it right that at a given time they should reveal the worst depths of human brutality and sadism. (1935/1940: 66)

There is another dialectical aspect to Mannheim's thinking. That is, not only does increasing functional rationality lead to an increase in certain irrationalities, but it also leads to the beginning of a rational sense that *planning* is needed to deal with these problems: not just piecemeal planning, but planning at the level of the whole of society. The rationalization of society, as well as its growing irrationality, have made planning inevitable, but a central issue for Mannheim is who will do that planning? Those who represent narrow interest groups, or those who have the interests of society as a whole in mind? Mannheim prefers that the latter do the planning, and they must be either sociologists or those who have the kind of totalistic perspective that only sociology can offer.

This sense of planning shows once again that unlike Weber, Mannheim does not realize that a fundamental source of the irrationality of rationality, a fundamental problem in society, *is* the organizations that undertake and result from such planning. It is such planning that will lead to greater functional rationalization and therefore to the irrationalities that inevitably accompany it. Thus, Mannheim favors greater functional rationalization even if it comes at the expense of substantial rationalization. He is willing to accept this because in his day, and from his vantage point, the main danger to society stemmed from irrationality. Mannheim's thinking was shaped by the disruptions of the Great Depression and the rise of Nazism. He tended to see these as productive of irrational outbursts, or as irrational in themselves. The answer to the problem of such irrational outbursts is planning which would presumably produce more functionally rationalized systems capable of controlling them.

In the end Mannheim fails to see the key problem that was so brilliantly illuminated by Weber and is so well illustrated by today's McDonaldized systems: that the central problem lies in *the irrationalities of such systems themselves* and not in some irrational force that threatens to disrupt them. *Mannheim's most crucial failure is his inability to see the irrationality that lies at the core of rationality.*

Of course, the nature of planning in a McDonaldized system is very different from the kind of planning envisioned by Mannheim. While Mannheim was thinking of centralized planning on a society-wide basis, McDonaldized societies are characterized by a high degree of centralized planning within specific sectors of society. With the death of communism, the kind of centralized planning discussed by Mannheim is of little significance in the modern world. Instead, what we see is an extraordinarily high level of planning within a range of specific sectors as exemplified by the careful and detailed planning associated with the creation and running of each McDonald's outlet. Such planning is far more effective and omnipresent than anything that could have been created through centralized society-wide planning. And the system runs itself rather than requiring a secret police to enforce compliance with its dictates.

For example, McDonald's has recently created a set of business practices in the form of a handbook it calls 'Franchising 2000' (Gibson, 1996). Here are some illustrations of the kind of centralized control exercised by McDonald's over its franchisees:

> One controversial provision requires franchisees to submit annual financial goals to the company's regional managers, who sign off on them. The document also revives annual A, B, C and F grades, with only franchisees receiving As and Bs eligible for more restaurants; some franchisees doubt the system's objectivity. In addition, McDonald's is using Franchising 2000 to try to enforce a single pricing strategy, so that a Big Mac, for example, will cost the same almost everywhere ... Those who ignore such guidelines and otherwise 'seek personal gain and advantage to the detriment of the system', as the new handbook puts it, risk losing their franchise when it expires. (1996: A10)

This kind of centralized control is characteristic of McDonaldized systems. Mannheim envisioned a system in which broadly trained sociologists and politicians (schooled in sociological thinking) do the planning for society. However, the fact that this planning occurs in narrow sectors in McDonaldized society means that it is specialists rather than wide-ranging thinkers who do the planning. By its very nature, this kind of planning cannot take the needs of society as a whole into account. In any case, the plans of those in control of one sector can come into conflict with, and act to the detriment of, plans promulgated in other sectors. It is unlikely that this type of planning can accomplish the goals foreseen by Mannheim.

Conclusion

In comparison to its Weberian counterpart, Mannheim's later thinking on rationality has a number of strengths and weaknesses, as well as a number of advantages and disadvantages. Mannheim's conceptualization of substantial and functional rationalities is neater and easier to use than the Weberian concepts of formal and substantive rationalities. The messiness of the latter concepts makes them more difficult to use, especially in terms of the key issue of relating them to one another. Of perhaps greater importance is the fact that Mannheim's sense of substantial rationality yields a clearer and more defensible problematic than Weber's notion of substantive rationality. To Mannheim, substantial rationality involves rational thought and it is easy to see how that is threatened by the march of functional rationality. Less easy to see, and especially to defend, is Weber's concern over the fact that substantive rationality, associated with human values, is threatened by the advance of formal rationality. It is clear why we should be concerned about the loss of rational thought, but far less clear why we should fret over the decline of value-driven rationality. After all, much harm has been done in the world in the name of such rationality.

While Mannheim's sense of the relationship between substantial and functional rationalities is a significant advance, his ideas on substantial and functional irrationalities appear to add little, largely because they are defined residually. Of mixed significance, at least from the point of view of McDonaldization, are his notions of self-rationalization and self-observation. These concepts are largely embedded in the era in which they were created and have little to do with the work life realities of McDonaldized society, or at least the McDonaldized sectors of society. However, they do have surprising applicability to the patrons of McDonaldized systems.

The most important issue is: what can we say about McDonaldization in light of Mannheim's conceptualization, in particular his later ideas on rationalization? McDonaldization involves an increase in functional rationality at the expense of a decline in substantial rationality. It is this decline, the deterioration of the ability of people in most, especially lower-ranking, positions to think rationally, that is the fundamental irrationality of McDonaldized systems. There is little room for, or interest in, self-rationalization and self-observation in McDonaldized systems, except in higher-level positions. While largely uninterested in the self-rationalization and self-observation of employees, McDonaldized systems have come to place great reliance on self-rationalization and self-observation to get patrons to behave as they are expected to. The kind of centralized planning envisioned by Mannheim would only serve to increase the irrationality associated with the declining ability of lower-ranking employees to think. The local and in many ways more powerful planning of McDonaldized systems has also, in fact, led to an increase in that irrationality.

In the end, our understanding of McDonaldization is enhanced by rethinking it from the point of view of Mannheim's theory of rationality.

Its most important contribution is to point us toward the threat to the ability to think, rather than the Weberian threat to human values, as the fundamental irrationality of McDonaldized systems. Clearly, the narrow niches that more and more people occupy within McDonaldized systems provide little scope for thought. We need to devote more theoretical attention to the implications of the declining opportunity for substantial rationality within McDonaldized systems. This is particularly important because side by side with the growth of these McDonaldized systems is the expansion of postindustrial systems demanding the complex thought processes associated with substantial rationality (Hage and Powers, 1992). This brings us to another contribution of Mannheim's approach to this issue – his reminder of the importance of the relationship of social stratification to all of this. We are well on the way to a society differentiated, to a large degree, between high-status, high-paying postindustrial occupations characterized by substantial rationality and low-status, low-paying McDonaldized occupations largely lacking in such rationality.

Mannheim's thinking on rationality and irrationality has a number of weaknesses, most notably the fact that much of it is tied to a particular time and place; in many senses it does not stand the test of time very well. However, in other ways it has strengths and continues to be of use for thinking about contemporary society. All in all, Weberian theory remains the prime resource for thinking about McDonaldization. This is largely because of Weber's realization that irrationality is directly linked to the advancement of formal rationality and to Mannheim's failure to see this, epitomized by his strong case for planning. In spite of this weakness, as well as others, there is much to be gained by supplementing Weberian theory with, and rethinking McDonaldization from, a Mannheimian perspective.

Notes

This is Chapter 2 of *The McDonaldization Thesis* (1998: 16–34).

1   As we will see, planning becomes increasingly central to Mannheim's thinking on rationalization.

2   I am here using a distinction I developed in *Toward an Integrated Sociological Paradigm: The Search for an Exemplar and an Image of the Subject Matter* (Ritzer, 1981b) between two microscopic (micro-subjective (consciousness) and micro-objective (action)) and two macroscopic (macro-subjective (norms and values) and macro-objective (social structures)) levels of social analysis; see Chapter 4 of this volume.

3   The postmodernist Jean Baudrillard (1990/1993: 122) describes this as the 'hell of the Same'.

13

THE McDONALDIZATION OF AMERICAN SOCIOLOGY: A METASOCIOLOGICAL ANALYSIS

This final chapter has three objectives. The first, and by far the most important, is to apply the concept of McDonaldization to sociology. Second, it seeks to embed this specific work within the sociology of sociology, or metasociology. Third, and much more briefly, this analysis is used to cast some new or at least different light on the current 'crisis' in sociology.

As we saw in Chapter 1, there are three basic types of metasociological, especially metatheoretical, work. They differ in terms of their fundamental objectives: better understanding, creation of a new theoretical perspective, and creation of a new overarching perspective, or metatheory. This chapter falls within the first category and uses a theoretical idea – McDonaldization – to enhance our understanding of sociology in general, and sociological theory in particular.

McDonaldization and Sociology

It is the thesis of this chapter that sociology can be seen as simply another aspect of the modern world and that it, like almost all others, is undergoing a process of McDonaldization.[1] As Bourdieu (Bourdieu and Wacquant, 1992: 181–2) says, in more general terms, the sociology of sociology 'can teach people [i.e. sociologists] always to be aware that when they say or think something, they can be moved by causes as well as by reasons'. McDonaldization is one of the key *causes* of some recent developments in sociology. However, not all aspects of the modern world are McDonaldized to the same extent. While sociology is clearly McDonaldizing, it is nowhere as McDonaldized as, for example, fast-food restaurants. In discussing the McDonaldization of sociology we are not saying that it is, or could ever be, fully McDonaldized, but that sociology has come to be characterized, at least to some degree, by the major elements of McDonaldization and that there is evidence that it is moving in the direction of further McDonaldization.

McDonaldization is one of the causes of a variety of *problems* that are plaguing the field. While I will focus on these problems in this chapter, it should be noted that, as with McDonaldization in general (Ritzer, 1996: 11–13), the rationalization of sociology is far from having only negative effects on the field. Many of the dimensions of McDonaldization to be discussed below bring with them a series of benefits to sociology, but it is unnecessary here to catalogue them since most other sources in the field concentrate on those advantages. The objective here is to highlight the negative aspects.

The key to extending the idea of McDonaldization to sociology is an application of its basic components to an analysis of current trends in the field.[2] Not only do these dimensions play an important analytic role in the discussion to follow, but the first four (calculability, predictability, efficiency, and increased control over human unpredictability through the substitution of nonhuman for human technology) also help us to explain *why* sociology, as well as much of the modern world, is McDonaldizing. These dimensions represent advantages to be derived from McDonaldization and, as such, they are sought out by many sectors of the modern world, including sociology. However, they have various disadvantages that will be our focus throughout this discussion. Furthermore, the fifth component, the irrationality of rationality, allows us to get at the negative aspects of McDonaldization more directly.

The remainder of this chapter is divided into three sections. In the first, and longest, I deal with the area of sociology, empirical research, that has been most affected by McDonaldization. I then discuss the McDonaldization of sociology textbooks. Finally, I will turn to a discussion of sociological theory and the ways in which it, too, has undergone this process, at least to some degree.

The McDonaldization of Sociological Research

Calculability, or an emphasis on things that can be quantified, on quantity rather than quality, is manifest in mainstream American sociological research in several ways. First, of course, there is an overwhelming emphasis in the major journals on studies that rely on quantitative, rather than qualitative, data or that are strictly theoretical in nature.[3] Many years ago in *Fads and Foibles in Modern Sociology*, Pitirim Sorokin (1956) labeled this 'quantophrenia' and it is far more widespread today than it was in Sorokin's day. Qualitative studies are seen as anachronistic and one finds few of them in the major journals. Even a journal like *Work and Occupations* which was founded, at least in part, to be an outlet for qualitative studies of work has come to find little place for such research in its pages (Abbott, 1993). Journals are likely to include a theory essay or two in most issues, but they rarely occupy center stage.[4] The lack of calculability of qualitative and theoretical essays makes them out of place in a McDonaldized sociology.

Research that is likely to be published in the major journals is apt to involve large rather than small samples. Such studies not only are seen as desirable in themselves, but more importantly are considered more likely to yield results that are statistically significant. This is the parallel of the Big Mac phenomenon in fast-food restaurants. Just as we assume that a Big Mac is good because it is big, or that McDonald's more generally must be good because it has sold so many billions of burgers, we assume that a research study is important if it involves a large sample and reports strongly significant results. In both contexts quantity becomes a surrogate measure of quality. In other words, in both fast-food restaurants and sociology (at least in terms of correlations and other statistical measures), 'bigger is better'.

This emphasis is also manifest in the significance placed on obtaining large grants which, at least in part, permit the collection of large data bases. Studies based on these are more likely to be published in the major sociology journals. This is because such studies are seen as desirable in their own right and because they are more likely to be based on large samples and to produce highly significant results.

Furthermore, both sociological research and McDonald's are affected by the idea that it is difficult to assess quality directly, so we must focus on quantity instead. This is another reason for the comparative paucity of qualitative studies and theoretical essays. How is a reviewer to evaluate the adequacy of a new theoretical perspective? Such judgments are made, but they are difficult to make and highly subjective. The result is that reviewers often differ greatly in their evaluations. Faced with widely varying opinions, journal editors are likely to pass when it comes to publishing theoretical essays or qualitative studies. In contrast, because of the objective character of the numbers and the statistics, quantitative studies are more likely to elicit similar judgments from reviewers with the result that it is easier for editors to decide which quantitative studies should, and should not, be published.

A third, and less important, quantitative factor is that articles tend to be of a fairly uniform length. Those that are very long or very short are less likely to be published.[5] Very short papers are often assumed to lack depth.[6] Very long essays simply do not fit into the rationalized format of most academic journals. Long papers that are deemed publishable are likely to be accepted with the proviso that they be shortened. Such reductions may well result in a decline in quality.

Length is also an important criterion in the publication of research (as well as theoretical) monographs. Given the escalation in the cost of publishing, the decline in the number of publishers in a highly competitive business, and the fact that few sociologists are willing to shell out $50 or more for a book, publishers have become more cost-conscious. Longer books mean higher costs. Publishers who are still willing to publish monographs often insist that lengthy ones be short-ened, sometimes quite substantially. Such reductions often hurt the quality of the work (although it is true that cuts sometimes help). In addition, some publishers establish word or page limits even before books are submitted for publication.

Fourth, there is an emphasis among American sociologists on pro-ducing large numbers of publishable papers. As Bourdieu (1984a: 125) argues, researchers 'sacrifice all to a display of the amount of work accomplished'. This is related to the American system of academic tenure and the fact that in many cases more attention is paid to the quantity of publications than to their quality. It is also linked to the fact that it is easy to add up the number of a scholar's publications, but difficult to assess their quality. Not long ago, the then President of Stanford University was disturbed by a report indicating 'that nearly half of faculty members believe that their scholarly writings are merely counted – and not evaluated – when personnel decisions are made'. He described this as a 'bankrupt idea' and sought to 'reverse the appalling belief that counting and weighing are important means of evaluating faculty research' (Cooper, 1991: A12). The emphasis on quantity rather than quality exists throughout academia and is not restricted to sociology.

Quantitative factors dominate American sociology just as they define our fast-food restaurants and the rest of our McDonaldizing society. And, while it is not inevitable, the emphasis on quantity often serves to affect quality adversely.

One aspect of the *predictability* of what Mullins (1973) called stan-dard American sociology has already been touched on: research arti-cles tend to be fairly uniform, and predictable, in length. As a result, readers can anticipate with great accuracy how long it will take to work their way through the typical research piece.

More importantly, virtually all research articles have a predictable format: review of the literature, hypotheses, methodology, results, tables, interpretation, conclusion, notes and references. Reading the typical American research article offers the same kind of gratification as eating a Big Mac for lunch. The sociologist knows exactly what to expect and where each component of the article will be found, just as the consumer knows that the Big Mac will include a bun, burger, pickle, relish, and 'special sauce', as well as where each element is to be found if one cared to deconstruct the burger. There is great satisfaction in knowing precisely what can be expected in one's lunch and in what one reads before, after, or even with that lunch. Since they are both highly rationalized, a Big Mac and the typical research article in an

American journal go well together at lunchtime. (In contrast, it would be ludicrous to try to read the latest, nonrationalized books of Pierre Bourdieu or Jürgen Habermas over such a lunch.) It is nice to know that there will be no surprises: Big Macs and research articles almost always deliver precisely what is expected, no less, but also – and most tellingly and damningly – no more.

The nature of the review process in sociology journals ensures this predictability. Reviewers tend to be leading contributors to the area with which the submission is concerned; in fact, they are often chosen *because* their own work is cited in the article under consideration. Reviewers tend to have a clear sense that a new submission should build upon their work as well as the 'intellectual' tradition of which they are part. Works that do not flow out of that tradition, that do not add a slight increment to what is already known about a subject, are likely to be seen as being 'off the wall' and rejected out of hand. Truly original pieces of work, those that are 'unpredictable', have a hard time finding their way into the journals. The products of normal science, those that offer only slight refinements of the dominant paradigm, are those that are likely to be accepted for publication.

Entire journal issues tend to be quite predictable. We know that each issue will be dominated by quantitative studies. We can also expect that because of criticisms of the preeminence of quantitative papers, many issues will have a token theoretical and/or qualitative essay.

The kinds of research articles described above are *efficient* in various senses. They can be read quite expeditiously. Since there is a clear pattern to the articles, the experienced reader can read through them effortlessly. Uniform works can be judged far more quickly than projects that differ wildly from one another in basic structure and format.

Such research articles can also be written efficiently. The author knows the component parts that must be there, and in which order, and those parts can be produced in quite an orderly fashion. In fact, in the likely event that a number of articles are to be produced from the same study, a series of component parts can be 'manufactured' and 'warehoused' – review of the literature, methods, various tables, references, and so on – and they can be carted out and inserted at the appropriate points in a variety of finished products. If this communicates the feel of an assembly-line process, it is meant to; and this is enhanced when a team of specialized researchers is involved in a project. The various parts can be assigned to team members and each can become a kind of specialist – the library researcher, the data analyst, the computer specialist, the writer, the 'theoretician', and so on. This is part of the reason why research articles in sociology seem to involve more and more coauthors.[7] As in the manufacture of automobiles, it is far more efficient for a group of specialists to produce research articles than it is for a single generalist, but such efficiency carries with it, as most studies of the automobile industry have shown, a series of dysfunctions. This perspective is similar to Bourdieu's view and critique of the *'social division of labor* which splits, reifies, and compartmentalizes moments of the construction of the sociological object into separate specialities' (Wacquant, 1992: 32).

All this serves to make for the efficient replication of studies. With all of the component parts included in the published article in the usual order, a researcher can rush to the mail, quickly scan a new journal for relevant studies, hurry off to the computer center in search of the same data set, and rerun the data adding a few new variables. Within a few weeks, a replication of a study, one with a decent chance of acceptance because it is likely to be reviewed by the author of the study being replicated, is in the mail and off to the journal editor. Repeated over and over, we have here a very efficient method for building up a body of 'knowledge' on a specific topic.

Implied above is a series of *nonhuman* technologies that have not only exerted external control over sociologists, but also reduced their importance in the research process. The most notable of these are the computer, the computer program, and the use of increasingly sophisticated statistics. Instead of being done by the sociologist, a large portion of a research study is in the hands of computers, computer programmers, canned programs, and statistical packages. These technologies tend to make studies more quantitative in character, more predictable since large numbers of people have access to the same nonhuman technologies, and more efficient to produce since a good deal of what one needs is in those technologies.

Bourdieu et al. (1991: 5) also describe the contemporary reliance in sociology on 'scientific recipes and laboratory gadgets', and critique the 'blind submission to technical instruments' (1991: 10), as well as their tendency to reduce or eliminate scientific creativity. They argue: 'Those who push methodological concern to the point of obsession are like Freud's patient who spent all his time cleaning his spectacles and never put them on' (1991: 5).

Research in contemporary American sociology has, and in my opinion to an increasing degree, the four basic characteristics of McDonaldization discussed above: sociological research, like most other aspects of contemporary society, has become McDonaldized, at least to some extent. However, as in the rest of society, rationalization leads dialectically to its mirror image – the *irrationality of this rational system* for producing and disseminating new sociological knowledge.

One of these irrationalities is the leveling of sociology around the world (see Ritzer, 1998: 52–8 for a more detailed discussion of this issue, at least as it applies to sociological theory). McDonaldization, in general, does have such a leveling effect. For example, the spread of fast-food restaurants throughout the United States has reduced the significance of regional cuisine. Those regional cuisines that are McDonaldized become so rationalized that they lose many distinctive characteristics: the Cajun food served by Popeye's is a far cry from its progenitor Louisiana. In the same way, in sociology the model of the American research article has tended to produce clones throughout the world: the research article published in a European journal looks like its American counterpart. Furthermore, the research teams and the research steps are very much the same on both sides of the Atlantic.

The most general irrationality or rationality is dehumanization. As Takaki (1990: ix) put it, as a result of rationalization: 'The self was placed in confinement, its emotions controlled, and its spirit subdued.' Fast-food restaurants are dehumanizing for both workers and diners; we have already touched on the assembly-line portion of research articles. More generally, what is leached out of the research process in a McDonaldized sociology is human creativity, the creativity of the individual sociologist (again, for more on this, see Ritzer, 1998). Bourdieu is a critic of the lost art of sociology in the face of the spread of numbing sociological routines. For example, he describes French academia in general as 'a world without surprises' (Bourdieu, 1984a: 153). This is very close to the predictable, McDonaldized world being described here. In contrast, Bourdieu (1990: 26) says, 'For me, intellectual life is closer to the artist's life than to the routines of an academic existence.' This emphasis on 'art' by Bourdieu (as well as by Richard Münch: see Ritzer, 1998) leads to the issue of whether this chapter is just another assault on the increasing emphasis on science in sociology, especially, in Kuhn's (1962; 1970b) terms, on 'normal science'.

Before we deal with that question, a broader issue needs to be addressed: *is* science itself under attack here? Science does have the basic characteristics discussed above: calculability, predictability, efficiency, and substitution of nonhuman technology. This should come as no surprise since science can be seen as one of the precursors of the rationalization process (see Chapter 2 in *The McDonaldization of Society* for a discussion of other precursors). There is no question that science (as well as each of its basic characteristics) has been, in the main, a highly positive development. Indeed, it is always important to recognize that in all realms rationalization and its elements have a wide variety of positive consequences. This should not blind us to the fact that in science in general, and in sociology in particular, rationalization also has negative effects.

The problem is not simply these characteristics, but the excessive reliance on them: an overemphasis on quantifiable research; the quest for ever 'bigger and better' studies and results; a careeristic concern with producing large numbers of publishable studies; the slavish dependence on a predictable format in the publication of research results; the overconformity enforced by excessive reliance on the peer review process; the focus on the production of works that are efficient to write, review, read; an overelaborate division of labor; too much emphasis on the efficient replication of previously published research; an increasing reliance on nonhuman technologies that tend to reduce the role played by human creativity in science. The problem in sociology is that it has often emulated the worst excesses of scientific rationality. As in all sciences, there are both advantages and disadvantages to rationalization, but in sociology the pendulum seems to be swinging dangerously in the direction of the disadvantages of scientific rationality. It may be that the reason for this is that the elements of scientific rationality work best in normal science. However, to do normal science there must be a paradigm and most observers agree that sociology lacks a dominant paradigm (Ritzer, 1975/1980). Without a paradigm, normal science becomes a kind of parody of itself. The rational trappings are there, but there is no 'true' paradigm to flesh out and develop. Furthermore, normal science presupposes previous breakthroughs and presages others. However, sociology lacks the previous breakthroughs leading to a dominant paradigm so it is highly unlikely that normal science will lead to later breakthroughs. In sociology, the ritualistic following of the rational canons of normal science does little more than militate against the kind of 'artistic' thinking needed to create a paradigmatic revolution, or more appropriately in sociology, the discipline's first 'true', at least in the pure Kuhnian sense, paradigm.

The rationalized practices of science, especially in their excessive forms, are *not* appropriate to contemporary sociology. Of course, they are a disadvantage in any science, but the established sciences can tolerate them better. Sociology seems to have adopted the rationalized trappings without the knowledge base, or paradigm, to build upon. Whether or not the reader sees sociology as a science, given the realities of contemporary sociology, there is too much reliance on McDonaldized procedures and too little non-McDonaldized artistic creativity. It should not be forgotten, however, that all good science involves a solid mix of artistic creativity (especially during revolutionary periods) and rational- ized procedures (especially during the normal science phase).

The McDonaldization of Sociology Textbooks

The preceding discussion has singled out empirical sociology as the bastion of McDonaldization in American sociology. While I think it is, it is also true that other aspects of American sociology have become rationalized. For example, elsewhere, (Ritzer, 1988d) I have attacked the production of what I called 'cookie-cutter' textbooks in sociology, especially introductory texts. Pressures on publishers, reviewers, and adopters lead relentlessly to a depressing sameness, a leveling, a high degree of predictability in cookie-cutter textbooks. Publishers are highly attuned to their competitors' bestselling texts. When a particular textbook, such as John Macionis's or Anthony Giddens's in introductory sociology, is a big hit, competitors seek to discover the factors that made it such a success and then set about publishing clones. When a draft of the 'new' book is eventually produced, prepublication reviewers are asked to look for certain things, especially those things that made the leading text such a great success. When reviewers uncover elements that are missing, the authors are pressed by the publishers to include them so that in the end the new text looks depressingly like its successful predecessor. Repeated over and over, many texts come to look like every other one. Adopters also play a key role in the leveling of textbooks. In many cases, adopters prefer to use well-worn lecture notes and this leads them to prefer to continue to use the same text, or if they change, to adopt a text that closely resembles and follows the previously used text.

Textbooks also tend to contain the other elements of rationalization. There is a strong emphasis on quantity in such things as length of chapters, length of the text as a whole, reading level (a 10th- or 11th-grade reading level is preferred, i.e. that of 16–17 year olds), and, most importantly, sales. Books that sell well, irrespective of quality, will go through multiple printings and editions. Books that are high in quality, but low in sales, quickly disappear from publishers' lists. Efficiency is manifest in the emphasis on books that are easier both to produce and to read. The use of several authors and even teams of authors, the construction of so-called customized books with each chapter written by a different author, and production of 'managed books' in which professional writers work from notes and outlines provided by one or more sociologists, all reflect the emphasis on efficiency. The books should also be efficient reading. Ideally, students should be able to sail through the text with the same kind of efficiency that permits them to glide past their favorite fast-food drive-in window.

It is difficult for publishers to use nonhuman technologies to dominate the production of textbooks, but there have been some incursions. For example, the success of an introductory textbook often depends as much or more on the technologies that are available with it than on the quality of the text itself. Such technologies include CD-ROMs, computerized testbanks, computerized student projects, video and audio tapes. While these, like all technologies, have been produced by people, they reach students as nonhuman technologies in which the student is left to interact with a computer-generated multiple choice test, a computer screen, or a video monitor.

This, of course, leads to the irrationality of the rationality of textbooks. Implied above is the dehumanization associated with modern textbooks. Textbooks tend to be products in which all traces of a distinctive authorial voice have been eliminated. A bland, readable, almost mechanical text is preferred to one that reflects an author's distinctive style. Dehumanization can also be associated with the increasing degree to which students interact with computer screens or video monitors, rather than with human instructors. But dehumanization, while it is the most extreme irrationality, is not the only irrationality associated with textbooks. For example, the quantitative pressure to produce books at a 10th- or 11th-grade reading level reinforces students' incapabilities rather than seeking to elevate them. To take one other example, the need to write down to students reduces demands on authors and therefore does not fully exploit their capabilities as writers and as sociologists. In other words, most textbook writers are capable of doing far more than they are permitted to do in the writing of textbooks. Other irrationalities associated with textbooks could easily be enumerated, but the above suffice for our purposes.

Before moving on it should be noted that textbooks *themselves* are a part of the process of McDonaldization. They reflect the view that it is inefficient for students to have to read original works. Instead, it is left to textbook authors to read those works, to summarize them, and to present them in a palatable way to students. Accustomed to reader-friendly textbook summaries, students will find it difficult, if not impossible, ever to read original works.

The McDonaldization of Sociological Theory

It would be easy to dismiss the views expressed above, especially on empirical sociology, since I am so involved in sociological theory. In order to make those views more credible, and to demonstrate the extent of the McDonaldization of sociology, let me turn now to its impact on sociological theory. Like Parisian croissants, it is difficult to think of theory becoming McDonaldized, but as with those croissants, that is what has occurred, at least to some extent.

It is possible to trace the current low state of American sociological theory, at least in part, to its McDonaldization. The major American theorists of the recent past were decidedly nonrational in the way they produced theory and in the theories they created. In most cases there seemed to be little concern for the amount of work produced or the maximization of the efficiency of its production. Most of today's non-human technologies were either nonexistent, or in their primitive stages, and the technologies of the day (mainly the typewriter) were controlled by the authors rather than the technologies controlling them. As a result of the minimal rationalization of theory production, there were few irrationalities of rationality associated with it. In the main, theory emerged, often tortuously, from the creative intellectual impulses of the theorists. For example, George Herbert Mead wrote relatively little in his lifetime; his major work, *Mind, Self, and Society* (1934/1962), was produced by his students, from class notes, after his death. Herbert Blumer also produced a relatively small number of essays in his lifetime. Robert Merton, although more productive, often described how slow, laborious and painstaking it was for him to produce his work. Erving Goffman's work is so idiosyncratic that it defies rationalization. Talcott Parsons, of course, produced a voluminous amount of work, but it too is highly idiosyncratic. Furthermore, it is hard to imagine his lengthy, convoluted prose being published today. Modern publishers would have made greater use of copy-editors to make the prose less abstruse and, more importantly, less distinctive.

But how, specifically, is McDonaldization manifest in contemporary sociological theory? After all, it is far more difficult to rationalize a theoretical work than an empirical study. Nevertheless, rationalization *has* affected theoretical works in various ways. For one thing, an array of pressures lead American theorists to devote more attention than their European counterparts to the production of journal articles rather than books. The race for tenure and promotion in American academia is dominated by the model created by empirical researchers and the need to have a certain number of articles in major, refereed journals. To compete with their empirically oriented colleagues, theorists are driven to try to produce a like number of articles. However, theoretical ideas are often difficult to collapse into the page limits imposed by the article format; the natural home for works of theory throughout the history of sociology, and in Europe today, is the book-length manuscript. However, the dictates of an empirically oriented discipline lead to the view that it is the article in the refereed journal that is the 'coin of the realm'. Furthermore, books are suspect in highly rationalized disciplines. They seem to belong more to less rationalized fields like literature, history, or philosophy than to a rationalized science.

Driven to write short articles, American theorists must use a modified version of the rationalized format employed by empiricists. They must take a set of complex ideas and divide them up into a series of bite-sized 'theory McNuggets'. While they may be tasty, more easily produced and more easily digested, such bits of theory are not likely to be as nourishing as the complex ideas developed in the more substantial theoretical monographs being turned out by their European peers.

In producing articles that include a theoretical nugget or two, and in submitting them to journals, theorists are subjecting their work to the same kind of review process that leads to the rationalization of empirical works. Theoretical essays that represent small increments in knowledge to an extant theoretical tradition are those that are likely to be accepted for publication. To have such works accepted, the author must be careful to till old theoretical ground in the prescribed way and to cite all the 'right' sources. In other words, theorists are pressed in the direction of conforming to the dictates of Kuhn's (1962; 1970b) 'normal science'. The result is that a good deal of the nonrational art and creativity of theorizing is drained from such work.

Rationalization has also led to the publication in American sociology journals of a particular kind of theory. One rarely sees in those journals original theories, or even novel theoretical ideas. What do get published are metatheoretical works that summarize and/or critique the work of other sociological theorists. Such works are largely exegeses on the work of theoretical ancestors and contemporaries within American or European theory. Such works are about theory, they are studies of theory, rather than being original pieces of theorizing. While new theoretical ideas can come from such exegeses (a good example from the past is Parsons's *The Structure of Social Action*, 1937), the fact is that the return in new theoretical ideas from recent essays of this genre has been slim, if not nonexistent.

There is, of course, also a peer review process in the publication of books devoted to theory. However, the nature of that review process is somewhat different, and reviewers of books look for different things than reviewers of essays for the major journals. This is true even when the same reviewer does both. To put it simply, more irrationalities are permissible in book-length manuscripts. Length and format are less important. There is enough space to develop more fully a new theoretical idea or perspective. While, as we saw above, book production has been rationalized, it (especially monograph publishing) has not been McDonaldized to nearly the degree that article production has been rationalized. The fact that American theorists are forced to devote far more attention to writing essays for journals, and less to book-length manuscripts, helps to account for the rationalization of American theory and explains why it has suffered in comparison to European theory.

Another aspect of the McDonaldization of American sociological theory is the fact that to succeed, an American theorist has had to be seen as part of an extant tradition. Historically, this has led to specialization within sociological theory: a theorist was identified as a structural functionalist, a conflict theorist, a symbolic interactionist, an exchange theorist, and so on. One worked within a theoretical tradition and built on it, again in the manner of normal science and empirical sociology. This specialization tended to rationalize the process of theory development. For example, it was highly efficient to add increments of knowledge to the tradition in which one was embedded. However, such specialization also had its limitations. To the degree that one was exposed to other theories, one was inclined to critique them, rather than to try to integrate their useful derivatives into one's own theoretical perspective.

European theory has rarely had such clear theoretical boundaries. As a result, European theories have traditionally been a blend of ideas drawn from many traditions. The emphasis is more on the production of truly original works that are distinguished by the fact that they are clearly different from their theoretical ancestors and from other contemporary theoretical products. This is best seen in French social science where the overwhelming pressure is to be different, to be original (Lemert, 1981).[8] The result is that, that tradition has, in recent years, given us the very inventive and distinctive contributions of social theorists like Bourdieu, Foucault, Derrida, Lyotard, Baudrillard, and Virilio. The idiosyncratic character of much of this theoretical work stands in stark contrast to the careful and measured extensions offered by the vast majority of contemporary American theorists. It is difficult, if not impossible, to think of a contemporary American theorist whose work rivals that of the best contemporary Europeans in originality and distinctiveness.

Of course, there are important changes taking place in contemporary American theory. We are witnessing the end of the clear boundaries around theories (see Chapter 7) and the emergence of more synthetic theories (Ritzer, 1990a). However, even here these syntheses are occurring from a base in one of our traditional theories. The best example of this is the work of Jeffrey Alexander (Alexander and Colomy, 1990) who is seen as being part of, and building on, the structural-functional tradition with his neofunctionalism. Similar extensions are being made by Fine (1990) from within symbolic interactionism, Cook et al. (1990) from a base in exchange theory, and many others. Like contributions to empirical knowledge, these are more like comfortable increments to extant theories, than creative new theories that ignore all boundaries.

Sociological theorists not only specialize in a particular kind of theory, but more generally specialize in theory; that is, they often do theory to the exclusion of empirical research.[9] Bourdieu is a severe critic of this specialization, believing that 'social theory has little to expect from ventures in "theoretical logic" that are not grounded in a concrete research practice' (Wacquant, 1992: 32). While I disagree with Bourdieu here and feel that pure theorizing can produce, and more importantly *has* produced, important advances in sociology, I do agree that the tendency to specialize in *either* theory *or* research has had adverse effects on sociology.

Conclusion

While the thrust of this chapter has been to describe the McDonaldization of sociology, sociology has not, and can never be,

McDonaldized to the degree that fast-food restaurants and other aspects of modern society have been. Yet the process has affected sociology and its impact is continuing to spread. The point of this discussion is both to describe this process for the general reader, and to warn sociologists about what is occurring and to urge them to practice, in Bourdieu's terms, vigilance concerning this development. Above all, again following Bourdieu and Wacquant (1992: 183), 'you [the sociologist] must learn to *avoid being the toy of social forces in your practice of sociology*'. Given its breadth and power, it is possible to become a mere toy in the larger process of the McDonaldization of sociology.

This brings us to the final objective of this chapter – its contribution to our understanding of the current crisis in sociology. There are some who see the closing of some sociology departments, and reductions in the size of others, as signs of deep problems in the field. These difficulties are seen as making sociology very vulnerable in a period of academic cuts resulting from budget shortfalls. While these fears are, in my opinion, overstated,[10] there *are* problems in sociology and McDonaldization will lead sociology further away from creativity and more toward predictability and uniformity of work on the 'academic assembly line'. To the degree that the work of sociologists becomes predictable and uncreative, more and more administrators will ask why they need such people, or at least why they need so many of them. Creative scholars are indispensable, but as on the nation's automobile assembly lines, the value of those who perform highly routinized work can be questioned more easily *and* they are easier to replace.

While the thrust of rationalization theory leads to pessimism, this author hopes that the theory is wrong, at least in this regard. After all, it is human beings who lie behind the production of rationalized society in general, and a rationalized sociology in particular. Humans produced this world historically, and they reproduce it on a daily basis. Hence, they have the capacity to change those products. Reified social structures have been produced, but as the history of the former Soviet Union demonstrates, reified structures can be demolished. However, it is important to note that the Soviet structures were distinctly non-rationalized and it may have been this that made them relatively easy to bring down. Rationalized structures, following Weber, are far more difficult to destroy. Sociologists *can* bring down those structures; they can in Goffman's term be 'dangerous giants'. In fact, it may be that because they understand the social process involved, because they can bring sociological tools to bear on sociology, they are in a truly distinctive position to destroy the structures produced, or at least to mitigate their worst effects. Sociologists often inveigh against a public that mindlessly accepts the rationalized structures in which they exist. However, those critiques cannot be seen as credible until sociologists themselves act to overcome the rationalized systems that constrain them and their work. Indeed, such actions may be the first of what could ultimately become a wide-scale assault on the rationalized systems that increasingly control every facet of our lives. I would be the first to accept the idea that such a scenario is far-fetched. However, a basic premise of sociology is that all social systems are human constructions and that they can therefore be deconstructed!

Unlike many similar efforts, the goal of this critique is not to bring sociology to its knees; there are already too many people and forces intent on attaining that objective. In line with Wacquant's (1992: 36) contention about Bourdieu's metasociology, this chapter 'seeks not to assault but to *buttress the epistemological security of sociology'*. The ultimate objective here is to help build sociology by warning of the process of McDonaldization and suggesting that its adverse effects can be minimized and controlled. In terms of his work, Bourdieu (Bourdieu and Wacquant, 1992: 211) says: 'I continually use sociology to try to cleanse my work of the social determinants that necessarily bear on sociologists.' Put in those terms, the object of this chapter is to help 'cleanse' the negative effects of one of the major contemporary determinants – McDonaldization – of what is taking place in the modern world in general, and modern sociology in particular.

Finally, a word about the sociology of sociology, or metasociology, and its bad name in the discipline. The sociology of sociology contributed to its poor reputation with the triviality of many of its works. However, there is another factor in its lack of acceptance: sociologists have long been resistant to applying their own tools to themselves, to seeing themselves as being affected by the same social forces that affect everyone else. Wacquant (1992: 43–4) makes this point in discussing Bourdieu's approach:

> Sociological reflexivity instantly raises hackles because it represents a frontal attack on the sacred sense of individuality that is so dear to all of us Westerners, and particularly on the charismatic self-conception of intellectuals who like to think of themselves as undetermined, 'free-floating', and endowed with a form of symbolic grace.

This chapter, as well as the sociology of sociology employed in it, is likely to 'raise the hackles' of sociologists by associating them with a trend of which most of them are likely to be critical and with which they do not wish to be associated. Yet, it is necessary for sociologists to recognize that they are not immune to this wide-reaching trend and that, in order to begin to counteract it, they must be aware of its incursions into the heart of their own discipline. A greater awareness of this will help sociologists to see the importance – indeed, the necessity – of turning their intellectual tools on themselves.

Notes

The source of the chapter is Chapter 3 in *The McDonaldization Thesis* (1998: 35–51). I would like to thank Mark Abrahamson, JoAnn DeFiore, and Ken Kammeyer for a number of useful suggestions on an earlier draft of this chapter.

1   Or, depending on one's perspective, the postmodern world (Lyotard, 1984; Shelton, forthcoming).

2   It should be noted that the trends to be discussed below represent, in the main, my subjective views about them. It would be useful for others to undertake research studies aimed at ascertaining their validity as well as the validity of the overall thesis about McDonaldization.

3   There are American journals such as *Qualitative Sociology* that publish qualitative studies and there is greater emphasis on such work in other countries (e.g. Britain).

4   One exception is the June 1992 issue of *Social Psychology Quarterly* devoted to theoretical essays.

5   Although, short research articles may be published as research notes.

6   Interestingly, sociology lags behind even more rationalized social sciences like psychology on the issue of paper length. In psychology the norm tends to be very short, highly routinized research papers that can be read very quickly and efficiently.

7   Once again, more rationalized fields like psychology seem to be 'ahead' of sociology on the number of articles coauthored by long lists of people.

8   Although, as we saw earlier, Bourdieu is also critical of French sociology for being a world without surprises.

9   There are, of course, exceptions to this (for example the work of Joseph Berger and his colleagues on the expectation states: Berger et al., 1989), as well as all other generalizations made throughout this chapter.

10   As I was quoted in an article on the state of the field, 'There's no question that there are problems in the field ... But I don't think they are problems that represent the imminent demise or dissolution or decline of sociology' (cited in Coughlin, 1992: A6–A7).

REFERENCES

Abbott, Andrew. 1993. 'The Sociology of Work and Occupations', *Annual Review of Sociology* 187–209.

Abbott, Carroll, Charles R. Brown, and Paul V. Crosbie. 1973. 'Exchange as Symbolic Interaction: For What?', *American Sociological Review* 38: 504–6.

Abel, Theodore. 1970. *The Foundations of Sociological Theory*. New York: Random House.

Abrams, Denise, Roger Reitman, and Joan Sylvester. 1980. 'The Paradigmatic Status of Sociology: Current Evaluations and Future Prospects', in George Ritzer (ed.), *Sociology: A Multiple Paradigm Science*, rev. edn. Boston: Allyn and Bacon. 266–87.

Adams, J.S. 1963. 'Toward an Understanding of Inequity', *Journal of Abnormal and Social Psychology* 67: 422–36.

Agassi, Joseph. 1960. 'Methodological Individualism', *British Journal of Sociology* 11: 244–70.

Agrich, George J., and Charles E. Begley. 1985. 'Some Problems with Pro-Competition Reforms', *Social Science and Medicine* 21: 623–30.

Albrow, Martin. 1974. 'Dialectical and Categorical Paradigms of a Science of Society', *Sociological Review* 22: 183–202.

Alexander, Jeffrey C. 1982. *Theoretical Logic in Sociology*. Vol. 1, *Positivism Presuppositions, and Current Controversies*. Berkeley and Los Angeles: University of California Press.

Alexander, Jeffrey C. 1982–3. *Theoretical Logic in Sociology*, 4 Vols. Berkeley and Los Angeles: University of California Press.

Alexander, Jeffrey C. (ed.). 1985. *Neofunctionalism*. Beverly Hills, CA: Sage.

Alexander, Jeffrey C., and Paul Colomy. 1990. 'Neofunctionalism: Reconstructing a Theoretical Tradition', in George Ritzer (ed.), *Frontiers of Social Theory: The New Syntheses*. New York: Columbia University Press. 33–67.

Alexander, Jeffrey C., Bernard Giesen, Richard Münch, and Neil Smelser (eds). 1987. *The Micro-Macro Link*. Berkeley and Los Angeles: University of California Press.

Alford, Robert R., and Roger Friedland. 1985. *Powers of Theory: Capitalism, the State, and Democracy*. Cambridge: Cambridge University Press.

Allen, Bruce H., Richard A. Wright, and Louis E. Raho. 1985. 'Physicians and Advertising', *Journal of Health Care Marketing* 5: 39–49.

Alpert, Harry. 1939. *Emile Durkheim and His Sociology*. New York: Russell and Russell.

Alston, Jon P. 1986. *The American Samurai: Blending American and Japanese Managerial Practices*. Berlin: Walter de Gruyter.

Althusser, Louis. 1977. *Politics and History*. London: New Left Books.

Althusser, Louis, and Etienne Balibar (eds). 1970. *Reading Capital*. New York: Pantheon.

Appadurai, Arjun. 1990. 'Disjunction and Difference in the Global Cultural Economy', in Mike Featherstone (ed.), *Global Culture: Nationalism, Globalization and Modernity*. London: Sage. 295–310.

Archibald, W. Peter. 1977. 'Misplaced Concreteness or Misplaced Abstractions? Some Reflections on the State of Social Psychology', *American Sociologist* 12: 8–12.

Arney, William Ray. 1982. *Power and the Profession of Obstetrics*. University of Chicago Press.

Aron, Raymond. 1965. *Main Currents in Sociological Thought*. Vol. 1. New York: Basic Books.

Aron, Raymond. 1967. *18 Lectures on Industrial Society*. London: Weidenfeld and Nicolson.

Avineri, Shlomo. 1968. *The Social and Political Thought of Karl Marx*. London: Cambridge University Press.

Back, Kurt. 1970. 'Review of Robert Burgess and Don Bushell (eds), *Behavioral Sociology*', *American Sociological Review* 35: 1098–100.

Baer, William C. 1986. 'Expertise and Professional Standards', *Work and Occupations* 13: 532–52.

Bailey, Kenneth D. 1987. 'Globals, Mutables, and Immutables: An Alternative Approach to Micro/Macro Analysis'. Paper presented at the Meetings of the American Sociological Association, Chicago.

Baldwin, John C. 1986. *George Herbert Mead: A Unifying Theory for Sociology*. Newbury Park, CA: Sage.

Bandura, Albert. 1969. *Principles of Behavior Modification*. New York: Holt.

Bandura, Albert. 1971. *Psychological Modeling: Conflicting Theories*. Chicago: Aldine.

Bandura, Albert. 1977. *Social Learning Theory*. Englewood Cliffs, NJ: Prentice Hall.

Barash, David P. 1977. *Sociobiology and Behavior*. New York: Elsevier.

Barbalet, J.M. 1983. *Marx's Construction of Social Theory*. London: Routledge and Kegan Paul.

Barthes, Roland. 1977. *Image–Music–Text*. New York: Hill and Wang.

Battistella, Roger M. 1985. 'Hospital Receptivity to Market Competition: Image and Reality', *Health Care Management Review* 10: 19–26.

Baudrillard, Jean. 1976/1993. *Symbolic Exchange and Death*. London: Sage.

Baudrillard, Jean. 1983. *Simulations*. New York: Semiotext.

Baudrillard, Jean. 1983/1990. *Fatal Strategies*. New York: Semiotext(e).

Baudrillard, Jean. 1990/1993. *The Transparency of Evil: Essays on Extreme Phenomena*. London: Verso.

Bauman, Zygmunt. 1989. *Modernity and the Holocaust*. Ithaca, NY: Cornell University Press.

Bealer, Robert C. 1990. 'Paradigms, Theories, and Methods in Contemporary Rural Sociology: A Critical Reaction to Critical Questions', *Rural Sociology* 55: 91–100.

Becker, Howard, and Blanche Geer. 1957. 'Participant Observation and Interviewing: A Comparison', *Human Organization* 16: 29–32.

Begun, James W. 1986. 'Economic and Sociological Approaches to Professionalism', *Work and Occupations* 13: 113–29.

Bell, Daniel. 1973. *The Coming of Post-Industrial Society: A Venture in Social Forecasting*. New York: Basic Books.

Bender, Frederick (ed.). 1970. *Karl Marx: The Essential Writings*. New York: Harper.

Berger, Brigitte, and Peter Berger. 1984. *The War over the Family: Capturing the Middle Ground*. Garden City, NY: Anchor Press/Doubleday.

Berger, Charles R., and Steven H. Chaffee. 1988. *Handbook of Communication Science*. Newbury Park, CA: Sage.

Berger, Joseph, Morris Zelditch, Jr, and Bo Anderson (eds). 1989. *Sociological Theories in Progress: New Formulations*. Newbury Park, CA: Sage.

Berger, Peter. 1963. *Invitation to Sociology*. New York: Doubleday.

Berger, Peter, and Thomas Luckmann. 1967. *The Social Construction of Reality: A Treatise in the Sociology of Knowledge*. Garden City, NY: Anchor Books.

Berger, Peter, and Stanley Pullberg. 1965. 'Reification and the Sociological Critique of Consciousness', *History and Theory* 4: 196–211.

Berki, R.N. 1983. *Insight and Vision: The Problem of Communism in Marx's Thought*. London: Dent.

Berlant, Jeffrey Lionel. 1975. *Profession and Monopoly: A Study of Medicine in the United States and Great Britain*. University of California Press.

Besnard, Philippe (ed.). 1983a. *The Sociological Domain*. Cambridge: Cambridge University Press.

Besnard, Philippe. 1983b. 'The "Année Sociologique" Team', in Philippe Besnard (ed.), *The Sociological Domain*. Cambridge: Cambridge University Press. 11–39.

Best, Steven, and Douglas Kellner. 1991. *Postmodern Theory: Critical Interrogations*. New York: Guilford Press.

Best, Steven, and Douglas Kellner. 1997. *The Postmodern Turn*. New York: Guilford Press.

Blalock, Hubert, and Paul Wilken. 1979. *Intergroup Processes: A Micro–Macro Perspective*. New York: Free Press.

Blau, Peter. 1960. 'Structural Effects', *American Sociological Review* 25: 178–93.

Blau, Peter. 1964. *Exchange and Power in Social Life*. New York: Wiley.

Blau, Peter. 1979. 'Levels and Types of Structural Effects: The Impact of University Structure on Professional Schools', in William E. Snizek, Ellsworth R. Fuhrman, and Michael K. Miller (eds), *Contemporary Issues in Theory and Research: A Metasociological Perspective*. Westport, CT: Greenwood Press. 141–60.

Bosserman, Phillip. 1968. *Dialectical Sociology: An Analysis of the Sociology of Georges Gurvitch*. Boston: Porter Sargent.

Bourdieu, Pierre. 1984a. *Homo Academicus*. Stanford: Stanford University Press.

Bourdieu, Pierre. 1984b. *Distinction: A Social Critique of the Judgment of Taste*. Cambridge, MA: Harvard University Press.

Bourdieu, Pierre. 1990. *In Other Words: Essays toward a Reflexive Sociology*. Cambridge: Polity Press.

Bourdieu, Pierre, and Loic J.D. Wacquant. 1992. 'The Purpose of Reflexive Sociology (The Chicago Workshop)', in P. Bourdieu and L.J.D. Wacquant (eds), *An Invitation to Reflexive Sociology*. Chicago: University of Chicago Press. 61–215.

Bourdieu, Pierre, Jean-Claude Chamboredon, and Jean-Claude Passeron. 1991. *The Craft of Sociology: Epistemological Preliminaries*. Berlin and New York: Walter de Gruyter.

Boutilier, Robert G., J. Christian Roed, and Ann Svendsen. 1980. 'Crisis in the Two Social Psychologies: A Critical Comparison', *Social Psychology Quarterly* 43: 5–17.

Braverman, Harry. 1974. *Labor and Monopoly Capital: The Degradation of Work in the Twentieth Century*. New York: Monthly Review Press.

Brewer, John, and Albert Hunter. 1989. *Multimethod Research: A Synthesis of Styles*. Newbury Park, CA: Sage.

Brodbeck, May. 1954. 'On the Philosophy of the Social Sciences', *Philosophy of Science* 21: 140–56.

Brodbeck, May. 1958. 'Methodological Individualism: Definition and Reduction', *Philosophy of Science* 25: 1–22.

Brodbeck, May (ed.). 1968. *Readings in the Philosophy of the Social Sciences*. New York: Macmillan.

Brown, Julia, and Brian G. Gilmartin. 1969. 'Sociology Today: Lacunae, Emphases, and Surfeits', *American Sociologist* 4: 283–90.

Brown, Richard. 1987. *Society as Text: Essays on Rhetoric, Reason, and Reality*. Chicago: University of Chicago Press.

Brown, Richard. 1990. 'Social Science and the Poetics of Public Truth', *Sociological Forum* 5: 55–74.

Brubaker, Rogers. 1984. *The Limits of Rationality*. London: George Allen and Unwin.

Bulmer, Martin. 1984. *The Chicago School of Sociology: Institutionalization, Diversity and the Rise of Sociological Research*. Chicago: University of Chicago Press.

Bulmer, Martin. 1985. The Chicago School of Sociology: What made it a School? *History of Sociology: An International Review* 5: 61–77.

Burgess, Robert. 1977. 'The Withering Away of Social Psychology', *American Sociologist* 12: 12–14.

Burgess, Robert, and Don Bushell. 1969. 'A Behavioral View of Some Sociological Concepts', in Robert Burgess and Don Bushell (eds), *Behavioral Sociology*. New York: Columbia University Press. 273–90.

Bushell, Don, and Robert Burgess. 1969. 'Some Basic Principles of Behavior', in Robert Burgess and Don Bushell (eds), *Behavioral Sociology*. New York: Columbia University Press. 27–48.

Callinicos, A. 1990. *Against Postmodernism: A Marxist Critique*. New York: St Martin's Press.

Camic, Charles. 1987. 'The Making of a Model: A Historical Reinterpretation of the Early Parsons', *American Sociological Review* 52: 421–39.

Caplow, Theodore. 1954. *The Sociology of Work*. University of Minnesota Press.

Cassel, Christine K. 1985. 'Doctors and Allocation Decisions: A New Role in the New Medicare', *Journal of Health Politics, Policy and Law* 10: 549–64.

Clarke, Simon. 1990. 'The Crisis of Fordism or the Crisis of Social Democracy?', *Telos* 8: 71–98.

Cohen, Ira J. 1981. 'Introduction to the Transaction Edition: Max Weber on Modern Western Capitalism', in Max Weber, *General Economic History*. New Brunswick, NJ: Transaction Books. xv–lxxxiii.

Colburn, Don. 1985. 'Antitrust Enforcement in Health Care: Ten Years After the AMA Suit', *The New England Journal of Medicine* 313: 901–4.

Colclough, Glenna, and Patrick Horan. 1983. 'The Status Attainment Paradigm: An Application of a Kuhnian Perspective', *Sociological Quarterly* 24: 25–42.

Cole, Jonathan R., and Stephen Cole. 1973. *Social Stratification in Science*. Chicago: University of Chicago Press.

Coleman, James. 1968. 'Review of Harold Garfinkel, *Studies in Ethnomethodology*', *American Sociological Review* 33: 126–30.

Coleman, James. 1970. 'Relational Analysis: The Study of Social Organizations with Survey Methods', in Norman Denzin (ed.), *Sociological Methods*. Chicago: Aldine. 115–26.

Coleman, James. 1986. 'Social Theory, Social Research, and a Theory of Action', *American Journal of Sociology* 91: 1309–35.

Collins, Randall. 1975. *Conflict Sociology: Toward an Explanatory Science*. New York: Academic Press.

Collins, Randall. 1980. 'Weber's Last Theory of Capitalism: A Systematization', *American Sociological Review* 45: 925–42.

Collins, Randall. 1981a. 'Introduction' to *Sociology Since Midcentury: Essays in Theory Cumulation*. New York: Academic Press. 1–9.

Collins, Randall. 1981b. 'Micro-Translation as a Theory-Building Strategy', in Karin Knorr-Cetina and Aaron Cicourel (eds), *Advances in Social Theory and Methodology*. New York: Methuen. 81–108.

Collins, Randall. 1981c. 'On the Microfoundations of Macrosociology', *American Journal of Sociology* 86: 984–1014.

Collins, Randall. 1985. *Weberian Sociological Theory*. Cambridge: Cambridge University Press.

Collins, Randall. 1986a. 'Is 1980s Sociology in the Doldrums?', *American Journal of Sociology* 91: 1336–55.

Collins, Randall. 1986b. *Max Weber: A Skeleton Key*. Beverly Hills, CA: Sage.

Collins, Randall. 1986c. 'The Passing of Intellectual Generations: Reflections of the Death of Erving Goffman', *Sociological Theory* 4: 106–13.

Collins, Randall. 1987a. 'A Micro–Macro Theory of Intellectual Creativity: The Case of German Idealistic Philosophy', *Sociological Theory* 5: 47–69.

Collins, Randall. 1987b. 'Interaction Ritual Chains, Power, and Property: The Micro–Macro Connection as an Empirically Based Theoretical Problem', in Jeffrey C. Alexander, Bernard Giesen, Richard Münch, and Neil Smelser (eds), *The Micro–Macro Link*. Berkeley and Los Angeles: University of California Press. 193–206.

Collins, Randall. 1988. 'The Micro Contribution to Macro Sociology', *Sociological Theory* 6: 242–53.

Collins, Randall. 1989a. 'Sociology: Proscience or Antiscience?', *American Sociological Review* 54: 124–39.

Collins, Randall. 1989b. 'Toward a Neo-Meadian Sociology of Mind', *Symbolic Interaction* 12: 1–32.

Collins, Randall. 1990. 'Conflict Theory and the Advance of Macro-Historical Sociology', in George Ritzer (ed.), *Frontiers of Social Theory: The New Syntheses*. New York: Columbia University Press. 68–87.

Collins, Randall. 1999. *The Sociology of Philosophies: A Global Theory of Intellectual Change*. Cambridge, MA: Belknap Press.

Connolly, William E. 1973. 'Theoretical Self-Consciousness', *Polity* 6: 5–35.

Cook, Karen S. 1987a. 'Emerson's Contribution to Exchange Theory', in Karen S. Cook (ed.), *Social Exchange Theory*. Beverly Hills, CA: Sage. 209–22.

Cook, Karen S. (ed.). 1987b. *Social Exchange Theory*. Beverly Hills, CA: Sage.

Cook, Karen S., Jodi O'Brien, and Peter Kollock. 1990. 'Exchange Theory: A Blueprint for Structure and Process', in George Ritzer (ed.), *Frontiers of Social Theory: The New Syntheses*. New York: Columbia University Press. 158–81.

Cooper, Kenneth. 1991. 'Stanford President Sets Initiative on Teaching', *Washington Post* 3 March: A12.

Coser, Lewis (ed.). 1965. *Georg Simmel*. Englewood Cliffs, NJ: Prentice Hall.

Costilo, L. Barry. 1985. 'Antitrust Enforcement in Health Care: Ten Years after the AMA Suit', *The New England Journal of Medicine* 313: 901–4.

Coughlin, Ellen K. 1992. 'Sociologists Confront Questions about Field's Vitality and Direction', *Chronicle of Higher Education*, 12 August: A6–8.

Crane, Diana. 1969. 'Social Structure in a Group of Scientists: A Test of the "Invisible College" Hypothesis', *American Sociological Review* 34: 335–51.

Dahrendorf, Ralf. 1959. *Class and Class Conflict in Industrial Society*. Stanford, CA: Stanford University Press.

Darling, John R., and Blaise J. Bergiel. 1983. 'Health Care Advertising: A Comparative Analysis', *Journal of Health Care Marketing* 3: 21–8.

Davis, Kingsley. 1959. 'The Myth of Functional Analysis as a Special Method in Sociology and Anthropology', *American Sociological Review* 24: 757–72.

de Certeau, Michel. 1984. *The Practice of Everyday Life*. Berkeley and Los Angeles: University of California Press.

Derber, Charles (ed.). 1982. *Professionals as Workers: Mental Labor in Advanced Capitalism*. Boston: G.K. Hall.

Derrida, Jacques. 1974. *Of Grammatology*. Baltimore: Johns Hopkins University Press.

Derrida, Jacques. 1978. *Writing and Difference*. Chicago: University of Chicago Press.

De Vos, George A. 1975. 'Apprenticeship and Paternalism', in Ezra Vogel (ed.), *Modern Japanese Organization and Decision Making*. Berkeley and Los Angeles: University of California Press. 210–77.

Diggins, John P. 1999. *Thorstein Veblen: Theorist of the Leisure Class*. Princeton. Princeton University.

DiMaggio, Paul J., and Walter W. Powell. 1983. 'The Iron Cage Revisited: Institutional Isomorphism and Collective Rationality in Organizational Fields', *American Sociological Review* 48: 147–50.

Dingwall, Robert. 1976. 'Accomplishing Professions', *Sociological Review* 24: 331–49.

Donougho, Martin. 1989. 'Postmodern Jameson', in Douglas Kellner (ed.), *Postmodernism, Jameson, Critique*. Washington, DC: Maisonneuve Press.

Durkheim, Emile. 1893/1964. *The Division of Labor in Society*. New York: Free Press.

Durkheim, Emile. 1895/1964. *The Rules of Sociological Method*. New York: Free Press.

Durkheim, Emile. 1897/1951. *Suicide*. New York: Free Press.

Durkheim, Emile. 1912/1965. *The Elementary Forms of Religious Life*. New York: Free Press.

Durkheim, Emile. 1922/1956. *Education and Sociology*. New York: Free Press.

Durkheim, Emile, and Marcel Mauss. 1903/1963. *Primitive Classification*. Chicago: University of Chicago Press.

Eckberg, Douglas, and Lester Hill. 1979. 'The Paradigm Concept in Sociology: A Critical Review', *American Sociological Review* 44: 925–37.

Edel, Abraham. 1959. 'The Concept of Levels in Sociological Theory', in L. Gross (ed.), *Symposium on Sociological Theory*. Evanston, IL: Row Peterson. 167–95.

Effrat, Andrew. 1972. 'Power to the Paradigms', *Sociological Inquiry* 42: 3–33.

Egan, Timothy. 1994. 'In Land of French Fry, Study Finds Problems', *New York Times* 7 February: A10.

Eisen, Arnold. 1978. 'The Meanings and Confusions of Weberian "Rationality"' *British Journal of Sociology* 29: 57–70.

Eisenstadt, S. N., and M. Curelaru. 1976. *The Form of Sociology: Paradigms and Crises*. New York: Wiley.

Elster, Jon. 1982. 'Marxism, Functionalism and Game Theory: The Case for Methodological Individualism', *Theory and Society* 11: 453–82.

Elster, Jon. 1985. *Making Sense of Marx*. Cambridge: Cambridge University Press.

Emerson, Richard M. 1981 'Social Exchange Theory' in Morris, Rosenberg and Ralph H. Turner (eds), *Social Psychology: Sociological Perspectives*, New York: Basic Books. 30–65.

Engels, Friedrich. 1890/1972. 'Letter to Joseph Bloch', in Robert C. Tucker (ed.), *The Marx–Engels Reader*. New York: Norton. 640–2.

Ermann, Dan, and Jon Gabel. 1986. 'Investor-Owned Multihospital System: A Synthesis of Research Findings', in Bradford H. Gray (ed.), *For-Profit Enterprise in Health Care*. National Academy Press. 474–91.

Falk, William, and Shanyang Zhao. 1989. 'Paradigms, Theories, and Methods in Contemporary Rural Sociology: A Partial Replication', *Rural Sociology* 54: 587–600.

Falk, William, and Shanyang Zhao. 1990. 'Paradigms, Theories, and Methods Revisited: We Respond to Our Critics', *Rural Sociology* 55: 112–22.

Farah, Douglas. 1995. 'Cuban Fast Food Joints Are Quick Way for Government to Rally Economy', *Washington Post* 24 January: A14.

Featherman, David L. 1972. 'Achievement Orientations and Socioeconomic Career Attainments', *American Sociological Review* 37: 131–43.

Feldstein, Paul J. 1986. 'The Emergence of Market Competition in the U.S. Health Care System: Its Causes, Likely Structure and Implications', *Health Policy* 6: 1–20.

Fendrich, Michael. 1984. '"Wives" Employment and Husbands' Distress: A Meta Analysis and a Replication', *Journal of Marriage and the Family* 46: 871–9.

Fine, Gary. 1990. 'Symbolic Interactionism in the Post-Blumerian Age', in George Ritzer (ed.), *Frontiers of Social Theory: The New Syntheses*. New York: Columbia University Press. 117–57.

Fischer, Claude. 1976. *The Urban Experience*. New York: Harcourt Brace Jovanovich.

Fiske, Donald W., and Richard A. Shweder (eds). 1986. *Metatheory in Social Science: Pluralisms and Subjectivities*. Chicago: University of Chicago Press.

Folland, Sherman T. 1985. 'The Effects of Health Care Advertising', *Journal of Health Politics, Policy and Law* 10: 329–45.

Foote, Nelson. 1953. 'The Professionalization of Labor in Detroit', *American Journal of Sociology* 58: 371–80.

Forsyth, Patrick, and Thomas J. Danisiewicz. 1985. 'Toward a Theory of Professionalization', *Work and Occupations* 12: 59–76.

Foucault, Michel. 1965. *Madness and Civilization: A History of Insanity in the Age of Reason*. New York: Vintage.

Foucault, Michel. 1966/1973. *The Order of Things: An Archaeology of the Human Sciences*. New York: Vintage.

Foucault, Michel. 1969, 1971/1976. *The Archaeology of Knowledge and The Discourse of Language*. New York: Harper Colophon.

Foucault, Michel. 1970. *The Order of Things: An Archeology of the Human Sciences*. London: Tavistock.

Foucault, Michel. 1975. *The Birth of the Clinic: An Archaeology of Medical Perception*. New York: Vintage.

Foucault, Michel. 1979. *Discipline and Punish: The Birth of the Prison*. New York: Vintage.

Freedman, Steve A. 1985. 'Megacorporate Health Care: A Choice for the Future', *The New England Journal of Medicine* 312: 579–82.

Freidson, Eliot. 1960. 'Client Control and Medical Practice', *American Journal of Sociology* 65: 374–82.

Freidson, Eliot. 1970. *The Profession of Medicine*. Dodd, Mead.

Freidson, Eliot. 1975. *Doctoring Together: A Study of Professional Social Control*. Elsevier.

Freidson, Eliot. 1980. *Patients' Views of Medical Practice*. University of Chicago Press.

Freidson, Eliot. 1983. 'The Theory of the Professions: State of the Art', in Robert Dingwall and Philip Lewis (eds), *The Sociology of the Professions: Lawyers, Doctors and Others*. Macmillan. 19–37.

Freidson, Eliot. 1984. 'The Changing Nature of Professional Control', *Annual Review of Sociology* 10: 1–20.

Freidson, Eliot. 1985. 'The Reorganization of the Medical Profession', *Medical Care Review* 42: 11–35.

Freidson, Eliot. 1986. *Professional Powers: A Study in the Institutionalization of Formal Knowledge*. Chicago: University of Chicago Press.

Friedheim, Elizabeth. 1979. 'An Empirical Comparison of Ritzers' Paradigms and Similar Metatheories', *Social Forces* 58: 59–66.

Friedrichs, Robert. 1970. *A Sociology of Sociology*. New York: Free Press.

Friedrichs, Robert. 1972. 'Dialectical Sociology: Toward a Resolution of the Current "Crises" in Western Sociology', *British Journal of Sociology* 13: 263–74.

Friedrichs, Robert W. 1974. 'The Potential Impact of B.F. Skinner upon American Sociology', *American Sociologist* 9: 3–8.

Frisby, David. 1984. *Georg Simmel*. Chichester: Ellis Horwood.

Fuhrman, Ellsworth R., and William E. Snizek. 1987. 'Finnish and American Sociology: A Cross-Cultural Comparison', *Sociological Inquiry* 57: 204–21.

Furfey, Paul Hanly. 1953/1965. *The Scope and Method of Sociology: A Metasociological Treatise*. New York: Cooper Square.

Gelfand, Toby. 1980. *Professionalizing Modern Medicine: Paris Surgeons and Medical Science and Institutions in the 18th Century*. Greenwood.

Gellner, Ernest. 1956/1973. 'Explanation in History', in John O'Neill (ed.), *Modes of Individualism and Collectivism*. London: Heinemann. 248–63.

Genosko, Gary. 1994. *Baudrillard and Signs: Signification Ablaze*. London: Routledge.

Georgoudi, Marianthi, and Ralph Rosnow. 1985. 'Notes toward a Contextualist Understanding of Social Psychology', *Personality and Social Psychology Bulletin* 11: 5–22.

Geras, Norman. 1983. *Marx and Human Nature: Refutation of a Legend*. London: New Left Books.

Gergen, Kenneth J. 1973. 'Social Psychology as History', *Journal of Personality and Social Psychology* 26: 309–20.

Gergen, Kenneth J. 1986. 'Correspondence versus Autonomy in the Language of Understanding Human Action', in Donald W. Fiske and Richard A. Shweder (eds), *Metatheory in Social Science: Pluralisms and Subjectivities*. Chicago: University of Chicago Press. 136–62.

Gerth, Hans, and C. Wright Mills. 1953. *Character and Social Structure*. New York: Harcourt, Brace and World.

Gerth, Hans, and C. Wright Mills (eds). 1958. *From Max Weber*. New York: Oxford University Press.

Gibney, Frank. 1982. *Miracle by Design*. New York: Time Books.

Gibson, Richard. 1996. 'McDonalds Accelerates Store Openings in U.S. and Abroad, Pressuring Rivals', *Wall Street Journal*, 18 January: A3.

Giddens, Anthony (ed.). 1972. *Emile Durkheim: Selected Writings*. Cambridge: Cambridge University Press.

Giddens, Anthony (ed.). 1984. *The Constitution of Society: Outline of the Theory of Structuration*. Berkeley and Los Angeles: University of California Press.

Gieryn, Thomas, George M. Bevins, and Stephen C. Zehr. 1985. 'Professionalization of American Scientists: Public Science in the Creation/Evolution Trials', *American Sociological Review* 50: 392–409.

Godelier, Maurice. 1972. *Rationality and Irrationality in Economics*. London: New Left Books.

Goldman, Steven L., Roger N. Nagel, and Kenneth Preiss. 1994. 'Why Seiko Has 3,000 Watch Styles', *New York Times* 9 October: 9.

Goldman, Steven L., Roger N. Nagel, and Kenneth Preiss. 1995. *Agile Competitors and Virtual Organizations: Strategies for Enriching the Customer*. New York: Van Nostrand Reinhold.

Goldstein, Leon J. 1956. 'The Inadequacy of the Principle of Methodological Individualism', *Journal of Philosophy* 53: 801–13.

Goldstein, Leon J. 1958. 'The Two Theses of Methodological Individualism', *British Journal for the Philosophy of Science* 9: 1–11.

Goldstein, Michael S. 1984. 'Abortion as a Medical Career Choice: Entrepreneurs, Community Physicians, and Others', *Journal of Health and Social Behavior* 25: 211–29.

Goode, William J. 1957. 'Community within a Community: The Professions', *American Sociological* 22: 194–200.

Gottdiener, Mark. 1997. *The Theming of America*. Boulder, CO: Westview Press.

Gould, Carol. 1978. *Marx's Social Ontology: Individuality and Community in Marx's Theory of Social Reality*. Cambridge, MA: MIT Press.

Gouldner, Alvin. 1958. *Introduction to Socialism and Saint-Simon, by Emile Durkheim*. Yellow Springs, Ohio: Antioch Press.

Gouldner, Alvin. 1965. *Enter Plato: Classical Greece and the Origins of Social Theory*. New York: Basic Books.

Gouldner, Alvin. 1970. *The Coming Crisis of Western Sociology*. New York: Basic Books.

Gramsci, Antonio. 1971. *Selections from the Prison Notebooks*. New York: Basic Books.

Gray, Bradford H. (ed.). 1986. *For-Profit Enterprise in Health Care*. National Academy Press.

Greenwood, Ernest. 1957. 'Attributes of a Profession', *Social Work* 2: 45–55.

Gurvitch, Georges. 1964. *The Spectrum of Social Time*. Dordrecht: D. Reidel.

Habermas, Jürgen. 1984. *The Theory of Communicative Action*. Vol. 1, *Reason and the Rationalization of Society*. Boston: Beacon Press.

Habermas, Jürgen. 1987. *The Theory of Communicative Action*. Vol. 2, *Life World and System: A Critique of Functionalist Reason*. Boston: Beacon Press.

Hage, Jerald, and Charles H. Powers. 1992. *Post-Industrial Lives: Roles and Relationships in the 21st Century*. Newbury Park, CA: Sage.

Halfpenny, Peter. Forthcoming. 'Positivism', in George Ritzer and Barry Smart (eds), *Handbook of Social Theory*. London: Sage.

Hall, Richard. 1983. 'Theoretical Trends in the Sociology of Occupations', *Sociological Quarterly* 24: 5–23.

Harvey, David. 1989. *The Condition of Postmodernity: An Enquiry into the Origins of Cultural Change*. Oxford: Basil Blackwell.

Harvey, Lee. 1982. 'The Use and Abuse of Kuhnian Paradigms in the Sociology of Knowledge', *British Journal of Sociology* 16: 85–101.

Harvey, Lee. 1987. 'The Nature of "Schools" in the Sociology of Knowledge: The Case of the "Chicago School"', *Sociological Review* 35: 245–78.

Haug, Marie R. 1973. 'Deprofessionalization: An Alternate Hypothesis for the Future', in Paul Halmos (ed.), *Professionalization and Social Change*. University of Keele. 195–211.

Haug, Marie R. 1975. 'The Deprofessionalization of Everyone?', *Sociological Focus* 8: 197–213.

Havighurst, Clark C. 1983. 'The Doctors' Trust: Self Regulation and the Law', *Health Affairs* 2: 64–76.

Hayek, Frederick A. von. 1955. *The Counter-Revolution of Science*. New York: Free Press.

Heberle, Rudolph. 1965. 'Simmels Methods', in Lewis Coser (ed.), *Georg Simmel*. Englewood Cliffs, NJ: Prentice Hall. 116–21.

Hegtvedt, Karen. 1988. 'Social Determinants of Perception: Power Equity and Status Effects in an Exchange Situation', *Social Psychology Quarterly* 51: 141–53.

Heller, Agnes. 1976. *The Theory of Need in Marx*. New York: St Martin's Press.

Henry, Michel. 1983. *Marx: A Philosophy of Human Reality*. Bloomington, IN: Indiana University Press.

Heritage, John. 1984. *Garfinkel and Ethnomethodology*. Cambridge: Polity Press.

Heritage, John. and J. Maxwell Atkinson. 1984. 'Introduction' to John Heritage and J. Maxwell Atkinson (eds), *Structures of Social Actions*. Cambridge: Cambridge University Press. 1–15.

Hewitt, John P. 1977. 'Comment: The Dissipation of Social Psychology', *American Sociologist* 12: 14–17.

Hilbert, Richard A. 1987. 'Bureaucracy as Belief, Rationalization as Repair: Max Weber in a Post-Functionalist Age', *Sociological Theory* 5: 47–69.

Hilbert, Richard A. 1990. 'Ethnomethodology and the Micro–Macro Order', *American Sociological Review* 55: 794–808.

Hill, Lester, Jr, and Douglas Lee Eckberg. 1981. 'Clarifying Confusions about Paradigms: A Reply to Ritzer', *American Sociological Review* 46: 248–52.

Hinkle, Roscoe. 1963. 'Antecedents of the Action Orientation in American Sociology before 1935', *American Sociological Review* 28: 705–15.

Hirsch, Paul, Stuart Michaels, and Ray Friedman. 1987. '"Dirty Hands" versus "Clean Models": Is Sociology in Danger of Being Seduced by Economics?', *Theory and Society* 16: 317–36.

Hockstader, Lee. 1991. 'No Service, No Smile, Little Sauce', *Washington Post* 5 August A12.

Hoecker-Drysdale, Susan. 2000. 'Harriet Martineau', in George Ritzer (ed.), *The Blackwell Companion to Major Social Theorists*. Malden, MA and Oxford: Blackwell. 53–80.

Homans, George. 1958. 'Social Behavior as Exchange', *American Journal of Sociology* 63: 597–606.

Homans, George. 1961/1974. *Social Behavior: Its Elementary Forms*. New York: Harcourt Brace Jovanovich.

Homans, George. 1971. 'Commentary', in Herman Turk and Richard Simpson (eds), *Institutions and Social Exchange*. Indianapolis, IN: Bobbs-Merrill: 363–74.

Homans, George. 1984. *Coming to My Senses: The Autobiography of a Sociologist*. New Brunswick, NJ: Transaction Books.

Horobin, Gordon. 1983. 'Professional Mystery: The Maintenance of Charisma in General Medical Practice', in Robert Dingwall and Philip Lewis (eds), *The Sociology of the Professions: Lawyers, Doctors and Others*. Macmillan. 84–105.

Horowitz, Irving Louis. 1983. *C. Wright Mills: An American Utopian*. New York: Free Press.

House, James. 1977. 'The Three Faces of Social Psychology', *Sociometry* 40: 161–77.

Hoy, David. 1985. 'Jacques Derrida', in Quentin Skinner (ed.), *The Return of Grand Theory in the Human Sciences*. Cambridge: Cambridge University Press. 43–64.

Huaco, George. 1986. 'Ideology and General Theory: The Case of Sociological Functionalism', *Comparative Studies in Society and History* 28: 34–54.

Hunter, J.E., and F.L. Schmidt. 1989. *Methods of Meta-Analysis: Correcting Error and Bias in Research Findings*. Newbury Park, CA: Sage.

Hunter, J.E., Schmidt, F.L., and G.B. Jackson. 1982. *Meta-Analysis: Cumulating Research Findings Across Studies*. Beverly Hills, CA: Sage.

Inkeles, Alex. 1969. 'Making Men Modern: On the Causes and Consequences of Individual Change in Six Developing Countries', *American Journal of Sociology* 75: 208–25.

Israel, Joachim. 1971. *Alienation: From Marx to Modern Sociology*. Boston: Allyn and Bacon.

Iwata, Ryuahi. 1982. *Japanese-Style Management: Its Foundations and Prospects*. Tokyo: Asian Productivity Organization.

Jameson, Fredric. 1984. 'Postmodernism, or the Cultural Logic of Late Capitalism', *New Left Review* 146: 53–92.

Jameson, Fredric. 1991. *Postmodernism, or the Cultural Logic of Late Capitalism*. Durham, NC: Duke University Press.

Jamous, H., and B. Peloille. 1970. 'Changes in the French University-Hospital System, in J.A. Jackson (ed.), *Professions and Professionalization*. Cambridge: Cambridge University Press. 111–52.

Jarvie, I.C. 1964. *The Revolution in Anthropology*. New York: Humanities Press.

Jarvie, Ian. 1972. *Concepts and Society*. London: Routledge.

Johnson, Chalmers. 1982. *MITI and the Japanese Miracle*. Stanford, CA: Stanford University Press.

Johnson, Terence. 1972. *The Professions and Power*. London: Macmillan.

Kalberg, Stephen. 1980. 'Max Weber's Types of Rationality: Cornerstones for the Analysis of Rationalization Processes in History', *American Journal of Sociology* 85: 1145–79.

Kalberg, Stephen. 1983. 'Max Weber's Universal-Historical Architectonic of Economically-Oriented Action: A Preliminary Construction', in Scott McNall (ed.), *Current Perspectives in Social Theory*. Greenwich, CT: JAI Press. Vol. 4. 253–88.

Kalberg, Stephen. 1994. *Max Weber's Comparative-Historical Sociology*, Chicago: University of Chicago.

Katz, Irwin, and R. Glen Haas. 1988. 'Racial Ambivalence and American Value Conflict: Correlational and Priming Studies of Dual Cognitive Structures', *Journal of Personality and Social Psychology* 55: 893–905.

Kautsky, Karl. 1927/1978. *The Materialist Conception of History*. New Haven: Yale University Press.

Kemeny, Jim. 1976. 'Perspectives on the Micro–Macro Distinction', *Sociological Review* 24: 731–52.

Kerr, Stephen T. 1985. 'Referral in Education and Medicine: Differing Patterns of Development in Specialized Professions', *Work and Occupations* 12: 416–36.

Klegon, Douglas. 1978. 'The Sociology of Professions: An Emerging Perspective', *Sociology of Work and Occupations* 5: 259–83.

Knox, John. 1963. 'The Concept of Exchange in Sociological Theory: 1884 and 1961', *Social Forces* 41: 341–6.

Kohn, Melvin. 1969. *Class and Conformity*. Homewood, IL: Dorsey Press.

Kohn, Melvin. 1989. 'Social Structure and Personality: A Quintessentially Sociological Approach to Social Psychology', *Social Forces* 68: 26–33.

Korenbaum, Mildred. 1964. 'Translator's Preface' to *The Spectrum of Social Time* by George Gurvitch. Dordrecht: D. Reidel.

Kroker, Arthur, Marilouise Kroker, and David Cook. 1989. *Panic Encyclopedia: The Definitive Guide to the Postmodern Scene*. New York: St Martin's Press.

Kuhn, Thomas. 1962. *The Structure of Scientific Revolutions*. Chicago: University of Chicago Press.

Kuhn, Thomas. 1970a. 'Reflections on My Critics', in Imre Lakatos and Alan Musgrave (eds), *Criticism and the Growth of Knowledge*. Cambridge: Cambridge University Press. 231–78.

Kuhn, Thomas. 1970b. *The Structure of Scientific Revolutions*, 2nd edn. Chicago: University of Chicago Press.

Kuisel, Richard. 1993. *Seducing the French: The Dilemma of Americanization*. Berkeley, CA: University of California Press.

Lakatos, Imre. 1978. *The Methodology of Scientific Research Programs*. Cambridge: Cambridge University Press.

Larkin, Gerald. 1983. *Occupational Monopoly and Modern Medicine*. Tavistock.

Larson, Magali Sarfatti. 1977. *The Rise of Professionalism: A Sociological Analysis*. Berkeley, CA: University of California Press.

Lefebvre, Henri. 1968. *The Sociology of Marx*. New York: Vintage.

Leidner, Robin. 1993. *Fast Food, Fast Talk: Service Work and the Routinization of Everyday Life*. Berkeley, CA: University of California Press.

Leinhart, Samuel. 1977. *Social Networks: A Developing Paradigm*. New York: Academic Press.

Lemert, Charles (ed.). 1981. *French Sociology: Rupture and Renewal Since 1968*. New York: Columbia University Press.

Lemert, Charles. 2000. 'Charlotte Perkins Gilman', in George Ritzer (ed.), *The Blackwell Companion to Major Social Theorists*. Malden, MA and Oxford: Blackwell. 279–301.

Lengermann, Patricia M. 1979. 'The Founding of the American Sociological Review', *American Sociological Review* 4: 185–98.

Lengermann, Patricia M., and Jill Niebrugge-Brantley. 1998. *The Women Founders: Sociology and Social Theory, 1830–1930*. New York: McGraw-Hill.

Levine, Donald. 1981. 'Rationality and Freedom: Weber and Beyond', *Sociological Inquiry* 51: 5–25.

Lévi-Strauss, Claude. 1966. *The Savage Mind*. Chicago: University of Chicago Press.

Liska, Allen. 1977. 'The Dissipation of Sociological Social Psychology', *American Sociologist* 12: 2–8.

Liska, Allen. 1990. 'The Significance of Aggregate Dependent Variables and Contextual Independent Variables for Linking Macro and Micro Theories', *Social Psychology Quarterly* 53: 292–301.

Lodahl, Janice B., and Gerald Gordon. 1972. 'The Structure of Scientific Fields and the Functioning of University Graduate Departments', *American Sociological Review* 37: 57–72.

Love, John, F. 1986. *McDonald's: Behind the Arches*. Toronto: Bantam Books.

Lukács, Georg. 1922/1968. *History and Class Consciousness*. Cambridge: MIT Press.

Lukes, Steven. 1973. *Emile Durkheim: His Life and Work*. New York: Harper & Row.

Lyotard, Jean-François. 1984. *The Postmodern Condition*. Minneapolis: University of Minnesota Press.

Lyotard, Jean-François. 1988/1993. *The Postmodern Explained: Correspondence 1982–1985*. Minneapolis and London: University of Minnesota Press.

Majoribanks, Kevin. 1989. 'Ethnicity, Ability, Aspirations and Social Status Attainment', *International Journal of Psychology* 24: 35–47.

Mandel, Ernest. 1983. *Introduction to Marxist Economic Theory*, 2nd edn. New York: Pathfinder Press.

Mandelbaum, Maurice. 1955. 'Societal Facts', *British Journal of Sociology* 6: 305–16.

Mandelbaum, Maurice. 1957. 'Societal Laws', *British Journal for the Philosophy of Science* 8: 211–24.

Mandelbaum, Maurice. 1965. 'The History of Ideas, Intellectual History, and the History of Philosophy', in *The Historiography of the History of Philosophy*. Beiheft 5, History and Theory. 33–66.

Mann, Michael. 1986. *The Sources of Social Power*. Vol. 1. New York: Cambridge University Press.

Mannheim, Karl. 1929/1936. *Ideology and Utopia: An Introduction to the Sociology of Knowledge*. New York: Harvest Books.

Mannheim, Karl. 1935/1940. *Man and Society in an Age of Reconstruction*. New York: Harcourt, Brace and World.

Marini, Margaret M. 1988. 'Sociology of Gender', in Edgar F. Borgatta and Karen S. Cook (eds), *The Future of Sociology*. Beverly Hills, CA: Sage. 374–93.

Marske, Charles E. 1987. 'Durkheim's "Cult of the Individual" and the Moral Reconstitution of Society', *Sociological Theory* 5: 1–14.

Martindale, Don. 1960. *The Nature and Types of Sociological Theory*. Boston: Houghton Mifflin.

Martindale, Don. 1979. 'Ideologies, Paradigms, and Theories', in William Snizek, Ellsworth Fuhrman, and Michael K. Miller (eds), *Contemporary Issues in Theory and Research*. Westport, CT: Greenwood Press. 7–24.

Marx, Karl. 1857–8/1964. *Pre-Capitalist Economic Formations*. New York: International Publishers.

Marx, Karl. 1857–8/1973. *The Grundrisse: Foundations of the Critique of Political Economy*. New York: Random House.

Marx, Karl. 1859/1970. *A Contribution to the Critique of Political Economy*. Vol. 1. New York: International Publishers.

Marx, Karl. 1867/1967. *Capital: A Critique of Political Economy*. Vol. 1. New York: International Publishers.

Marx, Karl. 1932/1964. *The Economic and Philosophic Manuscripts of 1844*. Edited by Dirk J. Struik. New York: International Publishers.

Marx, Karl, and Friedrich Engels. 1845/1956. *The Holy Family: Or Critique of Critical Critique*. Moscow: Foreign Languages Publishing House.

Marx, Karl, and Friedrich Engels. 1845–6/1970. *The German Ideology*. Part 1. Edited by C. J. Arthur. New York: International Publishers.

Masterman, Margaret. 1970. 'The Nature of a Paradigm', in Imre Lakatos and Alan Musgrove (eds), *Criticism and the Growth of Knowledge*. Cambridge: Cambridge University Press. 59–80.

Mauss, Marcel. 1954. *The Gift*. London: Cohen and West.

Mazlish, Bruce. 1984. *The Meaning of Karl Marx*. New York: Oxford University Press.

McKinlay, John B. 1973. 'On the Professional Regulation of Change', in Paul Halmos (ed.), *Professionalization and Social Change*. University of Keele. 61–84.

McKinlay, John B. 1982. 'The Proletarianization of Physicians', in Charles Derber (ed.), *Professionals as Workers: Mental Labor in Advanced Capitalism*. Boston: G.K. Hall. 37–62.

McMillan, Charles J. 1984. *The Japanese Industrial System*. Berlin: Walter de Gruyter. 195–220.

McMurty, John. 1978. *The Structure of Marx's World-View*. Princeton, NJ: Princeton University Press.

Mead, George H. 1934/1962. *Mind, Self, and Society*. Chicago: University of Chicago Press.

Mehan, Hugh, and Houston Wood. 1975. *The Reality of Ethnomethodology*. New York: Wiley.

Merton, Robert. 1949/1968. 'Manifest and Latent Functions', *Social Theory and Social Structure*. New York: Free Press. 73–138.

Merton, Robert. 1965. *On the Shoulders of Giants: A Shandean Postscript*. New York: Free Press.

Merton, Robert. 1968. *Social Theory and Social Structure*, enlarged edn. New York: Free Press.

Merton, Robert. 1975. 'Structural Analysis in Sociology', in Peter Blau (ed.), *Approaches to the Study of Social Structure*. New York: Free Press. 21–52.

Meszaros, Istvan. 1970. *Marx's Theory of Alienation*. New York: Harper Torchbooks.

Michael, Allen, Isreal Shaked and John Daley. 1985. 'The Proprietary Hospital Industry: A Financial Analysis, 1972–1982', *Social Science and Medicine* 21: 235–42.

Mill, John Stuart. 1843/1950. *Philosophy of Scientific Method*. New York: Hafner.

Miller, James. 1993. *The Passion of Michel Foucault*. New York: Anchor Books.

Mises, Ludwig von. 1976. *Epistemological Problems of Economics*. New York: New York University Press.

Mitchell, Janet B. 1985. 'Physician DRGs', *The New England Journal of Medicine* 313: 670–5.

Mitroff, Ian, and Warren Bennis. 1989. *The Unreality Industry: The Deliberate Manufacturing of Falsehood and What It Is Doing to Our Lives*. New York: Birch Lane Press.

Mitzman, Arthur. 1969. *The Iron Cage: An Historical Interpretation of Max Weber*. New York: Grosset and Dunlap.

Monk, Richard (ed.). 1986. *Structures of Knowing*. Lanham, MD: University Press of America.

Mowitt, John. 1992. *Text: The Genealogy of an Antidisciplinary Object*. Durham, NC and London: Duke University Press.

Mulligan, G., and B. Lederman. 1977. 'Social Facts and Rules of Practice', *American Journal of Sociology* 83: 539–50.

Mullins, Nicholas. 1973. *Theories and Theory Groups in Contemporary American Sociology*. New York: Harper and Row.

Mullins, Nicholas. 1983. 'Theories and Theory Groups Revisited', in Randall Collins (ed.), *Sociological Theory, 1983*. San Francisco: Jossey Bass. 319–37.

Murray, Topsy, Robert Dingwall, and John Eekelaar. 1983. 'The Professionals' Bureaucracies: Solicitors in Private Practice and Local Government', in Robert Dingwall and Philip Lewis (eds), *The Sociology of the Professions: Lawyers, Doctors and Others*. Macmillan.

Nass, Clifford I. 1986. 'Bureaucracy, Technical Expertise, and Professionals: A Weberian Approach', *Sociological Theory* 4: 61–70.

Needham, Rodney. 1963. 'Introduction' to *Primitive Classification* by Emile Durkheim and Marcel Mauss. Chicago: University of Chicago Press.

Nelson, Robert L. 1981. 'Practice and Privilege: Social Change and the Structure of Large Law Firms', *American Bar Foundation Research Journal* 97–140.

Nicolaus, Martin. 1973. 'Foreword' to *The Grundrisse: Foundations of the Critique of Political Economy* by Karl Marx. New York: Random House.

Nisbet, Robert. 1974. *The Sociology of Emile Durkheim*. New York: Oxford University Press.

Noblit, George W., and R. Dwight Hare. 1988. *Meta-Ethnography: Synthesizing Qualitative Studies*. Newbury Park, CA: Sage.

Oakes, Guy. 1984. 'The Problem of Women in Simmel's Theory of Culture', in *On Women, Sexuality, and Love* by Georg Simmel. New Haven, CT: Yale University Press. 3–62.

Ollman, Bertell. 1971. *Alienation*. Cambridge: Cambridge University Press.

Ollman, Bertell. 1976. *Alienation*, 2nd edn. Cambridge: Cambridge University Press.

Oppenheimer, Martin. 1973. 'The Proletarianization of the Professional', in Paul Halmos (ed.), *Professionalization and Social Change*. University of Keele. 213–27.

Ouchi, William. 1981. *Theory Z*. Reading, MA: Addison-Wesley.

Pampel, Fred. 2000. *Sociological Lives and Ideas: An Introduction to the Classical Theorists*. New York: Worth.

Parsons, Talcott. 1937. *The Structure of Social Action*. New York: McGraw-Hill.

Parsons, Talcott. 1937/1949. *The Structure of Social Action*, 2nd edn. New York: Free Press.

Parsons, Talcott. 1964. 'Levels of Organization and the Mediation of Social Interaction', *Sociological Inquiry* 34: 207–20.

Pegels, Carl C. 1984. *Japan vs. the West: Implications for Management*. Boston: Kluwer-Nijhoff.

Phillips, Dennis. 1976. *Holistic Thought in Social Science*. Stanford, CA: Stanford University Press.

Phillips, Derek. 1973. 'Paradigms, Falsifications, and Sociology', *Acta Sociologica* 16: 13–31.

Piaget, Jean. 1970. *Structuralism*. New York: Harper Colophon.

Picou, J. Steven, Richard H. Wells, and Kenneth L. Nyberg. 1978. 'Paradigms, Theories, and Methods in Contemporary Rural Sociology', *Rural Sociology* 43: 559–83.

Pieterse, Jan Nederveen. 1994. 'Globalization as Hybridisation', *International Sociology* 9.

Platt, Jennifer. 1986. 'Functionalism and the Survey: The Relation of Theory and Method', *Sociological Review* 34: 501–36.

Polit, Denise F., and Toni Falbo. 1987. 'Only Children and Personality Development: A Quantitative Review', *Journal of Marriage and the Family* 49: 309–25.

Pope, Whitney. 1973. 'Classic on Classic: Parsons' Interpretation of Durkheim', *American Sociological Review* 38: 399–415.

Pope, Whitney. 1975. 'Durkheim as Functionalist', *Sociological Quarterly* 16: 361–79.

Pope, Whitney. 1976. *Durkheim's 'Suicide': A Classic Analyzed*. Chicago: University of Chicago Press.

Pope, Whitney, and Jere Cohen. 1978. 'On R. Stephen Warner's "Toward a Redefinition of Action Theory": Paying the Cognitive Element its Due', *American Journal of Sociology* 83: 1359–67.

Pope, Whitney, Jere Cohen, and Lawrence Hazelrigg. 1975. 'On the Divergence of Weber and Durkheim: A Critique of Parsons' Convergence Thesis', *American Sociological Review* 40: 417–27.

Popper, Karl. 1950. *The Open Society and Its Enemies*. London: Routledge and Kegan Paul.

Popper, Karl. 1961. *The Poverty of Historicism*. London: Routledge and Kegan Paul.

Porpora, Douglas. 1989. 'Four Concepts of Social Structure', *Journal for the Theory of Social Behaviour* 19: 195–211.

Portes, Alejandro. 1973. 'The Factorial Structure of Modernity: Empirical Replications and a Critique', *American Journal of Sociology* 79: 14–44.

Price, Derek J. De Solla. 1963. *Little Science, Big Science*. New York: Columbia University Press.

Quintana, Jose B., W. Jack Duncan, and Howard W. Houser. 1985. 'Hospital Governance and the Corporate Revolution', *Health Care Management Review* 10: 63–71.

Radnitzky, Gerard. 1973. *Contemporary Schools of Metascience*. Chicago: Henry Regnery.

Rattansi, Ali. 1982. *Marx and the Division of Labour*. London: Macmillan.

Reiser, Stanley Joel. 1978. *Medicine and the Reign of Technology*. Cambridge: Cambridge University Press.

Relman, Arnold S. 1980. 'The New Medical-Industrial Complex', *The New England Journal of Medicine* 303: 963–70.

Relman, Arnold S., and Uwe Reinhardt. 1986. 'An Exchange on For-Profit Health Care', in Bradford H. Gray (ed.), *For-Profit Enterprise in Health Care*. National Academy Press. 209–23.

Riding, Alan. 1992. 'Only the French Elite Scorn Mickey's Debut', *New York Times* 13 April: A13.

Ritzer, George. 1975a. 'The Emerging Power Perspective in the Sociological Study of the Professions'. Paper presented at the Meetings of the American Sociological Association, San Francisco.

Ritzer, George. 1975b. 'Professionalization, Bureaucratization, and Rationalization: The Views of Max Weber', *Social Forces* 53: 627–34.

Ritzer, George. 1975c. *Sociology: A Multiple Paradigm Science*. Boston: Allyn and Bacon.

Ritzer, George. 1975d. 'Sociology: A Multiple Paradigm Science', *American Sociologist* 10: 156–67.

Ritzer, George. 1975/1980. *Sociology: A Multiple Paradigm Science*, rev. edn. Boston: Allyn and Bacon.

Ritzer, George. 1981a. 'Paradigm Analysis in Sociology: Clarifying the Issues', *American Sociological Review* 46: 245–8.

Ritzer, George. 1981b. *Toward an Integrated Sociological Paradigm: The Search for an Exemplar and an Image of the Subject Matter*. Boston: Allyn and Bacon.

Ritzer, George. 1983. 'The McDonaldization of Society', *Journal of American Culture* 6: 100–7.

Ritzer, George. 1987. 'The Current State of Metatheory', *Sociological Perspectives: The Theory Section Newsletter* 10: 1–6.

Ritzer, George. 1988a. 'The Micro–Macro Link: Problems and Prospects', *Contemporary Sociology* 17: 703–6.

Ritzer, George. 1988b. 'Sociological Metatheory: Defending a Subfield by Delineating its Parameters', *Sociological Theory* 6: 187–200.

Ritzer, George. 1988c. *Sociological Theory*. New York: Alfred A. Knopf.

Ritzer, George. 1988d. 'Problems, Scandals and the Possibility of "Textbookgate": An Author's View', *Teaching Sociology* 16: 373–80.

Ritzer, George. 1989a. 'Metatheorizing as a Prelude to Theory Development'. Paper presented at the Meetings of the American Sociological Association, San Francisco.

Ritzer, George. 1989b. 'The New Economy? The Perpetually New Economy: The Case for the Resuscitation of Economic Sociology', *Work and Occupations* 16: 243–72.

Ritzer, George. 1989c. 'Of Levels and "Intellectual Amnesia"', Sociological Theory 7: 226–9.

Ritzer, George. 1990a. 'The Current Status of Sociological Theory: The New Syntheses', in George Ritzer (ed.), Frontiers of Social Theory: The New Syntheses. New York: Columbia University Press. 1–30.

Ritzer, George. 1990b. 'Micro–Macro Linkage in Sociological Theory: Applying a Metatheoretical Tool', in George Ritzer (ed.), Frontiers of Social Theory, The New Syntheses. New York: Columbia University Press. 347–70.

Ritzer, George (ed.). 1990c. 'Symposium: Metatheory, its Uses and Abuses in Contemporary Sociology', Sociological Forum 5: 1–74.

Ritzer, George. 1990d. 'Metatheorizing in Sociology', Sociological Forum 5: 3–15.

Ritzer, George. 1991a. 'The Recent History and the Emerging Reality of American Sociological Theory: A Metatheoretical Interpretation', Sociological Forum 6: 269–87.

Ritzer, George. 1991b. Metatheorizing in Sociology. Lexington, MA: Lexington Books.

Ritzer, George (ed.). 1992. Metatheorizing. Newbury Park, CA: Sage.

Ritzer, George. 1996. The McDonaldization of Society, 2nd edn. Thousand Oaks, CA: Pine Forge Press.

Ritzer, George. 1997. Postmodern Social Theory. New York: McGraw-Hill.

Ritzer, George. 1998. The McDonaldization Thesis. London: Sage.

Ritzer, George. 1999. Enchanting a Disenchanted World: Revolutionizing the Means of Consumption. Thousand Oaks, CA: Pine Forge Press.

Ritzer, George (ed.). 2000a. The Blackwell Companion to Major Social Theorists. Malden, MA and Oxford: Blackwell.

Ritzer, George. 2000b. Classical Sociological Theory, 3rd edn. New York: McGraw-Hill.

Ritzer, George. 2000c. Sociological Theory. NY: McGraw-Hill.

Ritzer, George, and Richard Bell. 1981. 'Emile Durkheim: Exemplar for an Integrated Sociological Paradigm?', Social Forces 59: 966–95.

Ritzer, George, and Pamela Gindoff. 1992. 'Methodological Relationism: Lessons for and from Social Psychology', Social Psychology Quarterly 55: 128–40.

Ritzer, George, and Terri LeMoyne. 1990. 'Hyperrationality and the Rise of Japanese Industry: An Application of Neo-Weberian Theory'. Paper presented at the Meetings of the International Sociological Association, Madrid.

Ritzer, George, and David Walczak. 1986. Working: Conflict and Change, 3rd edn. Englewood Cliffs, NJ: Prentice Hall.

Ritzer, George, and David Walczak. 1988. 'Rationalization and the Deprofessionalization of Physicians', Social Forces 67: 1–22.

Ritzer, George, Wendy Wiedenhoft, and James Murphy. Forthcoming. 'Thorstein Veblen in the Age of Hyperconsumption', in George Ritzer (ed.), Explorations in the Sociology of Consumption: Fast Food, Credit Cards and Casinos. London: Sage.

Robbins, Derek. 1991. The Work of Pierre Bourdieu. Boulder, CO: Westview Press.

Robertson, Roland. 1992. Globalization: Social Theory and Global Culture. London: Sage.

Rogers, Mary (ed.). 1996. Multicultural Experiences, Multicultural Theories. New York: McGraw-Hill.

Rohlen, Thomas P. 1975. 'The Company Work Group', in Ezra Vogel (ed.), Modern Japanese Organization and Decision Making. Berkeley and Los Angeles: University of California Press. 185–209.

Rorty, Richard. 1978. Philosophy and the Mirror of Nature. Princeton, NJ: Princeton University Press.

Rorty, Richard. 1979. Philosophy and the Mirror of Nature. Princeton, NJ: Princeton University.

Rorty, Richard. 1989. *Contingency, Irony, and Solidarity*. Cambridge: Cambridge University Press.

Rosenberg, Alexander. 1988. *Philosophy of Social Science*. Boulder, CO: Westview Press.

Rosenberg, Morris. 1965. *Society and the Adolescent Self Image*. Princeton, NJ: Princeton University Press.

Rosenberg, Morris. 1989. 'Self-Concept Research: A Historical Review', *Social Forces* 68: 34–44.

Rosenberg, Morris, and Ralph Turner (eds). 1981. *Social Psychology: Sociological Perspectives*. New York: Basic Books.

Roth, Julius. 1974. 'Professionalism: The Sociologist's Decoy', *Sociology of Work and Occupations* 1: 6–23.

Rothman, Robert. 1984. 'Deprofessionalization: The Case of Law in America', *Work and Occupations* 11: 183–206.

Rothstein, William. 1973. 'Professionalization and Employer Demands: The Case of Homeopathy and Psychoanalysis in the United States', in Paul Halmos (ed.), *Professionalization and Social Change*. University of Keele. 159–78.

Saks, Mike. 1983. 'Removing the Blinkers? A Critique of Recent Contributions to the Sociology of the Professions', *The Sociological Review* 31: 1–21.

Schlesinger, Mark. 1985. 'The Rise of Proprietary Health Care', *Business and Health* January/February: 7–12.

Schmitt, Neal, Richard Z. Gooding, Raymond A. Noe, and Michael Kirsch. 1984. 'Meta-Analyses of Validity Studies Published between 1964 and 1982 and the Investigation of Study Characteristics', *Personnel Psychology* 37: 407–22.

Schonberger, Richard J. 1982. *Japanese Manufacturing Techniques*. New York: Free Press.

Schutz, Alfred. 1932/1967. *The Phenomonology of the Social World*. Evanston, IL: Northwestern University Press.

Schutz, Alfred. 1962. *Collected Papers 1: The Problem of Social Reality*. The Hague: Martinus Nijhoff.

Schutz, Alfred. 1964. *Collected Papers 2: Studies in Social Theory*. The Hague: Martinus Nijhoff.

Schutz, Alfred. 1966. *Collected Papers 3: Studies in Phenomenological Philosophy*. The Hague: Martinus Nijhoff.

Scott, K.J. 1961. 'Methodological and Epistemological Individualism', *British Journal for the Philosophy of Science* 11: 331–5.

Sears, David. 1969. 'Political Behavior', in Gardner Lindzey and Elliott Aronson (eds), *Handbook of Social Psychology*. Reading, MA: Addison-Wesley. 315–348.

Sewell, William H., and Robert M. Hauser. 1974. *Education, Occupation and Earnings*. New York: Academic Press.

Shea, Steven, and David Marguilies. 1985. 'The Paperless Medical Record', *Social Science and Medicine* 21: 741–6.

* Shelton, Allen. Forthcoming. 'Writing McDonald's, Eating the Past: McDonald's as Postmodern Space'.

Shils, Edward. 1970. 'Tradition, Ecology, and Institution in the History of Sociology'. *Daedalus* 99: 760–825.

Simmel, Georg. 1907/1978. *The Philosophy of Money*. London: Routledge and Kegan Paul.

Simmel, Georg. 1908/1950. 'Subordination Under a Principle', in Kurt Wolff (ed.), *The Sociology of Georg Simmel*. New York: Free Press. 250–67.

Simmel, Georg. 1908/1971. 'Subjective Culture', in Donald Levine (ed.), *Georg Simmel*. Chicago: University of Chicago Press. 227–34.

Simmel, Georg. 1921/1968. 'The Conflict in Modern Culture', in Peter K. Etzkorn (ed.), *Georg Simmel: The Conflict in Modern Culture and other Essays*. New York: Teacher's College, Columbia University: 11–25.

Singelmann, Peter. 1972. 'Exchange as Symbolic Interaction', *American Sociological Review* 38: 414–24.

Skinner, B.F. 1971. *Beyond Freedom and Dignity*. New York: Alfred A. Knopf.

Skocpol, Theda. 1979. *States and Social Revolutions*. Cambridge: Cambridge University Press.

Skocpol, Theda. 1986. 'The Dead End of Metatheory', *Contemporary Sociology* 16: 10–12.

Smart, Barry. 1993. *Postmodernity*. London: Routledge.

Smart, Barry. 2000. 'Michel Foucault', in George Ritzer (ed.), *The Blackwell Companion to Major Social Theorists*. Malden, MA and Oxford: Blackwell. 630–50.

Smelser, Neil. 1989. 'External Influences on Sociology', *International Sociology* 4: 414–29.

Snizek, William. 1976. 'An Empirical Assessment of "Sociology: A Multiple Paradigm Science"', *American Sociologist* 11: 217–19.

Snizek, William. 1979. 'Toward a Clarification of the Interrelationship Between Theory and Research: its Form and Implications', in William Snizek, Ellsworth Fuhrman, and Michael K. Miller (eds), *Contemporary Issues in Theory and Research*. Westport, CT: Greenwood Press. vii–ix.

Sorokin, Pitirim. 1928. *Contemporary Sociological Theories*. New York: Harper.

Sorokin, Pitirim. 1956. *Fads and Foibles in Modern Sociology and Related Sciences*. Chicago: Regnery.

Spencer, Herbert. 1904. *An Autobiography*, 2 Vols. New York: Appleton.

Spivak, Gayatri. 1974. 'Translator's Preface', in J. Derrida, *Of Grammatology*. Baltimore: Johns Hopkins University Press. ix–lxxxvii.

Staats, Arthur. 1976. 'Skinnerian Behaviorism: Social Behaviorism or Radical Behaviorism?', *American Sociologist* 11: 59–60.

Stanfield, Ron. 1979. 'Kuhnian Scientific Revolutions and the Keynesian Revolution.' *Journal of Economic Issues* 8: 97–109.

Starr, Paul. 1982. *The Social Transformation of American Medicine*. New York: Basic Books.

Stauth, George, and Bryan S. Turner. 1988. 'Nostalgia, Postmodernism and the Critique of Mass Culture', *Theory, Culture and Society* 5: 509–26.

Stinchcombe, Arthur. 1986. 'The Development of Scholasticism', in Siegwart Lindenberg, James S. Coleman, and Stefan Nowak (eds), *Approaches to Social Theory*. New York: Russell Sage Foundation. 45–51.

Strasser, Hermann. 1976. *The Normative Structure of Sociology*. London: Routledge and Kegan Paul.

Stryker, Sheldon. 1980. *Symbolic Interactionism: A Social Structural Version*. Menlo Park, CA: Benjamin/Cummings.

Stryker, Sheldon. 1989. 'The Two Psychologies: Additional Thoughts', *Social Forces* 68: 45–54.

Sturrock, John. 1979. 'Roland Barthes', in J. Sturrock, *Structuralism and Since*. Oxford and New York: Oxford University Press. 52–80.

Swartz, David. 1990. *The Reflexive Sociologies of Pierre Bourdieu and Alvin Gouldner and Metatheorizing in Sociology*. Paper presented at Miniconference on Metatheorizing in Sociology at the Meetings of the American Sociological Association, Washington DC, August 1990.

Swingewood, Alan. 1975. *Marx and Modern Social Theory*. New York: Wiley.

Szmatka, Jack. 1989. 'Holism, Individualism, Reductionism', *International Sociology* 4: 169–86.

Takaki, Ronald. 1990. *Iron Cages: Race and Culture in 19th Century America*. New York: Oxford University Press.

Tarlov, Alfin R. 1986. 'HMO Enrollment Growth and Physicians: The Third Compartment', *Health Affairs* 5: 23–35.

Tarter, Donald. 1973. 'Heeding Skinner's Call: Toward the Development of a Social Technology', *American Sociologist* 8: 153–8.

Taylor, Jared. 1983. *Shadows of the Rising Sun*. New York: Random House.

Tilman, Rick. 1984. *C. Wright Mills: A Native Radical and his Intellectual Roots*. Philadelphia: Pennsylvania State University Press.

Timasheff, Nicholas. 1967. *Sociological Theory: Its Nature and Growth*, 2nd edn. New York: Random House.

Tiryakian, Edward A. 1962. *Sociologism and Existentialism: Two Perspectives on the Individual and Society*. Englewood Cliffs, NJ: Prentice Hall.

Tiryakian, Edward A. 1979. 'The Significance of Schools in the Development of Sociology', in William Snizek, Ellsworth Fuhrman, and Michael K. Miller (eds), *Contemporary Issues in Theory and Research*. Westport, CT: Greenwood Press. 211–33.

Tiryakian, Edward A. 1981. 'The Sociological Import of Metaphor: Tracking the Source of Max Weber's "Iron Cage"', *Sociological Inquiry* 51: 27–33.

Tiryakian, Edward A. 1986. 'Hegemonic Schools and the Development of Sociology: Rethinking the History of the Discipline', in Richard C. Monk (ed.), *Structures of Knowing*. Lanham, MD: University Press of America. 417–41.

Tominaga, Ken'ichi. 1989. 'Max Weber on Chinese and Japanese Social Structure', in Melvin L. Kohn (ed.), *Cross-National Research on Sociology*. Newbury Park, CA: Sage. 125–46.

Toren, Nina. 1975. 'Deprofessionalization and its Sources: A Preliminary Analysis', *Sociology of Work and Occupations* 2: 323–37.

Turner, Bryan. 1986. 'Simmel, Rationalisation and the Sociology of Money', *Sociological Review* 34: 93–114.

Turner, Bryan. 1987. 'A Note on Nostalgia', *Theory, Culture and Society* 4: 147–56.

Turner, Jonathan H. 1984. *Societal Stratification: A Theoretical Analysis*. New York: Columbia University Press.

Turner, Jonathan H. 1985. 'In Defense of Positivism', *Sociological Theory* 3: 24–30.

Turner, Jonathan H. 1987. 'Toward a Sociological Theory of Motivation', *American Sociological Review* 52: 15–27.

Turner, Jonathan H. 1989. 'Can Sociology be a Cumulative Science?', introduction to Jonathan Turner (ed.), *Theory Building in Sociology: Assessing Theoretical Cumulation*. Newbury Park, CA: Sage. 8–18.

Turner, Jonathan H. 1990a. 'The Misuse and Use of Metatheory', *Sociological Forum* 5: 37–53.

Turner, Jonathan H. 1990b. 'The Past, Present, and Future of Theory in American Sociology', in George Ritzer (ed.), *Frontiers of Social Theory: The New Syntheses*. New York: Columbia University Press. 371–91.

Turner, Jonathan H. 1991. *The Structure of Sociological Theory*, 5th edn. Belmont, CA: Wadsworth.

Turner, Jonathan H., and A.Z. Maryanski. 1978. *Functionalism: An Intellectual Portrait*. Palo Alto, CA: Cummings.

Turner, Jonathan H., and A.Z. Maryanski. 1988a. 'Is "Neofunctionalism" Really Functional?', *Sociological Theory* 6: 110–21.

Turner, Jonathan H., and A.Z. Maryanski. 1988b. 'Sociology's Lost Human Relations Area Files', *Sociological Perspectives* 31: 19–34.

Turner, Ralph. 1988. 'Personality in Society: Social Psychology's Contribution to Sociology', *Social Psychology Quarterly* 51: 1–10.

Udehn, Lars. 1981. 'The Conflict between Methodology and Rationalization in the Work of Max Weber', *Acta Sociologica* 24: 131–47.

Udehn, Lars. 1987. *Methodological Individualism: A Critical Appraisal.* Uppsala: Uppsala University.

Venable, Vernon. 1945. *Human Nature: The Marxian View.* New York: Alfred A. Knopf.

Vidich, Arthur J., and Stanford M. Lyman. 1985. *American Sociology: Worldly Rejections of Religion and their Directions.* New Haven, CT: Yale University Press.

Vogel, Ezra F. 1979. *Japan as Number One: Lessons for America.* New York: Harper and Row.

Vraciu, Robert A. 1985. 'Hospital Strategies for the Eighties: A Mid-Decade Look', *Health Care Management Review* 10: 9–19.

Wacquant, Loic J.D. 1992. 'Toward a Social Praxeology: The Structure and Logic of Bourdieu's Sociology', in P. Bourdieu and L.J.D. Wacquant (ed.), *An Invitation to Reflexive Sociology.* Chicago: University of Chicago Press. 2–59.

Wagner, David. 1984. *The Growth of Sociological Theories.* Beverly Hills, CA: Sage.

Wagner, David, and Joseph Berger. 1985. 'Do Sociological Theories Grow?', *American Journal of Sociology* 90: 697–728.

Wagner, Helmut. 1964. 'Displacement of Scope: A Problem of the Relationship between Small-Scale and Large-Scale Sociological Theories', *American Journal of Sociology* 69: 571–84.

Wallace, Walter. 1969. 'Overview of Contemporary Sociological Theory', in Walter Wallace, *Sociological Theory.* Chicago: Aldine. 1–59.

Wallerstein, Immanuel. 1974. *The Modern World-System: Capitalist Agriculture and the Origins of the European World-Economy in the 16th Century.* New York: Academic Press.

Wallerstein, Immanuel. 1980. *The Modern World-System 2: Mercantilism and the Consolidation of the European World-Economy, 1600–1750.* New York: Academic Press.

Wallerstein, Immanuel. 1989. *The Modern World-System 3: The Second Era of Great Expansion of the Capitalist World-Economy, 1730–1840.* New York: Academic Press.

Walliman, Isidor. 1981. *Estrangement: Marx's Conception of Human Nature and the Division of Labor.* Westport, CT: Greenwood Press.

Wallwork, Ernest. 1972. *Durkheim: Morality and Milieu.* Cambridge, MA: Harvard University Press.

Warriner, K. Charles. 1956. 'Groups are Real: A Reaffirmation', *American Sociological Review* 21: 549–54.

Warriner, K. Charles. 1970. *The Emergence of Society.* Homewood, IL: Dorsey.

Waters, Malcolm. 2000. 'Daniel Bell', in George Ritzer (ed.), *Blackwell Companion to Major Social Theorists.* Oxford: Blackwell.

Watkins, J.W.N. 1952a. 'Ideal Types and Historical Explanation', *British Journal for the Philosophy of Science* 3: 22–43.

Watkins, J.W.N. 1952b. 'The Principle of Methodological Individualism', *British Journal for the Philosophy of Science* 3: 186–9.

Watkins, J.W.N. 1954. 'Methodological Individualism: A Reply', *Philosophy of Science* 21: 91–110.

Watkins, J.W.N. 1957. 'Historical Explanation in the Social Sciences', *British Journal for the Philosophy of Science* 8: 104–17.

Watkins, J.W.N. 1968. 'Methodological Individualism and Social Tendencies', in May Brodbeck (ed.), *Readings in the Philosophy of the Social Sciences.* New York: Macmillan. 254–68.

Watson, James. 1997. 'McDonald's in Hong Kong: Consumerism, Dietary Change, and the Rise of a Children's Culture', in James Watson (ed.), *Golden Arches East: McDonald's in East Asia.* Stanford, CA: Stanford University Press. 77–109.

Watt, Michael J. Robert Derzon, Steven Kenn, Cael Scheamm, James S. Hahn, and George D. Pillari. 1986. 'The Comparative Economic Performance of Investor-Owned Chain and Not-for-Profit Hospitals', *The New England Journal of Medicine* 314: 89–96.

Watts, Malcolm S.M. 1985. 'Some Side Effects of Science and Technology on Medical Practice', *The Western Journal of Medicine* April: 5–45.

Weber, Max. 1896–1906/1976. *The Agrarian Sociology of Ancient Civilizations*. London: New Left Books.

Weber, Max. 1903–17/1949. *The Methodology of the Social Sciences*. New York: Free Press.

Weber, Max. 1904–5/1958. *The Protestant Ethic and the Spirit of Capitalism*. New York: Scribner's.

Weber, Max. 1916/1964. *The Religions of China: Confucianism and Taoism*. New York: Macmillan.

Weber, Max. 1921/1958. *The Rational and Social Foundations of Music*. Carbondale, IL: Southern Illinois University Press.

Weber, Max. 1921/1968. *Economy and Society*, 3 Vols. Edited by Guenther Roth and Claus Wittich. Totowa, NJ: Bedminster Press.

Weber, Max. 1921/1978. *Economy and Society*, 2 Vols. Edited by Guenther Roth and Claus Wittich. Berkeley and Los Angeles: University of California Press.

Weber, Max. 1922–3/1958. 'The Social Psychology of the World Religions', in Hans H. Gerth and C. Wright Mills (eds), *From Max Weber*. New York: Oxford University Press. 267–301.

Weber, Max. 1927/1981. *General Economic History*. New Brunswick, NJ: Transaction Books.

Weber, Max. 1947. *The Theory of Social and Economic Organization*. New York: Free Press.

Weber, Max. 1958. *From Max Weber: Essays in Sociology*. Edited by Hans H. Gerth and C. Wright Mills. New York: Oxford University Press.

Weingartner, Rudolph. 1959. 'Form and Content in Simmel's Philosophy of Life', in Kurt Wolff (ed.), *Essays on Sociology, Philosophy, and Aesthetics*. New York: Harper Torchbooks. 33–60.

White, Hayden. 1973. *The Historical Imagination in Nineteenth-Century Europe*. Baltimore: Johns Hopkins University Press.

White, Hayden. 1978. *Tropics of Discourse*. Baltimore: Johns Hopkins University Press.

Wichtel, Alex. 1994. 'By Way of Canarsie, One Large Hot Cup of Business Strategy', *New York Times* 14 December: C1, C8.

Wilensky, Harold L. 1964. 'The Professionalization of Everyone?', *American Journal of Sociology* 70: 137–58.

Wiley, Norbert. 1979. 'The Rise and Fall of Dominating Theories in American Sociology', in William Snizek, Ellsworth Fuhrman, and Michael K. Miller (eds), *Contemporary Issues in Theory and Research*. Westport, CT: Greenwood Press. 47–70.

Wiley, Norbert. 1988. 'The Micro-Macro Problem in Social Theory', *Sociological Theory* 6: 254–261.

Wiley, Norbert. 1989. 'Response to Ritzer', *Sociological Theory* 7: 230–1.

Wilke, Arthur S., and Raj P. Mohan. 1979. 'Units of Analysis and Paradigms in Contemporary Sociological Theory', *Social Science* Winter: 28–34.

Williams, Francis. 1962. *The American Invasion*. New York: Crown.

Wolf, Frederick M. 1986. *Meta-Analysis: Quantitative Methods for Research Synthesis*. Beverly Hills, CA: Sage.

Worsley, Peter. 1982. *Marx and Marxism*. Chichester: Ellis Horwood.

Wu, David Y.H. 1997. 'McDonald's in Taipei: Hamburgers, Betel Nuts, and National Identity', in James Watson (ed.), *Golden Arches East: McDonald's in East Asia*. Stanford, CA: Stanford University Press. 110–35.

Zola, Irving Kenneth, and Stephen J. Miller. 1973. 'The Erosion of Medicine from Within', in Eliot Freidson (ed.), *The Professions and Their Prospects*. Sage. 105–16.

INDEX